The
CHARACTER
of
NATIONS

The
CHARACTER
of
NATIONS

*How Politics Makes and Breaks
Prosperity, Family, and Civility*

ANGELO M. CODEVILLA

BasicBooks
A Division of HarperCollins*Publishers*

For
David
Peter
Michael
Elizabeth
Thomas

FIRST EDITION

Designed by Joseph Eagle

Library of Congress Cataloging-in-Publication Data

Codevilla, Angelo, 1943–
    The character of nations : how politics makes and breaks prosperity, family, and civility / Angelo M. Codevilla.—1st ed.
        p.   cm.
    Includes bibliographical references and index.
    ISBN 0-465-08220-3
    1. Political culture.   2. Moral conditions.   3. Social values.
I. Title.
JA75.7.C63   1997
306.2—dc21   97–20119
                                                                  CIP

97 98 99 00 ❖/HC 9 8 7 6 5 4 3 2 1

"What the Prince does then do many for upon the Prince are the eyes of all."

—LORENZO DE MEDICI

Contents

Preface

A S AN ADOLESCENT ITALIAN learning to be an American in the
1950s, I gained a painful glimpse into the possibilities for change
in human beings. The Greek classics taught me that habit and circumstance make for very different ways of life. Plato and Aristotle's descriptions of how Lycurgus's laws made the Spartans dogged while
Solon's laws made the Athenians expansive made sense. So did Thucydides' account of the Macedonian barbarians adopting Greek ways
while any number of Greeks were degenerating into barbarism. And
what was Roman history if not the tale of human character and political institutions rising and falling intertwined? As I devoured books
about faraway times and places, I learned to wonder what it would take
for me to live like the people I was reading about and for my new
country to change into yet something else.

As a student, as a naval officer, in various civilian assignments with
the U.S. government, as a consultant, researcher, lecturer, tourist, I
have been privileged to poke into almost every corner of the world and
to talk about it with interesting people. This has strengthened my awe
for the countervailing powers of habit and contingency. By and large,
people live as they do primarily by following old patterns. Nevertheless, ways of life change because everywhere some make themselves
champions of "new modes and orders," which Machiavelli says is the
hardest thing in the world.

I confess to sympathy with John Adams's *A Defense of the American
Constitutions*, which surveyed the world's political systems, and found it
easy to imagine the world's peoples digging themselves deeper into
misery, despotism, depravity, and superstition, but more difficult to
imagine them raising themselves to the prosperity, civility, decency,
and piety in which the American people of his time found themselves.
Indeed, thought Adams, the Americans should realize how precarious
was their hold on the virtues responsible for their happiness. So, I believe that "new modes and orders" must work within cultural bound-

aries, and that they are not quite so likely to improve human character as they are to worsen it.

Political science, as founded by Aristotle, had as its principal object understanding the human consequences of certain forms and acts of government. The great tyrannies of our time challenge political science to explain why so many peoples have changed so much. When I first walked around Germany it was difficult for me to believe that the solid burghers I saw had been party to the Holocaust. What could have led them to do that? The political science I was studying in college hardly gave me a clue. But Hannah Arendt explained, much as Aristotle would have, how the regime had made evil banal. I read that the Soviet Union had murdered on an even grosser scale. Arthur Koestler and Aleksandr Solzhenitsyn, rather than political scientists, explained how. How could the superpolite Japanese people, who are filling the world with Sonys, have wreaked unspeakable cruelties around the Pacific? Douglas MacArthur explained how one facet of this people's character gave way to another. The Japanologists were otherwise occupied. From the outset of my career I have preferred the old political science to the new, and wanted to write a book on comparative government in the style of Aristotle and Montesquieu, of de Tocqueville, Walter Bagehot, Lord Bryce, and Ferdinand A. Hermens, a book that would also compare the rest of the world's governments with that of the United States.

After finishing *War Ends and Means*, I asked my editor, the late, venerable Martin Kessler, if Basic Books would be interested in a 1,200-page comparative government text that would describe each of the contemporary world's major forms of government, explaining how each affected the capacity of the people under it for economic prosperity, civic freedom, family and spiritual life, as well as for generating military power. I reminded him how important the ancients thought regimes are, and proposed that my book would describe the world's major regimes.

Kessler said no to the whole project, but convinced me to concentrate on reintroducing the concept of regime to modern readers, to forego detailed descriptions of the world's major regimes, and to develop the theme: peoples—nations—affect the quality of their lives by how they govern themselves.

Of course, the primary reason why we are interested in all this is that the character of the American way of life is up for grabs perhaps more than ever before, and that our government and the sectors of society associated with it—our regime—affects that character deeply. Paul Golob, my editor at Basic after Martin Kessler's passing, encouraged me to focus on America even more. Even as our regime is quietly bringing about vast changes in how we live, liberals and conservatives are trumpeting ideas for social engineering. This book is intended to give pause to all social engineers by making the case that the powerful levers they want to pull really are connected to living tissue, that each scheme for reform has reasonably well-known effects, and that one of these is what the American founders knew as the deadly disease of faction.

Since this is political science in the old style, it does not mean to prove anything. It is an essay that musters facts because the author thinks they point to interesting phenomena. Notes are to help the reader check quotes, provide the source of statistics, indulge some tangential thoughts, and to thank authors from whom I have learned much. This book contains no facts previously unknown. It does bring the experiences of faraway places and times to bear on choices very close to us.

In addition to Martin Kessler, I am indebted to a number of colleagues whose wisdom enriched and delighted me for a decade under the regime of Glen Campbell at the Hoover Institution, Stanford University: to the late Lewis Gann for his wisdom on Africa, Germany, and the English language; to Mikhail Bernstam and Robert Conquest for years of discussions on the Soviet regime; to Hilton Root for insights on economics in China and the Third World; and to Thomas Metzger and Ramon Myers for teaching me about the interaction of Confucianism and the West in Taiwan. I am also indebted to Thomas West of the University of Dallas, and the Claremont Institute in general, for discussions on the character of the American founding; and to Hernan Cubillos for countless conversations on the Chilean revolution of 1973–1990. I thank Tim Duggan, who ably handled the details for me at Basic Books. I thank also David Corbin and Matt Parks, graduate students, and Meredith Wilson, an undergraduate, at Boston University, who helped with the research. I alone am responsible for all interpretations and errors.

Introduction

Day by day, case by case [the Supreme Court] is busy designing a Constitution for a country I do not recognize.
—JUSTICE ANTONIN SCALIA,
Romer v. Evans

AMERICANS HAVE HAD REASON to be nonchalant about government—at least until recently. We know that government cannot make us rich or wise—never mind good—and we would like to think that neither can government corrupt us into poverty and degeneracy. Our common sense tells us that people make their own poverty or prosperity, their own freedom or servitude. Moreover, until recently, Americans thought that the choices bearing on what kind of people we are had been made once and for all a long time ago, and we did not suspect that as we wrestled with the problems of the day we were changing our habits for the long run. Whereas once we were sure that the future would bring only more wealth, freedom, and happiness, now we realize that the range of possibilities is much broader.

Anyone over forty is tempted to think of the America in which we live as a different country from that in which we grew up. The changes in the ways we make our living, in how we raise children, and in what we expect from the future dwarf the physical and technological changes. And when we ask ourselves why so much has changed, we usually wind up talking about government. We then wonder how we might change further and how the things that our government does or does not do might make the difference between our living in the land of our dreams or of our nightmares. Agree as we might that our character makes the biggest difference in how we live, we realize that government influences citizens' character, just as the character of citizens shapes the government. Regardless of where we begin, we are compelled to deal with the relationship between how we govern ourselves and how we live.

Consider a snapshot of life in New York City. In July 1994, after lengthy deliberation, the city government decided that a person riding the subway stark naked could be arrested—but only if the individual was smoking. Whereas an earlier generation of city officials would not have hesitated to protect the community against "indecent exposure," by 1994 it was difficult to find an official who would explain that concept. But there was broad agreement among officials that subway riders should be protected against secondhand smoke, something unknown to these officials' parents. The change from intolerance of public nudity to intolerance of public smoking is just a whiff of what amounts to a revolution in American public life.

Or consider this: Until the late 1960s, on any Friday night in late spring, the streets of New York were full of wandering prom couples in tuxes and long gowns. These couples would close the bars, open the bakeries, and watch the sunrise from the Staten Island ferry or from the city's big bridges. Few feared for their safety any more than for their sobriety. Nowadays, serving beer to eighteen-year-olds is a crime, and anyone wandering the streets of an American city until dawn would be suspected of having suicidal instincts.

Or think about this: Very occasionally, a teenage couple would generate a pregnancy, typically followed by a shotgun wedding—a lesson to one and all that, as people sang then, "love and marriage go together like a horse and carriage." Nowadays, the horse and carriage of sex (not to mention love) and marriage are increasingly uncoupled. Two-thirds of black children and one-fifth of whites are born out of wedlock.[1] If the young man causing the pregnancy is lower class and if he sticks around, he may share the girl's welfare payment. If he is above that, he normally joins in pressuring her to have an abortion, regarding the baby as an intrusion on bigger agendas. The very term "shotgun wedding" is hardly understood, and the compulsion to marital responsibility that underlay it is generally abhorred. This revolution of mores is just as evident in public life. While in the 1960s, Nelson Rockefeller never got to first base as a presidential candidate because his divorce shocked public morality, by the late 1970s cohabitation had become so widespread that divorce and remarriage seemed conservative by comparison. Thus, no one suggested Ronald Reagan's divorce and remarriage disqualified him as the leader of American conservatism—never mind for the presidency. Then again, an American who graduated from college before the mid-1960s might well have come across the words of Creon in Sophocles' *Antigone*: "He that is a righteous master of his house will be a righteous statesman."[2] To later graduates, such sentiments are as foreign as the text.

Or reflect on this: In 1965, four-fifths of the members of Congress were veterans of the armed forces, and an exemplary military record was essential for men to advance in society.[3] In 1992, the country elected a president who had made no secret of his disdain for military service, and any young man trying to succeed in the corporate world, the media, or academe found that if military service did not disqualify him outright, it marked him as a social stranger with unsavory lower-class odors.

Nor will it do to describe the changes among us as a loosening of rules. No, rules are as tight as ever and maybe tighter, as tight as anywhere. But they are different. Can one imagine an American television station today airing a drama about a repentant homosexual who confesses his sinful lifestyle to a priest? That is no more conceivable than a discussion of the sins of communism on Soviet television under Leonid Brezhnev. Modern America has its taboos no less than remotest New Guinea. But these taboos are ever changing. Some are brand new, while others are outright reversals of old ones. In our America, a single ethnic joke or even a remark merely susceptible of racial interpretation can cost a career. Thus, Howard Cosell's thirty years in sports broadcasting ended during a Monday night football game when he said of a great run by the Washington Redskins' Alvin Garrett: "Look at that little monkey go!" And although no law forbids the traditional English-language coverage of both sexes by masculine pronouns, nor has any law disestablished the words *Miss* and *Mrs.*, editors importune authors to use gender-neutral language, as well as the appellation *Ms.*

Today, unlike a generation ago, one can do what one pleases to an American flag, anywhere. But no one is free to pray publicly in a public school. Students have been suspended for singing Christmas carols.[4] Police forces today must warn criminal suspects of procedural rights, but unlike in former years, police and other government agencies can now seize property without ever bringing criminal charges. More officials than ever have the discretion to subject individuals to onerous procedures. A fire chief in Massachusetts who relieved a small flood was fined his net worth for breaching a beaver dam without a permit, a Florida homeowner was fined $10,000 for killing a squirrel that was eating his garden, and an eighty-year-old New York woman was put through "the process," including a strip-search, because a cop did not like her attitude. All that anyone needs to have his or her life wrecked in modern America is to become some bureaucrat's pet project or fit some agency's "profile." For example, people charged with sexual abuse of children can now get life in prison on the basis of testimony "recovered" from toddlers by experts, and a kindred expertise has turned spanking recalcitrant children, once the sign of dutiful parenting, into child abuse, about which the government solicits anonymous accusations. Above all, the list of things one can do today without some kind of permission from government is shorter than ever. So, not only does America "define deviancy down," in the words of Senator Daniel P. Moynihan, it also defines other kinds of behavior "up"—out of deficiency into normalcy—as well as creating wholly new categories of things that are praiseworthy or beyond the pale. In short, it will not do to describe our America simply as a place where "anything goes."

It is not necessary to protract the list of contrasts to see that our lives today differ more from those of Americans one generation ago than they do from those of our contemporaries in Western Europe. In short, we have changed enough to change countries. Some of us like the new country better than the old. All will prefer some feature of the old or of the new. But that is not the point. Since we are continuing to change, a generation from now we might well live in yet another kind of country. For this reason, we should ask: What can become of us? What kind of people do we want to become? Another question, more immediately to the point, arises: What are the long-term consequences of our political choices on our capacity to be prosperous and civil, on our capacity to defend ourselves, and on the quality of our family lives and our spirit?

This book is about how, in various times and places, systems of government, or regimes, affect the economic, civic, familial, spiritual, and military habits of those who live under them. It does not attempt to give "the whole picture" of what is happening regarding any given set of habits in any given country, much less in the United States. The full picture includes the various forms of resistance to the regime by various parts of society, the struggles, and how they come out. But this book has the simpler task of describing what regimes do. Its premise is that governments and the leading elements of society—which together comprise what are variously called "the Establishment" or "the regime"—have a lot to do with supporting ways of life, with tearing them down, or with building new ones.

Choices—Radical and Not So

The America described by Alexis de Tocqueville in the 1830s, when John Marshall was chief justice, Andrew Jackson was president, and Daniel Webster was in the Senate, left a lively record of a kind of life fostered by its own kind of rules. That life, based on propositions self-evident at the time—a sovereign God and a very limited government—is remote enough from us to provide if not a set of realistic options for political organization and economic and social policy in our own time, then an extreme pole by which to judge the direction in which we are moving. At the other extreme, and equally unlikely to be pursued wholeheartedly by the whole American people, is the life toward which much of mankind has been moving in our century. That life is based on the proposition, self-evident to many, that omnicompetent government as the executor of modern science can be the agent of unprecedented wealth, justice, and happiness. We err at our peril if by focusing on the bloody show of totalitarian regimes, we imagine that they were wholly extraneous to the great trends of our time or to what is happening among us. In fact, the century's kindred spirits of secularism, of statism and radical individualism, most clearly manifest in the totalitarian regimes, as well as our century's peculiar combination of pacifism and disdain for human life, have affected in some measure the rules by which we live. This triad shapes the choices that face us in the future quite as much as our heritage from de Tocqueville's America.

The twentieth century has retaught us the awesome power of governments to shape the character of the peoples living under them. The great totalitarian movements left a legacy even more fearsome and instructive than one hundred million corpses, namely, the changes they wrought in the mentality and habits of the people who survived them, which they are passing down to new generations. The joy that greeted the collapse of communism was followed by the realization that it would be harder for whole nations to take socialism out of themselves than it had been to take themselves out of socialism. Whereas after the end of Nazism's twelve-year reign the German people quickly recovered the capacity to run a free, prosperous economy in civil peace, restoring eastern Germany to productive and happy life after forty-five years of communism is proving to be far more problematic. In Russia, which suffered for three generations, we see even more clearly how the atrophy of moral faculties has mired able human beings in economic misery and crime, as if the Communist regime had killed something essential in the bodies it left standing and had created a spiritual Chernobyl.

Less dramatic, just as real, and perhaps more practically instructive are the effects of less polar forms of government, indeed, of individual policies by any government whatever. The histories of the Roman republic, for example, stress the litigiousness engendered by the redistributive "agrarian law." Well before our century, every kind of economic policy had compiled a record of its effects on wealth and on society, as had policies toward families and religion. Educated people have also long been acquainted with the effects on character of the various systems for organizing political competition. The debates surrounding the establishment of Germany's Federal Republic in 1949 were particularly replete with historical references to how government policy would affect the people's capacity to lead decent lives. All sides searched history for alternatives to the financial and political rules that had wrecked the Weimar Republic. But in their consideration of social policy, they sought different models. Konrad Adenauer sought to promote families in which the husband is the sole breadwinner, while Kurt Schumacher sought models of the good life based on communal raising of children. America's founding fathers had not lived through the horrors of our century, nor even yet through those of the French Revolution. Nevertheless, led by George Washington (whose favorite phrase might well have been "we have a national character to establish"), they combed history for lessons about the possible long-term effects of the arrangements they were considering. America's founding generation saw in God's lengthy warning in the Old Testament against Israel's adoption of monarchy a "common-sense" historical argument for the principle of human equality and for the practical proposition that big government is inherently wasteful, as well as corruptive of mores.[5]

Regimes and Character

The first part of this book begins with the argument, strange to modern American minds but a staple of ancient thought, that regimes— governments and the Establishment associated with them—make big differences in how people live.

The diversity of human habits dwarfs the physical diversity of human beings. Not much travel or reading is needed to grasp that some peoples glory in labor while others shun it; that modesty is the rule of life in some places but exhibitionism rules in others; that in some places you can go out at night without fear, whereas in others daylight does not reassure; that among some peoples a handshake seals a deal but among others signatures are worthless; that some peoples will fight and others will not; that family ties bind some peoples more than others; that some people are more restrained by fear of God than by fear of man and others respond vice versa, along with a host of other contrasts. In short, while all men might well have been created equal, they regularly live lives that are obviously different. Moreover, the habits that enable us to live as we do disable us from living otherwise. And yet people's habits change—cumulatively. Social science, including economics, gives unsatisfactory single-cause explanations for such differences.

The ancients, however, realized that changes in political rules favor one set of habits over others and lay down new layers of habits. We have difficulty understanding this because we are the intellectual heirs of Western Christianity, which made society and individuals less dependent on government than ever before or since. The twentieth century, however, took sovereign government to its logical conclusion. Nowadays, few governments spend less than one-third of their people's wealth. Nearly all have become the chief makers and breakers of fortunes and reputation, even becoming the arbiters of truth. They create wholly new professions and sustain entire classes of people. In short, we now understand perhaps better than at any time since the fall of Rome what the ancients meant by "regime": an arrangement of offices and honors that fosters a peculiar complex of ideas, loves, hates, and fashions and that sets standards for adults and aspirations for children.

Attention to our surroundings leads to a practical grasp of the differences that regimes make in lives and how they go about making them. Well-traveled professionals, whether doctors, professional athletes, corporate or military officers, or journeymen mechanics, readily sense differences in the incentives and disincentives—the "climate"—established by those who dominate any given workplace. Indeed, most regimes—whether corporate or national—broadcast the tone they wish to set, for example, by requiring or banning certain items of clothing (the Muslim veil, the white shirt and tie that J. Edgar Hoover imposed on the FBI) or certain types of architecture, music, and art. Such outward signs are usually good indicators of the priorities that regimes press onto people. Often, governments leave the setting of the regime's tone to private elements. Sometimes they do this intentionally, as when the Chilean military let the country's free-market reformers set the tone of Chilean life between 1973 and 1989.

Particular regimes bring out some of the potential inherent in any given civilization while suppressing others. Civilizations so limit the influence of regimes that, for example, in civilizations where the God-given equality and worth of individuals is not self-evident we may not properly use the term *democracy* to describe movements for spreading political power. Nor may we discuss the economic effects of regimes as if motivation to labor and allergy to corruption were spread equally throughout humanity. Because civilizations truly are different, talk of spreading capitalism to the ends of the earth is downright meaningless.

Within the bounds set by any given civilization, the various broad categories of regimes—tyranny, the several kinds of oligarchy, and democracy[6]—have peculiar effects on the capacity of peoples to be prosperous and civil, to live spiritually meaningful lives in families, free from foreign domination.

The hallmark of the politics and economics of tyranny is cronyism. Wealth is just another of the privileges that flow from connection to the tyrant. The differences between modern party dictatorships and ancient tyrannies lie primarily in the much greater size of the retinues that society is compelled to support and obey today, as well as in the modern dictatorship's intentional degradation of family and spiritual lives. In military matters, tyrannical regimes are marked by special units with privileges far superior to those of the (usually very large) regular armed forces. The loyalty of such units is both the arrow and the Achilles' heel of the regime. The differences between oligarchies, regimes built to enrich the rulers, lie in the attitudes of the rulers regarding the wealth of others. On one extreme are what we might call Mafia oligarchies such as post-Communist Russia, where the rulers regard others' prosperity as a threat to their own and where friendship is restricted to families. Religion is pressed into superstition, and armed force is something used to rub out rivals. Then there are defenseless free ports, like Singapore, where the rulers thrive within systems of law and low taxes that encourage large numbers of people to think of nothing but making money. At the other extreme are grand oligarchies such as those of nineteenth-century Britain, ancient Carthage, and medieval Venice, all of which hired armies, built empires, and spread refined manners along with wealth.

Because democracies have no character except that which their regimes and their peoples combine to give them at any particular time, they can exhibit any of the features of other regimes. And they can change rapidly. The history of the Roman and Athenian democracies, to name but two, is replete with swings between valor and cowardice, poverty and prosperity, freedom and tyranny, piety and sacrilege, harmony and civil war. While no people is ever spared the choices by which it defines its character, democratic peoples face those choices constantly. Alas, history teaches that when democracies find themselves astride the world, their enemies vanquished, they tend quickly to destroy the remnants of the habits that had made them great.

Few peoples have ever been in the position we are: to hope with some confidence to live with prosperity, limited only by our effort; to strive for government to be our servant rather than our master; to live in families undisturbed; and to overawe our enemies even as we walk humbly with our God. What can we do in our public lives to foster in ourselves the kinds of habits that make possible such an exalted wish list? What are the main choices through which we will create the character of our nation?

By deciding on the size of our government, we will decide to what extent we give in to the temptation typical of the waning twentieth century to substitute power for voluntary relationships. Economic regulation affects civil society even more than the production of goods. To the extent that government squeezes civil society's autonomy over moral matters, it forces people to seek moral satisfaction through power. Governmental services provided to families tends to relieve them of their functions. In practical terms, the autonomy of civil society means chiefly the latitude of local government. But local discretion diminishes the power of society's most powerful and tests everyone's tolerance of diversity.

We define ourselves by what we argue about and by how we structure our competition. Arguing about which interest group gets what is conducive neither to prosperity nor to civility. As Lincoln taught and as the contemporary controversy about abortion shows again, arguing about who shall be defined into and out of the human race is a recipe for civil war. Finally, whatever else we do, if we do not habituate the country's leading classes to sacrifice comfort and risk their lives in the country's defense, we will fall to the first serious military challenge.

The Differences Regimes Make

The second part of the book describes the manifold ways in which governments have affected their peoples' capacity for prosperity, civility, family and spiritual life, as well as for military defense.

Mindful of the hallowed logical principle that the search for understanding of the good must begin with contemplation of the awful,[7] the section begins with consideration of the Soviet regime—whose destructiveness and failure are now more acknowledged than understood. The Soviet regime trained its people to waste labor and investments by teaching them through practice that political connections rather than productivity are the keys to the good things in life. The Soviet economy was a very efficient model of a pervasive patronage machine. Like the rest of society, the economy ran by one supreme law: The politically strong do what they can and the weak suffer what they must. The prevalence of officially sanctioned caprice accounted for much of the mutual spite that characterized life in the Soviet empire. The regime also tried to destroy families outright. Only the fear of a demographic crash in the 1930s stopped it. Nevertheless, the regime's conscription of female labor, its usurpation of men's duties as heads of households, and its use of abortion for birth control fostered in men the characteristics we associate with ghetto youths, sowed distrust between men and women, and built an unhappy matriarchy. By contrast, the regime's even more consistent campaign against religion failed utterly to destroy the people's longing for God. In the end, religious and nationalist symbols replaced those of communism. Longing and symbolism notwithstanding, post-Soviet life is characterized by religious ignorance and irreligious practice. Finally, no failure of the Soviet regime is more remarkable than that of its military, to which it had devoted the best of its material and moral resources. It failed mortally in what was supposed to have been its surest strength, the loyalty of the special units that were supposed to do its dirty work—and refused to.

Worldwide since World War II, crafting formulas for national prosperity has been almost as popular as selling financial advice to individuals. During the 1960s, the Third World model was in vogue, followed in the 1980s by the so-called Japanese-Asian model. But the flow of goods and money into the Third World has created classes of powerful parasites there, while in Japan, the mighty production of goods has left many people with Third World comforts. Quite simply, prosperity lies in producing more butter than guns, more widgets than lawsuits, in minimizing the "cut" that nonproducers take from producers, and above all in treating the economy's various participants equally under law. Yet regimes often place production far down on the scale of activities they reward, and they redistribute at will.

Note how different are the skills, attitudes, and lifestyles fostered by various countries that from time to time are held up as economically imitable. The Chinese government's occasionally permissive, consistently predatory regulatory climate creates less prosperity than privilege. Business in China consists effectively of granting and using the privilege to hire labor for next to nothing. The system runs not on property rights secured by law but on the expectation that various officials will be content with the bribes they have received. Thus, the most talented Chinese will continue to prefer gatekeeping and rent seeking to the making of real prosperity. In Europe, dirigisme—the cozy relationship between government regulators and established business—and welfare, jointly dominate economic life. Europe's welfare culture has grown fastest at the top as well as at the bottom of society in areas already inured to clientelism, as in eastern Germany and southern Italy. It grows alongside the tendency of workers to start careers later, to end them earlier, and to work ever-fewer hours. One reason that work is becoming less attractive than working the system is that dirigisme, plus high taxes, make favors and lottery likelier paths to wealth than work.

By contrast, Chile, under the government of General Augusto Pinochet, set out to separate political power from economic life as well as to replace habits of group competition with habits of individual responsibility. To wean people from seeking favors, Pinochet reduced the state's power to grant them, while outlawing the simultaneous practice of politics and business. To foster habits of personal responsibility, he substituted consumer sovereignty for traditional state services while turning the state social security system into individual retirement accounts. In short, the Pinochet regime used economic means for political ends. Chile's subsequent economic and political well being is less significant than the change in attitudes on which it is based.

Nothing so affects economic life, civic life, or, for that matter, family and spiritual life as whether the rulers are bound by law or rule by discretion. The rule of law—and citizenship—arise from the habitual belief that people have things and freedoms by right rather than by anyone's leave. This is problematic in modern governments that recognize none but positive law, where millions of unelected officials write and administer countless pages of rules, and where the broad scope of administration inevitably leads to arbitrary enforcement. The pretense that voting for national officials makes citizens out of people who in practice do nothing but obey and wheedle engenders nothing but cynicism. In practice, law and citizenship tend to grow or wither along with property rights and local prerogatives. The politics of redistribution has been destructive of citizenship precisely because it makes positive law—a thing without inherent limit—into a partisan tool. Some kinds of political parties engender more partisanship than others. Parties based on officials elected independently of one another have tended to be less destructive of law and citizenship, whereas parties that are controlled by their own apparatus have fostered the rule of men. The rule of law is a necessary but not sufficient condition of citizenship.

Since 1949, the Communist Chinese regime has largely succeeded in breaking down much of their people's Confucian respect for traditional virtues and order. But it has failed to inculcate any habitual respect for itself, never mind any of its ideals. Instead, it has trained ordinary people to imitate the leadership's use of power for personal satisfaction. As the regime has aged, it has granted to more and more people the franchise to take advantage of those below them—so long as they pay those above them for the privilege of doing so. In Taiwan, by contrast, the regime began by observing property rights and went on to build something like a civil society on Confucian foundations. The leaders of Singapore, the third regime within Chinese civilization, argue that the Taiwanese regime is doomed by the habits of indiscipline it has legitimized, while Singapore is nipping those habits in the bud. But while the future of citizenship in Taiwan may be shaky, few would argue that Singapore's inhabitants are any more than satisfied consumers of competent government.

The regimes of contemporary Europe from North Cape to Crete also present themselves as nonpolitical administrators of the only reasonable agenda—social security. Because Europeans largely accept that agenda, politics in Europe is dead. Although Scandinavians and Germans largely accept the government's good faith and Italians mostly do not, and although the currency of influence varies from north to south, all Europeans accept their roles as subjects—as entitled consumers of government services. The real citizens of Europe, from whom power and to whom privilege flow, are society's corporations, whether big business, unions, political parties, or the complex of bureaucrats and the interest groups they finance. Because of this, Europe's regimes differ only quantitatively from any number of non-European ones. The Mexican regime, for example, is not based on law but on what Mexicans call their national institution—the *mordida*, the "bribe." Like most modern regimes, Mexico claims socioeconomic expertise and co-opts the country's main private interests while ruling through informal networks. Mexico differs from most modern regimes not because its voters have so much less power over their lives or because the amount of favor brokering is so much greater than elsewhere, but rather because most Mexicans are wholly without illusion about law and citizenship.

Modern Western regimes are inherently enemies of families because their intellectual fashion dictates that all human relations (except those between sovereign government and each individual) are purely consensual. Marriage, the foundation of families, is everywhere a creature of law. Laws support the natural symbiosis of men and women when they protect the marriage contract and the party most faithful to it against the other party's evasion or abuse of responsibility. But when they favor the other party, laws tend to erase the essential difference between marriage and consensual relationships. By tilting to one side or the other, laws affect the character of men and women and families. Twentieth-century governments have also interposed themselves between parents and children, ostensibly to protect the latter but in fact diminishing habits of mutual responsibility between generations. To see radically different treatments in our time one must go outside the West, for example, to Japan and to Saudi Arabia.

Sweden shows the epitome of the tendency of Western regimes to atomize families into individuals whose primary recourse is to the state. The Swedish regime has achieved relations between the sexes similar to but less contested than those in the old Soviet Union. Its tax system makes sending women to work the most efficient way to raise a couple's income. Schools teach that marriage is just one of many lifestyles and encourage sexual uninhibitedness as the most socially acceptable expression of freedom. Government policy, implemented from day-care centers to the workplace and expressed even in the design of apartments, is designed to feminize men and androgynize women while reducing intergenerational contact. One of the consequences of such social policies is that by 1980, 63 percent of Stockholm's inhabitants lived alone. Japan's government, by contrast, believes that the country's success and its very identity are due to the cohesion of its families. And so, Japanese tax laws encourage one-earner households, while the authorities back society's ostracism of co-habiting couples and unmarried parents. Japan's illegitimacy rate is one-fiftieth of Sweden's.[8] However, Japanese authorities have begun to pay at least lip service to modern European ideals of relations between the sexes, and Japanese public opinion tends to follow its leaders. The Saudi government, always under pressure by Muslim brotherhoods and various intellectuals to become more Islamic, is enforcing Islamic marriage laws that require equal treatment of multiple wives—something that is difficult even for the very rich and, some say, inherently impossible. Hence, as the government is being pushed ideologically, it is pulling its people toward practical monogamy.

The most contentious and consequential issues touch religion. Modern government's relationship with religion has been one of rivalry. Although there is not now and never has been a better predictor of prosperity, family, and civility than the practice of Judaism and Christianity, modern Western governments have used their power over education to teach secularism at first, followed by various anti-religious dogmas and, most recently, lifestyles repugnant to religious morality. The fundamental Judeo-Christian teaching is that mankind lives under a single, objective set of laws equally binding on all. As governments drain Western societies of religious preferences, they introduce new beliefs based on relativism, that is, on the basis of power. Hence, nowadays nihilism does battle for Western souls with a thin, ill-fitting combination of self-worship and earth worship. The stark alternatives in the relationship between religion and political power have clear effects. Outright persecution (unless it is total) strengthens religion, while embrace usually suffocates it. More interesting are the effects of nuanced approaches.

Rome approached religion differently at various points in its long history. In early republican times, the city revered its gods and the oaths to them with a strictness greater than that of the Homeric Greeks. But since its focus was on the city's victory in war, the Roman religion never developed a complex philosophic or ethical component. Thus, it lent itself to becoming a mere motivational tool and quickly lost respect. During the Roman Empire, official religion became irrelevant, while each of the contending nonofficial cults fostered its own way of life. In modern northern Europe, established Protestant churches have acquiesced first in the government's secularization of society and even in the teaching of official antireligion. In Catholic Europe, the Christian Democratic movement, the principal reaction to militant liberalism, gave up advocacy of Christian causes, refused to take clear stands on the major issues of the day, immersed itself in day-to-day administration, and died. Throughout the European continent, then, politics has trained people to forget the soul. In Israel, the official religion is observed by perhaps one-fourth of the population. The most important part of Judaism's legal status is the autonomy it inherited from the laws of the Ottoman Empire. On behalf of a large majority of religiously indifferent Jews (and a substantial minority of antireligious ones), the Jewish state runs separate schools for the religious and accommodates some of their sensibilities about the Sabbath and marriage. But as the religious increase in number and assertiveness, some secular Jews feel their irreligious Jewishness so outraged that they commit acts of mockery against their religious brethren. This helps neither Israeli souls nor Israel's chances of winning the next war.

The capacity to fight and win wars is the ultimate test of character, and nothing so characterizes a people or determines its fate as the way in which it draws military power from itself. In ancient republics, military service was synonymous with citizenship. The ultimate political question always and everywhere is which people will risk their lives to uphold the regime. Israel excuses its Arabs from military service, even as the South Africa of apartheid did not draft blacks: The regime could not expect to rely on them when it might need them most. Citizen soldiers and veterans have attitudes of ownership toward their regimes and are less likely to endure treatment as subjects. Regimes that purchase military service or compel it from subjects nevertheless have to ensure the loyalty of military cadres and satisfy their claims. Nothing so destroys any regime as soldiers' sentiment that their lives are being toyed with. A look at three regimes shows how their military establishments have shaped their very different characters.

Great Britain in the eighteenth and nineteenth centuries fashioned effective, reliable naval and ground forces out of men taken almost exclusively from the bottom of society for their entire useful lives. Officers from a gentry and bourgeoisie schooled severely in duty and in the glories of empire provided the forces' connection to the regime. In sum, the military functioned like the other parts of Britain's oligarchy and satisfied its measured aims. In Napoleonic France, by contrast, the military was the template of the regime. Just as the democratic nature of the armed forces enticed men to unlimited promotion by merit, the civil service and the educational system in general adopted exams as the key to advancement. The Napoleonic institution of schools of engineering, mines, and public works, and even the numbering of houses was designed to facilitate the conscription of all of society's resources to serve the regime's unlimited thirst for glory. Charles de Gaulle noted that Napoleon ended up breaking France's sword by striking it senselessly. The Swiss, for their part, have marshaled their forces perhaps as fully as anyone ever has, though without striking, for two hundred years. Male service is universal, as are high-quality weapons. Bank presidents are colonels. Training is fierce. Units are as local as their mission. Thus, today's Swiss are still as Niccolo Machiavelli described them half a millennium ago—"most armed and most free."

Our Character

The third part of the book considers the struggles by which the American regime is reshaping itself and its people. In order to see how different the foundations of America's prosperity, civility, military defense, family, and religious life are from those of others and in order to see how new shoots are being grafted onto its stem and how newer ones yet might be, we must begin by looking closely at the regime's point of departure—de Tocqueville's time, when the sapling was young and most unique.

The economy of early America was not designed by anyone, and America's founders did not think of themselves as its managers. The vigor of the economy came from the freedom and equality of scattered farmers and artisans. Having been hurt by Britain's mercantilism, Americans were viscerally committed to free trade. In short, American capitalism was not a doctrine but rather the consequence of the country's religious, family, and civic institutions. Religion, wrote de Tocqueville, was the first of America's political institutions. A kind of Judaized Christianity filled every nook and cranny of the public square and set the regime's tone, because both political and ecclesiastical authority was exercised by, of, and for a Bible-toting people. Clergymen, unlike today, were forbidden to hold office and taught that all men were equally under God's injunction to be virtuous—or else. The American people's love of liberty was anything but morally empty libertarianism. De Tocqueville explained the American devotion to law and civic duty as a commitment to equality and to doing the right thing.

The old American regime's uniqueness may be grasped by the fact that the national Constitution does not even contain the most important word of modern government—"sovereignty"—meaning the prerogative to define one's own power. Habituated to making and respecting their own laws, to being their own police and their own militias, early Americans were wary of the notion that anyone, even the whole people, could exercise broad, ill-defined powers. The laws that principally shaped their private lives had to do with marriage. American laws punished adulterers and fornicators of either sex, as well as husbands who failed to support their families. Early Americans hanged rapists. De Tocqueville reported that Americans also viewed marriage from the standpoint of the economic principle of the division of labor and distinguished the roles of men and women much more than Europeans. In sum, Americans saw their ways as part of the naturally and divinely ordained path to the good life.

In recent years, many Americans have adopted laws, customs, and habits that contrast sharply with those of America's founders. Others have sought to adhere to older ways. At any rate, today's America is substantially another country. The U.S. government and the regime it leads are not entirely responsible for this. But neither have they been spectators in the culture wars. On the contrary, they have lent growing force to those who have urged a rather coherent set of changes.

America's prosperity is being affected less by the kinds of forces mentioned in economics courses than by changes in the American people's economically relevant habits. Although there has been much talk of how the government expands irresponsibility among the poor by making acceptable the abandonment of responsibility, government-fostered changes in the habits of Americans in the middle and at the top of society are even more significant. As government imposes ever more rules and exceptions and gains greater power to endow and impoverish, it trains us to get ahead through official channels rather than through productive activities. It undermines middle-class responsibility through programs that promise more for less (alas, while delivering less). Above all, government corrupts America from the top by trading priceless access to power for the support of the wealthiest. Thus, the country is dividing between politically potent beneficiaries and the politically impotent who pay for them.

Big government is depriving Americans of self-rule by making un-elected judges supreme over even referenda and by empowering them to legislate on whatever they choose. It is depriving us of the rule of law by multiplying bureaucrats who make, execute, and enforce rules. Bureaucrats and judges, along with well-connected labor unions, have well-nigh eliminated citizens' control over the education of their children. Having set out to right social wrongs by giving advantages to women and blacks, the government has spread habits of mutual recrimination. Having emasculated the police powers of localities, the government has curtailed citizens' capacity to protect themselves with firearms. Having made public places unpleasant, the leaders of the American regime have largely abandoned them. Not surprisingly, the country is filling up with people who like one another less—but who dislike the government most of all.

One reason for antigovernment sentiment is that government has become the main weapon of those who want to denigrate and diminish the role of family and religion in American life. This is not to say that government has campaigned directly to increase the rate of divorce or to decrease that of church attendance. But government did institute no-fault divorce, has mandated sex education that abstracts from families, has weakened parental control by spreading the presumption that families abuse children, has made abortion into the most absolute right in the land, and has campaigned for the proposition that all forms of human relationships are at least as valid as that of the natural family. Government has effectively driven religion out of America's public schools and indeed out of almost all public spaces. The odor of illegitimacy attached to public expressions of religiosity has largely caused the very word "Christmas" to be replaced with "holiday" on the airwaves and in public discourse. The government has established, at public expense and with a host of privileges, a secular priesthood of judges, social workers, psychologists, intellectuals, and artists, all of whom teach a contrary gospel. The result has been not only a host of social pathologies ranging from increased abuse of children and the elderly but also a growing split between those who live in natural families and by biblical religion and those who live in alternative arrangements and by the regime's new gods.

Can the new American regime defend itself? Since the Vietnam War, the U.S. armed forces have stood on an ever-shakier social base. The leading elements of society, which opted out of the armed forces during the war, also rejected for themselves the whole complex of personal habits and attitudes involved with killing and being killed. They have consented to dispose of military forces composed of hired personnel who have that complex of habits. But the tensions between the U.S. armed forces (as well as the subculture from which they come) and the regime are sure to continue growing.

Our objective here is not to predict the outcome of the struggles over the habits of Americans. Rather, it is to note the directions in which the current regime is pushing those habits. Nevertheless, it is worthwhile to note two of America's deeply rooted habits that surely affect those struggles. First, America's very bones are pluralist. Americans tend to move away from people they cannot stand and to congregate with those they can. Thus, complete victory in the culture wars by any side is less likely than is the increasing separation of the people who worship the God of the Bible from those who worship the gods of the regime, of those whose views of marriage and child raising are anathema to one another, of those who march to different drummers. Of course, such growing separation will accelerate the trends that have thus far restricted civic life in America. And needless to say, all this casts a shadow over the country's capacity to face major challenges from abroad. Second, however, America is incorrigibly moralist. Not for nothing do historians point to the Civil War as the most telling event in our history. When two sets of Americans believe that their fundamental freedom to live righteously is being violated by the forces of darkness, they tend to the kinds of passion against which Abraham Lincoln warned—unsuccessfully.

Part I

REGIMES AND CHARACTER

Chapter 1
REGIMES

How small, of all that human hearts endure / That part that laws or kings can cause or cure.

*—*Samuel Johnson, in Oliver Goldsmith,
"The Traveller"

Since the city is a partnership of citizens in a regime, when the form of the government changes and becomes different, then it may be supposed that the city is no longer the same, just as a tragic differs from a comic chorus, although the members may be identical. In the same manner . . . every union or compound is different when the form of their composition changes.

*—*Aristotle, *Politics*

THE OLDEST GERMANS ALIVE at the end of the twentieth century lived in five radically different countries without ever leaving their homes. Born under the Wilhelmine monarchy, among the most polite, orderly environments imaginable, they were young adults in the anything-goes, irreverent, inflationary Weimar Republic. In their most vigorous years, these people lived by Nazi standards. They spent their middle age trying to approach the ideals of the Adenauer republic—bourgeois respectability, family, church, and hard money. Their old age has been passed in a country characterized by sex shops and environmentalism, where the ways of the Adenauer republic are ridiculed. By comparison, their contemporaries who emigrated to the German enclaves of southern Chile before World War I have hardly moved at all.

But the range of human possibilities, of course, dwarfs the German experience. Those who travel the world can hardly avoid asking themselves: What would it be like to have to make my way here, among peo-

23

ple like these, living by their rules and customs? Could I stand it? Yet few go further and ask how the locals can stand it, how they got to live as they do, and how perhaps we, too, might wind up living like that.

Why the Differences?

The variety of human conditions is as striking today—and as baffling—as it was when the ancient Greeks began to try to account for it. We see poverty of many types: clean, orderly, and striving in Turkey and Korea; hopeless, in India; violent, in West Africa. Wealth appears in clean, crime-free Japan or on trashy crime-ridden U.S. college campuses. We see rich Singaporeans whose parents had been poor, and poor Argentineans whose parents had been rich, poverty in the midst of Brazil's grand natural resources, and wealth on Japan's stingy land. We see peace in racially heterogeneous places and strife within the same race, as well as the opposite. We see people living as if freedom were the most natural thing in the world, and we see others who put up with subjection to misery just as normally. And we ask: Why? What makes for the vast differences in the ways people live?

Academic disciplines do not help much because they consist of various sets of blinders. The cutting edge of modern social science presses convenient bits of reality into mathematical models and disregards the rest.[1] Older social science suffers from another kind of procrustean urge. Marxists teach a tripartite historical progression of human society—from slave through feudal to capitalist—based on different arrangements of the means of production. Freudians explain civilization as variations on the theme of repression of instincts. Some liberal theoreticians ascribe the differences among peoples to various stages of the progression of freedom, while others say it is equality that bears all other good things in its train. But viewing complex realities through chosen lenses distorts them.

The most common error today is believing that everything depends on how the economy is organized. And indeed we saw that the socialist countries' peculiar economic arrangements produced not just shoddy goods but also people whose motto was "They pretend to pay us and we pretend to work," people habituated to seeking and granting favors rather than producing and inured to regarding positions of power as opportunities to steal. In Hong Kong, by contrast, a population disciplined by a brutally free market developed characteristics very different from those of people living under socialism. Yet as the shadow of Communist rule lengthened over them, the people of Hong Kong began to exhibit many of the clientelistic ways of the mainland—the best apartment buildings were being bought up by bureaucrats from the mainland, and businessmen, mindful that civil liberties were being repealed, sought out patrons in the new power structure. Still, human beings are not mere bundles of incentives. Hence, merely changing economic policies—tariffs, tax policies, subsidies, and regulations—will not remake a people. History is full of government programs that crashed on the rocks of entrenched habits. But where do habits come from?

A common answer is that "it is all in the genes." Since race is the most obvious human characteristic, it makes superficial sense to associate how people live with what they look like. As Thomas Sowell has shown,[2] every people carries along its peculiar ways wherever it migrates. Germans, it seems, are inveterate engineers and military officers, whether they move to South America or to Russia. In Africa, Ibos are professionals and Zulus are fighters. Italians and Chinese are known for their skills in cooking and small business. Thus, few would be surprised if when the first spaceship lands on Mars, it found Chinese and Italian restaurants already open for business. But there was a time when Roman cooking was, well, Spartan, and when Germans had to learn engineering from the British. Yet the British seem to have lost many of the skills they once taught to others. Then, of course, there is the fact that people who are equally Chinese live very differently in Taiwan, Singapore, and mainland China. Italians in Switzerland's Ticino are just as Italian as the Milanese who live just down the hill, but their attitude toward public life could not be more different. Since gene pools change over many centuries rather than in a few decades and since they are quite unaltered by location, biology seems an insufficient explanation. We may therefore presume that the habits we correctly associate with ethnic groups are somehow acquired in particular circumstances. But how?

It is fashionable today to explain happiness and misery in the world according to the different ways in which various peoples come to grips with their environment. By this token, growth in population and depletion of natural resources bring all bad things, whereas the opposite brings good. This is the view of Robert D. Kaplan in his thoughtful 1994 article "The Coming Anarchy."[3] Kaplan draws scenes of hellish cities, where children drink from sewers, where disease is endemic, violence routine, and the vestiges of any civilization are dissolving. He concludes that it is all somehow due to populations exceeding the carrying capacity of the land. Yet it is obvious that any land will carry fewer hunter-gatherers than farmers, fewer farmers than producers of computer software, and that no land at all can long carry a population that trashes it. Just as obviously, cities in Japan and the Netherlands are groomed gardens compared to the less-crowded Hobbesian plasma that Kaplan found in Africa. Because man makes his own environment, slums everywhere are sets of people rather than places. But how do people get to be destroyers or groomers of their surroundings?

Another explanation has to do with intelligence. Richard Herrnstein and Charles Murray have shown that all sorts of social pathologies are associated with lower test scores, while decent patterns of life are more often associated with higher scores.[4] By the same token, economists have long counted high levels of education as one of the principal assets any nation can possess—and rightly so. But Charles Murray has also pointed out that what he considers the mother of pathologies—namely, out-of-wedlock births—has tripled among American blacks and has grown tenfold among American whites in recent decades. It is not unfair to note that while this pathology was gestating, test scores for whites were not falling tenfold and those for blacks were increasing a bit. It is also true that between 1950 and 1980, Argentina slid from the First World to the Third World as the educational level among its population rose. Clearly, the important factor is not so much intelligence as how it is used. But why do some peoples in particular times and places use it to their advantage while others use it to their disadvantage? Could it be their upbringing?

Is it true then that "the two-parent family is the most successful health, education and welfare program ever invented?"[5] Was the prime minister of Japan correct when he predicted that his country would outcompete the United States in the long run because Japanese families are more cohesive than American ones?[6] A wealth of data stretching back to ancient Rome supports the contention, first argued by Xenophon,[7] that the two-parent, patriarchal family divides human labor most efficiently and fosters in all its members the habits most conducive to their and the polity's happiness. But where do strong families come from? And what weakens them?

Is society responsible for our behavior toward our families, our jobs, and everything else? No one would deny that the strictures of society are important. Jonathan Rauch has argued persuasively that as societies age, they accrue layer upon layer of special privileges.[8] This progressively diminishes the opportunity for talent and the return for effort. Growing rigidity depresses and corrupts. A similar line of reasoning proposes that societies live or die according to the flow of information through their networks. The Soviet Union, by this reckoning, was killed by a flow of information that overwhelmed its structures.[9] Apparently believing something of this sort, the Islamic Republic of Iran has outlawed TV satellite dishes and China has followed a schizophrenic stop-go policy toward them. During the 1996 campaign, President Bill Clinton promoted, as a safeguard for America's mores, a device by which parents could prevent television sets from receiving certain types of programs. Nevertheless, none of this tells us how all societies come to establish certain privileges and not others and how some societies draw life from the free flow of information while others poison themselves with it. How can both occur?

One answer is so obviously true that it explains nothing at all: "It's the culture!" Well, of course it is. But what is a culture other than a way of life—T. S. Eliot's "all the characteristic activities and interests of a people"?[10] Eliot defined the English culture of his time in terms of Derby Day, the Henley Regatta, the music of Elgar, dartboards, and boiled cabbage. And no doubt contemporary American culture cannot be defined without football and Big Macs. Could anyone describe life in socialist countries without reference to hours spent in line at stores? Anyone who grew up in Japan would surely mention the stylized lunch boxes at school. The lists of such peculiarities are endless. But they say nothing about why one society is rich and another poor, self-governing or not, more or less moral. More telling in these regards would be a list of peculiar attitudes. The heart of any culture is a *forma mentis*, a set of attitudes expressed in life's most important behavior patterns. No Western visitor to Saudi Arabia or to Hindu India, for example, can help but be impressed by the prevailing contempt for labor and those who perform it. By the same token, the American underclass has been best described as a set of attitudes antithetical to the bourgeois virtues of discipline, fidelity, frugality, and so forth.[11] Travelers arriving at West African airports confronted by customs officials who demand bribes reach reasonable conclusions about what awaits them downtown. Visitors to Italy instantly notice that the locals consider the state the enemy, while no visitor to Japan should be surprised to hear that narcotics are not a problem there, because they are against the law.

We Make Our Differences

What then makes for the attitudes and patterns of behavior that make the crucial differences in how we live? Moses' conveyance of the Law from Mount Sinai is unique in that it sought to define the Israelites' entire way of life in one act. But, so the Bible says, even divine action could not remake a people who were already "stiff-necked" about their existing habits. Experience teaches that other peoples are pretty stiff-necked, too. The birth, change, and death of cultures is gradual. Above all, most cultural norms do not come down from heaven to any extent. We ourselves make them, change them, and break them, and we do so at will.

We choose for ourselves what we think and how we live. Surely, any choice at any given time is conditioned by previous choices. We are indeed creatures of habit. But human habit, as distinguished from animal instinct, is somehow tied to conscious choice. "In order to discover the character of any people," wrote St. Augustine, "we have only to observe what they love."[12] Among the most important of the choices we humans make, among the most definitive ways that we show what we love and what we abhor, are the ways in which we govern ourselves. Those who wrote the classics had no doubt that forms and acts of government are the clearest reflection and among the strongest influence on what people do and what they think, that they both reflect the souls of people and form them. Ethics, according to Aristotle, is a branch of politics. The Greek word *ethos* translates as "custom." Thoughts and actions repeated become habits. In our time, an "ethos" has come to mean a culture. Aristotle would not have objected to the notion of culture as an accumulation of habits. But where do habits come from if not from choices repeated and ingrained?

Politics, thought Aristotle, is one of the most powerful influences on our habits—but by no means the sole or omnipotent influence. No message of Aristotle's is clearer than that it is futile to try to govern barbarians as if they were Greeks. Habits make people, and any new act must inevitably contend with accumulated habits. In this vein, when Jesus was asked why the law of Moses permits polygamy while he proposes monogamy, he answered that Moses could not have asked more of his sinful people. Culture, the accumulation of habits of heart and mind, sets limits to government. Those limits are sometimes so obvious as to lead one to conclude that government does not matter very much. Well, sometimes it matters little, and sometimes a lot.

The Impact of Government

The strongest argument for the point of view that government is of little consequence is that here and there in history one finds small governments ruling over strong, autonomous societies. But much of history is full of big governments ruling over societies that either never had vigorous lives of their own or whose independence had long been crushed by the weight of government. As parochial Westerners with short memories, we are wont to think that the natural state of mankind is to live under limited governments that treat everyone alike. But most of the world's peoples have no history of equality under the law. Their lot has been to be subjects of empire, with rulers who empower some subjects to take advantage of others. Because each ruler made a different world for his subjects, most of mankind has measured time from the beginning of the reign of particular rulers. The strength of the proposition that government does make a difference in people's lives today becomes unmistakable when we consider how very different from our own are the historical circumstances in which it made the least difference—the Christian Middle Ages. During this period, roughly between A.D. 800 and 1450, rulers were constrained as never before or since.

In ancient times, no distinction had existed among religion, society, and government. The rulers of each city or empire were also the most prominent men as well as the chief priests. One set of rules, flowing from the same authority, commanded or forbade everything from the planting of crops to the sacrificing of human victims. When a city was conquered—assuming it was not annihilated—its gods were changed and its moral universe was refashioned. The attraction of the great ecumenical empires—of which the greatest was Rome's—was that they tried to leave the gods and lives of their subjects as untouched as possible. But they certainly imposed new bureaucracies, new tax structures, and new mores that changed with each emperor. Alexander's empire seduced the educated classes of the East into Hellenic culture. After the Roman conquest, these same classes absorbed Roman ways, though often in Greek. Yet those ways changed substantially with each emperor. While Rome under the Antonines spread the habits of the rule of law, under Commodius and Maximus it forced people to live by the law of the jungle.

Plato and Aristotle thought that there is a direct, causal connection between any given form of government and the kind of human traits that flourish under it. Yet these philosophers—the twin fountainheads of our way of life—taught us to differentiate between the demands of rulers and the demands of nature. This distinction, which implies that rulers can be objectively unruly, theoretically diminished the scope of government to a heretofore unimaginable extent. Jesus' injunction to "render unto Caesar the things that are Caesar's and to God the things that are God's" left no doubt that rulers could no longer lay claim to spiritual authority. The Christian commentators combined Jesus' command with Platonic-Aristotelian natural law and gradually produced what might be called the social doctrine of the Christian Middle Ages—a set of ideas and practices that limited the consequences of government as never before or since.

Medieval kings could ask for more or less money from their subjects, but they had no right to the property of their subjects. The different outcome of passionate struggles over the legality of royal financial requests in medieval England, France, and Spain eventually made the crucial difference between European societies ruled by law or by administrative edict. Moreover, the daily lives of ordinary people surely were affected by the personal character of the kings, noblemen, and clergy with whom they came in contact. Thus, Shakespeare's Henry V could say: "O Kate, nice customs court'sy to great kings. Dear Kate, you and I cannot be confined within the weak list of a country's fashion: we are the makers of manners, Kate."[13] But in Spain as in England, kings and peasants were enmeshed in a network of canon law, civil law, and above all customary law. At the base of all the rules and customs lay one principle: Only God is sovereign. Every family, every village, every contract, and indeed every human being and every human institution depends on Him. Hence, every human association, like every human being, is endowed by its Creator with its own particular place and purpose in the divine order. It was as improper for anyone to interfere with its life as to snuff it out. Powerful Christianity made for weak rulers and strong societies. The notion that kings might issue rules on the conduct of farming or the raising of children, that they might require an annual universal act of financial confession, or that they might force people to fight in their armies would have been regarded as both ridiculous and impious. And in fact, when radical movements seized political power in the thirteenth century, seeking to force the church and society in general to conform to virtuous models, society rose up and burned these movements' leaders at the stake.[14]

After the Reformation, government became more powerful. Hence, a change in rulers might mean either Catholic or Protestant dominance. In Ireland, dominion by another branch of Christianity went along with economically exploitative rule. But this was the exception. In most of Europe, the rulers' profession of transubstantiation or consubstantiation made no difference in the wealth or poverty, the decency or depravity, the vigor or the decadence of public life. The quality of public life differed widely, ranging from Spain's warrior regime to England's model feudalism, Venice's imperial republicanism, and the predatory monarchies of Naples. Yet nowhere in medieval and Renaissance Europe did government make the kind of difference in people's lives that it had in the ancient world or that it would later in the modern world.

Nevertheless, rulers always had an impact on society, and no one has ever denied the power of examples from on high. Even trivial effects are instructive. Why do the French—except for some non-elites in the South—pronounce their "r's" gutturally instead of rolling them in the Latin manner? Because in the seventeenth century, France had a Danish queen who could not manage the Latin "r." Courtiers affected to speak as she did, noblemen affected court speech, and soon failure to growl one's r's became a sure sign of unsophistication. Four hundred years later, from the Boulevard Saint Germain to Tahiti, it still is. No historian would deny the importance of the sobering effects on the church and society of Pope Gregory VII's imposition of austerity on the worldly clergy of the eleventh century, any more than a scholar would contest the notion that the luxurious papal court at Avignon two centuries later helped spread corruption, and eventually revolution, in Europe. Nor did anyone ever deny the power of princely patronage. Cathedrals, and the priceless works of art in European museums, testify to the magnificent taste of Renaissance rulers—a taste that set standards for ours. The influence of patronage, however, depends in part on its size. To commission a handful of artists is one thing, while creating whole classes of people who live by patronage is another phenomenon, quite beyond the premodern imagination. Finally, the Renaissance saw an outpouring of a genre of neoclassical literature called Mirror of Princes, which pointed out the character traits that the prince should cultivate in himself and, by example, in his subjects. But in premodern times, the notion that princes should be partisans in what Bismarck called *kultur kampf* was incomprehensible.

The power of constitutional-legal incentive to spread ideas and habits was always well known. The grand political struggle of the Middle Ages between the pope and the emperor called forth the treatises of Marsilius of Padua and John of Paris, as well as commentaries by Thomas Aquinas and Dante. Both sides of the quarrel, though, accused the other of trying to wield power over matters that were not properly its own and thus of taking the first big step to arbitrary rule.[15] Similar arguments surrounded the big constitutional questions of the Renaissance—who should appoint bishops, and what should be the relationship between crown and nobles? Because all sides in these controversies ultimately founded their claims on God and natural law, all agreed that every part of society had its legitimate powers, none absolute, and that all were obliged to sustain the complex of customs of the *Cristianitas.*

Following the Reformation, however, the struggles for power between Catholic and Protestant nobles, and the persecution of religious dissent, reintroduced the notion that culture and politics were linked. The rise of nation-states convinced millions that the cultural differences between the French, the Germans, the Russians, and so on were very important, and this introduced governmental authorities into cultural matters. The first few years of the French Revolution, with its transformation of churches into temples to the fatherland, new calendars, and social purges not seen since the Roman civil wars, shocked the world.

What Is a Regime?

Still, until our time, most Westerners simply could not understand what Aristotle had meant by "regime" or "constitution." How could the very same country be one thing before a political change and something totally different afterward? Also, because the individuals or projects likely to take power in Western countries were just not that different from one another, Westerners could not understand what Socrates had meant when he said that every city was the "writ-large" version of the particular kind of human being dominant within it.[16]

Having lived through the twentieth century, we find Plato and Aristotle much easier to understand. The century began with boundless faith in the capacity of government, as the agent of modern science, to engineer health, wealth, and happiness. Yet we have lived to see not just Germany but also Russia, China, and countless other places turned into hells-on-earth. The list of ills inflicted on the human heart by twentieth-century regimes is very long. When we read Thucydides's account of how the revolution in Corcyra accustomed a people to ever-higher levels of mutual slaughter, it is all too easy to think of modern parallels, from the Russian Revolution to Bosnia and Rwanda.[17] We have also seen countries wrecked without significant violence. Thus, in the 1930s, Argentina might have been the world's second-richest country per capita. But by the 1980s, after a succession of populist regimes, it experienced food riots. Algeria, once an exporter of food and wine and a bastion of worldliness within Islam, was driven to hunger and to seeking after Islamic purity by three decades of secular socialism that had rendered its people intolerant of corruption. By the same token, we have seen Japan turn from militarism to commerce; parts of China turn from socialism to energetic enterprise; Taiwan become the first democracy in the five-thousand-year history of the Chinese people; and Singapore become the first physically clean city in the long history of the vast Chinese cultural area. We know that modern Germany was built on de-Nazification and modern Japan on the radical reversal in the sociopolitical importance of soldiers and businessmen. The agents of these changes have been regimes that very consciously encouraged certain habits in their peoples while discouraging others. In sum, we have regained some of the ancient philosophers' sober appreciation of the capacity of regimes for good and for ill.

But what exactly are regimes? According to the classics, regimes are arrangements of offices and honors.[18] Each set of arrangements answers the question "Who rules?" as well as "For the good of whom?" and "To what end?" Aristotle, remember, had divided regimes into two broad categories—those that rule in the interest of the rulers only and those that rule in the interest of the whole polity.[19] Within each category, however, he pointed to the existence of rule by one man, rule by few, and rule by many. Each kind of regime served a different purpose and fostered a particular kind of human being. All this makes sense because there are any number of character traits within each human being. Depending on which of these traits are fostered and which suppressed, people can be tyrannical or law loving, rapacious or virtuous, dissolute or civic minded. For the classical tradition from Socrates to Cicero, the whole point of discourse on politics was to figure out how to structure regimes that would foster the appropriate character traits in a given set of circumstances. George Will claimed no originality when he wrote in 1983 that statecraft is soulcraft.[20]

The classical philosophers knew that the prominence of oligarchs who spent their time accumulating wealth would increase the polity's concern with wealth. If the rulers were engaged in trade, they would be tempted to confuse their interests with the public business.[21] They knew that where the generals' mentality dominates, the city becomes an armed camp,[22] while entrusting the city to especially virtuous men would involve the society with moral concerns.[23] They also knew that prominent men could use virtue as a cover for greed. They knew that cooperation between classes was heartily to be desired and could be encouraged by giving each class a share in the government. But they also knew that when different interests combine, they have a propensity to raid the treasury. Given the character of its citizens, each city needs a particular prescription to bring out the best and suppress the worst of its potentials. Arrangements of offices and honors were designed to bring to prominence certain kinds of men, whose examples would help form their fellow citizens. Laws would also legitimize some practices and delegitimize others. Finally, the laws would offer outright incentives for some activities, like showing up at assemblies, and penalize others, like sacrilege. This, in sum, is classical political science.

Regimes, however, cannot be reduced to official acts of commission or omission. They are the sum of what is prominent in society—the reigning ideas, loves and hates, fashions and phobias, hymns and epithets. They are embodied in prominent persons—the Establishment. Holy men and entertainers, generals and the rich, rulers and ruffians—every society has its makers of standards, the ones whom children imitate and adults wish they were. Sometimes—rarely—the governmental establishment imparts to society standards very different from those of the private establishment. In post–World War II Poland, for example, the Communist Party monopolized all the commanding heights of society except one—the Roman Catholic Church. Over the course of forty years, the church gradually ousted the party from civil society, and eventually from government. But this sort of thing is rare. In most instances, official and unofficial establishments are mutually supporting and evolve together. Thus, the phenomenon known as the U.S. "counterculture" of the 1960s, for example, embodied the maturation of attitudes that had been growing among American elites, in and out of government, for several generations. Consequently, though the nominal American Constitution remained the same during this era, the actual American regime changed profoundly.[24]

Nowadays, regimes are often confused with mere arrangements of constitutions and laws. This is because our medieval Christian heritage leads us to separate politics from civil society—family, business, and professional life, the realm of knowledge, faith, and morals. And in fact, no modern regime has the unchallenged moral authority of pre-Christian, pre-philosophical polities. But even the most liberal modern governments have material powers beyond the imagination of ancient tyrants. Modern governmental and nongovernmental elites are integrated everywhere as they have not been since the third century A.D. So, like it or not, the stakes of modern politics include the character of civil society.

Today, in much of the world, the state has taken over from churches (largely by default) the role of arbiter of morality. By taxing and spending to provide for retirement and medical care, government has preempted individual providence for the elderly and has taken on the role of older children in families. By providing sustenance to people who cannot or will not work, government has preempted private charity and assumed the role of husband and father in the lives of countless women and children. A framework of laws regulates family life. Not only in Sweden, which, as the saying goes, has laws on everything from raising children to walking dogs, parents may raise their children only so long as government does not choose to take them away. By becoming the principal financier and regulator of education, research, and professional qualifications, government has effectively become the arbiter of truth. Even in the United States, religious schools must be licensed. In other countries, churches themselves must be licensed. It is difficult to find any government on earth that spends less than one-third of its people's total product. Most spend about one-half. Government is the biggest employer, awards the most contracts, and legislates so as to make all occupations expend significant amounts of effort to comply with its regulations (which are further shaped to its advantage). Government is the biggest maker of winners and losers in society. The world is abuzz with governmental schemes to remedy the ravages of governments. In 1927, when France's government was perhaps one-third of its present size, Charles de Gaulle wrote that the regimentation it imposed "would have revolted our fathers."[25] But whether one is revolted or thrilled by modern regimes, no one can deny their enormous effect on the lives of those who live under them.

How Regimes Lead

Regimes lead by example, by precept, and through the power of the purse. Adolf Hitler knew what he was doing when, campaigning against the Weimar Republic, he contrasted its archetypes—politicians whose daily business seemed to be the buying and selling of principle—with the man he presented as the model Nazi, Hermann Göring, the clean-cut hero who had routinely offered his life for his country in the skies over the western front during the Great War. Later, Göring came to personify the regime's degeneracy. Addicted to narcotics and to every imaginable perversion, the obese Reichsmarshal played while the regime was sending millions to their deaths.

Like ships, corporations, or athletic teams, regimes tend to take on the personality of their chiefs. By deploying incentives, chiefs can even manage to make subordinates put forth initiative. Napoleon thus instituted what amounted to nationwide contests for honors and rewards to be earned on the battlefield. Much as Peter the Great had done in Russia, he thereby established a new class of nobles. Most leaders ask less, and subordinates are happy enough to find out what it takes to please. De Gaulle used to say that people instinctively bend themselves around power. Indeed, the effect of leaders may be likened to that of the sun, which has only to move for the sunflower to follow.

Organizations and regimes develop what the Romans called the *cursus honorum*—the path to power and profit. In the early centuries of the Roman republic, the cursus inevitably began with service in the army, followed by several levels of elective office, and ever-higher military commands. But during the later republic, fewer patricians bothered with the military part, a trend that continued into the empire, until the Emperor Gallienus actually forbade senators and their immediate families from serving in the army. By then, of course, patricians had ceased to be powerful. They were merely rich men, groveling before every rough-hewn emperor whom the legions made and unmade.

Different paths to the top favor different kinds of people. Today's Japan is ruled by people who made their way by studying for exams and by conforming to a culture of production and service. These leaders are very different from those of the 1930s, who had become successful in peacetime by adhering to the warrior's code of *bushido*. Either kind of person would find it hard to succeed in the other's regime, just as most people who had made successful careers in the hierarchical culture of IBM would have found it difficult to succeed in the Apple corporation's freewheeling early years.

The founders of regimes quite consciously try to foster certain qualities. Thomas Jefferson thought that the self-reliance of farmers who work their own land was the indispensable foundation of American freedom. Founded on rebellion, the American regime could not remain the same if the American people lost the capacity to rebel. Jefferson did not esteem farming for its own sake, but he did not know any other nursery of independence. De Gaulle thought that his people were too prone to division. Hence, he thought that a serious electoral system that compelled voters to choose governments and a serious constitution that obliged governments to govern would help make the French people more coherent and much more serious. By contrast, President George Bush's wish for a "kinder and gentler" America was unrelated to what the voters remembered as his administration's principal initiative—raising taxes.

The personal behavior of leaders is always important, but not always in the same way. During the 1960s, for example, the Central Intelligence Agency surreptitiously filmed the goatish sexual practices of Indonesia's dictator, Sukarno, in the mistaken belief that he would fear their revelation. These same officials shielded the equally goatish practices of their own president, John F. Kennedy, fearing, correctly, that their revelation would destroy Kennedy politically. They did not understand the difference between the American republic and the Indonesian empire, whose subjects expect their despots to use their positions for all sorts of gratification. By the 1990s, however, the American people seemed to tolerate President Clinton's adultery almost as if they had become Indonesians. Similarly, while the Roman regime of the first century B.C. demanded that Julius Caesar and his wife be above suspicion, Roman emperors only a few generations later were not politically inconvenienced by engaging in any debauchery whatever. Standards change, and much depends on those who set them.

The common practice of naming regimes, or even epochs, after the individuals that shaped them most makes some sense. True, Marxist theory and Leninist practice fully prescribed and initiated murderous totalitarianism. Nevertheless, the Soviet Union's massive network of officials who lived in constant fear of Siberia or worse was the work of Josef Stalin. The Soviet Union really was Stalin writ large. When his successors tried to run the Soviet system by different rules—without terrorizing the ranks of the Communist Party—the system began to break down. Likewise, the presidency of the United States was designed to fit George Washington, who consciously set precedents for his successors. His refusal to serve more than two terms in office, his avoidance of pomp, and his narrow interpretation of his powers indelibly distinguished the American regime from monarchy or empire. But since World War II, the U.S. government has taken on imperial trappings. Recent presidents, like the early Roman emperors who used to play the role of mere elected officials on ceremonial occasions, have called photographers to show them eating common foods, carrying their own luggage, or making simple purchases. It remains to be seen how long the contradiction between the ways of Washington, D.C., and the presidents' pretenses of Washingtonian simplicity can endure. In the same manner, the Ayatollah Khomeini created Iran's Islamic republic in his own image. Therefore, it will endure only as long as Khomeini's successors maintain the sense of wounded, avenging righteousness that he engendered.

Regimes are also defined by the spirit of their laws. Some laws or constitutional provisions clearly aim to define the regime. The organic law that accompanied the Chilean Constitution of 1981, for example, specifically prohibits any person from holding office simultaneously in a political party and in a business or professional association. Thus, the drafters sought the regime's primary goal: the separation of economic and political life. Sometimes regimes make laws that give them new identities. For example, after the 1948 victory of the National Party, South Africa made laws to enforce what it called "separate development" of the races within its borders. Eventually, apartheid became South Africa's consuming preoccupation. Italy's First Republic (1946–1994) was defined above all by its electoral system, which allowed parties, but not individuals, to stand for parliament. The natural result was an oligopoly in which party bosses were the only people who counted.[26]

Sometimes contending factions so strongly support or oppose a law that the outcome of their struggle is sure to alter the regime, if not to redefine it outright. This was surely the case in the United States in the late 1850s. For supporters of the Supreme Court's decision in the case of *Dred Scott vs. Sandford*, the essence of American freedom came to be the capacity to take their slaves wherever they wished, whereas to opponents, the long-term existence of freedom for whites became incompatible with the long-term existence of slavery for Negroes. As Lincoln said, the house divided could no longer stand.[27] The issue of slavery had become so important that both sides agreed the entire regime would be defined by its resolution, one way or the other. The same is probably true of America's division over abortion and euthanasia in the late twentieth century. For some Americans, the legality and propriety of these acts have become the touchstone of the good life, while for others, the definition of decency begins with the protection of life from conception to unassisted death. Regimes have been defined by less-weighty controversies.

Laws that do not define regimes nevertheless help shape them as well as shape important aspects of people's lives. In the Roman republic, the paterfamilias had the absolute power of life and death over everyone in his household, whether slave or free, as well as the right to adopt anyone into the household. The emperors gradually took away that power, even over slaves. This was done neither out of tenderheartedness nor out of hostility to strong families. The emperors just wanted to make their courts the arbiters of as many disputes as possible, not least for the purpose of increasing their revenue. While we cannot ascribe the decline of the patrician family to the father's loss of this power, it is undeniable that with the exception of Marcus Aurelius, the emperors left no record of tender concern for family life. Similarly, while one may not blame the decline of the family in modern Sweden exclusively on government, it is undeniable that the Swedish government, like the Roman emperors, tries to reach each individual as if the family did not exist.

Laws that shape economic life affect the regime in very special ways. Most of the world, for example, does not prohibit what in the United States is known as insider trading. Consequently, in most of the world the trading of securities is practically confined to individuals who have or think they have privileged information. Such conditions train the average wary investor to regard investment in publicly held companies as a trap for the unwary and hence to retreat to one's own insider realm—family-held companies.

Today, one school of economists recognizes the concept that government can shape habits through material incentives. This school's premise is the homo economicus of eighteenth-century European liberalism, the individual who coolly calculates how to optimize his material position and maximize the latitude of his choices. Raise taxes so that workers get to keep less of what they earn, and homo economicus will work less. Lower the difference between the rewards of positions requiring more and less effort, and homo economicus will gravitate toward the ones that require less. For this school, strengthening families is merely a matter of finding the right tax advantages or crafting just the right welfare plan. To say that few actual human beings fit this model is not to argue that most people are irrational but rather to say that the ends of eighteenth-century liberalism are not the sole or even the highest objectives of reason. This school overestimates the power of government incentives. Quite simply, not all human behavior is for sale. Still, governments have always been able to buy some people, and modern governments have an awful lot of money to spend. Hence, in practice, the straightforward statement of what one might call the "Gary Becker school"—that governments get what they pay for—is true for the most part in modern liberal societies.

Consider that before Benito Mussolini, the chief source of income and status of the southern Italian middle class was renting land. This class was already well practiced in the habits of buying and selling sinecures and lesser favors. Mussolini easily turned the members of this class into bureaucrats, their main qualification being that the Fascist system was willing to hire them as administrators for the regulatory and welfare state it was building. By the same token, the southern Italian sharecroppers who lived by their landlords' favors had never been clients of the state. But when their landlords-turned-bureaucrats offered government money in exchange for allegiance, the sharecroppers quickly transferred their old social skills to these more profitable arrangements.

The very power of the state to direct floods of money into some social sectors and not into others achieves what farmers do by watering and fertilizing certain fields rather than others. The very occupation of social worker, for example, never existed in all of history until our time, when Western governments instituted this secular priesthood and paid uncounted thousands to practice it. By the same token, decisions by vast state-funded medical plans to pay or not to pay for treating psychiatric or social dysfunctions mean that thousands of people will or will not spend their lives attempting to live by certain sets of standards and advising others to do the same. In the United States, the National Defense Education Act of 1958 was based on the premise that the country needed to increase vastly the percentage of young people who graduated from college in science and engineering to meet the Soviet Union's challenge to a race in outer space. Because that race was won within a decade, the people who went to college because of the legislation proved irrelevant to it. Moreover, the government paid for more people to teach and study "soft" subjects than it did for people to study the hard sciences. To boot, the United States soon abandoned the objective of dominating space. Notwithstanding any of this, the National Defense Education Act helped to quadruple the ratio of college graduates to nongraduates, vastly enlarged the professorate, virtually created a class of administrators of higher education, swelled and enriched university towns, and made politically significant the heretofore marginal tastes of half-educated intellectuals.

The tastes of any regime's ruling element are on display in society's public places. Today's rulers no less than ancient ones commission statues and murals, music and theater. The rulers' choices permit some artists to live by their art, while the artists not chosen must make it the hard way. Each set of patrons, artists, and products of art embodies a viewpoint on which human possibilities are good and which bad. No European regime today would build a cathedral, any more than their thirteenth-century predecessors would have commissioned twisted hunks of metal to adorn public squares. Modern states have ministries of culture and education. There are less direct ways of gauging what the regime is about than laying side by side the proposals and job applicants to which these ministries give money and those to which they do not.

In our times, no less than in ancient ones, political regimes correspond to ways of life. The relationship between them is like that of the chicken and the egg: It matters less where we begin to examine it than that we do so.

Chapter 2
TONE AND CHARACTER

Perhaps the easiest way of making a town's acquaintance is to ascertain how the people in it work, how they love, and how they die.

—ALBERT CAMUS, *The Plague*

I N MOST PLACES, the tone of life is obvious, as if a giant tuning fork were setting the surroundings to vibrate at its frequency. No one driving into Las Vegas, Nevada, could possibly mistake the fact that the place hums to the tune of the casinos that dominate the landscape any more than visitors to the old Soviet Union could miss the point of the giant inscriptions that proclaimed the glory of the Communist Party, the oversize statuary to its heroes, and the traffic lane reserved for party functionaries that ran down the middle of major streets: namely, this place is ours, and if you want to get along here, it is going to be on our terms.

Businessmen who travel a lot learn quickly to discern the "business climate" wherever they land—what are the local rules for making money and who makes them? While it is unimaginable to do business in China without paying bribes, to offer one in Japan is the greatest of faux pas—yet nevertheless one must be prepared to grant Japanese business associates other forms of privileged treatment. To judge foreign climates, businessmen use skills honed, antennae developed to discern corporate cultures. Diplomats are taught explicitly to home in on the sources of power in the vastly different places to which they are posted during their careers. Before getting down to writing official reports, they are taught to act like Alexis de Tocqueville—to take walks, look, listen, get the feel of the place. Following these examples, the sociologist Edward Banfield walked the streets of a small Mormon town in southern Utah and those of a comparable small town in southern Italy. In his book *The Moral Basis of a Backward Society*, he noted that while the tone of Mormon life was set by cooperation and mutual assistance, that of the southern Italian town was set by mutual jealousies.[1] Thus, he observed that while the Mormons led prosperous, gregarious, and happy lives, the southern Italians lived lives that fulfilled Thomas Hobbes's formula: solitary, poor, nasty, brutish, and short.

Almost always, the ruling culture and the formal government are symbiotic. Seldom does any major faction of the culture exist despite the regime. When it does, it is most noteworthy. With a little reflection, it is easy enough for any perceptive adult to make sense of a human situation, to listen to its tune, and than to begin to understand its elements. Having heard the main tone and seen the flow of the main stream, he may then perceive the parts of the melody, the dissonances, and the countercurrents.

Tone and Government

The tone that strikes the newcomer is almost always intended. The leaders of most regimes—regardless of whether the regime is part of, say, Christian, Muslim, Confucian, Hindu, or Japanese culture—believe that sending certain signals about what is approved and disapproved is central to what the regime is all about. That is because regimes usually establish themselves by winning wars, whether civil or international; because a given regime may believe that it is barely winning the struggle to be what it wants to be; or simply because it wants to rub in its victory. In 1979, the Islamic republic that the Ayatollah Khomeini installed in Iran forbade women to be seen in public without a veil or scarf over most of the face. It is a commonplace that century after century the history of Iran boils down to a struggle between the way of life depicted in the *Shah Nameh*, the book of the ancient, secular kings, and the Muslim Koran. By imposing the veil, closing businesses on Fridays, and so on, Khomeini wanted to leave no doubt as to who had won the latest round in that struggle. By contrast, the leaders of modern Turkey rightly consider the increasing voluntary use of the veil by Turkish women—including lawyers and members of Parliament—to be a threat to the regime established in 1923 by Mustafa Kemal, the central point of which was that the Muslim muezzin would no longer sound the main tone of Turkish life. Turkey would be a secular, western state. To that end, Kemal's regime not only banned the veil but ordained that the Turkish language—heretofore written in Arabic characters—would now be written with the Latin alphabet. Thus, he made it impossible for ordinary literate Turks to read the Koran in the original. Indeed, in much of the Islamic world, there is an important struggle between leaders for whom the Koran is either not terribly important or downright alien, and less powerful people for whom secular leaders are foreigners. Hence, anyone looking for an indicator of fundamental trends in any Islamic country might note whether more or fewer women wear veils and who those women are.[2]

Travelers to Israel, too, have noticed over the years that the proportion of men wearing yarmulkes or even black hats has risen and that the number of people who say that this makes them uncomfortable has risen as well. The dominant tone nowadays is one of discord. Until the 1980s, visitors to Israel noted the acerbity of its politics but also observed that just about all kinds of people came together in the army. That institution sounded a loud tone. Most of Israel's founders had been secular Western socialists but had been so committed to gathering the world's Jews to the Promised Land, so seared by the Holocaust, and so pressed by neighbors who forced Israel to fight for survival that they embraced military service. By the late 1980s, however, the army seemed less near to the hearts of the kind of secular Jews who founded Israel. Many, like their fellow leftists in the West, had taken to pacifist fashions. It seemed equally clear that the central preoccupation of the Israelis who count most had shifted from a united, forceful affirmation of Zionism to a divisive question: Who are the true Israelis? And since they seemed to have decided that the country's tone would not be set and the country's defense would not be inspired by the Judaism of the Torah, it was not clear whether it would be inspired by anything at all.

Whereas a generation ago travelers to India were struck by the sad, flat note of sleepy misery under a mildly corrupt post-British bureaucracy, today they cannot help but be struck by powerful, dissonant tones that come from a revival of Hindu identity (for Hinduism is not, strictly speaking, a religion) and from a widespread popular lament for some kind of liberation from government-imposed misery. The Hindu revival seems directed less at any sort of piety than at growing resentment of Muslims. And just as in the Islamic world, religion is a convenient weapon with which to attack officials who flout their secularism.

Travelers to China also cannot help but be struck by dissonance. On the one hand, the regime shouts the language of Communist egalitarianism and practices naked tyranny on an appalling scale. The tanks that rolled over demonstrators in Beijing's central square in June 1989 and the various officials who collect protection money and force abortion and infanticide on one billion people sound a frightening tone. On the other hand, the very fact that so many officials are so obviously for sale and in business for themselves sounds a tone of openness and possibility.

Visitors to the United States are usually on guard against the disorienting effects of its diversity. Nevertheless, even casual tourists get the main points. Touring the White House, they are struck that such great power should be wielded from a place exceeded in splendor by any number of palaces in their native lands. This tone of republican simplicity, reinforced by the austere neoclassical architecture of state and local governments around the country, touches the heart of the matter. Although the contemporary U.S. government resembles an empire more than it does the republic described by de Tocqueville a century and a half ago, the tradition of limited government is still the most important feature of American public life—a feature that politicians ignore at their political peril. Almost all foreigners are mystified by the American people's intolerance of politicians' public moral failings and by the fact that regardless of their beliefs, American politicians, especially aspirants to the presidency, overwhelmingly profess to be practicing Christians. Well-traveled visitors know that most Americans no longer live in small towns dominated by a clapboard church or two, a little red schoolhouse, and a modest town hall. But they realize that American minds are still tuned to the emanations of those powerful symbols.

In every country, the largest buildings—the most prominently located buildings, and the public buildings—are a powerful sign of who rules and why. This is as true in our day as it was in the time of ancient civilizations, as true in the West as in the East. The Mesopotamian, Egyptian, and Mayan temples made clear that those who lived in their shadows saw in them the meeting of heaven and earth and the unity of all authority. By contrast, in China, India, and Japan, the majesty of the rulers' palaces has always overshadowed religious shrines. In Western civilization, from the Middle Ages until very close to our own time, the biggest, best-located, and most-frequented buildings in every city and village were churches. In eighteenth-century France, government buildings began to challenge churches for size, splendor, and prominence. But until the 1960s, the Cathedral of Notre Dame continued to dominate the low-rise skyline of Paris. In the twentieth century, beginning in America, business buildings became so prominent that it is almost impossible to pick a cathedral out of a modern American skyline. The Soviet Union demolished churches to make room for its signature buildings—offices for bureaucracies and apartments for bureaucrats. But the most prominent feature of the Moscow skyline today is the rebuilt cathedral of Christ the Savior. In today's America, though, the most luxurious buildings being built (of marble, brass, and rare woods) are federal courthouses.[3]

Statues in front of buildings help set the tone. France requires all localities to clear all statues with the central government. Had it not done so, the Paris suburbs would once have been filled with statues of Stalin. Other countries are not so formal. Nevertheless, in a given time and place the standards are clear. Whereas during the Renaissance Western sculptors immortalized saints and figures from classical antiquity, the most common statues from the seventeenth through much of the twentieth century have been of generals on horseback and of political founders—signifying the primacy that peoples during this period placed on combat and nationhood. No one walking the Soviet Union's public squares could have failed to sense the regime's tones. Even bolder than the tone sounded by the ubiquitous memorials to heroes of war and socialist labor was that sounded by statues of Pavel Morozov, the boy who informed Stalin's police of his parents' political incorrectness. Changes in statuary are really a rather accurate social indicator: Though much of the Communist legacy survived the Soviet collapse, all forms of intentional state pressures against families did not. When the regime fell, Russians pulled down the statues of Morozov even faster than they did the ones of Feliks Dzerzhinsky, the founder of the secret police. Since 1992, the statues of Dzerzhinsky, Stalin, Leonid Brezhnev, and many others have lain mutilated in a weed lot behind a Moscow art school. The ones of Morozov are nowhere to be found.

In America, a sort of unofficial code has ensured that all but a handful of statues erected between circa 1960 and 1985 consist of twisted shapes, the significance of which may be known only by those who manufacture them and the government officials who pay for them. Since the mid 1980s, the dominant genre of American statuary celebrates women, people of color, and even white men—if they happen to be crippled. In the 1990s, U.S. courts have entertained suits alleging that the failure to take down statues to confederate soldiers is an intolerable insult to the plaintiffs. In the same vein but more significant is that the U.S. Supreme Court has forbidden any statuary or manifestation of any kind to convey any Christian or Jewish themes on public ground. The city of San Diego, California, tried to prevent the removal of a cross that had stood in a city park for as long as anyone could remember by giving the land it stands on to a private group. But it seems the Court will not allow the transfer of property. Nevertheless, without explanation, the Court has allowed the city of San Jose, California, to place in its public square a statue not of the saint after which the city is named, but of the Aztecs' bloodthirsty god, Quetzalcoatl.

Who Sets the Tone?

Often, governments leave it to others to set society's main tone. Visitors to Saudi Arabia are impressed by the high walls that separate the royal family's sumptuous Western-style life from society's daily Koranic rigor and by how the nongovernmental religious police dictate dress, manners, and morals on the streets. In Western civilization, too, until recent decades public authorities left responsibility for marriages and morals to churches and synagogues. In America, argued de Tocqueville, religion set the rules of life more powerfully than anywhere else because it did so on its own authority, apart from the state. Moreover, de Tocqueville argued that America controlled common crime more successfully than other countries because the American people took upon themselves the responsibility of keeping public order and pursuing criminals rather than leaving it to the authorities.[4]

Since few of the world's civil authorities are actually strong enough to rule the streets by their own power, they all must do so to some extent by preferring the order set by one class of private persons over that of others—in other words, by acting as if certain people have the presumption of right over others. Alan Erenhalt's moving description of the orderliness of ethnic white Chicago neighborhoods in the 1950s makes no mention of policemen—only of priests, nuns, teachers, and adults, all of whom were confident that they could inflict summary corporal punishment as well as verbal admonition on any youth they thought deserved it.[5] If asked who ruled the world, any teenager in

New York in the 1950s might well have answered that it was the shop owners and building superintendents who hose off the sidewalks in summer and shovel the snow in winter. They determined whether you could play stickball or not, along with whatever else was allowed and prohibited. The police, the judges, the mayor, and heaven itself just seemed to echo the "supers"—just as the authorities in Saudi Arabia back up the religious police and the authorities in Ireland backed the church in family matters until recently.

In many places, leaving society to police itself means simply that it is left prey to its most disorderly elements. James Q. Wilson shocked many who should have known better with his observation that broken windows left unrepaired quickly change the character of a place by spreading the message that the vandals are in charge.[6] As we will see in later chapters, the presumption that those who are likely to commit violent crimes have as much right to the streets as anyone else has reshaped American life. Some have even argued that the power that violent young black men wield on America's streets has led other sectors of society to imitate their clothing—from fancy sneakers to baggy pants. Because—by default—their hairstyles, their music, and their manners have come to symbolize virility, those who do not imitate them telegraph the kind of weakness that attracts violence. Such a mixture of incentives and disincentives has spread from the inner cities to all parts of American society. One is as likely to find teens with shorts down to their ankles in small-town America as in New York City—the home of the successful cable television network MTV that spreads the "gangsta" gospel. Even in the glossy pages of the *New York Times Magazine*, trendy advertisements for expensive clothes feature young people properly disheveled, with just the right expression of resentment and menace. The government, it seems, has let street toughs corner the market on manliness.

But there are places in the world where the tone of violence is even louder and deadlier. In Sicily, the streets are full of small knots of people speaking quietly, glancing over their shoulders, ready to tell anyone who asks that they do not know anything about anything. Neither the church nor the state has been able to disabuse most Sicilians of the assumption that the sine qua non of prosperity, peace of mind, and long life is to pay respectful attention to what the Mafia's self-proclaimed "men of honor" say. In post-Communist Russia, the copycat "Mafiyas" wear something of a uniform—1930s Chicago-style clothing with expensive jewelry—but they carry the same message as their Sicilian models: Officials answer to us, not we to them. In Chelyabinsk as in Palermo, the mafiosi are the regime: attractive to women, the envy of men, and models for the next generation.

Government and society usually also speak the same language—using the same terms of praise and blame. Because the terms of public discourse are the lifeblood of the body politic, they sound perhaps the most telling of all. Contrast, for example, any newspaper or barroom conversation circa 1990 in Yugoslavia and in most of the European Union (EU). Throughout Yugoslavia, people were eager to explain how their kind had been good but had been victimized by that other evil nationality. In fact, the visitor would soon conclude that any number of people in the bar would just as soon kill as play chess. By contrast, none of their counterparts in Western Europe expressed the kind of resentment against other groups that might justify killing them. Indeed, their talk did not contain the kind of passion about anything, whether nationhood or religion, not even soccer, that might have led anyone in any EU country to forceful offense—or, alas, to defense of anything. Moreover, one got the impression that the very unfamiliar sight of a weapon might produce debilitating shock.

The tone in Europe's bars is reflected at the highest levels of Europe's government. Reading the annual defense white papers of the North Atlantic Treaty Organization's (NATO) major European members, one is struck by the euphemisms and circumlocutions the writers use to avoid discussing the heart of the matter: that certain foreign peoples might do things that are so unacceptable that preparing to kill them in large numbers is both prudent and morally necessary. All such papers reiterate that the most important thing to be done is to maintain "the transatlantic link." No uninitiated person would venture to say that this disembodied term means that in certain circumstances, Americans should be willing to blow up millions of human beings with nuclear weapons on Europe's behalf. Even the initiates would hardly guess what these circumstances might be, why Europe might ever benefit, or why any Americans in their right mind might do such a thing. Victorian discussions of sex were more graphic and enlightening than contemporary European discussion of war. In contrast with their shyness about warfare, none of these governments is at all shy about presenting on their government-controlled television networks graphically explicit discussions of how people contract the HIV virus. In fact, government-sponsored discussions of sex in Western Europe are almost as explicit, as lengthy, and as boring as discussions of the distribution of government benefits. Just as it is in most places, the tone of the regime is loud and clear.

Regime and Civilization

Regimes do not spring up with particular sets of characteristics just anywhere on the planet. Strong as the influence of regimes on people's lives is, the influence of civilizations tends to be greater. Civilizations set the bounds within which regimes exercise their powers over human habits. The best predictor of the quality of life in any given regime is the civilization in which the regime exists. The random baby born in Africa is likely to have a life very different from that of a counterpart born in North America. Indeed, a European child will have a very different life depending on whether that baby was born east or west of a line that starts at the Baltics and stretches southward along Poland's eastern border, down Slovakia's western border and along the eastern border of Hungary, then continues down through the middle of Bosnia to the Adriatic Sea. West of this line are relatively prosperous Catholics and Protestants; east of it, there are mostly poor orthodox Slavs, who live in what Steven Schwartz has called the India of the North. The world's major civilizations are more or less coterminous with its major religions and, much more roughly, with its major races.[7] Western civilization surely covers Australia, North America, the southern cone of South America, and in some mixture most of the rest of the Americas as well, in addition to that part of Europe lying west of the line that divides Western Christian from Orthodox-Slavic civilization. South and east of both, from the Atlantic coast of Saharan Africa to Indonesia, is the world of Islam. South of that, black Africa is a mixture of the effects of other civilizations' imperfect recruiting and tribal memories that are mostly lost. Asia, of course, contains the Hindu, Confucian, and Japanese civilizations. Each civilization is a package of habits and precepts that not only affects the way people live but to some extent defines what it means to be happy.

Nevertheless, although every civilization determines much of this, each is open to a wide range of possibilities. Indeed, the struggles within civilizations are even more bitter and significant than those between them. In every historical circumstance, the regime—the arrangement of honors, offices, and priorities particular to the time and place—realizes some of the potentials in each civilization and pushes the others to the side. In every civilization, there are undeniable examples of poverty and wealth, family breakdown and cohesion, and civic peace with relative freedom. There have been circumstances in which Muslims, Slavs, Europeans, and Japanese have been willing and able to draw military effort from themselves and circumstances in which they have not. Some civilizations and some cultures within them seem more malleable by circumstance and regime than others. None have given greater evidence of malleability than the Japanese, who, within a century after their leaders' decision to abandon feudalism and isolation, were led rather easily to adopt three ways of life vastly different in tone and substance: obedient pupils, aggressive militarists, and single-minded producers. Yet, as we have seen, peoples belonging to other civilizations have changed their ways of life as well.

The Thrust of Regimes

It is not necessary here to describe the political cultures of the world's main civilizations—there are many within each. Rather, it is sufficient to point out that within each and all there are regimes that foster certain kinds of behavior and personality over others.

The terms used here to describe political phenomena do not have precisely the same meaning across the world's civilizations. Democracy, in contemporary discourse, describes rule by the majority of citizens, all of whom count alike and all of whom can expect to be both voters and officeholders at some time in their lives. Willingness to rule and to be ruled presupposes willingness on the part of both rulers and ruled to abide by the same laws. This whole idea makes sense only insofar as one believes that every citizen, regardless of power or status, is both equal and worthy in some fundamental way. With every passing year, however, fewer and fewer within Western civilization believe this.[8] The success of John Rawls' *Theory of Justice*—in which justice is defined in terms of the power-dependent concept of fairness—shows how far we have come in redefining the intellectual basis of democracy.[9]

Outside the West, practically no one believes that people have any right to equal treatment. What then can be the long-term future of democracy? The few Chinese, Japanese, and Muslims who yearn for democracy and citizenship based on human equality (assuming they understand the meaning of such words) want things foreign to their civilization. Within Confucian civilization, the many can be fulfilled in an ethically worthy organization. Equal acceptance of social order is Confucian. But the interchangeability of roles is not, nor is the equal worth of each member. The Islamic *umma* (the people) can be united in "the house of peace" (that is, under any truly Islamic, supranational government—something inherently problematic) or "in the path of God" (that is, fighting for one). Any Muslim's claim to leadership is as good as anyone else's. But in the Islamic world, the status of leader and led is incommensurable. The normal mode of Japanese participation is consensus, irrespective of how it is achieved. The same is true wherever Japanese cultural influence reaches—even in Korea. But this kind of consensus is consistent with winner-take-all politics. Thus, South Korea has changed governments simply because of elections. But it seems not to have shed the notion that political losers are to be jailed or worse.

Thus, when we think about how regimes foster or hinder civil life, and about the role of equality in civil life, we should think about what is possible in the context of any given civilization. We should also consider how the changes taking place within our civilization make problematic the continuation of our own democratic institutions.

Similarly, when we think about how regimes may foster prosperity, we should think beyond the economic institutions of economically successful countries and consider what attitudes and policies foster economic activity in a variety of contexts. For instance, consider that the culture that supports American economics could not survive were the U.S. government somehow to attempt to impose the kind of high-level favoritism—Americans call it corruption—that is a major feature of life in the successful economies of East Asia. How favoritism affects East Asian economies is another question. Consider also that desire for one's own economic betterment is not the *summum bonum* (highest good) in all the world's cultures. Often, the ruling passion is to be better off than one's neighbors in relative terms. This was certainly so in Edward Banfield's southern Italian village and is very much so in much of the Middle East and India. The point here is that we must think through to those features of any regime anywhere that foster economic activity and then try to understand what kind of economic satisfaction they foster.

The various kinds of regimes—tyrannies, revolutionary dictatorships, various kinds of military empires, theocracies and other kinds of oligarchies, and various kinds of democracies—exist within most civilizations, though seldom in pure form.[10] It makes sense, however, to begin by examining how some of the pure types affect prosperity, civility, and family; how they raise and lower the human spirit; and how they affect the capacity of a people to defend themselves among others.

Tyranny

All civilizations are familiar with tyranny—that is, with regimes organized to satisfy the desires of the ruler. The tyrant may rule over a great European power, as with Hitler, over a medium-sized one in the Middle East, as with Hafez Assad and Saddam Hussein, or over a small African country, as with Idi Amin. The tyrant's passions may be petty or grand. But the results are remarkably similar: economics reduced to favor seeking; politics reduced to flattery, intrigues, betrayals, and purges; families destabilized, spirits degraded, and people killed by repression and war.

The tyrant's desire to control and to take overrides any concern he might have for the prosperity of the people under him.[11] That is why it makes no sense to describe such regimes as nationalistic. From Syria to Haiti, such rulers want to make sure the people closest to them get special advantages over the mass of unconnected people. This provides incentives to those closest to the tyrant to continue seeking his favor, and makes it more difficult for people who are not connected with the tyrant to muster the economic means to oppose him. Thus, in Syria, Cuba, and Iraq, the right to import various necessities of life (as well as the privilege of importing and transshipping narcotics) is reserved exclusively for family and close friends of the tyrant. The efficient practice of tyranny, however, requires that the tyrant cause some turnover in the ranks of the privileged, both to keep the competition for favoritism lively and to prevent any of the privileged from acquiring too much wealth and too many constituents. Hence, Assad, Castro, and Hussein, like the rest of their kind, regularly disgrace some of their favorites—Assad even included his brother among those purged—for corruption.[12] Various other kinds of economic privilege—bank credit, licenses, captive customers—are the normal coin with which tyrants pay supporters. Hence the most remunerative economic act in tyrannies is one that satisfies the person closest to the source of privilege. In most tyrannies, the laws specifically protect private property. But since the only real law is the will of the tyrant, property is held and disputes about it are resolved strictly through favor.[13]

Cronyism is also the mark of tyrannical politics. The whole point of tyranny, of course, is that either there are no laws or, more likely, there are so many laws that willful officials can construe whomever they choose to be in violation. Hence, each official does to the powerless—and to other officials—what he thinks will advance his own personal fortunes with the one and only source of law. The only relevant political question is who depends on whose favor and why. Therefore, the politics of tyranny is, above all, self-ingratiation and palace intrigues aimed at building up or tearing down the influence of favorites. As Hilton Root's reports to the World Bank about African governments have shown, the politics and economics of tyranny are two sides of the same transaction. Privilege is the coin that pays for support, and vice versa. But since the logic of the competition leads to the search for better deals up and down the line, its logical end is the coup d'état.

The other major coin of tyrannical politics is the appearance of personal affection. Procuring women as well as providing derogatory information on real and imagined enemies are the age-old means of self-ingratiation. This is the coin that the *Book of Kings*, the manual of Persian courtiers, suggested to those who would make their fortunes at tyrants' courts centuries ago. It seems to be the currency of choice in the tyrannies of our time. Obviously, pursuit of success by such radical commitments to pleasing the boss or the boss's secretary is incompatible with respect for anyone's family, including one's own. Religious leaders, too, face the choice between public irrelevance, death, or prostitution. Whichever they choose, the tyranny makes obvious the dominance of willful self-seeking over matters of the spirit.

Tyrannies have special relationships with military force. Whether in high-tech Nazi Germany, in the Soviet Union and its satellites, or in the primitive conditions of Eduardo Macias's Equatorial Guinea, they follow Machiavelli's model of distrust for citizen militias and reliance on professional "special units." Such units live apart from regular armies and, in exchange for special privileges, do the regime's dirty work, engage in the brutal repression that others refuse to do, and, of course, purge and prod regular armies. The privileges are sometimes petty. Before the Polish government sent its ZOMO forces to crack down on the Solidarity trade union in 1981, it issued them chocolate bars—some people will do a lot for a little. But there is seldom anything petty about what such units do. Thus, in both the Gulf War and the war with Iran, Saddam Hussein's special units followed the Soviet practice of sowing land mines behind their regulars to discourage retreat. But because such armed forces are optimized for internal repression and have little stomach for real fighting, they are of little use when foreign enemies threaten. Moreover, they are unwilling and unable to call on the help of the citizenry. The more tyrannical a regime, the greater the percentage of its military forces that is devoted to containing other domestic military forces and the weaker the ensemble. Thus, when the Kenyan army invaded Idi Amin's Uganda, it faced little organized resistance. For this reason, tyrannies typically die either because they cannot summon the strength to withstand foreign arms or as a result of coups hatched within the professional armed forces.

Modern revolutionary dictatorships have taken tyranny to new levels. Because they rule through parties, the number of tyrants, and their appetites, is multiplied manifold. Because they aim to reshape society, they infect all of it with the ethos of tyranny.

The economics of "real socialism" as practiced from Havana to East Berlin and Moscow to Hanoi and Pyongyang had nothing whatever to do with any egalitarianism. Soviet Communist leaders lived "like gods and tsars," as Russians often say,[14] or rather, like the Communist bosses of East Germany and every other such state, secure in their own suburbs, eating special foods. Indeed, the dietary consequences of the economic stratification of "real socialism" were evident in the physical appearance of the population. The elites looked much like Westerners who eat balanced diets that include meat and fresh vegetables all year round. Below the very top were thick, shiny officials who obviously had regular access to meat, but not to greens. The upper levels of the masses had the sort of pasty complexion that comes from lots of starch, while the gaunt pastiness of the rest of the people suggested they had trouble getting even enough starch. The Cuban, Chinese, and Nicaraguan Sandinista governments even empowered their grassroots officials to make sure that ordinary people did not consume more than the allotted number of calories per day. In Tanzania, Julius Nyerere's Ujamaa villages got inmates to work by withholding food from the recalcitrant. Thus, on the lowest as well as the highest levels, economic life under "real socialism" consists of an unremitting effort to be among the rule makers and enforcers rather than among those who must live by the rules. Unlike standard tyranny, modern socialist tyranny forces everyone, low as well as high, to seek special treatment through special arrangements. No commodity has a natural price. No labor has intrinsic worth. No one has title to anything. Each and all can expect to enjoy neither more nor less than what they can get the authorities to agree to at any given time.

Stalin—with Machiavelli's *The Prince* by his bedside—set the tone for the politics of the socialist world: purge, so that no one might ever feel secure in his position and hence so that everyone might be obliged to constantly seek the party's favor at everyone else's expense. The Soviet system eventually collapsed because Leonid Brezhnev's encouragement of officials at all levels to become "rooted" in their posts turned the Soviet Union into a feudal state that was increasingly unresponsive to the center. When Yuri Andropov and Mikhail Gorbachev tried to take the party in hand again, they did so through purges backed not by bloodshed but rather by fostering popular criticism of their enemies in officialdom. That violated the basic rule of tyranny that Stalin had epitomized: Only the tyrant—not any autonomous agency, and least of all public opinion—purges officials, rewards friends capriciously, and kills enemies ostentatiously. The Communists who have followed that rule have kept control. Fidel Castro managed to hang on to power by mastering his subordinates' intrigues and betrayals through bloody purges of the best of them and by practicing indiscriminate violence against opponents. Thus, he convicted and executed the popular General Osvaldo Ochoa of drug trafficking, ordered the machine-gunning of people who try to flee the island, and made sure that the officials who are close to him at any given time have privileged access to the dollars from the tourist industry.

The policy of the socialist world toward families has been straightforward hostility. China went so far as to herd peasants into communes and there to physically separate the men, women, and children into barracks, granting conjugal time as a reward for work or favor but decreeing the killing—before or after birth—of more than one child per couple. Meanwhile, of course, many officials did what they could through the exchange of favors to foster the fortunes and privileges of their children. The fabulous wealth of the families of Leonid Brezhnev and Deng Xiaoping is well documented. Nevertheless, for many more officials the *banda*, or bureaucratic group, through which they pursued their fortunes became more important than biological families. The decline of family loyalties in socialist countries is less remarkable than their survival.

The degradation of the human spirit has been no less a policy of modern revolutionary dictatorships. Although the Nazi regime could not practically consider the physical elimination of Christians, its enmity toward the idea of Christianity was only somewhat less virulent than its attitude toward Judaism. As for the Soviet Union, as late as September 1984, *Pravda* editorialized that the most mortal of the perils the system faced was the recrudescence of religion. The Chinese government closed all but thirteen out of some 6,500 monasteries in Tibet. Other Communist governments closed smaller percentages— from about 90 percent of the churches in Russia to only 20 percent in Poland. But everywhere they put religion under ministries whose purpose was to banish it from public life first, then from private life as well. To all this, one must add that such regimes are always calling on the people to join in portentous programs to improve the material lot of mankind, to do wondrous things in science, and to rid society of certain perennial ills. Yet because such calls to greatness and appeals to generosity are counterfeit, they produce mean-spiritedness. These regimes produced no art, and the only worthwhile literature has been inspired by opposition. It is not surprising then that perhaps the most obvious feature of postsocialist countries is a lack of morality, sometimes described as a moral vacuum.[15]

If socialist states excelled in anything, it was in their armed forces, which absorbed upward of one-third of their economies. The Soviet military had more major modern weapons systems (except aircraft carriers) than the rest of the world combined. James L. Payne has shown that in Communist countries, the ratio of men under arms, as well as that of major weapons systems to the number of citizens, was several times that in the rest of the world.[16] And yet, next to suppressing religion, nothing so preoccupied Communist leaders as controlling the ever-present threat of dissension within the armed forces and creating a commitment that they knew was not there to fight for the regime. In the Soviet Union, as in Poland and every other tyrannical system, the leadership relied on special units. But in its last days, the Soviet regime could not find any special unit willing to fight another. Regimes that live by special units die of them as well.

Oligarchy

Most of the world's regimes, regardless of what they call themselves, are oligarchies—that is, some kind of arrangement by which relatively few people rule for the purpose of enriching themselves. Oligarchies come in numerous varieties. One kind consists of Mafias, tightly knit groups that share the loot from the meager economies of poor, small countries. Occasionally, the disorganization of large countries—such as today's Russia—lets them be governed this way for a short time. Mafia economics is short-sighted because it is purely extractive. The oligarchs' gains come from others' losses. For the few, the road to prosperity lies in fealty to a gang. For the many, selective servility and general passivity are the best way of getting by. Families thrive under Mafias because fortunes tend to rise and fall jointly and retribution also falls jointly on families. In such systems, family members are the only people one can trust. But from Palermo to Moscow, the spirit of life is mean, and religion approaches superstition.

Another kind of oligarchy has ruled the world's free ports, from ancient Phoenicia to yesterday's Hong Kong and most of today's Asian Tigers. Since these rulers' raison d'être is to take shares of expanding trade and since they know that trade can go elsewhere, they tend to run scrupulously fair systems of commercial law, except of course for occasional interventions to secure moderate privileges for themselves. Such places also usually underpin civil order and safety with draconian laws. In such places, the path to riches lies in keeping one's nose clean, keeping one's dealings simple and productive. Here, economics is least fettered by politics, and economics rewards families that pool resources to invest in business or professional education. Those close to the regime sometimes take a cut, though not often enough to raise the real cost of doing business above that of competing sovereignties. Such places are seldom known for spiritual growth, not because the governments have anything against religion but because the inhabitants are in a hurry to make money. They had better be, because history teaches that such governments have short lives—primarily because their own citizens have neither the skill nor the inclination to form powerful armed forces. Hence, they must depend for their existence on the good will and protection of great powers—things that great powers seldom give for free or for long.

A third kind of oligarchy ruled ancient Carthage, the late Roman republic, Renaissance Venice, and early modern Britain. Its common feature is the tendency of its leaders to engage in great enterprises. They enforce privilege for themselves at home to foster vast commerce abroad. They build magnificent cities for themselves while fostering law, industry, the arts, and human excellence in general. And though they infrequently draw the bulk of their citizenry into the military (most such regimes have been naval powers), they organize great military enterprises.

In any given instance, however, these regimes can foster very different kinds of lives. In the eighteenth century, economic life in Great Britain was characterized by mean-spirited protectionism and exploitative mercantilism. The turn-of-the-century debates in the House of Lords over the impeachment of Warren Hastings, the chief delegate of the East India Company, laid out the conflict between economic life based, on the one hand, on restricting imports and granting special privileges to certain companies, and, on the other hand, on the economics of equal opportunity. Although Edmund Burke and Adam Smith carried the day intellectually, the great debate was not resolved until the Corn Laws were repealed in 1847, almost two generations later—after the Reform Act of 1832 had broadened participation in political life, affirmed the principle of equal treatment under law, and set Britain on the road to democracy. Venice, too, experienced a major shift in economic life in the fifteenth and sixteenth centuries. When Turkish conquests around the Black Sea gradually closed down the silk trade with China (which had been conducted by a small number of chartered importers), a host of unregulated small businesses sprang up that produced silk domestically. This in turn broadened the base of the oligarchy and changed the basis of Venice's prosperity. Political life in such regimes, then, depends substantially on economic arrangements. As these become less restrictive, political power tends to spread as well. Magnificence sometimes follows.

The habits of adherence to law and impartial procedure that are essential to commerce tend to spread to politics. Compare, for example, the conditions under which young Winston Churchill rose in late nineteenth-century Britain with those under which his ancestor, John Churchill, later the duke of Marlborough, had risen two hundred years before. John had succeeded in currying favor in no small part because his sister was the mistress of the king's brother. Accounts of Marlborough's *cursus honorum* remind the reader of the Persian *Book of Kings*. Winston, by contrast, rose less through family connections than by the very bourgeois skill of self-advertising. Clearly, however, oligarchic regimes of this kind can as easily evolve toward the licentiousness of the very rich as toward sober bourgeois meritocracy.

The seeking after great things that suffuses such regimes extends first to the arts—in no other regimes do so many people pay so many artists for so many works of adornment and entertainment—and then to enterprises of the mind and spirit. The lasting fruits of such regimes are the works of Cicero, Virgil, William Shakespeare, Edward Gibbon, and those of the entire Venetian school that adorned the churches at which millions of tourists now gaze, as well as the civilization that they spread to the far corners of the world.

Democracy

Democracies, however, have no character except the character of the demos or its leaders at any given time. Thus, in practice, democracies can resemble any other regime—even any kind of oligarchy or tyranny. While some democracies have failed to muster the cohesion necessary to defend themselves, others have created and run military empires, sometimes moderate and other times not. Whole peoples have given themselves over to the pursuit of religious perfection, while others, just as democratically, have perfected debauchery. De Tocqueville marveled that, in America, democracy had brought domestic and international peace, civility, prosperity, and morality, whereas in France, it had brought precisely the opposite. When we consider how moderate the very same generation of Athenians was when it listened to Pericles, how cruel when listening to Cleon, how blindly and self-destructively ambitious when listening to Alcibiades, we are reminded of how easily and how often the German people effectively changed their character during the twentieth century, and we are led to ask how American democracy, the American regime, is changing.

Knowing that changes in our regime can change our capacity to be prosperous, to live as members of healthy families and communities, to raise our minds and spirits, and to protect ourselves in the world and knowing that the social and political choices we face are sure to change our regime, we want to understand what the harbingers and the consequences of such changes might be.

We wonder what aspects of our character, of our history, which symbols, will set the tone of our lives. There are more than enough clashing alternatives. Every April 19, Americans, especially in New England, are asked to celebrate the anniversary of the day in 1775, now known as Patriot Day, when a bunch of embattled farmers near Concord, Massachusetts, "fired the shot heard round the world." By killing the soldiers of a government that had grown too demanding and inaccessible, Americans established their right to freedom. But on April 19, 1993, the U.S. government used tanks to assault a small group of cultists in Waco, Texas, resulting in the deaths of 80, including 25 children. Two years later, a former soldier, incensed at the Waco killings and resentful of the U.S. government's growing arrogance, exploded a truck bomb outside the federal building in Oklahoma City, killing 168 people, including 39 children. Though there was precisely no evidence that any militia was involved, the President of the United States, followed by like-minded politicians and editorialists, blamed opponents of big government for the blast and have since made it part of national lore that America is threatened by militia terrorism. Hence, the U.S. government closed off Pennsylvania Avenue in front of the White House, and has made the general public pass through metal detectors to get into federal buildings. Not least of the questions we must answer is, Which of the legacies of April 19 will set the tone among us? Or will the legacy be merely one of strife?

Chapter 3

THE CHARACTER
OF DEMOCRACY

*Free nations, remember this maxim: "Liberty may be acquired
but never recovered."*

—JEAN-JACQUES ROUSSEAU,
The Social Contract

WHEN FRANCIS FUKUYAMA wrote in 1989 that liberal democracy's triumph over communism had ended history, he was following a long tradition.[1] End-of-history theses have always been
popular because they promise something like "and ye shall live happily
ever after"—perpetual relief from war—and above all because they
suggest that peoples will be spared momentous choices about how
they shall live their lives. In fact, however, no people is ever spared the
choices by which it continues to define itself. When the Romans finally erased Carthage from the face of the earth in 146 B.C. and found
themselves in a world without major enemies, they had reason to think
that their republican way of life was safe. But they could not have been
more mistaken: It was not safe from themselves. They themselves immediately set about adopting new ways and in the process undid the
civic, economic, familial, and religious institutions that had made
Roman republicanism so successful. The Romans did not intend to
start a century of civil wars, much less do away with their own freedom
and decency, and, eventually, their prosperity as well. Yet the Romans'
new habits inexorably brought loss of self-government, moral decadence, and the division of society into few lords and many paupers. It
took a while, but these new habits also eventually undermined the Romans' capacity for self-defense.

Liberal democracies are more subject to changing their character radically than any other kind of regime.[2] That is because the character of liberal democracy so totally depends on the character of the people and because the people's character depends so substantially on how they freely choose to mold it. In short, today, no less than during the Cold War, we must choose what aspects of our way of life we will defend, modify, or jettison. The momentary lack of military pressure from abroad merely leaves us freer to change ourselves for better or worse. But what do we want for ourselves? At first glance, the list seems modest.

As good liberal democrats, we want our rulers to work for us rather than the other way around. Rather than legions of bureaucrats, we want few laws that are equally applicable to all. Because we would rather be neither predators nor prey, we do not want our prosperity to depend on favors granted at the expense of others; rather, we want to be limited only by our own labor. We want to live in families, to care for our children as we choose, and to have them care for us. We want to be decent people, who treat one another as we would like to be treated—people whose spirits rise above the requirements for getting by in the world, who walk humbly with God but who overawe our enemies. Far from being modest, however, this wish list is so ambitious, so far out of the ordinary experience of mankind, that few peoples have ever been granted anything like it, and then only for short periods of time and always as the result of uncommon habits bolstering rare institutions.

The questions that we Americans—and indeed all the other liberal democratic peoples—must decide about our public lives touch the very heart of the habits and institutions that make us citizens or subjects, rich or poor, that make or break families, that elevate or abase souls, and that make for military might.

Size, Scope, and Purpose

The biggest set of questions we must decide regarding our civic life concerns the size of government and its competence. Size makes certain that government will weigh—or will not—on a host of choices. Although size does not ensure that government will have the capacity to fulfill any particular set of responsibilities, let alone be able to carry them out well, size is a gross measure of government's incidence on civil society. In *Federalist Paper* no. 46, James Madison underlined that the American regime could not be understood merely by focusing on the Constitution. The Constitution had to be seen in its proper context—as a small island of government in a big sea of civil life. Madison wrote:

> The adversaries of the Constitution seem to have lost sight of the people altogether in their reasoning on this subject; and to have viewed these different establishments not only as mutual rival and enemies, but as uncontrolled by any common superior in their efforts to usurp the authorities of each other. They must be told that the ultimate authority, wherever the derivative may be found, resides in the people alone, and that it will not depend merely on the comparative ambition or address of the different governments whether either, or which of them, will be able to enlarge its sphere of jurisdiction at the expense of the other. Truth, no less than decency, requires that the event in every case should be supposed to depend on the sentiments and sanction of their common constituents.

The bigger government is, the smaller must civil society be.

Max Weber accustomed us to dividing human relations between *gemeinschaft*, the things we do out of personal obligation, and *gesellschaft*, our arm's-length economic activities. But our lives contain a substantial measure of what we might call *machtschaft*, namely, the things that we do to others and others do to us through the power of government. This compulsive power exists alongside and intermingled with the things we do to make a living as well as with our voluntary activities as members of families, churches or synagogues, and professions. But while government is necessary to civil society, its power has always offered itself as a tool for trumping civil society. In the twentieth century, the typical temptation has been to try to substitute government for both voluntary social and economic relationships.

Thus, our questions about the role of government must begin with the basic ones about its size: Of the many things that we do, which should require some kind of license or permission from some government agency? What should we be able to do solely on our own account? All can agree that we want government to test the performance of drivers and airline pilots. But to what extent do we wish to put the performance of other professions under the tutelage of government? Every government has the power of eminent domain, to take private property for public use. But to what extent should government be able to restrict or determine the use of private property that it does not take? How much and what kind of regulation is proper—not for economic health but for the very existence of civil society? No one denies that government should punish murder or robbery even when committed by one member of a family against another. Certainly marriage, the contract that constitutes new families, is public business, as are its terms. But to what extent are the relations between husband and wife, between parents and children, reviewable by government? Do we want government to issue and revoke parenting licenses subject to some test? At what point are governmental attempts to supplant or to second-guess relations between individuals wrong ipso facto?

In Western societies, judgments about right and wrong traditionally belonged to religion. As stated earlier, the Western tradition of government is one of minimal interference in the moral judgments of families and other organs of civil society. Traditionally, civil and criminal law consciously reflected society's religious judgments and indeed lent secular strength to them. Since the sixteenth century, however, most Western governments (the United States being the most notable exception) have claimed the right to make laws out of the sheer sovereign power to do so. In his classic commentary on the laws of England, Sir William Blackstone wrote that the British Parliament could do anything not naturally impossible, such as turning a man into a woman. Nevertheless, until recently, only revolutionary governments (preeminently those of the French Revolution and the Soviet and Nazi regimes) wilfully departed from the rule that secular law never contradicts the fundamental tenets of religious law. Recently, however, as *machtschaft* has expanded and civil society has shrunk, governments throughout the West have tended to act as if they could make up standards as they go along and have increasingly treated religion, which they call "fundamentalism" whenever it asserts itself, as the enemy of secular order rather than as its basis.

What then is to be the role of religion among us? How do we want to divide the power to set moral standards between civil society and government? How should government regard the special claims of religion? Are religious citizens in the West to face the choice that modern regimes in the Islamic world force on their citizens, namely, that so long as secularists hold government power, their alien standards will push religion to the margins of society, make public life a mockery of everything you deem holy, and lead your children to mock you? But if you want your surroundings and your children to reflect your judgments about right and wrong, you must seize government power and impose Koranic law on everyone. If you do not want to be degraded, you must degrade others. As Western governments squeeze civil society's traditional autonomy over morals, they willy-nilly force individuals to seek moral satisfaction through government. The alternative would involve a renunciation of a sizable share of the claims of modern government.

Who shall run the schools—and determine what is to be taught? In 1995, 1.5 percent of American parents—all of whom paid school taxes—did not send their children to school at all, while another 13 percent paid twice to send theirs to some kind of private school. Countless more wish they had the money or the courage to detach their families from the public schools. Theirs is a harsh judgment on the academic and moral competence of the government's schools. Comparison of test scores indicates that they are correct.[3] But if government is rightly and fully sovereign and if education is the foundation on which government rests,[4] then those parents who teach standards different from those taught in the government's schools are subversives by definition, while by that very definition government schools are right and proper regardless of what they teach. Hence, every effort should be made to stamp out private education in general and home schooling in particular. For much of the twentieth century, certainly in Europe, government schools were the very standard of civilization. The authority of government over education was seldom questioned. But today, as the competence of government to set intellectual and moral standards becomes obviously questionable, we also wonder what civil society loses by putting education into the realm of compulsion.

Traditionally, the inherent tension between government and civil society has been cushioned by a level of public life that partakes of civil society as well as of *machtschaft*, namely, local government. The idea that lots of responsibility at the level of government closest to the people makes possible the coexistence of extensive government with civil society, the core of James Madison's *Federalist Paper* no. 10, an idea often attributed to Baron de Montesquieu or even to Edmund Burke,[5] is actually far older. Large ancient cities, including Athens and Rome, were divided into tribes. Each tribe occupied a part of the city, had its own gods, and settled most civil and criminal matters within its own ranks. And of course feudal society was nothing but a welter of local privileges, obligations, and particularisms. Recently, economists have found that countries where there exist a variety of regulatory and tax jurisdictions tend to be more prosperous than countries with unitary systems. This is so because diversity spawns competition among the various local units and competition drives each unit to be more favorable to economic activity than it would otherwise have been. In sum, there is little need in the Western tradition and none at all in the American tradition to make a theoretical case for the goodness of strong local institutions.

The question for us (as it has always been for those who have decided the fate of vast countries) is the extent to which we are willing to take responsibility for running the affairs of our local community and how willing we are to tolerate communities in our country that live differently from us. Not long ago in America, public schools were run by units of government so small and so peculiar to the particular individuals involved that they functioned more as private than as public associations. The parents' exercise of power over them by vote over minute matters was arguably more effective than the power that private school parents today exercise by paying or withholding tuition. By the same token, whereas the First Amendment to the U.S. Constitution prohibited the federal government from establishing any religion on the national level, religion was fully established in eleven of the thirteen states. It remained fully established (at least by contemporary standards) in countless localities, especially in the public schools, until our time. Now, of course, small groups of neighbors have power over almost nothing.

Thus, the choice with regard to schools, or social and economic matters, is clear enough: Since only a tiny percentage can take significant part in public affairs at the national level, most citizens will take part in local affairs or not at all. But they will take part only if the jurisdiction of local governments is both very small and quite powerful. Note that de Tocqueville made the important distinction between centralized government and centralized administration. In his discussion of the different systems in place in England, France, and the United States, de Toqueville wrote:

In America the power that conducts the administration is far less regular, less enlightened, and less skillful, but a hundred fold greater than in Europe. In no country in the world do the citizens make such exertions for the common weal. I know of no people who have established schools so numerous and efficacious, places of public worship better suited to the wants of the inhabitants, or roads kept in better repair. Uniformity or permanence of design, the minute arrangement of details, and the perfection of administrative system must not be sought for in the United States; what we find there is the presence of a power which, if it is somewhat wild, is at least robust, and an existence checkered with accidents, indeed, but full of animation and effort.[6]

However, if many different sets of people decide big questions, they will surely decide differently. Some local governments would legalize drugs. Others would institute Singapore-style caning for their occasional use and death for salesmen. Rules regarding abortion would surely be different. Before the 1850s, Americans tolerated differences about slavery. But after the Dred Scott decision, toleration became impossible for all sides. How much diversity, how much freedom can we now tolerate, and on what basis?

Defining Issues

Much depends on the issues. Abraham Lincoln taught that politics, whether at the national or local level, cannot help but be nasty if its object is to decide who is to be defined into the human race and thus protected and who is to be left defenseless. That is why he thought that the very process of making detailed rules about slavery would corrupt the American people. Questions about who gets what, where, and how, and at whose expense, as well as questions about which classes of people are to be somehow "protected," subsidized, or entitled, also naturally lead to combat. The point here is that we define ourselves whenever we decide what we shall argue about and how we shall conduct the argument. As Montesquieu wrote, the health of republics depends on public life being dominated by questions that foster rather than destroy virtue. But how do we tell the difference between issues, and how do we foster the right kind among ourselves?

Addressing the second question leads to a better understanding of the first. Even mere formalities matter. Do we—in each of our electoral districts and in our governors and presidents—want to be represented by single individuals or by parties? Since a single officeholder is responsible for everyone who voted, regardless of whether the voter voted for or against that person, and since a party is responsible only to the voters who cast their ballots for it, it is no surprise that countries where the electors must choose between party lists tend to argue over more divisive issues and do so more divisively than countries where the voters choose individuals directly. Different electoral systems also bring to the fore different kinds of politicians.

Each electoral system also tends to create its own particular kind of political party. Do we want "strong" parties that can be "responsible" for turning their promises into actions by government? Or do we want parties that are only agglomerations of individuals with no power over their members and little capacity to carry out their promises?[7] Each kind has virtues and vices. "Responsible" parties tend to be filled with professional politicians, meaning professional dispensers of special privileges, lots of expertise, lots of power, and little need to care about anyone outside their own organization. Or do we want to limit the number of terms our politicians can serve, making them less expert and more responsive, if less responsible? If parties are held together by transient affiliations between blocks of voters, politicians may broker interests without care for principle. If parties are based only on ideas, they may be unable to compromise at all. Some combination of interest and principle seems to be necessary. But the twentieth century's peculiar disease has been parties organized to live off society and to oppress their enemies therein in the name of lofty principles.

Expertise is one of the perennial bones of contention in republics. Do we want to be governed by people such as judges and career government employees whose claim to rule is that they know better than the rest of us? Is their detachment from politics—especially local politics—likely to make them fairer and more enlightened?[8] It is even conceivable to detach administration from powerful interests in society, given that it is the very access to *machtschaft* that makes these interests so powerful? Are we better off with mandarins who administer specific laws according to strict rules, with administrators who have wide discretion to achieve broad objectives, or is fair impersonal administration simply incompatible with government that sets out to achieve big goals with huge resources?

According to perhaps a majority of academic opinion, the wealth of nations is the result of wise management by rulers whose powers are equal to their task. According to this view, the peoples of the Pacific Rim have achieved prosperity because of what Chalmers Johnson calls "state-directed capitalism." Others call it "industrial policy," or "neomercantilism." With no little irony, the Communists in power from Beijing to Moscow to Belgrade who claim to be following this model call it "market economy." In a nutshell, this means that government officials, who often have interests and always have friends and enemies in business, decide which ventures to favor by direct subsidies, protective tariffs, contracts, or tailored regulations. Peoples who export more high-tech goods than they import, so goes the argument, wind up with more money and with a better share of the world's high-paying jobs than others whose governments have not been so wisely active. Regardless of what else happens, officials and their friends benefit.

According to another view, however, state-directed capitalism is even more dysfunctional socially than it is economically. Indeed, advantages bestowed on companies and individuals tend to corrupt them and to pervert economic life from production to favor seeking. According to this perspective, government fosters prosperity by safeguarding property rights, as well as by providing a level playing field and fair, inexpensive settlement of disputes. The first approach requires a big government that takes much and gives much with wide discretion, while the second requires a government as small and law-bound as possible. As we choose between the two, we choose, at the very least, how much of our economic activities we should channel into seeking favor from government.

As we decide the role of government in foreign trade, in business and professional regulation, in tax policy, and in providing for old age, ill health, and misfortune, we are also deciding about what kinds of lives we will live. To what extent shall we be protectionists or free traders? This involves more than the economic question of whether wealth can be created by protecting high-wage jobs. Rather, it centers on what habits and ways of life protectionism protects and what ways of life free trade imposes. Is it the objective of economic life, in addition to earning a living, to earn it in roughly the same way in the same place throughout one's lifetime and perhaps to pass the entire situation on to one's children? When we decide that some among us will be protected while others will face competition, do we also decide who shall have the power to make such decisions and everything else that such power implies?

To what extent shall our governments regulate? The necessary premise of the tens of thousands of pages of regulations that flow from modern governments each year is that government knows more about the right way to build widgets than do widget makers or that although widget makers might be knowledgeable, only the hand of government prevents them from using their expertise to exploit the public. But of course since government draws its expertise by involving business in the regulatory process, government inevitably rules all widget makers through its favorite widget makers. Moreover, it makes a big difference, for example, if the people being regulated can be certain about what satisfies and does not satisfy regulations and be sure of the extent to which they must depend on discretionary rulings. The formal and informal ways in which the regulated influence the regulations also make a big difference. Do officials live in fear of overstepping their bounds, or do they swagger?

Choices about taxes are obviously about incentives and disincentives. By taxing the proceeds from the sale of businesses, we discourage transforming old businesses into new ones. By taxing any activity more, we discourage it more. By taxing it less, we decrease the discouragement. This applies to everything from the formation and size of families to charitable contributions, home ownership, savings, investment, the use of restaurants, cars, computers, and so forth. Thus, all schemes of taxation imply not just different levels of economic activity. They ensure that some activities, some ways of life, will be surer pathways to wealth than others.

When, at the turn of the twentieth century, Western governments embarked on becoming the major providers of assistance in old age, health, and personal failure, only a few imagined that government might thereby supplant rather than support the role of families in society.[9] Few foresaw that it would bring about vast changes in the composition of the labor force and even contribute to reducing the number of births to below that of deaths. Today, the economic and social consequences of pursuing social welfare through government raise questions long eclipsed by faith in government. For example, what difference does it make who is responsible for basic decisions about how much medical care we receive? Is it really good for us to make the government instead of our families the beneficiary of whatever part of our retirement savings we leave behind? Who is to judge who is worthy of charity, and who should get it?

Not the least of the economic questions before us is the extent to which we want to pay for a class of government employees, in effect subsidizing a class with a unique relationship to power. Is it anything but surprising that throughout the world the most heartfelt arguments for any function of government come from the people who are paid to perform that function and that government employees are everywhere the most determined political supporters of statist parties? Two generations ago, the U.S. government dealt with this fact by passing the Hatch Act, which prohibits certain kinds of political activity by government employees. Of course, the size and weight of this political constituency—today in America more people are employed to govern than to make things—has overwhelmed the Hatch Act. Surely, among the greatest questions with regard to any economy is the relationship between government power and economic life.

But government affects economic well-being even more by influencing the "human capital" that is the principal ingredient of any economy. Do we want government leaders and government policies to strengthen or to weaken in people's minds the basic connection between work and reward—that is, that people end up getting what they earn—or do we want them to promote the practical tenet of modern entrepreneurship that achievement consists of orchestrating the good graces of powerful patrons? Much has been made recently of the proposition that a people's economic success is proportionate to its level of trust, that those who can trust only members of their families will cooperate only with them, whereas extending trust farther allows economic cooperation to spread farther. While government cannot legislate trust, governments certainly affect the level of trust in society by the degree of evenhandedness and transparency with which they enforce their own rules.

Since human capital grows in families, the character of families may well be the primary element in the creation of prosperity, not to mention its enjoyment.[10] One of the great debates concerning economic efficiency is precisely whether it is best for most women to take part in the world of work interchangeably with men, sharing both housework and child care equally with men, while leaving children in some kind of day care, or whether it is best for everyone to have women devote themselves to caring for their own children in their own homes. According to some, the Japanese people work more diligently than the citizens of other developed countries in part because Japanese families are much less affected by divorce, illegitimacy, and uncertain roles for men and women. By the same token, Mikhail Gorbachev has noted that the economic contribution of women in the Soviet economy was more than canceled out by the decline in the quality of women's principal product: well-brought-up children and motivated men. On the other side, Scandinavian societies manage to do reasonably well economically with rates of illegitimacy fifty times as high as those of the Japanese. The point here is that the debate over what kind of family we should promote amongst ourselves is very much an economic debate as well.

Economic prosperity is so often linked to national power and happiness that people assume their equivalence. But that is not so. Innumerable cases, from sixteenth-century Spain to contemporary Saudi Arabia, have shown that neither money nor productive capacity necessarily translates into power, much less into civil peace or happiness. Plato was only the first to note that some forms of wealth tend to separate men from their community by reducing them to mere earners and consumers while cutting ties of responsibility with their neighbors. He called wealthy people who neither care for nor command others "drones" and considered them an element of decay. He also considered as elements of weakness those whose livelihood—at whatever level of prosperity—is rendered so precarious that they have no time for public affairs or who are so dependent on the favor of government that their involvement in public affairs consists of currying favor. As we ask how to foster prosperity, we must keep in mind the ways in which it can bring a people together or pull it apart.

The human content of an individual's home and family affects the quality of life far more than any material contents. Conversely, the character of families is much affected by government policy. But what is a family? Today, there is considerable objection even to defining the family in natural terms: as the union of a man and a woman that normally produces children. The alternative definition is conventional: A family is any group of individuals who live together with some degree of intimacy and commitment.[11] Although the difference between the two basic approaches to families is rooted in part in the opposition between heterosexuality and homosexuality, the difference is deeper and wider: Ought we to recognize or reject the way of life of most of mankind, namely, the division of labor between men and women, as well as the responsibility of men for their children and for the women who bear them—and its logical concomitant, the special authority of husbands over wives and children? The traditional Christian and Jewish marriage rituals stipulate different duties for husbands and wives. Until recently, our laws roughly followed these stipulations. About a generation ago, new laws and other signals from on high began trying to mold society according to the notion that neither man, woman, nor child had any particular obligation to anyone else. While there is a general recognition today that something has to be done about strengthening families, the several recipes proposed are based on radically different premises and would drive families in very different directions.

Perhaps the most prominent vision of the family is that the whole nation is a kind of extended family or "village," in which a variety of governmental institutions help raise the children, as well as provide for the sick, the old, and the indigent. According to this vision, the good society is filled with high-quality day-care centers so that women can work without guilt; with after-school programs and even midnight basketball leagues to keep children busy when they are not in school; with organized activities for senior citizens to make sure they remain independent of their adult children; and with counseling centers for all sorts of social dysfunctions, backed by teams to investigate cases of abuse and to intervene therein with education or law enforcement. Staffing such assistance to families properly would require building up the social service profession to Scandinavian levels and increasing taxes correspondingly.

At the opposite pole is the view that further pursuit of such family policy amounts not to assistance but to substitution for the family and that we ought rather to reverse the incentives that government has thus far instituted to dissolve the patriarchal family. Under this category are proposals to stop taxation to get money that is now spent on hiring people to do for others' parents and children what they might be doing for their own. There are also proposals to remove disincentives to marriage and to raising children from the tax code, which would reduce the pressure on women with young children to work. But the main proposals under this category have to do with the legal status of marriage and birth. Thus, if the family, defined by marriage, is the only proper place for children to be conceived rather than just another alternative, then causing a pregnancy outside marriage must be punishable; and if fathers are to be held responsible for their children, it makes no sense to give to mothers the absolute right to abort them. Different images of the family, of course, are the most prominent parts of different images of human decency.

The most fundamental struggle of all will be precisely over the meaning of decency. Every set of elites has its set of basic commandments, of actions that define good people and bad. The United States was founded by a group of men who held certain truths to be self-evident. The Declaration of Independence listed a small number of the truths that its signers and their neighbors accepted as guidance for their lives. The more extensive list surely would have begun with the Ten Commandments. Although the American founders would not have thought of translating most of those commandments into law any more than they thought of legislating the pursuit of happiness, their list made all the difference.

Were a time machine somehow to cause any community of the founders' generation magically to appear among us, contemporary American elites would surely find it in violation of the most basic laws of the land—which now enjoin actions once prohibited and prohibit actions once enjoined. They would find the founders' intolerance of pornography and their mixing of religion in public life violations of the First Amendment, their treatment of criminals in violation of the Eighth. They would deem pathologically anarchic their tolerance of firearms and their distrust of government. The founders, for their part, would likely beat a hasty retreat to their time machine, pointing their muzzle loaders at the atheist, servile folks who had perverted their republic.

Today, those who make laws in Western society find no truths to be self-evident, and their concept of decency is a grab bag of conflicting elements. We thus see government relieving millions of people of economic responsibility, telling them that happiness is doing whatever pleases them, and then putting some of them in jail for pleasuring themselves through drugs. The content of the list of moral imperatives by which we live has become a contest of tastes decided by trials of political force. Nevertheless, this public contest over the content of our souls determines the outcome of all the other contests we must wage.

Part II

WHAT DIFFERENCES REGIMES MAKE

Chapter 4

THE SOVIET UNION

He that soweth discord in his own house shall inherit the wind.
— PROVERBS 11:29

One of the most difficult things to convey to a Western audience is how disgusting the rank and file of the old Soviet ruling class really were—how mean, treacherous, shamelessly lying, cowardly, sycophantic, ignorant.

—ROBERT CONQUEST,
"The Importance of Historical Truth"

THE SOVIET UNION'S FAILURE is more acknowledged than understood. How could a system that organized its people so thoroughly end up so disarticulated economically and politically, with its people spiritually starved, snapping at each other on the streets and in their homes, unable even to make use of the armed forces into which it had poured material and human resources most unstintingly? The Soviet Union collapsed without being pushed when millions of human relationships failed. They failed because the regime's logic had produced its full effects on rulers and ruled alike. Karl Marx and Friedrich Engels had preached the incompatibility of human interests: All relationships, whether in government, business, family, or faith are exploitative. Following Marx's practical guidance to socialist parties, Lenin sought a government that would rule so exclusively and oppressively in the interests of its class that it would obliterate all other classes. As an instrument of this war of annihilation, he established a party of specialists in conflict—above all internal. The Soviet Union, in short, was at war with itself from the top to the bottom of society, from its first moment to its last. St. Augustine reminds us that even bands of thieves survive by fostering peace amongst themselves. But having sown discord, the Soviet Union reaped a terrible human harvest.

The Economics of Taking

The Soviet economy and its principal result, a contribution to the degradation of Russia's human capital, may best be understood in terms of warfare, especially by noting that the German word for warfare is *Kriegen*, which is also the verb "to take." Marx's voluminous writings nowhere contain any affirmative description of a socialist economy. Their central theme, however, is that control of the means of production is inescapably exploitative and that the driving force in life is everyone's struggle to control the means of production so as to exploit everyone else.[1] The natural corollary of both Marx's and Lenin's bellicose legacies is that the primary purpose of economic activity came to be to ensure the primacy of the Communist Party. In short, Marxist economics is much more about taking and keeping from others than about producing.

In the Marxist scheme of things, economic goods are important primarily as a weapon—once a class is deprived of its economic base, it cannot defend itself, cannot feed itself, and ceases to exist. From the outset, the Soviet regime sought to deny bread to its opponents. Every Communist regime has done the same. Second, economic goods are useful for producing military goods. Third, production itself is best organized according to the principles pioneered by Walter Rathenau in Germany during World War I: through concentration to achieve maximum economies of scale, with each factory producing only one item at maximum capacity and the central authority allocating both capital and labor. Thus, in the Soviet Union, Communist bosses allocated resources and labor for the whole country from Party headquarters—not because Marx had so prescribed but because they blindly followed an inappropriate example, and because doing so allowed the Party to crush enemies, reward friends, and secure itself.

Communist managers of farms and factories, for their part, hoarded labor and materials out of proportion to economic need not because any Marxist text told them to but because control over people and goods meant power, status, and privileged use for themselves. "Nothing but the best for the Proletariat" was the cynical principle by which people at any given level of power took what they could. To secure themselves from above and below, Communist officials made sure that basic foods (and medical care and vacations) were subsidized and effectively rationed. Such a system gave workers some controlled incentives to work, while avoiding the kinds of sporadic riots that always brought vulnerability to the officials on whose watch they occurred. Hence, the purpose of the Communist economy was not so much to produce goods and services—much less happiness for the masses—as to use economic means to maximize the Party's control over itself and over ordinary people. Thus, according to its own standard, the Soviet economy performed brilliantly.

A regime at war with its own people and with the world could base its economy only on compulsion: compulsion of rural populations into industrial occupations (the last of many great drives occurring in the 1960s), compulsion of women into the labor force (90 percent participation), and compulsion of the population in general to accept uneconomically low wages—effectively a kind of slave labor. Agriculture was based on compulsory collectivization and on the compulsory sale of produce at uneconomically low prices—again, effectively a kind of slavery. Industrial production was organized monopolistically, conferring on a few state enterprises the exclusive right to produce certain products, effectively compelling the public to buy whatever came out. In Gorbachev's Soviet Union, some 46,000 firms accounted for all industrial production. (By contrast, the United States at the time had some 2.7 million industrial proprietorships, partnerships, and corporations.) But socialist managers used their monopoly powers to coerce the state as well as consumers. They pressured state planners with demands for ever more materials and labor, plus, of course, housing, food for special stores, access to clinics and resorts, and so forth. Like any monopolists, they charged more while producing proportionately less. In practice, the state was caught between its natural bent to compel production and the compulsive power it had given to producers as a consequence of that bent.

Stalin resolved this dilemma by violent purges, and his successors by unbloody ones. But with every resolution, producers got ever more, consumers got ever less. In 1928, finished consumer goods accounted for 60.5 percent of Soviet industrial production. By 1987, these goods accounted for only 24.9 percent of Soviet industrial production. This downward trend persisted, regardless of peace, war, changes in leadership, and five-year plans.

As the years passed, ever-greater proportions of all things were wasted. The Soviet regime's preference for military things cannot account for the discrepancy between the high output of Soviet industry and the country's effective poverty. While official U.S. estimates for Soviet military spending of 12 percent to 18 percent of GDP are certainly too low, it is difficult to imagine the military taking up much more than about one-third of GDP or industrial production. What happened to the other forty-odd percent that civilians did not consume? The official Soviet answer was "investment." Official Soviet figures for investment in the economy as a whole come to 33 percent.[2] By contrast, in Western economies, some 15 percent of industrial production is devoted to capital investment. Investing more than twice as much as the West should have brought the Soviet Union wondrous growth. And indeed, when Soviet leaders threatened to bury the West economically, the Westerners who believed it had in mind the high rate of Soviet investment. Instead, Soviet industrial investment amounted to, as Mikhail Bernstam has written, "machines that produce other machines in order to produce other machines which exact other resources in order to produce more machines."[3] In other words, waste.

But the inefficiencies went beyond that. During the 1970s, socialist countries used one and one-half times as much steel and energy per $1,000 of GDP as capitalist countries. By the mid-1980s, they were using three and one-half times as much. Using roughly as much grain for animal feed as the United States, the Soviet Union produced one-half the meat.[4] Moreover, the Soviet economy's use of primary commodities continued to increase even as the production of finished goods declined. Much waste, it seems, was systematic: Materials and labor were directed by powerful producers to ends unrelated to the desires of powerless consumers.

Certainly, unmeasurable parts of "lost" production were the result of individuals appropriating state property for their own use. But this sort of thing was not waste. The satisfaction of human desires made economic sense. And it made sense, too, in terms of the system. After all, in appropriating public property, lower-ranking people were only imitating the top leadership. Hence, it was altogether reasonable that the personnel of Aeroflot reserved first-class seats for people who paid them directly and that to get nonharmful attention from medical personnel one had to pay them personally, usually with goods or access thereto. Also, given the system, why blame the farmer who considered the state's tractor his own to plow his private plot but not his own when it came time to fix it?

Although impossible to quantify, the human waste must have been greater than the material waste. The overstaffing of factories, offices, restaurants, garages, and so on paralleled the excess of material inputs.

Even worse was the employment of countless people in economically useless jobs. Legions were employed to check on others, who checked on them—chief assistants to the assistant chief, secretaries and drivers and janitors for functions like "political work," which no one would pay for voluntarily. Nevertheless, some of these functions, like Communist Party posts, had so much economic value within the system that people sacrificed significant portions of their lives to achieve them. But while valuable to individuals, such jobs redistributed wealth rather than creating it. Forcible redistribution also had a more direct cost: moral degeneracy.

Like every other economy, the Soviet economy had managers, engineers, teachers, and plumbers. But in addition, there were some jobs unique to the Communist system. The *nomenklaturists* were the high-level people on whose decisions projects, fortunes, and careers hinged.[5] Then there were the *tolkachi*—the fixers, the people worth their weight in gold who brokered favors, bargained bribes, arbitrated claims, found apartments, jobs, materials, and places in school, who procured permissions and loans and all manner of documents. The state guaranteed a place in a maternity clinic and a grave site. But the *tolkach* actually made such things available—for a price. And there was the art of the *stukach*, the stool pigeon, who would make derogatory reports about someone who stood in the way at the office. Just about anyone who got anywhere did it either by using that art or by successfully guarding against it. But part of the art consisted of gauging the predisposition of the authorities to whom the report was made to take action against the accused—in other words, being sure the report went to an enemy of the accused, but only if the accused was judged friendless enough to be got. The Soviet economy, then, degraded the economic usefulness of its participants by rewarding vile people.

There was social mobility aplenty in the old Soviet Union. After 1938, nearly all people in the ruling class were the sons of peasants. Throughout the regime's seventy-four years, countless penniless people moved up the ranks of society and acquired opulent lifestyles. Some did it on the level playing fields of sport, others on the nearly level fields of technology or the military. But the mass of those who profited from purges of others, who ingratiated their way up ladders of patronage, who made fortunes as brokers of favor, did so by excelling at the low arts of nepotism, betrayal, bribery, and flattery. Neither prosperity nor anything else worthwhile can be built on these qualities.

Plus ça change—

Because the Soviet system was not replaced by another, the post-Soviet Russian economy is being run by nomenklaturists, to whom the Soviet economy was essentially gifted. These people usually occupy the same offices they did before 1991. Regardless of the titles on their business cards or the political labels they may now sport, they brought "their habits with them."[6]

The new Russian economy bears no relationship to free enterprise. "The Nomenklatura," wrote former Soviet dissident Lev Timofeyev, "both acquired the freedom of private initiative and preserved their entire distributive power over state property."[7] Georgii Arbatov has explained how the system worked: "An enormous and parasitic apparat gives or takes away, permits or prohibits, can fine anybody, demote anybody, often even throw him in prison or, on the contrary, raise him up."[8] It still worked this way in post-Soviet Russia, except that the regime's factions had multiplied and become independent.

Who prospers in today's Russia? At the bottom of the prosperous heap are those gangsters who exact protection money.[9] These are not merely private individuals, because they work with the approval of the various police authorities—approval they must purchase. Gang wars come about when one gang pays some or all of the authorities a higher percentage of the take than other gangs are willing to pay. Thus, the Moscow police swept away the Georgian gang that had been running the used car lot by the river south of Moscow on behalf of a Chechen gang that was willing to cut them a bigger share of the business. If the Georgian gang had been on top of things, it would have matched the offer or bought the help of another of the state's security services, in which case the battle would have taken place among uniformed men, as sometimes happens on Russian streets. That is the sort of business acumen that makes fortunes in Russia. Millions of Russians produce goods and services, from bread to train rides, metals, and energy that are inherently valuable. But such people do not receive rewards proportionate to their work any more than they did under communism.

This is why people in business worry first and last about their official *protektsiya*, their "protection." This is not part of the business: It is the only real business. It yields the right to operate banks that recycle moneys from Western drug cartels back into Western economies, the right to buy all kinds of assets—from real estate to oil and gas to specialty metals at prices regulated below world market levels and the right to sell them on the world market.[10] It enables one to buy and sell currencies and securities armed with foreknowledge of events that will surely affect their value. It also enables one to receive "soft financing" from the state, just as during Communist times. And only *protektsiya*, of course, makes it possible to tap foreign money through joint ventures, as well as to administer billions of dollars and deutsche marks in foreign assistance.

True, the bigger the business, the bigger the share that officials demand of it. Prime Minister Viktor Chernomyrdin, a former minister of the Soviet gas ministry—and the private proprietor of 10 percent of *Gazprom*, its privatized successor—has reportedly amassed a private fortune amounting to $5 billion.[11] Those who manage to be the instruments of such officials literally do not have to know or do anything else to prosper. Deputy chairman of the Russian State Duma Mikhail Yuryev claimed to me that he owns every gas station in Moscow and that he does millions of dollars of business all over the world. He did not build his business on satisfying customers. His main business resource is power. Such people do not add value. Having rid themselves of the responsibilities that they used to exercise for the welfare of their employees and having added to their privileges, these nomenklatura-turned-bizhnesmeny reap without sowing. Compared with such pure parasites, the thugs who run protection rackets work for a living and sometimes actually come close to providing real service.

Engineering Discord

Just as socialist poverty and prosperity come from exchanges between people with different degrees of access to power, socialist politics consists of competitive oppression. This produced in the Soviet people a set of characteristics that Andrei Amalrik described as follows:

> [T]he idea of self-government, of equality before the law and of personal freedom—and the responsibility that goes with these—are almost incomprehensible to the Russian people. . . . To the majority of people the very word "freedom" is synonymous with "disorder" or the opportunity to indulge with impunity in some kind of anti-social or dangerous activity. As for respecting the rights of an individual as such, the idea simply arouses bewilderment.[12]

The perennial Russian practice of an autocratic, centralized empire whose only contact with the citizens consisted of taking produce or sons, surely taught only one law: The strong do what they can, and the muzhiks suffer what they must. In other words, Russia was all too well-suited temperamentally for Communist totalitarianism. The counterargument, which also makes sense, is that the Russian people's instinctive disbelief in government actually tempered the rigors of communism. Imagine, so goes the argument, if Communist tyranny had sprung up among Germans credulous enough to give it their hearts.[13] Be that as it may, because the Soviet regime embodied the denial of all law, it wrecked human relationships by overdosing them with power.

On the surface, Soviet society was more thickly overgrown with human organization than the northern Italian cities that Robert Putnam took as his model of civic life.[14] In 1960, the Soviet trade unions had some 75 million members; the Komsomol youth organization, 32 million; the various cooperatives, 28 million; 2 million served as part-time deputies to various Soviets; and another 20 million were classified as "activists" who organized everything from chess tournaments and amateur drama to school ceremonies and sporting events.[15] People were incessantly mobilized for the widest variety of causes—from helping with the harvest to "storming" (a kind of forced volunteer overtime) at work or on civic projects. The artificial character of this human interaction exacerbated the combination of obedience and resentment for which Russians are famous. Nevertheless, some Russians remember it fondly.

Whereas according to the classical and Christian traditions, family, clan, friendship, village, and profession are natural and occur prior to politics, Lenin considered them either obstacles to be razed or "transmission belts." Stalin called them "gears and levers" by which "the realization of dictatorship is made possible."[16] Hence, the Soviet Union broke natural ties to locality, profession, and so on by adding to the injury of despotism the insulting pretense that the subjects approved of it enthusiastically. That is, the Soviet regime forced people to lie to one another's face. According to Aleksandr Solzhenitsyn, mutual lying lowered people in their own eyes and in those of others, making impossible both normal society and the Communist parody of it as well.[17]

The Communist Party was the basis of that artificial society. As befits people at war with the world, the Party designated from its own ranks a never-ending stream of traitors, wreckers, conspirators, and the criminally incompetent. Since no one could know what or who might be thrust tomorrow into the categories of the politically incorrect, everyone learned to distrust everyone else. For leaders at all levels, lack of trust meant delegating power to subordinates as little as possible. Thus, despite its nominally extreme bureaucratization, the Soviet Union was not run by formal bureaucracy. Rather, higher officials tended to descend (physically or otherwise) onto lower ones, involving them in special working groups. By practicing the equivalent of the tsars' flogging of officials (or of Cesare Borgia's dismemberment of his lieutenant, Remirro Orco) they earned the love of vengeance-hungry subjects. Stalin was the teacher of this and other techniques for hoarding personal power, including fostering competing bureaucracies among whose chiefs he arbitrated. In this way, Soviet officials devalued bureaucratic rules—not to mention laws. Much as during the Roman republic's decadence, Soviet public lives were built on the exchange of loyalty for the expectation of lawless favors, and lesser men were defined by the *khvost* (the tail, meaning the extended entourage) to which they belonged, while the princes were defined by the power of their "tails."

The greatest change in Soviet politics between the Russian Revolution and the rise of Mikhail Gorbachev occurred when Leonid Brezhnev curtailed the prerogatives of the central administration to interfere in the affairs of republic and oblast divisions of the Party. After 1968, as the personal "tails" acquired a local character and semiformal rules came to govern the trading of patronage, Soviet public life became almost feudal. The system had always allocated material goods to satisfy various groups. The constant shifting of favor had exacerbated ill feeling among ethnic groups. By regularizing the system of preferences, Brezhnev's reforms tended to give this system the feel and color of law. For many, this was a safe, comfortable way of life. This is the system that Gorbachev attempted to undo. But the botched undoing reminded everyone of their resentments, weakened arbitrary authority, and snowballed into the destruction of the Soviet Union. But that is another story. The point here is that even under Brezhnev, but especially before that, the substitution of power for law and the personalization of power demeaned and embittered everyone. Solzhenitsyn ends *The Gulag Archipelago* with this comprehensive snapshot of how these effects made Soviet life lawless:

Only in those few cases (15 percent perhaps?) in which the subject of investigation and judicial proceedings affects neither the interests of the state nor the reigning ideology nor the personal interests of comfort of some office holder—only very rarely can the officers of the court enjoy the privilege of trying a case without telephoning somebody to seek instructions; of trying it on its merits and as conscience dictates. All other cases—the overwhelming majority: criminal or civil, it makes no difference—inevitably affect in some important way the interests of the chairman of a kolkhoz or a village Soviet, a shop foreman, a factory manager, the head of a housing bureau, a block sergeant, the investigating officer or commander of a police district, the medical superintendent of a hospital, a chief planning officer, the heads of administration or ministries, special sections or personnel sections, the secretaries of district or oblast party committees—and upward, ever upward. In all such cases, calls are made from one discreet inner office to another; leisurely lowered voices give friendly advice, steady and steer the decision to be reached in the trial of a wretched little man caught in the tangled schemes, which he would not understand even if he knew them, of those set in authority over him. The naively trusting newspaper reader goes into the courtroom conscious that he is in the right. His reasonable arguments are carefully rehearsed, and he lays them before the somnolent, masklike faces on the bench, never suspecting that sentence has been passed on him already.[18]

Solzhenitsyn's passage applies this portrait of the rule of influence exclusively to judicial proceedings. But it applied to Soviet public life in general, and the average Russian was painfully aware of how the system worked. Because they knew the rules well, Soviet subjects cowered insofar as they did not have the right connections, and they swaggered when they did. They lived in fear of trouble but rejoiced in their capacity to cause trouble for others.

Another portrait, this one of the lower ends of Soviet life, clinches the point. The journalist Hedrick Smith noted:

I would have thought that with all the nuisances burdening ordinary Russians that they would instinctively have banded together to ease the strain of life. Within their own narrow circles they do. Yet Soviet society in general is peopled by mini-dictators inflicting inconvenience and misery on the rest of their fellow citizens, often it seems as a way of getting back at the system for the hardship and frustration they themselves have suffered . . . I have heard Russians in more recent years describe this phenomenon as a mass settling of scores on a personal level. . . . "Put a Russian in charge of a little plot of ground or a doorway, somewhere," a bespectacled scientist ruminated sadly to me, "and he will use his meager authority over that spot to make life hard on others."[19]

To these systemic harassments, humblings, and houndings that one can avenge but not bring to justice, Smith ascribed "the quiet erosion of the spirit that takes place daily."[20] Spirits thus reduced to voluntary self-abasement, to nurturing connections by which they mean to mitigate abasement at the hands of some by inflicting it on others, are barely able to conceive of standing up for one's own rights under the law, much less for the rights of others. And for right or truth in general? Nonsense. That would be neither smart nor wise, and certainly contrary to the practical training the regime imparted to its subjects.

Soviet society practiced negative selection of human qualities because, having made political power the arbiter of religion, science, and human relations in general, it became much easier for sleazes and frauds to find protectors than critics. Fortunately for the world, this habit led the Party to acquiesce not only in patent scientific frauds such as T. D. Lysenko's genetics but also in Mikhail Gorbachev's patently self-destructive politics. The regime's preference for worse human types over better ones finally caught up with it. As the regime was dying, a Russian told Robert Conquest: "We've been ruled by morons for forty years, and this is the first time it's paid off."[21]

Fouling the Nest

The Soviet regime was as unfriendly to natural families as it was to other natural human institutions. But the regime's ideologically motivated campaign to wreck Russian families lasted little more than a decade. By 1936, for pragmatic reasons, Stalin introduced a set of material and psychological incentives to marriage and procreation. Nonetheless, the requirements of tyranny maintained the regime's pressure against family life. The regime's structural bias against family life was, if anything, accentuated by both the liberalization of the regime in later years and by the regime's collapse into lawlessness.

Next to religion, Lenin's Bolsheviks considered the family as the most important pillar of bourgeois society. A basic tenet of Marxism is the extreme Darwinian position that all human characteristics result from adaptation to external conditions. Hence, the proletarian revolution that would overthrow the material bases on which all societies had ever existed would resolve the "contradictions" between man and woman as well as those between town and country, intellectual and manual labor, and so on. The Marxist image of the family is doubly negative: It is both a den of mutual exploitation (like the rest of present-day society) and the place where the next generation is trained to perpetuate all the evils of contemporary society. The Bolsheviks went out of their way to mock marriage almost as much as they mocked religion. That grim lot were libertines in principle rather than for fun.

The first Soviet Constitution contained a statement on women's rights even more detailed than the Equal Rights Amendment proposed for the U.S. Constitution in the 1970s. The Soviet state effectively pushed women to take jobs, and it initially instituted workers' housing with the kind of communal living dormitories and refectories that exiled Bolsheviks had seen among the radical socialist workers' settlements in Western Europe. In the new industrial zones and on the first collective farms, no other kinds of living arrangements were available.

By the 1930s, the Soviets' desire to break down the family quickly gave way to more pressing ones, like industrialization. The Party went all-out (almost) to increase births. Like other Soviet producers, mothers were awarded medals designating ever-higher ranking, depending on the number of children they turned out. And parents who produced children got preferential treatment for new apartments. But the regime did not in the least relax the pressure on mothers to work, nor did it let fathers exercise any authority over their families. It was Stalin, after all, who built the cult of the boy who had reported on his parents to the secret police. The Soviet state might encourage men and women to copulate. But men and women would prosper or hang separately according to the whims of the Party. Men and women together might produce children. But children would belong to the state.

In short, the regime stripped the family of all sources of social support. The Russian people's veneration of virginity, abhorrence of adultery, and reverence for life, as well as their belief in the responsibility of the strong for the weak had all come from the church. Yet all connected with the church now was off-limits. So was literature favorable to bourgeois ways. And so, under material and moral pressures, those ways declined. Women conscripted into labor, under double pressures of work and home, aborted most of their children (estimates of the average number of abortions by each Soviet woman hovers between five and ten) and put the survivors in day care. Life was not any more family-friendly for the new Soviet man. Knowing that he could gain nothing for his family by sweat, brains, or integrity and that he had nothing to say about whether his children would live or die, Homo Sovieticus became increasingly superfluous to women and children.

The accounts of Western visitors, whether reporters, feminists, or religious conservatives, contain the same judgments by Russian women on their men: They are boorish cads. "They seem to have no sense of responsibility at all. . . . Seventy years of Soviet rule have taught men to be selfish and passive."[22] At work, they are lazy intriguers. At home, they practice what they learned at work: The more powerful take what they can from the less powerful. Many live with their wives only so long as they are served and the children are not too bothersome. Then they leave. They do not encounter moral censure for it, for after most of a century of relativism and fraudulent male role models, moral censure is in short supply in Russia, whether on the upper end of society or low. Some men agree to have children in order to qualify for an apartment. Then they push them out. Some observers claim that men have been conditioned by experience to think of good grades in school, hard work, and responsibility as female traits, which they shun.[23]

The collapse of the Soviet regime did not erase the marks it had left on conjugal relations any more than it erased its consequences for economic and civic behavior. The condition of women in Russia is as obviously appalling to the casual visitor today as that of American Indian women was to the pioneers. Male janitors and street cleaners are practically unknown, as are male road construction crews. The nonmechanized aspects of agriculture are women's work, too, as is assembly-line work. One-half of the female workforce does heavy "drudge" work. Men, though stronger, reserve the lighter tasks for themselves. The medical (paid very badly) and teaching professions are also heavily female. And women from the highest to the lowest in rank bear this burden: They do not really expect men to do anything other than impregnate them and leave. Thus, hard-working Russian janitors and doctors share an experience that in the West is thought to pertain only to unemployable, semiliterate, incontinent lower-class girls. However, the defining characteristic in the lives of Soviet and post-Soviet women is that they live as single mothers even with men in the house.[24]

Among Russian women, there seems to be a desire to return to the sex roles of old. Women eagerly practice cooking, the arts of house-keeping, and almost invariably dress with greater attention to style and attractiveness than American women of comparable socioeconomic status. They want to have more children and spend more time with them. Because of this, only one in five Soviet children under two is in the state day-care system, and over the last decades of the Soviet Union, the state gradually increased the amount of post-childbirth (half-pay) leave a woman could take to eighteen months, meaning that the biggest state-imposed obstacle to large families was really the size of apartments. But there seems to be no corresponding movement among men to support women and children, to take responsibility for families. There is no Russian counterpart to the American promise-keeper movement (whose members pledge fidelity to their families) and something of a consensus that childbirth and abortion are women's business. The ideal of manly life in Russia seems to have shifted from Party hack to Mafiya-connected "biznesmen." Conse-quently, Russian women have taken to advertising in America for real husbands who want real wives.

One man who agrees with this trend in female opinion is Mikhail Gorbachev, who wrote:

[Because they have jobs] women no longer have enough time to perform their everyday duties at home—housework, the upbring-ing of children and the creation of a good family atmosphere. We have discovered that many of our problems—in children's and young people's behavior, in morals, culture and in production— are partially caused by the weakening of family ties and slack atti-tude to family responsibilities . . . we are now holding heated debates . . . about the question of what we should do to make it possible for women to return to their purely womanly mission.[25]

On January 20, 1988, at the height of his power Gorbachev told a radio audience the same thing, only more emphatically:

I think it is time to review the role of women as mothers versus as workers. Women are more important as producers of good peo-ple than as producers of fabric or whatever. I am going to propose a system of economic benefits through childhood for each child born so that it becomes economically possible for women to devote more of themselves to their families.

Unfortunately, while experience shows all too well that government can help wreck families, experience contains no guide for policies that might restore them. The main asset of Russia's families seems to be a widespread realization that socialist ways brought only misery.

Degrading the Spirit

Fyodor Dostoevsky and Nikolai Berdayev had foreseen it: The socialist movement would forcibly banish God from the Russian soul and would fill Russia with nihilists. The physical near-annihilation of the church did not destroy the Russian people's quest for transcendence and indeed lent urgency to their desire for "normalcy." But the regime's antireligious efforts did reduce the opportunities for the organized, mutually supportive practice of religion and for the moral discipline that is essential to religious practice.

Lenin seemed to have taken in earnest Voltaire's jocular remark that the era of human happiness would begin when the last king was strangled in the entrails of the last priest. And so Lenin and Stalin destroyed or diverted to the use of the Soviet state over 90 percent of Russia's 96,000 churches and killed over 90 percent of its 112,000 Russian priests.[26] The rest were thoroughly infiltrated by the Cheka and its follower, the KGB, and were forbidden to proselytize or even to preach. And indeed, this remnant church did its best to function as a transmission belt for the regime, persecuting priests who took their jobs seriously. The Bible and religious literature were banned. Meetings for religious purposes or religious conversations were cause for one-way trips to Siberia. All but old people were effectively prevented from going to church. In the Catholic parts of the Baltics and in the western Ukraine, measures were even harsher. Anti-Semitism—the fight against "rootless cosmopolitans"—was also official policy.

Hence, the extent to which the regime succeeded in destroying the spiritual bases of family, faith, property, and law is less interesting than the reasons why it did not succeed even more. The short answer seems to be that the campaign quickly drove millions of Russians to nihilism and that nihilism is unendurable for very long. Visitors to the Soviet

Union in the era of glasnost encountered cynicism so deep and widespread, misanthropy so bitter, that even the most ardent communists had become frightened of it. By the late 1980s, when communists spoke of "moral renewal," they no longer meant just the old saws about increased party discipline and "socialist morality." But they did not know quite what they meant.

The barely surviving remnants of religion supplied the meaning. Generations of Soviet rule had never quite purged the official Russian Orthodox Church of every vestige of Christianity. The church's very existence drew to the seminaries four times as many applicants as there were places. A few priests here and there actually practiced the faith. The constant flow of priests beaten and jailed for trying to do their job and the very existence of churches that were obviously muzzled reminded the masses that there was an alternative to the regime's morality, more attractive because forbidden. The regime *said* that Christianity was corrupt. But the masses *knew* that the regime was. Serious students of Marxism were equipped with a serious philosophical case against Christianity. But to the extent that they understood that case, they also understood the concept of natural law and the extent of Christianity's conformity to it. Such people had firsthand, guilty knowledge of the Party's betrayal of its own mores. For their part, the masses, which never heard anything but unsophisticated, antireligious agitprop, found the glimpses of the faith's solemnities positively alluring.

Although the regime did not recognize the Christian holidays (people had to report to work), anyone walking by churches, especially on Easter, found them surrounded by large crowds, pressing against the police cordons, striving for a look at the procession and to listen to the chants. The regime used to send squads of "spontaneous" hecklers to disrupt the services. But starting in the 1970s, the crowds tended to shut them out and shout them down. Sometimes, the crowds, which were substantially made up of young people, would break through and join the congregation of old folks. When asked by strangers what they were doing, such onlookers replied that they were just curious or interested in a historic or cultural phenomenon. But it was more than that. Again, beginning in the 1970s, summertime visitors to Russia could see that many young women were wearing crosses around their necks. Visitors to the apartments of scientists or even government officials began to notice that religious icons were proudly displayed on the walls. "Oh, they are just art, part of our cultural patrimony," the owners would say. And whereas in previous years Westerners had been able to buy icons at good prices, by the 1970s demand had driven prices up. That interest in religious things was part of renewed attachment to timeless Russia was not a merely prophylactic explanation. By ostentatiously defining itself as the negation of the Russian past, the regime had made every scrap of the past into an instrument with which the people could deny the regime.

Personal religious practice also rose, at least superficially. Apparently, by the mid-1970s, "as many as half of the newlyweds in some areas, including Moscow, were having church weddings, and more than half of the newborns were being baptized."[27] In 1973, *Pravda Ukrainy* reported "that while one party official was lecturing on atheism, his children were being taken for baptism by his wife and mother-in-law."[28] Note well: This happened without proselytizing. The priests found themselves mobbed despite themselves. When we ask whence came this power, we are tempted to recall Machiavelli's account: While the barbarians who had defeated the Roman Empire were riding around renaming towns, they were naming their own children after Christian saints.[29] Of course, this did not transform them into instant Christians any more than the Russians who availed themselves of the church's sacraments thereby shed the spiritual habits of a lifetime under Communism.

One must also recognize that yearning for religion is not religion. Consciousness of a vacuum does not fill it; much less do official declarations, especially when made by politicians jumping on bandwagons. Algidras Brazouskas, the reformist first secretary of the Lithuanian Communist Party who lost his country's first post-Soviet presidential elections in 1991 for being too closely tied to the past, "revealed" during the 1995 campaign that he had always been a practicing Catholic. Likewise, in March 1995, General Pavel Grachev, the Russian defense minister who started the war against Chechnya, had himself baptized in public.[30] He followed former foreign minister Eduard Shevardnadze, the butcher of Tbilisi, by one year. By 1990 Boris Yeltsin had already announced in his memoirs that his mother had had him baptized as a child. Before leaving for his 1992 summit meeting with President George Bush, Yeltsin publicly received the blessing of Patriarch Alexis II. The patriarch also blessed the opening session of the Russian Parliament in 1994. None of this, however, seems to have suffused Russian public life with the substance of Christianity.

The reasons go beyond hypocrisy. Christianity (like Judaism and

Islam) is a vast complex of intellectual concepts that can be learned only through study, and of moral practices that can be adopted—if at all—only with the prompting and vigilant support of a community. The Soviet regime succeeded in reducing the circulation of religious ideas to almost nothing. Without them, rituals and sacraments lose much of their power over human souls and become mere adjuncts to nationalism and elements of opposition or, at best, nostalgia. In addition, because of near-universal ignorance of what Christianity is supposed to mean for political life, discussions among Russians on how to repair the damage of communism take place on the sterile soil of economics. Everyone knows that the Soviet regime was even more an assault on the soul and the family than it was about a certain vision of economics. But there is not enough knowledge of spiritual matters to sustain an intelligent discussion about the ethical prerequisites of classical economics or of decent politics. The contemporary Russian discussions of market economics bear no resemblance to those of Adam Smith or Wilhelm Ropke—both of whom were themselves well-read Christians. Contemporary Russian discussions of the terrible state of family life also tend to be couched in terms of modern sociology rather than in terms of transcendental obligations. Nor is it clear that such knowledge will be forthcoming, because of the quality of religious instruction in the seminaries.

The cultivation of the soul is inherently a social enterprise. Ordinary people do not soar to heights of spirituality, and all but the most extraordinary need others as examples and counselors. Outside of well-led communities, even well-motivated individuals let their mental discipline lapse. That is why there are churches and synagogues. Moreover, that is why those that are successful stress personal conduct, lest men slacken their efforts to apply spiritual guidance to their own lives in the family, on the job, and in the city. The habits of the soul are formed by the habits of the whole person. It is nonsense to speak of spiritual renewal where economic practice has more to do with theft than with production, where fathers leave and mothers abort. The shortcomings of the churches might be less significant if the laws of Russia were actively promoting family, civility, and mutually beneficial economic behavior. But the regime of post-Soviet Russia is promoting quite the reverse.

Why did Soviet totalitarianism fail to eradicate religion? The reason seems to be that when any set of ideas is pressed violently upon a people, that people then associates those ideas with unpleasantness.

That is why the Italian Communist Antonio Gramsci, perhaps the most perceptive theorist of totalitarianism (whose sons became Soviet citizens), advocated mostly nonviolent cultural hegemony. With reasoning drawn from Machiavelli, Gramsci urged Communists to act as if alien ideas did not exist, while materially driving them from society without raising too much of a fuss. In effect, Gramsci advocated the kind of antireligious campaign later waged by the Swedish regime. Because the Soviets did not follow Gramsci's advice, they left the Russian people the goading memory of evil so unmixed that it can serve as a reliable, if negative, guide to the renewal of the soul.

Rotten Arms

Considering all of the Soviet regime's other failures, the Soviet armed forces' botched coup d'état on August 19–21, 1991, intended to save the tottering regime from an opposition possessed of negligible physical force, was in character. And yet the disarticulation of the Soviet armed forces is most remarkable because the regime had put all its heart, all its strength, and all its mind into building them up and keeping them loyal. The forces were big and abundantly equipped, and the apparatus by which the regime controlled them unprecedented. Nevertheless, they suffered from the brittleness common to the armies of tyrannies—once the sovereign began to totter, its corrupt members minded only their most private interests.

The Soviet armed forces were the world's largest and best equipped. Just under 4 million men managed more of just about every type of major weapon (aircraft carriers excepted) than the rest of the world combined. Nor did the Soviets lack quality. The list of Soviet weapons that set the world's standard begins with the AK47 rifle, moves to the BMP series of infantry fighting vehicles, to the Akuka all-titanium submarine, and on to the world's finest artillery and rocket engines by far. The SS24 mobile missile as well as the SA12B mobile antimissile system put to shame their American counterparts, the MX missile and the Patriot and THAAD antimissile systems, respectively. The Soviets had the world's only antisatellite systems, radar ocean reconnaissance satellites, naval bombers, and much more. They compensated for areas of technical inferiority, such as noisiness of submarines or relative inaccuracy of missiles, by well-conceived tactics for employment, by greater quantities or with bigger explosive yields. The privilege of rejecting the products of their industrial suppliers and lavish pay made the armed forces an island of capitalism that attracted the best of the country's talents. Discipline in the ranks was exemplary, enforced by cruel hazing and backed by superior officers' authority to summarily execute recalcitrants. In operational military thought, the Soviet armed forces led the world. Had the Soviets fought a war against the West, they probably would have won.[31]

Even more awesome was the apparatus by which the regime controlled its arms. Yet since that apparatus consisted of preparations for various parts of the armed forces to fight one another for the regime's sake, it contained the seeds of its own destruction. The regime had been born in 1917, thanks to its recruitment of criminal individuals (the men in black leather jerkins) and small units of the Imperial Navy to act as the Party's killers. It had survived its earliest trials because a special unit of sailors and another of Latvian riflemen had been willing to fight larger units of the old Russian armed forces and to slaughter the regime's enemies as no regular forces would ever do. Also, the liveliest historical image in Bolshevik minds was that the French Revolution ended when some members of its directorate brought Napoleon into their quarrels. Against the danger of Bonapartism, the Bolsheviks deployed an unprecedented variety of special units to do three critical jobs: to make sure that the regular armed forces stayed loyal by being able to kill anyone among them at any time; to be able to kill any dissident elements in society, no matter how large; and, finally, to keep one another in check.

During the Cold War, the Soviet regime had more men in some sort of special unit (some three-fourths of a million) than were in the whole U.S. army. Lower on the food chain were the armed forces' own commando units, including the Alpha force that decapitated the Afghan government in 1979. At the bottom were the Ministry of the Interior's troops, specialized in putting down riots. Then, interspersed within the regular armed forces was a cadre of political officers answerable to the secret police, or KGB. One part, the Third Chief Directorate, seeded all military organizations with informants and had the power to make or break careers. The other, the Border Troops, numbering some 300,000, enjoying independent supply lines and equipped with tactical nuclear weapons, could go to war with anyone. The lines of command and control purposely crossed and overlapped. Third World regimes yearned to be shown how to set up similarly ironclad guarantees for themselves.[32]

It is an understatement to say that the Soviet armed forces were a cockpit of intrigue and grudges. The regulars hated the special units, the specials hated one another, and that collective hatred as well as individual selfishness rather than trust ran up and down the tangled chain of command. But the mutual fears worked as intended even when (and, indeed, especially when) Stalin purged 90 percent of general officers and three-fourths of field grade officers in the 1930s, as well as in World War II, when Soviet units were taking 50 percent casualties. That was so because the chances of being killed for perceived disloyalty were 100 percent. When the regime stopped projecting the image of murderous resolve, the system of mutual fears and hatreds began to work in reverse. The reasons why under Gorbachev the regime was willing to kill only by the tens, whereas under Brezhnev it had killed by the hundreds, under Khrushchev by the thousands, and under Stalin by the millions, are beyond our scope. The point is simply that the human qualities that had held together the military system exceedingly well under one set of circumstances destroyed that system when circumstances changed.

The Soviet Union's war in Afghanistan was never popular. But the Soviet population endured it. Then, when the authorities did not use mass executions or one-way trips to Siberia to crush servicemen's expressions of dissatisfaction, they created a little space for dissent. That space grew quickly. By the late 1980s, the regime allowed the public to disparage not just the Afghan War but many other things that Gorbachev unwisely thought he could impute to his predecessors and political enemies. The regime's subjects had a long list of complaints. The ones in and against the military were relatively minor. Thus, it apparently did not occur to the regime that voicing such complaints could set off a deadly chain reaction. In fact, that reaction moved with blinding speed.

Beginning in 1990, when the regime began to call on various military units to quell disturbances breaking out from the Baltics in the Northwest to Tadzhikistan six time zones southeastward, the units and their commanders vied with one another to minimize their own exposure. The regime unwittingly fostered this disastrous competition. When one unit attacked Georgian demonstrators with shovels, the regime responded to popular outrage with punitive investigations of the unit. So when the regime called up reservists to send large numbers of troops to do something similar in Azerbaijan, an uproar by their mothers was enough to get the order reversed.[33] The Alpha unit killed one dozen people on "bloody Sunday" in Vilnius and thought it did not get the unanimous praise it deserved. Eighteen months later, when asked to storm the Russian Parliament in the climactic act of the regime's climactic moment, it refused. Nor did any other group of habitual murderers put itself in the slightest danger to rescue the regime.

Chapter 5
PROSPERITY

Commerce is the profession of equals . . . the most miserable [of peoples] are those whose prince is in business.
    —Baron de Montesquieu, *Spirit of the Laws*

Things, money, and the capacity to enjoy them flow from human skills, which in turn flow from attitudes. Every political system sets premiums on certain skills and attitudes while discouraging others. And every system fosters the economic advantage of certain kinds of human beings over that of others. What kinds of economic behavior do some of the exemplar political systems of our time bring forth? The modern Chinese system secures the power and wealth of officials and their friends, while inculcating favor seeking in its subjects. The modern European welfare state has spread power and privilege to so many that within it, work offers no hope for anything more exciting than somnolent lives. By contrast, since 1973 the government of Chile has been trying to separate economic life from political power, believing that the connection corrupts both.

Recipes du Jour

Advice about how to make whole peoples rich is almost as common as guides to wealth for individuals. Someone is always pointing to the experience of some country as the model. During the 1960s, the Agency for International Development and the World Bank, following Walt Whitman Rostow's *The Stages of Economic Growth*, prescribed a formula to the governments of what they then called "developing countries": Use foreign aid to strengthen and centralize government, to build roads, dams, steel mills, and other infrastructure. Use land reform and taxation to break up traditional patterns of agricultural land use and traditional society. Raise tariffs and subsidies to foster industrialization and urbanization. Secure popular support through secularization, liberalization, and the expansion of government patronage. Thirty years later, there is no doubt that this recipe helped produce economic, social, and political disaster. Ruling parties from Chad to Chile used it to build political clienteles for themselves. Secularization fostered the rise of fundamentalism (especially in the Islamic world). Land reform and other wrongs done to agriculture caused hunger and pushed people into increasingly dysfunctional cities. The industrial policy of "import substitution" raised prices while developing classes of workers dependent on government favor. The epitome of the "nation-building" movements was a set of ruling classes from Burma to Burundi, guarded by goons and riding through worsening poverty in their Mercedes 600s.

Today, from Moscow to Mexico City, experts from the International Monetary Fund teach the new catechism of the Harvard and Stanford economics departments: Eliminate governmental budget deficits by raising taxes and privatizing state-owned firms. Make exports cheaper while discouraging imports by devaluing currencies and cutting real wages. Rely on cheap labor and high interest rates to attract foreign investment. But devaluing currencies has brought inflation, while high interest rates have discouraged internal investment and low wages have hurt both producers and consumers. And while high taxes may mean prosperity to those who reap the revenue, they are less obviously a sign of prosperity for those who pay them. Nor is privatization synonymous with prosperity, since the government often transfers monopolies, like telephone companies, into the hands of its friends, monopoly powers and all. In short, this recipe often makes the rich richer and the poor poorer by strengthening the power of privilege.

Some argue that the amount of privilege that governments grant is not the point, because what matters is whether the government is elected. Thus, Stanford University scholars Kenneth A. Schultz and Barry Weingast have argued that democracy makes people more competitive because they are better credit risks and can therefore attract more capital.[1] William Safire has written that even corruption on the scale of India is not a bar to prosperity because democracy simply unleashes enough human creativity to overcome its ill effects. But no evidence links elections per se with prosperity.

In the 1980s and early 1990s, the most fashionable model was the

Japanese. Lester Theroux, Chalmers Johnson, James Fallows, Clyde Prestowitz, Ronald Morse, and Alan Tonelson[2] among many others have argued that the Japanese discovered the secret of perpetual high-rate economic growth: namely, a combination of protectionism and directed investment at home and aggressive pursuit of market shares abroad. It became conventional wisdom that the Japanese economy would surpass the United States by the year 2000. Japan's economic morass since 1989 has merely led devotees of the model to broaden its terms to include other countries of the Pacific Rim, including China. Like Japan, they could be expected to outperform America because they had discovered the efficiencies of solidarity between management and labor, as well as the wisdom of allowing astute public officials to manage the private economy strategically. This seems to be the Holy Grail of modern political economists: to somehow conjoin the individual incentives of free enterprise with the superior wisdom of planners. Indeed, modern American discourse is full of references to the need for partnership between government and business in order to compete with the dynamic managed economies of Asia.

In the wake of communism, the concoction of recipes for prosperity mushroomed into an industry. Beginning in 1990, Eastern Europe was full of emissaries touting economic models as varied as those of Sweden and Chile, but especially that of the European Union. Moscow particularly became the battleground for contrasting Western schools—Jeffrey Sachs of Harvard University and Edward Lazear of Stanford's Hoover Institution headed two of the better-connected groups. Their proposals differed concerning the extent and timing of privatization and decontrol of prices, as well as in regard to monetary and fiscal policy. But they shared the premise that if the right formulas were applied, Communist sows' ears could be turned into capitalist silk purses. Yet although different recipes have been tried in different countries, not even the best results—those in the Czech Republic—resemble the kind of prosperity that burst forth in West Germany after World War II or that is routine in the United States.

This leads us back to the proposition that the details of economic policy are less important than a population that is habituated to property rights and to the rule of law.[3] First, laws about property must be stable, transparent, and equally enforced. People will work harder and more efficiently, so goes the argument, to the extent that they are not deprived of the fruits of their labors by gangsters, arbitrary officials, or high taxes. Second, there must be a currency whose value is constant or, at any rate, predictable. Third, there must be equal access to the market—meaning that tariffs on imported goods must be both low and equal among products, that the government will not otherwise interfere with prices and wages, and that it will not play favorites among people and businesses. But these prerequisites cannot be established simply by some parliament passing a law. They are themselves a rare and fragile set of beliefs and habits. The question therefore comes full circle, except that we search for ways of fostering these basic beliefs and habits. That search must begin with a consideration of the factors that make it so difficult: Different regimes (and indeed different observers) have different standards for gauging what constitutes prosperity. Just as important, each and every political arrangement promotes the economic well-being of some kinds of people rather than others.

What Is Prosperity?

What constitutes prosperity is not self-evident. We laugh too easily nowadays at the U.S. government economists who wrote in the *Statistical Abstract of the United States* in 1987 that the per capita GDP of East Germany was substantially equal to that of West Germany. They accepted local figures because these reflected the value that the local authorities place on activities in their country—an error inherent to reducing different economic activities to a common measure. While citizens of the West might well have placed negative values on East Germany's vaunted day-care system and police force, these and other services were legitimately counted as part of the "goods and services" enjoyed by East German citizens. The same abstract showed the per capita GDP of the Soviet Union as three times that of Argentina, even though poor Argentineans enjoyed steaks and vegetables that all but the richest Soviets could only dream about. But the Soviet Union was opulent in modern weaponry. Here is the point: In any country, perusal of anything like the yellow pages reveals a variety of activities, from abortion and agriculture to X-ray supplies and zoning consultants, each of which carries with it a certain lifestyle. A city of farmers will differ from one of shopkeepers, and a city of sophisticates will differ from one of soldiers. Therefore, founders and leaders of regimes know that the various occupational activities of their people make a big difference. Thus, when we speak of prosperity, it behooves us to remember that there are many ways of being rich and different distributions of wealth.[4]

Since time immemorial, observers have remarked on the wealth and splendor of Oriental civilizations. Economists have always known that peaks of Oriental opulence rested on broad bases of misery. But they have been tempted to suppose that only passing circumstances prevented the ordinary people who produced Taj Mahals from turning their genius and industry to their own benefit. Hence, predictions seem to be perennial that the numerous and hard-working Orientals would inherit the earth. Whereas in the past, prominent observers—Montesquieu in the eighteenth century and Karl Wittfogel in the twentieth—described in some detail how the division of labor in "Oriental despotism" was part of inherently limited cultures of masters and slaves, modern writers typically discount cultural differences. Paul Kennedy, for example, discussed the prospects for China's and India's economic growth as if the Chinese or Indian masses were purely composed of Homo economicus and their leaders were primarily interested in maximizing economic growth for everyone's benefit.[5] Even when describing the economies of states like Saudi Arabia, where vast amounts of money, largely unearned by anyone in the society, flow to unelected rulers who spend it on themselves, economists nowadays write as if whole peoples were working for some kind of common economic well-being.

Clearly, however, prosperity is less a matter of arithmetic than of value placed on various kinds of human activity. It was enough for Harvard economist John Kenneth Galbraith to walk Soviet streets in 1984 to judge the Soviet Union a vibrant and prosperous society. Galbraith, remember, had long chastised American society for "public squalor amidst private wealth."[6] Even though wealth in America is remarkably widespread, Galbraith called American life squalid because he did not think that the things that Americans do with their time and energy are particularly worthy. On the other hand, because he had higher esteem for the things that the Soviet regime directed its citizens to do with their time and energy, he deemed their undeniable relative material privations as a kind of uncomplicated virtue.

Thus, prosperity is neither money nor things. If it were money, then the Kuwaitis, Bahrainians, and Bruneians would be among the world's richest peoples. But much of the money in these regimes pays for the extravagant lives of thousands of princelings. Other moneys go to grossly uneconomic schemes, such as producing wheat in the desert, irrigated by desalinated water. The entrepreneurs make money not from the wheat but from the subsidy. But does such money at least result in some local citizens acquiring skills? No, because work is usually done by workers imported from Pakistan, the Philippines, or Palestine, while the locals' contempt for labor makes them ever-less-fit to earn a living. Even more certainly, prosperity does not consist of things. Some islanders in the Pacific came to believe that the ships and planes that brought the goods of civilization had been sent by the gods, and that they would come more often if the proper sacrifices were performed. Surely, however, prosperity consists of the capacity to make money and things. But production cannot be an end in itself. Mercantilists regard investment, production, and commerce as a kind of war. Following Aristotle and the Bible, we tend to think that production is for the sake of use and enjoyment. But whose?

In practice, most political systems define economic goals substantially in terms of the advantage of their most influential members. To the extent they so define it, it matters little whether they call themselves capitalist, socialist, or anything else. The Washington-based free-market Heritage Foundation has rated every country in the world in terms of economic liberties, while the Berlin-based Transparency International, interested less in freedom and more in administrative efficiency, has produced an interesting index for rating the degree of corruption in any given country.[7] How one rates any given country is less important than the realization that everywhere the playing field is tilted in some direction to some degree. The point here is that all political systems affect hearts and minds in economically significant ways.[8]

Who Profits?

The economic character of a people is affected not only by the goods and services they produce but also by the extent to which they let goods and services circulate among those who produce them rather than channeling those goods to powerful nonproducers. Thus, although the habits that produce the things that make life more comfortable are important to prosperity, the habits of equality under law that protect the wide and just spread of these things are just as important. This means that to promote prosperity any regime must encourage production and discourage rent seeking. Unfortunately, most regimes tend to do the opposite.

In the aftermath of World War II, Western economists and politicians asked how the masses of Africa, Asia, and Latin America might be brought to Western standards of living. They rejected as racist all facts indicating that prosperity and poverty are due to human character. So the British, French, Belgian, and Dutch constructed a comprehensive economic recipe, the centerpiece of which was the raising up of native elites—mostly people like themselves, alumni of the leading Western universities—to whom they turned over a major portion of mankind. But none of these elites had the slightest knowledge of or interest in production. They were masters of political patronage. Americans promoted the same people through the CIA, the World Bank, and the Agency for International Development.[9] By the 1990s, Western elites reluctantly recognized that most of the "developing countries" were not about to develop—and the ones that had developed had done so by empowering people very different from the kinds to whom the West had given its colonies. David Landes wrote in *The New Republic*: "people are different," and "this makes the story of [economic] growth very different." Landes mentioned some of the cognitive skills and personal habits that economists now recognize as the keys to economic performance and concluded that some peoples "don't like them; they don't want them, they are discouraged from learning them, if they learn them, they want out, etc."[10] True as it is that some cultures value cognitive skills, hard work, and honesty less than others, no one should forget the fact that Western assistance essentially empowered parasites and their habits over producers and theirs.

The habits that Western policies fostered in the countries that became known as the Third World are a set of human possibilities that any people anywhere may adopt at any time. Indeed, elements of these habits were present in the Soviet Union, in post-communist countries, and are growing within Western countries. Nor has the source of these habits ever been a mystery. By the time development economists touted the Third World model as the *dernier cri*, the recipe's effects were already well known. The following description of Mexico while it was still a colony of Spain could be applied to any current Third World regime:

The interventionist and pervasive arbitrary nature of the institutional environment forced every enterprise, urban or rural, to operate in a highly politicized manner, using kinship networks, political influence, and family prestige to gain privileged access to subsidized credit, to aid various stratagems for recruiting labor, to collect debts or enforce contracts, to evade taxes or circumvent the courts, and to defend or assert title to lands. Success or failure in the economic arena always depended on the relationship of the producer with political authorities—local officials for arranging matters close at hand, the central government of the colony for sympathetic interpretations of the law and intervention at the local level when conditions required it. Small enterprise, excluded from the system of corporate privileged political favors, was forced to operate in a permanent state of semiclandestinity, always at the margin of the law, at the mercy of petty officials, never secure from arbitrary acts and never protected against the rights of those more powerful.[11]

In a nutshell, Western economists found a set of drunkards and proposed to sober them up by prescribing that they drink more of what had intoxicated them in the first place.

The characteristics of Third World economic life are easy enough to outline. Public employment is high, desirable, and obtainable only by favor. When Robert Mugabe became president of Zimbabwe in 1980, the bureaucracy employed 62,036 people. By 1990, it employed 181,401. Paying the bureaucracy's salaries and operating expenses consumes just over one-half the gross national income of this country of eleven million people. In Ghana, 74 percent of nonagricultural employment is in the bureaucracy. In Tanzania, it is 78 percent, and in Zambia, 81 percent. Public sector wages exceed per capita income by an average factor of 4.6.[12] But the expense of their salaries is the least of the burdens that bureaucrats place on the economy. They expropriate farms, set prices for agricultural products, and force farmers to sell their produce to the state; they control admission to universities and in general determine society's winners and losers. The loot flows upward, according to the principle "from each according to the privileges granted him." Naturally, the biggest winners are the most powerful, their families, and their friends. Almost invariably, the higher one goes in Third World governmental hierarchies, the wealthier one gets. In the Third World, the richest person or family and the most powerful such is often the same. Thus, Zaire's longtime President Mobutu Sese Seko, who started public life as a sergeant, is one of the world's richest men. Mexico's former presidents Luis Lopez Portillo and Miguel de la Madrid are generally acknowledged to have looted somewhere between $3 and $5 billion apiece. The family of their successor, Carlos Salinas de Gortari, may have made off with twice that. The richest man in post-communist Russia may well be Prime Minister Viktor Chernomyrdin.

Moreover, the power to loot flows downward according to a corresponding logic: "to each according to his worth as a supporter." Hence, for example, the lowest-ranking officers in Uganda were paid up to thirty times the average wage. Sometimes pay consists of the franchise to engage in a particularly lucrative business, like smuggling drugs, or the franchise to collect bribes in a certain field.[13] But ordinary commercial concessions, such as a protective tariff or the ruin of a competitor are just as valuable. Tax rates are high, but taxes are collected only from those not well connected with the regime. Thus, an effective pyramid of taxation is established. What Edward Gargan reported about Indonesia is true of dozens of other countries:

> Take a cab here or a local flight, stay in a hotel, smoke a clove cigarette, watch a private television station, make a cellular phone call, buy a Mercedes or a Kawasaki motorcycle, put sugar in your coffee—in each case, some of the money lands in a business controlled or owned in whole or in part by a relative of President Suharto.[14]

In Aristotelian terms, this is not corruption but rather the logic by which regimes of a particular kind maintain themselves. Therefore, when we read that a Third World ruler has prosecuted one of the regime's pillars for corruption, we must think in Aristotelian terms: The prosecution is likely to be for the only act that really rots the regime, namely, disloyalty. When President Carlos Salinas of Mexico sent army troops to arrest Joaquin Hernandez Galicia, known as La Quina, the powerful head of the oil workers' union, he did so not because of Hernandez's well-known habit of translating his power into money but because of his equally well-known ties to Salinas's opponent, from whom Salinas had stolen the election of 1988.[15] Since power is for the personal benefit of those who hold it, it is logical that those who take it away also try to strip their predecessors of their gains—to their own benefit, of course.

To survive predatory behavior at the top, those below adopt certain habits. Business skills in the Third World consist primarily of knowing the people who make the rules and doing what is necessary to get along with them—meaning knowing who is part of whose network and what payment or demonstration of loyalty will propitiate whom. Since these matters are seldom entirely explicit, wisdom in the Third World consists of trying to fathom conspiracies. Hidden combinations and occult motives are behind every rise and every fall in fortunes. Every event is somebody's thrust or parry. Explanations in terms of proper recompense for value received are reasonably considered eyewash for fools. The classroom questions that my students at the DUXX Business School in Monterrey, Mexico, ask tend to be of this sort: "We have read the published version of this event. Please tell us the real story."

The Third World mentality predates Third World governments. As Lincoln said, the notion that some men are born with saddles on their backs and others booted and spurred to ride them is as old as the hills. The chief problem with Third World regimes is that they fit and foster this mentality so well. They endow certain social institutions, whether business or labor unions, with state power—sometimes arbitrary and always self-interested. Thus, labor unions in Mexico and Argentina, to name only two places, collect enormous dues (in Argentina they administer the proceeds of a 50 percent payroll tax) and run social services at their discretion. As in the Soviet Union, ordinary people have to wangle the services to which they are nominally entitled. The very size, power, and inherent partiality of Third World bureaucracies have made them pillars both of subjection and of entitlement and have strengthened the widespread feeling that those who know only how to work are unfortunates or fools.

Japan

The contrast between shiny Japanese products and Third World shabbiness should not obscure the similarities that come from the similar, fateful mixture of economic and government power. That power has resulted in habitual behavior on the part of corporate and government bureaucrats that is as ruinous of prosperity as any in the world. Japan has confounded Western economists because Japanese workers are rewarded for some of the world's best labor with lifestyles all too reminiscent of the Third World. And yet they keep on working. Only three in ten of the (cramped) Japanese houses has central heating—never mind air conditioning, in a country that makes Washington, D.C., summers feel cool by comparison. By the end of the 1980s, although Japan's per capita GDP was 12 percent above that of the United States, the purchasing power of the average Japanese was not greater than that of the average American but rather 30 to 40 percent lower. In a sense, then, the Japanese people are getting only about one-half of the fruits of their labors. Therefore, although the Japanese people produce lots of wealth, they are not prosperous—but they are content.[16]

The cultural premise of capitalist economics—that the personal status of buyers and sellers, producers and consumers, does not affect the price of goods and services; that individuals will treat one another equally and demand equal treatment from others as they seek the best economic deal for themselves; and that economic goods are earned to be enjoyed—are even more foreign to Japan then they are to the Third World, though for different reasons. In Japan, people regard one another as the occupants of particular stations in life, each of which comports certain duties and privileges. In addition, the Japanese people believe that they are unique and compelled to cooperate in the struggle for collective survival in a hostile world. That is why there is less outrage in Japan than in the West at officials who enrich themselves and why the officers of companies, banks, and the Ministry of Finance have exercised the kind of economic power over the kind of people that the rest of the world's planners can only dream about.

In business, the Japanese are unequal in what matters most: access to power. The great Japanese corporations were started with privileged privatizations of government property, were immediately protected from foreign competition, and have received various forms of subsidy from time to time.[17] All sectors of business are protected by legal impediments to entry. Small shopkeepers are protected by barriers against large retail outlets. Construction of houses and businesses is regulated by the *dango* system, which fixes the level of bids. And the prices of agricultural commodities are supported by restrictions on imports. Beyond overt protectionism, the Ministry of Finance and the Ministry of Trade and Industry lend further support for high prices by encouraging companies in each sector to cooperate rather than compete—from farming to industry (the Keiretsu network of companies, affiliated through reciprocal ownership of stock and interlocking directorships) to wholesale and retail sales. Mussolini's most ambitious designs for the corporate state were a pale shadow of Japanese reality, while the results he achieved with the Italian people were even less than that.

The results should not be confused with prosperity. The Japanese people pay $1 for a strawberry, $7 per pound for rice, $50,000 per square yard for office space, and more for Japanese goods than they are sold for abroad.[18] By the late 1980s, the value of all real estate in Japan exceeded that of all the United States by a factor of four, the average stock on the Tokyo exchange sold for ninety times yearly earnings, and companies competed with one another for extravagant expense accounts while buying famous real estate abroad at fabulous prices. Most such investments have lost money, and since 1989, the value of Japanese stocks has dropped by more than one-half. Economists should have noted other classic signs of a bubble economy: Companies were bidding up prices of stock and real estate. Perhaps they thought all was well because the inflated value of stock and real estate was secured with loans from the Bank of Japan, approved by the Ministry of Finance.

Indeed, the ministry's wise men may have been the bubble's prime inflators. Why? Beyond reasons of comity is the fact that the expansion created posts into which government officials retire, posts so lucrative they are called *amakudari-saki*—places into which to descend from heaven. In 1989, when the Bank of Japan stopped giving away money for less than the rate of inflation, the inflationary bubble burst, leaving a highly inflexible economy in which manufacturing costs are twice as high as in America. In sum, acting as sorcerer's apprentices, Japan's big businessmen and bureaucrats have been wasting their people's considerable talents.

The traditional Japanese response to this, namely, squeezing each employee to produce even more, is beside the point. As Akio Morita, the man who built Sony, has noted, the problem with Japan is not that its people should be working harder or better but rather that the system does not allow them to enjoy the fruits of their labors. The fundamental Japanese willingness to sacrifice does not itself impose fruitless sacrifice. That is imposed by an economic system in which honest, productive labor is a ticket to places of power but where power is oriented to the satisfaction of a network of privileges. That network produces a myriad of high stakes, bad bets, and uneconomic preferential deals that make the difference between the high productivity of Japanese labor and its low consumption. Japan is lucky, however, that wholesale corruption at the top has not undone the retail honesty on which its wealth, if not its prosperity, rests.

China

The economy of the People's Republic of China has been growing strongly since the late 1970s, averaging 9 percent per year. The World Bank has forecast that at this rate and in this way, China will become the world's biggest economy, if not the most prosperous, by the year 2002.[19] In 1997, optimism about the Chinese economy continued unabated.[20] This Chinese miracle is supposedly due to an artful combination of "market economics" or "capitalism" with political socialism. In fact, it has nothing to do with either. Socialism is an economic concept, the heart of which is production for consumption rather than profit, as well as the assurance that everyone's material needs will be met from the cradle to the grave. To pursue these economic goals, governments aspiring to socialism have assumed more power over society than governments that do not aspire to socialism. But statism is supposed to be a means to socialism, not an end in itself. To call a government "socialist" merely because it is big and harsh shows how thoroughly the means of socialism became its ends. The proper name for big, nasty governments that enrich their favorites and oppress opponents is oligarchy (of the Mafia kind). The Chinese regime now claims to be socialist only in the political sense. In other words, it admits to being such an oligarchy.

At best, Chinese officials' references to socialism and capitalism are code words, denoting positions on the central question: How shall we, the oligarchs, get richer while maintaining control? The theoretical answer reached by a group of well-connected Chinese economists in 1993–1994 is a "shared cooperative system."[21] According to Hilton Root, this amounts to "legitimizing for the first time diverse forms of property rights but not identifying the socialist market economy with any particular form of property right."[22] In other words, a lot of people will be allowed to do a lot of things, so long as they pay a cut to those above them in the Communist Party, the army, or other parts of the state. But no one can be sure precisely what the rules are today or how they will change tomorrow.

The contemporary practice of business in China is less confusing than the theory. The essence of that practice is the proliferation of ways in which individuals manage to exercise some of what we call property rights. All these ways, however, have one thing in common: They all involve either direct ownership by a part of the government or Communist Party—a unit of the police or the army; a local government (township or village enterprises accounted for 30 percent of industrial production) or a branch thereof. Specifically, property rights can be exercised by officials and by those somehow connected to officials. In sum, the regime acknowledges its own great and growing pluralism and permits its various members to enrich themselves subject only to respect for the regime itself and the hierarchy within it. This results in the exercise not of property rights as we know them but of what Root calls "loyalty rights."[23] Sheryl WuDunn has described the phenomenon as follows: "[T]he price of capital, [indeed, she might have said 'of anything else'] in China isn't interest. It's a bribe. Or it's the work that has gone into cultivating *guanxi*, or connections with the bankers and local officials."[24]

The innumerable examples of this practice all point in the same direction. In a typical situation at the outer edges of entrepreneurship, an ambitious young man struck up a friendship with the manager of a large pharmaceutical factory. The manager agreed to illegally slip him part of the production, in exchange for a cut of 20 percent of the sale price. Then the entrepreneur found a purchaser for a hospital who was willing to buy illegally from him, for a cut of 50 percent. The entrepreneur was delighted with the remaining 30 percent.[25] And rightly so, because if any other government official had found out, he would have exacted a cut of his share. As it was, he paid a 70 percent tax. But he invested nothing and put in little labor. Not a bad deal. Then there are the officials of ministries and counties, who have gone into business for themselves, encouraging various kinds of businesses as well as making problems for them with various kinds of regulations and then solving them for a price.

In sum, the legal system is identical to the administrative system and broadly overlaps with the economic system itself. At the top, Deng Zhifang, the youngest son of Deng Xiaoping, set the standard by advertising his brokerage services, sealed by a picture, for the price of 5 percent of any deal. As his father's death approached, however, the value of his services declined and the prospect of prosecution for "corruption" arose. In another way, counties and ministries become owners of factories established by foreign investors under specified conditions and then abandoned after local officials or labor brokers changed the terms and made the deal unprofitable. This bureaucratic "death by a thousand cuts," involving shutdowns of electricity or water, the unavailability of transportation, or labor troubles was epitomized in a *New York Times* headline: "China, the Art of the (Raw) Deal."[26] According to Root, the Chinese economy seems to be developing as "an administratively managed economy much like that of India, designed to enrich the gatekeepers at the expense of both consumers and producers."[27] The system's incentives are obvious: Produce if you cannot avoid it. Consume at your peril. But if you can, become a gatekeeper.

Nevertheless, in contrast with the former Soviet Union, contemporary China produces substantial amounts of real wealth. There are three reasons for this. The first, and perhaps in the long run the most important, is the sheer multiplicity of the phenomenon of greater economic freedom, especially among the urban middle classes. Since 1992, when the government began sanctioning the practice of "leaping into the sea," meaning leaving one's job and starting one's own business, uncountable masses of people have leapt into growing networks of families and local officials engaged in a bewildering variety of activities based on innumerable special deals. Stories of success feed the optimism that seems inherent in so many Chinese. The result is that something that looks like economic civil society is taking hold, for which the government is eager to claim credit.[28]

Still, what is evolving in China is not an economic civil society, because there is no such thing as business unconnected with some kind of official power. Moreover, one of the reasons that so many Chinese are in such a hurry is that they have reason to fear that their own special deals will not last.

The second and less important reason is the regulatory climate. The bulk of Chinese growth has taken place in the special economic zones decreed in 1978 along the southern coast, to which Shanghai was added in 1992. Here, local enterprises doing business with foreign companies are exempted from official taxes, while the foreign companies are supposed to receive tax holidays and duty-free imports of raw material. Neither locals nor foreigners, however, are exempt from the undisciplined bureaucrats intent on drawing maximum rent from the new economic activity, and who may well kill the geese that lay the golden eggs either by squeezing them too hard or by fighting one another over the privilege of squeezing.[29] War between lords of neighboring regions for the right to each other's plunder is very much in China's tradition, as are officials who extort without caring that other sets of officials are already extorting from the same people.

It is certain, however, that long-term capital cannot be raised for ventures where there is no law but the caprice of the sovereign—especially where the sovereigns are many and prone to violent quarrels. That is why so much of the investment that Western companies make in China (American companies have invested roughly $3 billion per year in the 1990s out of a total of about $35 billion per year) is guaranteed by their own governments. Still, these sizable sums are tiny compared to the ones that come to genuinely free economies through genuinely free stock markets that draw unsecured capital from widespread sources. But such markets exist only under the rule of law.

The current Chinese investment climate has less in common with nineteenth century "wild" Western capitalism and the prosperity it brought than it does with the kind of investment that took place in China a century ago. Note that between 1902 and 1931, the Shanghai region was a magnet for foreign investment. The foreigners enjoyed their privileges and some Chinese made lots of money, but most benefited little. Note also that Hong Kong's reversion to being just another of China's special zones has begun to drive out the kind of ordinary, unsecured investment and economic activity that had made the city some *forty times* more prosperous than the rest of China on a per capita basis ($21,500 versus $520).[30]

The final and, for now, most important reason for China's surge in productivity was stated succinctly by Peter Topp, the supply manager for the largest joint venture in China, Shanghai Volkswagen: "For all practical purposes, the cost of labor in China is nothing."[31] Just as in the days of the foreign concessions of the nineteenth century, Chinese officials are willing to rent out Chinese workers to foreign companies that are willing to pay them for this privilege. Wage controls in the interior regions that make the "nothing" wages in the new economic regions seem generous continue to pull workers. At the same time, these workers are being pushed off the farm by unscrupulous local officials who had tyrannized farmers collectively in camplike communes, and thereafter on their leaseholds, squeezing them individually for protection money. Thus, individual Chinese sacrifice mightily to move to the coastal regions and to acquire marketable skills. Foreign factories in China, unlike foreign companies that did business in South Africa during apartheid, help the Chinese government keep its grip on the population—including helping it to enforce the one-child policy.

Thus, the wealth of China is as firmly based on coolie labor, coolie drivers, coolie salesman, coolie renters, and buyers of coolie products as it ever was. Volkswagen, Mattel toys, and other foreign renters of labor are simply taking advantage of the fact that power is the most valuable commodity in China, rather than helping to change that fact. Hence, for all the aforementioned reasons, China's prospects are as limited as ever.

The European Way

Technocratic dirigisme and paternalistic social providence have come together in Europe in this century. Although they are distinct phenomena that create different sets of incentives, each in its own way takes power and responsibility from individuals and society, and pushes people to rely on state power. Together, these two sets of incentives have produced populations with a penchant for starting careers later in life and ending them earlier, working fewer hours of the day, and taking longer vacations, while looking to the state for improvement in their economic conditions.

The European welfare state has grown mutatis mutandis under every party and ideology that has ruled Europe in this century—laborism, fascism, Christian democracy, radicalism, and various kinds of conservatism. Regardless of country, it has had pretty much the same components—pensions for old age and disability, unemployment compensation, health care, schooling and day care for children, and housing benefits, plus progressive taxation meant to pay for it all and to flatten disparities of income. The programs share an ideological and a practical element. Because they proceed from an integral vision of society, they are not aimed primarily at relieving the lot of the poor but rather are meant to apply to everyone, including the very rich. But because the distribution of money stimulates group interests, each program focuses benefits on those who were able to fashion the program in the first place at the expense of the wider public.

Given the great number of programs, everyone in society is both a winner and a loser—both at the same time and during different stages of life. In most circumstances, it is difficult to know whether one is getting more net benefit than one is paying for or vice versa. In some cases, however, it is all too clear. When the ratio of people who will enter the workforce in coming decades to currently active workers is inferior to the current ratio of active workers to retirees, pay-as-you-go pension systems are obviously a bad deal for contributors.

Who gets the most out of social programs? Those who have had a hand in targeting the system to their own needs—those who have the best knowledge of how the system operates, who have the greatest affinity with the people who run the system, and who have devoted themselves to working the system. Such people fall into several categories. Everywhere, it seems that the welfare state gives members of the upper middle class some of the more expensive things they most seek to enhance their lives. In Sweden, a place in a child-care center is worth some $12,000 per year. Places in public universities are expensive everywhere. (In the United States, universities cost more than $20,000 per student per year.) Such services are used disproportionately by well-off professionals. As in other systems, the welfare state creates well-paid occupations peculiar to it, such as directors of child-care centers, officials of departments of social services, benefits counselors, ombudsmen, lawyers, and so forth. These places are also filled by upper-middle-class types. Overall, it should surprise no one that the distribution of income in states that devote a higher percentage of GDP to social programs is, if anything, somewhat more skewed in favor of higher-income groups than in states that devote a lower percentage of GDP to welfare.[32]

It also seems that everywhere some of the people near the lower end of the socioeconomic scale have learned to make unemployment and disability benefits, and even public subsistence, the basis of their lives. Unemployment in the European Union—rising inexorably through all phases of business cycles over more than a generation—now averages 13 percent, meaning that one worker in eight receives a high percentage of the salary from the previous job while supposedly looking for a job or retraining. Europeans rightly consider unemployment their number one economic problem. In Spain, the unemployment rate is one in four. In Greece, it is one in six. The rate also varies by region. In eastern Germany it is one in five; and southern Italy, it is one in three. Yet unemployment notwithstanding, the European Union has a labor shortage so great that (with the exception of Germany) it semiofficially accepts illegal immigrants from the Third World, disproportionate among them working men. These amount to perhaps 5 percent of the European Union's population and a far greater percentage of its workforce. They are admitted simply because they are desperately needed. Although the size of the unemployment rolls is due to some extent to government policies that will be discussed below, some unemployment is also due, by definition, to the unwillingness of Europeans to do at least the jobs done by non-Europeans. Some of those on the unemployment rolls do nothing but collect. Many more, however, especially in southern Europe, also hold jobs and simply use unemployment as an extra source of income. The same goes for disability pensions. It is no coincidence that the regions reporting the highest rate of unemployment also report the highest rate of disability. In some Italian provinces, 40 percent of the working age population is officially disabled. In one Calabrian town, the rate reached 75 percent. Of course, many of them work, too.[33]

Working the system, it seems, is a skill like any other—most easily acquired by example and in an atmosphere of approval by one's neighbors. Hence, the welfare state culture grows as its subcultures are fed. Generous benefits are sure to tempt anyone. But when they are offered to societies such as those of eastern Germany, southern Italy, Greece, or Spain, where people are already accustomed to making the most of circumstances by clientelism, such benefits are certain to swell the welfare subculture.

The culture of entitlement also pervades the European workplace to the detriment of productivity. In Germany, for example, it is no secret that the 10 percent of the people who purchase health insurance outside the state system of "alliances" pay premiums that average 25 percent less than the state system's, without the latter's queues and restrictions on care. Furthermore, the administrative cost per capita is twice as high in the state system as in the private one.[34] But the German people are not about to get better service for less, because precisely those excess administrative personnel are there to work the system to keep the "alliance" system mandatory for most people, and the rest of German society is sympathetic enough to let them succeed. After all, so many others have their own special deals. The same goes for French railroad workers who strike to demand continued subsidy of featherbedding, or to truckers who demand to retire on full pay at age fifty-five and receive support from the public.

Dirigisme might well be described as welfare for the upper classes.

Its two pillars are various kinds of direct subsidies to producer firms, plus the indirect subsidy of protective tariffs and regulatory restraints. While direct public ownership of producer firms went out of fashion in Europe after the 1960s, total public support for big business has risen through "industrial policy." In France, dirigisme goes back to the privileged relationships between fifteenth century kings, bankers, and manufacturers of cannons.[35] With some variation, similar relationships existed throughout Europe. At the end of the nineteenth century, these relationships of privilege, patronage, and military utility began to be invested with the hope that they might fulfill the socialist goal of production for social use rather than profit. In the 1920s, Mussolini introduced the practice of consultation between management, labor, and government officials—who came to the table with credits, contracts, and regulatory powers. In the aftermath of World War II, most European countries adopted in one way or another what had been the Fascist system of cooperative consultation, otherwise known as "indicative" or "soft" planning. Governments and political parties came to like it because it offered power and patronage. Labor unions liked it because it guaranteed patronage and support for employment. Businessmen included in the system liked it best of all—because their inclusion guaranteed success and wealth for themselves without having to worry too much about competition, domestic or foreign. The result has been the rise of a class of businessmen like the Agnellis of Italy's Fiat, whose profits are their own (through huge salaries and stock options) but whose losses are hidden or absorbed by the state, along with the emergence of politicians who rely on them for favors, both political and personal.

The numbers of Europeans who make a lot of money in business is small. In Sweden in 1986, for example, only 1,100 people had an after-tax income above 200,000 kronas (nine times the average physician's salary) whereas 1,435 Swedes won at least that much in lotteries and other kinds of gambling.[36] The incentives to gamble are much greater than those to go into business, because the chances of going from poverty to wealth through business are much smaller than the numbers indicate. It is just not possible in Europe to rise from running a shop in one's garage to ownership of a multinational, simply because at each stage in the growth of the business, the owner would not have the political pull to be included among those invited to consult cooperatively at a level sufficiently high to get the contracts and the credit necessary to reach the next level. To rise to the top in European business, one must work one's way up in an organization that already has ties with the state or one must become involved through politics.

Hence, it is not surprising that so much of the news in the European press is about trades of official power for money, and vice versa. This is commonly called corruption. In Italy, some three thousand leaders of big business and government were indicted between 1992 and 1994. In Spain, the list begins with the governor of the Bank of Spain and two cabinet ministers. In France, the season opened in 1992 with the arrest of the minister of justice, and the careers of a prime minister and a presidential candidate were ended. The particulars are always the same: Money paid in exchange for lucrative government contracts or favorable regulatory treatment. The organization of the European Union may be supranational, but it is in the same business of dispensing valuable favors as are national governments. Since the European Commission's bureaucrats in Brussels have been setting standards for everything from bacteria in cheese to the length of condoms (15.2 cms.) they have become the focus of Europe's most lucrative lobbying. By one estimate, one-tenth of the EU's budget of $84 billion goes directly for fraud.[37]

That is why it is difficult to blame the European farmers who cut one ear off their cows to turn in as proof of slaughter so that they can collect the EU incentive payment for reducing milk production while they continue to produce milk. Like so many others in Europe, they know that their measure of prosperity depends on adjusting to government programs. The name of the game is to benefit from them and, if one can, to influence them. For now, the game yields some returns.

In the coming decades, however, the European economic game is sure to be played for diminishing returns but increasing individual stakes, because two countervailing trends will squeeze Europe. Although the welfare state's inherent dynamic is to expand and although interest groups do not normally tolerate cuts in benefits, drastic cuts are becoming more inevitable because the biggest pillars of the European welfare state—old age pensions and medical care—are collapsing under the weight of Europe's demographic inversion.[38] Twenty-five years from now, four out of ten Europeans will be sixty years of age or older, and there will be scarcely more than one active worker per retiree. The huge effort that will be required to pay some percentage—but not nearly all—of the benefits under these two headings will force other claimants into unprecedented combat. In sum, the Europeans' deep injection of the state into the production and distribution of economic goods seems to have produced a set of habits peculiarly incompatible with the pursuit of prosperity in the twenty-first century.

Chile

Chile's experience under the government of General Augusto Pinochet (1973–1990) is interesting not because the country became more prosperous (which it did, with per capita GDP rising 50 percent during the period and growing at 7 percent per year since) but because of the way in which the government sought prosperity: Countering the logic of most of the world's economic organization in the twentieth century, the Chileans sought to separate political power from economic life. A group of Chicago-trained economists found not just the military junta but broad sectors of Chilean society responsive to their argument that two generations of increasing state interference in the economy had inculcated habits of interest group competition that had led to poverty and civil strife and that reversing the country's economic fortunes would require a new set of habits. Thus, they aimed their reforms, whether obviously related to the economy or not, at shrinking the state and making it more difficult to translate political power into economic gain. It is important to underline that the reformers thought changing habits for the long run was more important than compelling behavior in the short run.

Chileans found arguments in favor of liberal economics convincing because between 1964 and 1973 the full logic of interest group redistribution had been visited upon them with a vengeance—especially under the Marxist regime of Salvador Allende (1970–1973). In 1964, Chile's Christian Democratic Party, with little objection from the Conservative Party and much assistance from the United States, began what was touted as a major effort to develop the Chilean economy. To stimulate agricultural production, the government expropriated 1,408 large farms,[39] but instead of giving title to the tenants, it turned them into collectives. Almost immediately, Chile became an ever-larger importer of food.[40] The government raised tariffs to protect and stimulate domestic industries, used foreign aid to build public housing, increased social benefits, and increased public employment. But as taxes and inflation rose, economic growth fell to one-half the Latin American average and lagged behind population growth.[41] The only clear winners were those closely tied to the Christian Democratic government. As the contest for redistribution turned more bitter, so did partisan strife.

The election of Salvador Allende in 1970 came about because he promised to do more for greater numbers of people by pursuing the same approach more energetically. With the backing of the Christian Democrats and the Socialists, he promised the country "empanadas with red wine." But only his followers got them. He officially expropriated 3,628 farms,[42] while fostering the unofficial expropriation of countless more, and raised some tariffs to 700 percent. As food and other goods disappeared from normal circulation, he tried to set up a rationing system run by local committees of his partisans. People were lining up for jobs on these committees. Within a year, housewives in Santiago were in the streets banging empty pots, and some people were finding jobs as *coleros*, place holders in waiting lines. By the end of his regime, the central government had 650,000 employees (in a country of 11 million) and controlled 75 percent of GDP. It did this for the benefit of friends at the expense of enemies. The economists who wrote *El Ladrillo* (meaning "the brick," the book that roughly served as a guide to the military regime's reforms) chronicle what political patronage came to mean to business: "Concessions on taxes or tariffs, permission or prohibition on the import of spare parts, the approval or disapproval of loans."[43] In practice, the reign of patronage meant that those who had better connections could do whatever they wanted to those whose connections were worse. And if a citizen managed to get a court ruling against the government or one of its friends, the government ignored it. It ignored some seven thousand court rulings.[44] Relief from all this is what the Christian Democrats, along with the vast majority of Chileans, sought from the military when they asked for a military coup.

They got more than they bargained for, not just because the coup set off a simmering guerrilla war with the Left but because senior military officers had decided that they did not want to take power to run the system and perhaps become its dominant rent collector or to enforce a time-out, after which the system would function as before. The military regime defined what it wanted by imagining the reverse of what Allende had put the country through. Its leaders knew that their only chance to change long-term habits was to change a deep-rooted mentality. Although the desire to make such changes set the tone for the military government's reforms, the reforms did not occur according to any plan but rather happened in short bursts (1975, 1978–1981, and 1987–1988), usually when events left no choice between disaster and leaping ahead.

Above all, and in direct contradiction to the logic of Third Worldism, the military government shrank the size of the state. By the time Pinochet left office in 1989, the Chilean people had only 150,872 central government officials to support and to obey—one-fourth of the burden they had carried sixteen years before—and the government's direct consumption of GDP was down to 8.6 percent.[45] Just as important, the government officials who remain have far fewer favors to give and far less discretionary power than their predecessors. Bitter experience had taught Chileans contempt for the notion that the power to elect a government is a satisfactory substitute for the freedom to run one's daily life. Thus one of the main objectives of each of the reforms was precisely to reduce the intrusiveness and discretionary power of government. For example, the reformers decided to reduce tariffs on nearly all items to an equal, insignificant 11 percent, in large part because they wanted to do away with the power of government to make or break fortunes. If government did not have the power to grant such favors, it would not call forth from within society people who specialized in seeking them. They also transferred some inherently governmental services—roads and sanitation—from ministries to local governments, less for reasons of economic efficiency than to make it possible for citizens to approach the providers of services not as favor seekers, but as employers.

The military regime actually increased traditional welfare state benefits for the very poorest of the poor, but virtually eliminated them for everybody else. The reason went far beyond saving money and struck directly at the view that government can be a source of economic benefit. For citizens, there would be no employment as grantors of benefits and no premium in learning the complex paths to maximizing benefits. It would be more difficult for bureaucrats or politicians to draw rents or build clienteles by granting favors.

The substitution of private but compulsory retirement accounts for social security was excellent economic policy because it created a huge pool of investment capital and yielded higher returns for contributors. But it was even more significant for people's habits because it gave the contributors themselves, rather than bureaucrats, control over their own money. Thus it turned workers' attention from the arcana of government rules to the fortunes of the funds in which their contributions are invested. The institution of private medical care and a voucher system for primary and secondary education was based on the same view that consumer sovereignty produces better services and much better people.

The reformers sought to cut the link between power and money by requiring labor and professional organizations to elect their leaders openly and by prohibiting people in such organizations, as well as officers of corporations, from simultaneously holding office at any level of government or in any political party. Along with the diminution in the size and scope of government, these restrictions struck at the mutual attraction that everywhere exists between politicians and businessmen as well as at the way in which political parties in most of the world have been organized in the twentieth century (more on this in chapter 6). The result of these and other measures that reduced the capacity of political parties to reward their adherents both high and low was predictable. Whereas in 1973 one out of ten Chilean voters had been a dues-paying member of a political party, by 1990 only four out of one hundred were.[46] Since the parties could give less, fewer people were inclined to give them money.

It is important to stress that since the Chilean military's objective, especially regarding economics, was to establish equality before the law while building barriers against privilege, its success depended substantially on restraining its own members from taking advantage of their power. It did this by keeping to a bare minimum the number of officers involved in government, excluding them entirely from detailed administration, and not allowing the civilians whom they appointed to govern to build a government party per se.

There was something more than a little anomalous about a government that had taken power by the gun and that was carrying on a bloody war against armed opposition, a war that involved torture and "disappearances,"[47] trying to establish the rule of law. Nevertheless, that was the objective. First, the regime succeeded in separating the civil war from the economic-constitutional reforms because the war was not about policy—it was about the mutual and very personal hatred between the country's entrenched Marxist subculture and the military. Second, the economic metamorphosis succeeded despite the regime's inherent illegality because the military sincerely sought to base liberal economics on liberal legality, both through reforms that by their very character removed room for arbitrariness and through its own scrupulous adherence to its own rules, including timetables for a transition to democracy.

Power, Producers, and Takers

Government action cannot easily transmute the cognitive skills and work habits of any people, whether Swedes, Congolese, or Japanese. But it affects all such qualities everywhere at the margin. Government fosters hard work when it gives people reason to believe that they will not be deprived of its fruits. And it fosters the fruitfulness of human action when it channels that action toward pursuits inherently productive—both of economic goods and of respect for others' property.

Thomas Jefferson is renowned for claiming that he did not know of an occupation other than yeoman farmer that was as reliable a nursery for the human qualities of enduring prosperity and liberty. Jefferson may or may not have been correct about the ill effects of commerce. But his general point is unexceptionable: Some occupations foster better qualities than others. Just as the U.S. government's 1876 history of the whaling industry reasonably claims that perhaps its principal product was a set of exceptionally hardy, adventuresome, and industrious people, so historian Robert Conquest cites morally degenerate men as perhaps the main product of the Soviet economy. It matters a lot that so many governments effectively steer so many talented people to master the art of the courtesan, the fixer, and the exploiter. It matters that Japanese students compete so hard for posts in the Ministry of Finance, from whose merited heights they dispense unmerited favor. It matters that public employment, based more on personal status than on productivity, sets the tone for the European workplace and that in Chile it does not. Hence, we must ask the following of any government: How does it affect its people's choice of occupations among the productive, the wasteful, and the counterproductive?

Government influences economic life primarily by deciding what role coercive power will play in it. To the extent that power is a factor in any transaction, it is a part, negative or positive, of the price of the good or service traded. To the extent that one can bring power to bear on any transaction, he need bring less of any other value to it. That is, if one side can coerce the other into acquiescence without delivering the goods, why deliver them? The involvement of power in any transaction (unless it be for the neutral purpose of keeping all coercion away from it) will therefore lower the total economic value of the transaction. It is no accident, then, that government involvement in economic activity tends to be inversely proportional to productivity. The reason for that, however, is that government power destroys the equality of economic actors. Even power applied for the ostensible purpose of creating legal equality where social inequality prevails is problematic.

Because government is naturally the creature and ally of the strong, it is practically incapable of intervening on behalf of the weak. That, of course, is why the greater the level of government intervention in the economy, the more difficult it is for poor individuals to rise economically by economic means. That is true irrespective of the ostensible purpose for intervention. Hence, the great difference between systems of political economy is in how they make people into producers or takers.

Chapter 6
CIVILITY

Men of Athens I love you, but I must obey the god rather than you.

—SOCRATES, *The Apology*

Who can do what to whom?

—LENIN

NOTHING SO AFFECTS ECONOMIC LIFE—or for that matter family and spiritual life—as whether rulers are bound by laws or whether they rule by discretion. Almost as important is the extent to which people govern themselves in their own localities, and the range of things people can do without some official's permission. When people enjoy such ordered liberty, they tend to take a proprietary interest in their surroundings and may properly be called citizens. But rule of law, strong local government, and space for civil society result from the long exercise of rare habits.

In turn, habits of self-restraint and self-reliance are formed by politics that do not involve mutual depredation, demonization, or millennialist goals. And such politics are made much easier by political institutions that tend to repress the natural tendencies to centralize and tyrannize while bringing out such noble and moderate inclinations as any set of people might have. Yet, of course, such institutions do best where the rule of law, local autonomy, and limited government have already taken root.

In five thousand years of history, the Chinese people have not enjoyed citizenship. Yet the People's Republic seems to have eroded the Confucian habits on which citizenship might be built, while the Taiwanese regime seems to have built both the rule of law and a modicum of self-government, partly by strengthening and partly by weakening Confucian habits. On the same cultural base, the Singaporean regime has built the rule of law while excluding citizenship. In most countries, however, well-established combinations of public and private power make greater or lesser mockeries of the rule of law and self-government. We see only quantitative differences in the regimes of Italy and Mexico, which we are accustomed to think of as differing qualitatively in these respects. But first, let us look more closely at the principles of law and self-government.

Law and Discretion

Oaths of office are so common in Western culture, so often mouthed cynically, so often aped in civilizations to which they are truly foreign that we tend to forget their momentous meaning: The official takes power by an act of submission to a greater power. The kings of Castile used to receive their crowns while acknowledging a chorus of nobles saying, "Thou shalt be King if thou workest justice, and if thou does not do so, thou shalt not be King." Like all medieval European monarchs, they pledged allegiance to uphold and administer customs and immunities of which they were not the authors. When King John of England transgressed feudal law, the barons met him with swords at Runnymede in 1215 to write in the Magna Carta the law that he was supposed to have been obeying all along.[1] The difference between the king's theoretical and practical adherence to law was the subject of John Fortescue's distinction (1385–1479) between England's *dominium politicum et regale* and the increasingly lawless *dominium regale* of Spain and France. In the nineteenth century, King Mongkut of Thailand startled his subjects by answering their pledges of allegiance to him with a pledge of allegiance to them. The magistrates of the Roman republic—including the dictators—began and ended their offices by ritual submission to the laws that had been made by the various assemblies of the Roman people. Later, even the emperors pledged (sometimes even sincerely) to follow the laws that they themselves dictated.

The ruler's adherence to law, even laws of which he is the author, gives even unto slaves some of the dignity of citizens. Aleksandr Solzhenitsyn and Andrei Sakharov knew how big (and how destructive of the system) was their seemingly modest demand that the Soviet Union enforce its own laws. Any rule book can be a powerful bulwark. The sailor harassed to show deference can read that he is supposed to salute a superior within 30 feet and can measure a circle around his station beyond which he need not worry. The worker whose employee manual lists the things he must do to stay out of trouble knows that "working to rule" is a fearsome weapon in his hands. Even American Negro slaves figured out that the slave codes that bound them to servitude had loopholes—property rights—that the most ambitious could use to buy their freedom. By 1820, some 2,500 former slaves had bought slaves for themselves.[2] By the same token, despite apartheid's oppressive laws, South Africa enjoyed a net in-migration of blacks from nearby countries who found unfriendly laws preferable to thoroughly lawless rulers.

A multiplicity of laws abets lawlessness by increasing the number of officials and maximizing their discretion, as well as by reducing the number of fields in which ordinary individuals, families, and churches—in short, civil society—can act at *their* discretion. The sense of ownership that is at the heart of citizenship comes only when people freely join together in common enterprises, when the categories of rulers and ruled are blurred. The rule of law is fostered not by statutes that grant privileges but rather by ones that recognize the rightful limits of government. Freedom of religion, for example, is fundamental to the rule of law because it is the threshold indicator of whether there is any human activity at all on which the rulers will not trespass. And if the rulers recognize the root—the fact that man is not government's creature—then they may also respect the trunks and branches of that fact in civil society. To the extent that they do not recognize limits in what they may do to civil society, they are unlikely to respect the rules they themselves impose. Let us now look at some of the major ways in which regimes affect civic habits.

LAW AND LOCALITY

The Christian and classical traditions agree that the good man, the whole man, must fulfill responsibilities to the community—and that the highest form of relationship with the community is ruling and being ruled in turn.[3] But in just about all of today's nominally self-governing countries, life for all but a few individuals is a series of acts of obedience to regulations affecting every aspect of life in whose making the citizen's involvement is purely theoretical, and to officials with whose appointment or removal he is prohibited by law from interfering. Although the officials are called civil servants, citizens soon learn that the only way to avoid trouble and get what they want from them is to treat them as the masters they really are. Once every several years, citizens are supposed to feel like masters because they can vote for or against a few people, none of whom have a direct bearing on their lives.[4] If they resent this, they are told to work for social mobility, so that someday they or their children might become part of the ruling class. And to top it off, the rulers chastise the people for feeling "alienated." Since habits are the residue of repeated action and since in just about all of today's self-governing countries citizenship is a pretense, the tendency of citizens to become cynical, wheedling subjects is unsurprising. Hence, for all but a few, the only scope for citizenship lies in whatever latitude modern governments give to localities.

Rarely do the powers of local government proceed from the presumption that citizens of a locality have the right to deal with any matter at all. On the contrary, in most cases the central government delegates particular tasks to its subordinate units (provinces, departments, oblasts, states, and municipalities). Sometimes it also imposes on local authorities the political burden of raising whatever taxes may be necessary to carry out these tasks. But always it hands down the rules by which to proceed, and local officials are usually responsible more to the central government than to the locals who elected them. This makes all the difference between citizens with habits of spontaneous cooperation and subjects with the habits of consumers of services. Nothing is so futile as giving the label "community leaders" to individuals whose standing among their neighbors depends on passing down orders or patronage from the central government, nor is anything so self-contradictory as prohibiting localities from legislating on important matters and thereafter bemoaning the disarticulation of the community.

LAW AND RIGHT

What leads people to hold governments to law and to exercise individual and local autonomy? Very ancient history teaches us that people used to stick to customs for which they sought no explanation. Certainly, Confucius's *Analects* are exegeses of customs rather than explanations of why the customs are right, and there is no non-Roman account of the liberties of the Germanic tribes, much less any Germanic argument about why liberty was good for the Germans. By contrast, among the children of Jerusalem, Athens, and Rome, social practice has been intertwined with reason for two and one-half millennia—and living by law has depended on understanding the natural affinity of man for the way things ought to be.

Much explanation of law throughout history has been of the positive kind and has rested, as Plato's Thrasymachus put it in Book 1 of *The Republic*, on the judgment of society's strongest about what is most advantageous to themselves.[5] Following this tradition, U.S. Chief Justice William Rehnquist recently argued that, over time, such judgments "assume a general social acceptance neither because of any intrinsic worth nor because of any unique origins in someone's ideas of natural justice, but instead simply because they have been incorporated in a constitution by a people."[6] Yet the branch of the Western tradition that comes from Socrates—as well as from the Bible—and is lodged in the American Declaration of Independence notes that the judgment of any sovereign can be mistaken. It describes law as a set of rules that are to be accepted to the extent that they are intrinsically good, and rejected to the extent that they are not.

We can see what this means as regards the Ten Commandments by asking whether the lifestyle promoted by the list that came down from Mount Sinai is arbitrary or natural, whether it is inherently a better or a worse guide to human fulfillment than one made up of its opposites: Thou shalt have many gods and take their name in vain; never take a day to reflect; dishonor your father and mother; kill; steal; copulate competitively; envy your neighbor for everything. Or by the same token, we can ask whether the "natural rights" to life, liberty, and the pursuit of happiness, with which the Declaration of Independence says "all Men" are equally "endowed by their Creator," are noteworthy only because once upon a time a set of people found it useful to rally around them or whether they are so because, as the Declaration's authors said, they are "self-evident" truths valid at all times and in all places. One need only imagine how different America would have been if it had rallied around the opposite of these propositions. And of course, had the Americans confused law with right, there would have been no independence.

PROPERTY RIGHTS AND THE RULE OF LAW

Consider that self-interest can be both the foundation of the rule of law and its destruction. Self-interest was certainly in the minds of the historic defenders of law and civil society—the barons at Runnymede in 1215, the authors of the Glorious Revolution of 1688, and the authors of the Declaration of Independence in 1776. But these greats defended their interest in law based on their recognition that it was naturally proper for them to live a certain way and that it was right for them to have what others were trying to take away. Had they understood their self-interest to lie elsewhere, the results would have been different. In short, consciousness of natural law arises from living naturally, while living unnatural ways makes it difficult to understand nature.

Consider property rights—the idea that individuals or families who possess things are right to have them, defend them, and dispose of them. Living as if one had property rights is far from a universal human experience. In ancient Egypt and other Near Eastern empires, as well as in Russia until the nineteenth century, all land belonged to the sovereign, while its occupiers were mere renters. The renters' attitude—a short-term outlook, bad stewardship, and disinterest in cooperation with others to defend it—is the rule rather than the exception on the planet. It is all too easy to foster a renter's attitude in anyone. High property taxes effectively transfer to the government the presumption of ownership. Yet as the case of nineteenth-century Argentina shows, the attitude typical of renters can also exist where taxes are low, and people who are able to take responsibility for the property from which they are making money choose not to because it is too much trouble. A poet was able to write the verse that follows because many of those who came to the Argentine pampas sought exportable profits rather than to make the land truly their own:

> No one planted a tree
> And on the farms there were no sheep.
> Birds did not sing, the soft murmur
> Of bleating lambs was absent.
> Mothers raised sad children.[7]

The attitude of many people who took huge private profits from Argentina differed little from that of Russian serfs—the effective difference was the rate of return on labor. The point here is that private profit, which renters and investors can take as well as owners, is something very different from private property, which involves the duties of stewardship and defense.

By contrast, the reverential attitude toward property that Homer described in the *Odyssey* or that Fustel de Coulanges described in *The Ancient City* is a mixture of sacred right (often because ancestors were buried on the family farm) and the sacred obligation to develop and defend it, both singly and along with one's countrymen.[8] Private property is something that has to be respected and defended by the community—including, of course, by its leaders. European kings had to ask nobles and commoners for material sustenance because customary law and canon law already recognized the rightful existence of private property and because Europeans at the time were ready to fight for it. The development of the common law was substantially due to centuries of adjudication of disputes about property—disputes that presupposed general respect. The habit of exercising stewardship over property, of having one's right in property respected and of respecting others' such rights—a restrained combination of jealousy and generosity—naturally leads people to make and respect mutually satisfying rules about other aspects of public life.

However, whereas private property habituates people to the rule and defense of law, Plato taught that the mere possession of wealth does not. In Book 8 of *The Republic*, he drew an ominous portrait of society (or rather what passes for society), based not on the citizen but on the consumer. The merely wealthy man, he said, lives with all the outward trappings of social power but has none because he spends his life merely making money and enjoying it. Perhaps the regime allows no other ambition. He does not know his neighbors for any civic purpose. He is not part of any voluntary, nonprofit endeavor.[9] He could not lead and would not follow in peace, but he especially could not and would not do either in war. He is a human drone.

The Politics of Redistribution

Because weakening the habits of citizenship is easier than strengthening them, the policy agendas that affect such habits are easier to describe negatively than positively. Surely the Roman republic up to the second century B.C. is the most prominent example of habitual civic virtues, and Montesquieu's summation of the process by which those habits were lost is the most concise: Having been accustomed to despoiling foreigners, they began to despoil one another like foreigners.[10] That is, until the end of the Punic Wars, foreign wars had overshadowed the ordinary self-seeking of patricians and plebeians alike, setting the tone of political life and ensuring that honor in war and public service—that is, citizenship—would be prized above the private enjoyment of wealth. Thereafter, as wealth became the measure of success, the Romans' habitual capacity for forceful acquisition became the means of domestic politics. Livy wrote that whenever the city took up the question of limiting landed property to the equivalent of the ancient standard of two good hectares, or of distributing captured lands, the city was turned inside out.[11] To sort out justice and seek advantage in the face of ambiguous law and powerful opposing interests, the relationship between patron and client became the most powerful political tie. Politics was reduced to the question of "who is to get what, when, and how." The result was ever more demanding clienteles, ever higher taxes, ever weakening civic responsibility, civil war, proscriptions unto death, and, finally, the transformation of Roman citizens into imperial subjects.

Long before Rome's political agenda of redistribution engendered partisan violence, Plato's *Republic* and Aristotle's *Politics* had explained why violence is the natural end of redistributionism. Since there is no natural guide to who should have what, and because human wants are inherently unlimited, the inescapable conflicts can be settled only by force. Two thousand years later, Abraham Lincoln was telling Stephen Douglas and his Illinois audience nothing new when he declared, "as I would not be a slave, so would I not be a master"[12] and made the point that taking labor or the fruits thereof from some for the benefit of others is a game that anyone can learn to play to everyone's disadvantage. He also explained that race is only one of many possible bases on which the lawless invasion of property can be pursued.

As Jonathan Swift reminded us, almost any excuse will suffice to lead men to disregard law and to crush the individual and collective liberties of their enemies. The strife in seventeenth-century Britain (or for that matter in twentieth-century Northern Ireland) identified enemies in terms of religion. But surely, strife between the English, Irish, and Scots predated the Protestant Reformation; and surely, the oppression of Low Church Scots was as vigorous as that imposed on Catholic Irish and was not limited to the disinterested inculcation of the fine points of Anglican orthodoxy. It always involved the addictive pleasures of economic exploitation. Long before communism, whenever groups came to power to improve the character of the people by imposing purer lifestyles on them, they quickly came to enjoy the power inherent in their vast task to take, reward, punish, uplift, and humiliate. And none of the rulers wound up poorer than the ruled.[13] The saying about New Deal politicians in Washington—they came to do good and they stayed to do well—is applicable generally. Our point, then, is that respect for private property is the beginning of the rule of law, and that excuses for disrespect are never lacking.

Parties and Representation

Political agendas that build up or undermine liberty and the rule of law are often embedded in or are the logical consequence of political parties and the legal-constitutional structures in which they exist. In the twentieth century, some parties, for instance, America's Republicans and Democrats, have been more loosely organized than social clubs, with barely an agenda. But the trend of the century has been toward parties organized more tightly than military units to pursue wars more total than the ones armies wage—wars aimed to bring down whole cultures. Some have provided their members physical sustenance and moral certainty. As early as the turn of the twentieth century, Socialist parties in Europe were keeping clergymen away from workers' housing, filling the resulting spiritual void with lectures on modern mores. Since then, parties organized on the socialist model have become laws and polities unto themselves in many countries, eclipsing the government at all levels, so that individuals' relationships with parties have counted for more than formal rights and duties of citizenship. Socialist parties possessed this century's modernist faith explicitly and organized to manufacture their members' unanimous support for it. Their programmatic focus, their practical power, and the congruence between the structure of the party and the character of modern government has strongly influenced most of the world's parties.

What is to be the relationship between citizens and the governments that claim to represent them? This question first arose in the modern world in the aftermath of England's Glorious Revolution of 1688, when people realized that their representatives held the absolute powers that had been the king's during the previous century. Edmund Burke was the first to warn that the new order would be a despotism of the constituencies—worse than royal absolutism—if members of Parliament were to subordinate judgment about law and right to their constituents' instructions. Burke barely imagined party organizations that would organize a majority of the constituencies and literally reduce members of Parliament to being their employees. James Madison, who feared the prospect of such organizations, thought that since legislators would come from a vast country and represent diverse and shifting interests, they could not coalesce to preempt property rights and the citizenship that flows therefrom. Madison's *Federalist* no. 10, however, does not mention the one feature of America that eventually contributed most to his design's success: Each individual legislator came from a district diverse enough to make it difficult for any legislator to be captured by a single organized interest. Much less could any such interest organize masses of legislators into disciplined battalions.

The Socialist parties changed everything because they organized to capture government in the name of an interest, namely, that of industrial workers, whom they claimed had no town and no country, enjoyed the protection of no laws, and were oppressed even by religion. Thus, the Socialists set up societies among workers to provide insurance against unemployment and sickness, to organize leisure time, and to preach the rejection of present-day ideas, mores, and allegiances. The Socialists sent delegates to Parliament without regard for the common good, which they thought illusory. Even pressing for workers' interests within society took a backseat to doing battle with other interests. It is tempting to say that the Socialists were setting up alternative civil societies. But since every Socialist club ultimately depended on the Party, there was less civility in them than power.

The rise of socialism coincided with that of the notion—best articulated by John Stuart Mill—that representative government had to represent all of society's opinions and interests and that legislatures ought to mirror interests rather than localities.[14] In other words, out of all the aspects of any person's life, legislatures ought to represent just one: the individual's interest in a party—which in essence means none of the aspects of life that bind individuals as neighbors but rather the one aspect that tends to set the individual apart because it depends on individual choice alone. This meant rather than awarding seats one by one to whichever individual got the most votes in each district, seats would be distributed to parties in lots equal to the percentage of the vote they received. This system of proportional representation (PR) discourages voters from coalescing with other differently motivated voters behind an individual who will represent them all tolerably well. Rather, it encourages them to back the party that will promote their particular interests at the expense of others'.

Edmund Burke and James Madison had worried that individual legislators, once in office, would get together to pursue factional interests. But parties based on legislators who are elected individually and by their own efforts (or those of people bound to do the bidding of a particular locality) must be loose, ever-shifting coalitions—as indeed all British parties were up to the mid-nineteenth century and as American parties remain to this day. By contrast, legislators who arrive in office by virtue of proportional representation are already bound together to pursue factional interests because they are the mere creatures of the party. They are elected from lists compiled by the parties. The very existence of these lists presupposes and calls forth the party leaders who compile the lists. Under proportional representation, the leaders are all-powerful because they decide who is to be on the list and above all who will occupy the places on the list that are high enough to guarantee election, given the party's likely share of the vote. Under proportional representation, legislators work for the party leaders, who may not even be legislators themselves or who may hold no public office at all. Such leaders are elected by party officials whose careers they control. Thus insulated against pressure from the general public, party leaders under PR are powers unto themselves. Proportional representation makes them the only truly enfranchised citizens, and gives them incentives to set the several parts of civil society against one another.

The existence of growing Socialist subcultures represented by parliamentary factions whose discipline magnified their forces beyond their number led other European parties to imitate the Socialists' grassroots organizations and to support the introduction of PR so that they, too, might impose discipline on their members. Although Britain never did adopt PR and France did so only for the twelve years of the Fourth Republic from 1946 to 1958, both countries experienced a strengthening of party organizations at the expense of other political entities through the middle of the century, and passed the strong-party legacy on to their colonies, usually along with PR.

Italy and Germany, however, adopted PR immediately after World War I. The result was prototypical: Amid fragmented parties that had partially adopted the new Socialist-style organization (local sections controlled by regional and central committees, directorates, general secretaries and politburos, plus affiliated labor, youth, and women's organizations), the more compact, more fully disciplined Socialist parties were able to maneuver more adroitly to capture targeted sectors of the electorate and make and unmake coalitions. But the newest, most radical Socialist parties—the Fascists and the Communists—enjoyed the greatest advantages because they had carried organization, discipline, and antagonistic ideology to their logical conclusion: the establishment of armed gangs that brought "extra-parliamentary" pressure to bear on the political process. The black- and brown-shirted thugs who beat rank and file political opponents in the streets, whose leaders watched and quaked, became the only real citizens of the budding new regimes.[15]

It is important to note that the full logic of modern political parties and its effect on the habits of citizens living under them could manifest itself only *after* these parties had taken hold of state power and used it to feed and discipline their own organizations. Prior to that, even when Benito Mussolini himself, for example, ran afoul of the Socialist party in 1915 and was cut off from his party job (as editor of the party newspaper), he remained free to get another job and to organize his friends into a rival party. But once Mussolini's Fascist Party took state power, no other job would be available to apostates from the party, much less the freedom to organize opposition. Once upon a time the party's affiliated labor unions had worked with the party in the expectation that the party would advance the unions' own goals. But when the party gained power to prohibit alternative unions as well as to reward and punish the unions' officials more than the members could, the unions became (in the terminology of the Communists) "transmission belts" for orders from party chiefs to union officials bound to obey them. The rank and file became ciphers. The same goes for all other "sectoral" or "mass" organizations affiliated with the party.

Far from being confined to the Nazi and Communist parties, colonization of the economy and the presence of the transmission-belt syndrome in social organizations—the choking of civil society—is the rule in modern big-government states. Only the tightness of the grip and the degree of colonization are different. Since giving jobs and favors is a powerful tool of party discipline and government power in the modern world is nothing if not power over jobs, modern parties have aggressively sought involvement in the economy precisely to "colonize" both government and private employment, to reward the friends and punish the enemies of the party. From Israel to Italy and Japan, regimes that employ PR tend to have parties that are more disciplined, whose control of the social organizations associated with them is greater, and whose colonization of the economy has gone farther than parties that do not live under PR. In such regimes, elections do not determine who governs. Interparty deals do. Consequently, in such regimes, voters are less able than elsewhere to "throw the rascals out." How can they, when the "rascals" in the several parties fight as they might over the division of society's spoils and tend to cooperate, especially to shut out competition from upstarts. Throughout the Western world, for example, budgets are passed by comprehensive deals between the leaders of all major parties.

In sum, citizenship and the rule of law are problematic throughout the modern world, and most problematic in the regimes that most partake of modernity.

CIVILITY, REAL AND FAUX

Except when in the throes of revolution or civil chaos, peoples everywhere exhibit some kind of order: Robberies and rapes are less common than peaceful behavior, and at least some people spend their lives under arms to defend the regime. Yet we know that only in a minority of regimes can large numbers of people take part in public affairs on the basis of equality, and that in most regimes, order and the defense thereof result mainly from compulsion. Nevertheless, travelers and readers of history are struck by the fact that even the subjects of tyranny not only observe the laws but also sometimes genuinely cheer the regime and lay down their lives for it. Thus, while keeping in mind the distinction between citizens and subjects, it is important to draw still another distinction—between the patriotism that arises from a common ownership of the regime, and adherence to some of the regime's goals—which usually include its survival against enemies, foreign and domestic.

In modern times, nationalism has most often masked the absence of citizenship. Recall that the French Revolution endowed French people with the title "citizen" and sought to recreate the pre-Christian communities of ancient Greece and Rome.[16] The French revolutionaries did succeed in raising consciousness of national differences to levels unprecedented since the Dark Ages. And no doubt the lively sense of patriotism they worked so hard to build helped the regime to draft and discipline its armies as well as to compel its brand of civil order. But that is just the point. Despite their talk of the natural rights of man and of society's corporations, the French revolutionaries sought to use towns, churches, professional associations, and the schools they built as instruments to kill all of the above as well as individuals insofar as they were not bent to the service of the state. The practical point of de Tocqueville's *Democracy in America* was to disabuse his French countrymen of any illusions that the revolution had turned them into citizens. By describing the genuine American article, he showed Frenchmen that their patriotic enthusiasm did not in the least affect their status as subjects of an administrative state.

Between the French Revolution and World War I, the European regimes that more or less aped France succeeded brilliantly in identifying themselves with the nation. By the end of the nineteenth century, the peoples of Europe had bound themselves emotionally and uncon-ditionally to their regimes. The ties were so strong that even the So-cialist parties of Germany and Austria, for all their antimonarchist talk, never dared to try to break their members' solid habits of civil obedi-ence. When the war came, predictions of resistance to the draft proved unfounded. In August 1914, resistance averaged 1.5 percent through-out Europe.[17] Like everybody else, the Socialists marched into the meat grinder with merry patriotic hearts—just because the order to do so had come down from the top. The spirit of self-sacrifice was over-abundant. By and large, the European regimes of the nineteenth cen-tury were beloved. For the most part, they were the most law-abiding regimes of all time—the "state of law" having become something of an object of worship in Germany, more or less imitated elsewhere. And yet the fact that these Europeans loved the machines in which they were cogs did not make them any less cogs. It masked the fact that they had long since lost the habits of self-starting citizens. When the stu-pidity of World War I discredited nationalism, the European regimes were left to rule masses of mere claimants.

The Fascist movement after World War I was an attempt to resur-rect the prewar regimes by multiplying the dose of nationalism. Mus-solini was the last Jacobin. By militarizing society's rituals (there were "wars" on crime as well as on low productivity), by focusing the peo-ple's attention on enemies foreign and domestic, by radically expand-ing the welfare system to secure the "home front"—and not incidentally, by increasing the size and brutality of the state's adminis-trative apparatus—the Fascists managed to put some order into politi-cal processes that were degenerating into chaos. Thus, Mussolini's Italy—and even Hitler's Germany until the outbreak of war—gave the impression of order, purposeful energy, and widespread patriotism. But these regimes had no citizens. Mussolini's Fascists abandoned him as soon as it became profitable to do so, while the German people, having been seduced by the Nazis until 1939, thereafter submitted to ever-more-violent rape. Civic enthusiasm was absent.

After World War II, too many Europeans failed to see that the na-tionalist pageantry with which Third World leaders were surrounding themselves was a bad copy of fascism. Some Europeans, aghast at the increasing lack of civic commitment in their own sleepy welfare states, were tempted to envy what seemed to be the civic vitality of the Third World. The most renowned European political scientist, Sir Ralf Dahrendorf, even envied the patently fraudulent civic vitality that East

Germany had built with the aid of the Berlin Wall.[18] True, Third World regimes have little trouble whipping up crowds and raising armies. But, whereas citizenship is full partnership in a regime, the masses of the Third World are partners only in being exploited and manipulated into ethnic hate. At least in the Communist world, ordinary people learned to hate communism.

The Chinas

Despite the vast differences between Chinese and Russian cultures, the Communist regime in the People's Republic of China has fostered human habits distressingly similar to those produced by Communist rule in Russia. By contrast, the two non-Communist Chinese states, Taiwan and Singapore, have regimes very different from Communist China's, and they have promoted very different human qualities.

THE PEOPLE'S REPUBLIC

Even more than the Soviets, the Chinese Communists tried to destroy the moral basis of society as well as the material basis. After killing landowners and forcing peasants out of their family hovels into the sex-segregated barracks of agricultural communes, they lectured the inmates about the evils of Confucian ethics while trying to inculcate a new morality based on devotion to the state. During Mao Tse-tung's time, the public—especially the young—were exhorted to emulate Liu Weuxue, a young man who reported a landlord who had stolen what were now the people's peppers from his former field. In the 1990s equivalent, schoolchildren are forced to buy books about Lai Ming, a boy who reported on two of his classmates, who had struck up a romance before the age permitted by the state.[19]

Like the Russians, the Chinese had been the subjects of empires that had toyed with lives and property. But in China, unlike in Russia, emperors had not claimed to own all the land, and the Chinese Confucian tradition had been an even stronger support than Eastern Orthodox Christianity for the idea that righteousness and political power are not identical. True, the Confucian tradition has little to say to individuals except that they should conform perfectly to a virtuous social order. But Confucian demands on the virtue of rulers are so exacting that through the ages, those who claimed that any given regime had lost the "mandate of heaven" found it little more difficult to make their case than those who claimed the mandate. Moreover, the counsels of perfection that Confucius extended to individuals tend to make them almost as morally self-possessed, almost as likely to stand aside from government and criticize it, as Christians or Platonists. And although China had been ruled by a centralized empire, its very vastness also gave it some experience of local autonomy. In short, then, although China was not accustomed to living under the rule of law and did not have social institutions (other than the family) independent of rulers, it was not wholly bereft of bases on which law and civil society might have arisen. Communist rule, then, was even more disruptive of Chinese ways than it was of Russian ways.

The effect of absolute power on those Chinese who exercised it was roughly the same as the effect on their Russian counterparts. Recent accounts by Mao Tse-tung's physician reveal that Mao's taste for young girls was as insatiable as his thirst for power,[20] while biographies of other top Communists stress the groveling and betrayals that they had to practice on one another to survive. Change the proper names, and Chinese Communist stories would be interchangeable with Soviet ones. The story of Kang Sheng, for example, could easily be a composite of the biographies of the most murderous chiefs of the Soviet KGB.[21] The method of governing in Communist China was—and remains—what Kenneth Lieberthal has called "fragmented authoritarianism,"[22] the familiar Soviet pattern of bureaucrats responsible both to the chain of command leading to central party headquarters and to the local network of interests. And as in the Soviet Union, the bureaucrats resolve the conflict by forming informal networks through which they seek their personal interests regardless of law. In China as elsewhere this means total corruption at the retail level.

The effects on those who must put up with a government just as lawless as the Soviet but more intrusive—the enforcement of the government's one-child policy, as we will see (in chapter 7), marks a new low in the history of tyranny—may have been best described by Chinese visitors to the mainland from Taiwan. They noted that mainlanders are not conscientious in their work, that officials live well and demand bribes from the poor, that anything including admission to schools may be had for a bribe, and that "lack of sincerity," cheating, and extortion are prevalent. They noted that "many long-haired jobless youth loiter about, and some rob people" and that there had been a general decline in traditional Chinese virtues.[23] It takes no special sophistication for a traveler to see that everything is for sale, from immunity for one's self to the ruin of one's enemies.

No doubt, the People's Republic of China can make soldiers out of such human material—indeed, such deracinated people may be recruited by any number of military factions within the Chinese regime. And since the regime itself has no purpose other than the competitive enrichment of its members, there is every reason to believe that persons so habituated will hasten the recurrence of the Chinese cycle of civil war. The very concept of citizenship, however, clashes with Chinese reality.

TAIWAN

The Nationalist regime on Taiwan differs from the mainland Communist regime not so much in the degree of brutality involved in its founding[24] as it does in regard to purpose and organization and therefore in the habits it has fostered. Chiang Kai-shek shaped the Nationalist regime according to the ideas of Sun Yat-sen, who founded the Nationalist Party, and according to the bitter experiences of the civil war, which Chiang had lost. Sun had tried to blend the Confucian tradition, Western political philosophy, and Christianity.[25] The intellectual incoherence of that syncretic blend is less important than the fact that Sun's successors wanted to preserve the Confucian way of life and to somehow graft Western, liberal politics onto it. Also, Chiang knew he had lost the civil war in large part because his regime had been captured, paralyzed, and betrayed by corrupt interest groups in both cities and countryside. So, reason and necessity pushed him to found his regime on Taiwan in a way that would fuse Confucianism with Western ways, discourage the rise of corruption, and lay the bases for broad support, freely given.

Chiang's first constitutional act, like Mao's, was the expropriation of large estates. But Chiang performed this revolutionary act for a conservative purpose. That unlawful act could become the foundation of law because, like Machiavelli's model prince, Chiang's first harmful act was his biggest and nearly his last. He divided lands among peasant farmers, to whom he gave full title, while to the former owners he gave bond payments that made them stakeholders in Taiwan's budding industrial economy. Only time, however, could redeem Chiang's promise to respect property rights scrupulously and to depoliticize the economy. But that respect eventually became the foundation of the rule of law on Taiwan. The free, honest market in agriculture immediately provided a measure of prosperity for the native Taiwanese, and that, in turn, foreclosed serious opposition. Since the regime was not at war with the population or with its customs, it raised no barriers to upward mobility—including involvement in the ruling party and, eventually, in the free opposition that the party promised from the beginning. The government decided to own and operate primary industries so that it could ensure that the economy met its military needs without having to develop corrupting links to private wealth. The private industry it encouraged would be small: "In essence the decision to 'go small' was the industrial equivalent of land reform. Both policies preempted the rise of powerful interest groups."[26]

The effective constitution of Taiwan, then, presupposes the Confucian ideal of the autonomous and virtuous individual in harmony with the community; the Chinese tradition of large, hardworking, patriarchal families that seek (and in Taiwan have found) a minimum of interference with their affairs; and the consciousness that the country has to "make it" if it is to withstand the threat from its huge neighbor. These are not the Western foundations of the rule of law. The Taiwanese regime owes nothing to any idea of human equality, because Confucianism both ancient and modern is a culture of different duties for different stations in life rather than an exegesis of a nature common to all humans. Still, the rulers of Taiwan chose from the beginning to institute equal treatment by law regarding economic matters. When habits of economic equality had taken root, they chose to follow their logic to equal treatment regarding political matters as well. Yet the notion that fathers and sons should have equal standing before the law in social matters would be regarded as totally subversive, if anyone thought of it.

Although Taiwan calls itself the Republic of China, Chinese culture does not contain the idea of a republic, much less Montesquieu's notion that the chief political requirement of republics is a virtuous population. Nevertheless, the Confucian tradition knows even better than the Western that virtue is essential to all political life. Hence, it fears freedom, above all because of its often corrosive effects on virtue. Since Taiwan has been completely free for less than one decade, it is difficult to tell whether or to what extent freedom is undermining the good habits that undergird its constitution. The divorce rate, though not high by Western standards, has doubled since 1980 (thus becoming the highest in Asia) and alarms the Taiwanese.[27] Also, since both politics and economics on Taiwan are free, they have begun to mix freely. The newspapers are full of stories about the purchase of votes, and the rising price of influence indicates that its value must be rising, too. Finally, no Confucian composure could fail to be shaken by the indecorous sight of legislators fistfighting on the floor of Taiwan's National Assembly. Taiwan is the first Chinese republic. But the diseases of violent faction and redistributive economics can kill Taiwan's adherence to the rule of law just as surely as in any other republic anywhere.

SINGAPORE

Singapore's rulers argue precisely that their suppression of political freedom is the precondition for the maintenance of the rule of law and, therefore, of all other good things. The People's Action Party, led by Chief Minister Lee Kwan Yew, uses the powers of the state, including such machinations as lawsuits against political opponents tried before biased judges and the government's official influence over business, to effectively shut out the opposition. Anyone else is treated with scrupulous fairness under laws that make perfect sense in terms of both Confucianism and capitalism. Civil society exists by sufferance. The chief minister, his family, and the ruling party's main functionaries are paid very well, but they are not the richest men in the country and no one has charged them with using their power to skim the profits of business. Machiavelli would have been surprised at the regime's success in this very difficult feat, but not at the results of its having done so. The residents of Singapore are doing fine and have few complaints besides the high cost of the good life.[28]

But although they are satisfied as consumers of government, they have no experience of citizenship. Lee may be right that Taiwan's freedom is destroying the virtues needed to maintain the rule of law and the good life.[29] It is quite another thing for him to argue that those virtues are now safe in Singapore. Since he, their guardian, is someone Confucius might well have approved of, they are safe enough with him. When he dies, they will be in the hands either of his heirs, whose virtue is anyone's guess, or of the Singaporeans, whose expertise as consumers of mostly lawful government should not be confused with any capacity to produce it.

Does citizenship mean reliable reception of government services or does it mean self-government? Throughout the twentieth century, governments have justified their power by claiming to deliver more and better services. Some deliver better than others. But it seems that governments run as providers of services train those who live under them to be subjects rather than citizens.

Mexico

When we draw sharp lines between modern Western democracies and less democratic modern regimes, we are too kind to ourselves. To a greater or lesser extent, all modern regimes promote themselves as nonpolitical administrators of the only reasonable agenda: the assurance of ever-improving economic circumstances in a socially liberal, secular society.[30] Some regimes take more than others, and some preside over more orderly material well-being than others. Regardless of performance, however, modern regimes foster among those who live under them similar habits of social and political atrophy.

The Mexican people's habitual acquiescence to authority is rooted in the ways of the pre-Columbian Aztec and Mayan subjects, who became the servants of Spanish conquerors. One can notice the difference in the degree of social deference between most of Mexico, where this legacy of servitude is strong, and the northern deserts, where Spanish settlers found no one to enslave and had to work themselves.

In both Mexico and modern Europe, the only theoretical question in public life is who has the formula for general prosperity, while the only practical question for individuals is how to make the connections needed to ensure the maximum flow of favor. Yet the Mexican people do not believe their leaders' claims of technocratic expertise and benevolent disinterestedness as much as do modern Europeans. In Mexico, elections do not matter because the one and only ruling party has co-opted society's leading interests (including the opposition parties, to a considerable extent) and has endowed the regimes as a whole with monopoly power. But elections do not matter much in modern Europe, either, for much the same reasons: The parties have incorporated and institutionalized society's interest groups, and the bureaucracy is so big that it is out of reach of elected officials, except through party channels. The unconnected individual counts for as little in Europe as in Mexico, and in both places, the practical route for redress of grievances and pursuit of profit is less the legal structure than the political parties' "mass organizations." The cash bribe is the Mexican regime's currency. But since the color of a simple man's money is the same as that of a well-connected one, a Mexican who wants to get along need invest only cash—less of himself than a European. If anything, in Mexico the possibility of citizenship is less remote than in Europe because the Mexican people only act as if they believed in the system. In fact almost no Mexicans believe in technocracy, whereas a few Europeans still do.

The dictator Porfirio Diaz (1877–1911) began the practice of bolstering his government's prestige by claiming that he had put it in the hands of *los cientificos*, the scientists (that is, the economists) who knew best how to lift the country out of poverty. Of course, this was merely thin cover for kleptocracy. The several revolutionary factions that overthrew him fought the revolution that ended in the presidency of Lazaro Càrdenas in 1934 and coalesced into the Institutional Revolutionary Party (PRI). Just as kleptocratic as its forebears, the PRI claimed to have a surefire recipe for prosperity that was just as scientific: the nationalization of petroleum and other basic industries and the distribution of land to peasants (without title). The government would administer the oil and the land. The essence of the party and thus of the regime was an alliance of the labor movement, which was based mainly in the nationalized sector, of the government agency that controlled the peasants, and of the major industrialists. No law prohibited the formation of alternative labor unions or of opposition parties. But no law would protect them from bureaucrats whose main concern became preserving the monopoly of the PRI's affiliated social organizations. Without competition, the official unions ensured that the workers would continue to accept low wages. Opposition parties were either bought off or cheated in the vote counts.[31] Meanwhile, the PRI politicians began to pass themselves off as more scientific than *los cientificos*.

The main characteristic of Mexican public life is its lawlessness—especially at the highest levels. Mexico does not lack laws. But enforcement is a commodity to be bought and sold. Those who enforce regulations have wide discretion. One must get at the enforcers through the "right," meaning extralegal channels. However, in Mexico, the *mordida*, the "bribe" (literally, "the bite") is monetary rather than social.[32] The reason that officials and judges demand it so insistently is that they hold their patronage positions insecurely and thus must cash in while they can. Bureaucrats get along fine with the businesses they regulate because they get paid off, as do their superiors. The judges decide on the basis of payment and pressures on either side of the case, and the police are in business for themselves like everybody else. However, regardless of whether a person is an official of a labor union, a government employee, a big businessman, or an official of any of the countless "popular organizations," that individual is effectively a member of the PRI establishment and must pursue personal enrichment with due regard for the interests of others in other parts of the same hierarchy. That is the "law" that governs unofficial as well as official relationships.

The result is a population highly deferential and eager not to run afoul of the system. No conviction is more widespread in Mexico than that "the deal," whatever it may be, has already been agreed on by higher authority behind closed doors and that it is futile to fight it. But perhaps because so many Mexicans get deals that are so patently unfair, there is a lot more external acquiescence than internal. Mexicans perceive the unfairness partly because over the past forty years, fewer and fewer of them have belonged to the party-state's official organizations. Hence, the proportion of those who pay the system but receive nothing at all from it has risen. The official labor movement has not been able to organize the millions of employees in the *maquiladoras*, the factories near the U.S. border that produce for export to the United States. In addition, local sentiment and idealized images of civic life in the United States have fed opposition movements, especially in the northern states and cities of Mexico.[33] Whereas fifty years ago millions of Mexicans would have given their lives to resist absorption into the United States, nowadays they risk their lives to go there. The PRI's powerful administrative controls[34] have not been able to stem the steady decline in habits of deference. One reason is that unlike in Europe, the Mexican regime had gradually given up its pseudo-scientific pretenses and has therefore lost its grip on people's minds.

Italy

The Italian regime is a variant of a type found from Crete to the shores of the Arctic. But while the differences between Italians and Swedes are as great as those between Europeans and Mexicans, and each regime came to be by peculiar historical paths, all share common features: The relationship between parties and interest groups is more important than that between voters and parliaments; local government is powerless; government has colonized society; and the only law (other than cash) is political connection.

Modern Italy might seem peculiar because it is still largely dominated by parties organized under fascism and nourished in the Fascist-Communist way by "mass organizations" throughout civil society and because colonies of patronage posts are spotted throughout the public and private sector. In Italy this happened because the victorious Allies did not dismantle the Fascists' organs of control for the economy and society. Rather, the resurgent Communist and Socialist parties sought to substitute their own apparatuses for the Fascists'. But though the parties of the extreme left lost the 1948 elections decisively to Christian Democrats, Liberals, Social Democrats, and Republicans, the winners subsequently reorganized themselves even further along Fascist-Communist lines—instituting general secretaries, central committees, and so on—and invaded the economy in a hunt for patronage as competitive as the Oklahoma Land Rush.

The case of the Christian Democrats stands out because they chose specifically to shift their base of support, relying ever less on independent organizations of Catholic laymen and ever more on networks of recipients of patronage. They did this because they believed—like the Communists and Fascists—that politics is about taking away from enemies to give to friends and that only support that is bought and paid for can be relied upon. The Christian Democrats and their allies wanted to rely as much as possible on things they could control, like patronage and organization, and as little as possible on the variable opinion of voters. To disenfranchise voters even further, they developed the habit of cooperating with the opposition, both in or out of government, in a practice called *consociativismo*, loosely translated as "bipartisanship." As a result, voters got the same result regardless of who they voted for. Citizens who wanted favors could work through any party—Catholic or Communist. But anyone who wanted impartial treatment had nowhere to go. The result has been a half century of economic, political, and moral corruption.

But Italy is not unique. In Sweden, which never experienced fascism, the Social Democratic Party and its popular organizations loom even larger over economy, society, and Parliament than do all the parties in Italy combined. The tradition of nonconfrontation, of effacing differences among leaders, is much stronger in Sweden than in Italy. And the basis of the Italian regime's legitimacy, no less than that of Sweden, Germany, or France, is the assumption that government can deliver security, prosperity, and fairness. Italians, however, have fewer illusions.

The modern Italian political agenda has consisted of redistribution— wholesale among the parties, retail among their adherents. On the wholesale level, formal and informal additions to the governing coalition are "paid for" by grants of exclusive rights to patronage. Thus, the Socialists' payment for supporting the government in 1963 began with the right to staff the electric power industry. However, it certainly did not end there. The first installment payment for Communist support in 1974 was the addition of a third channel to the state TV network, for the Communists' use as a propaganda tool and as a fount of patronage. Below the highest level, each of the parties' "mass organizations" lobby for places and control of the countless contracts that the state issues for everything from moviemaking to welfare. Socialists and Communists own labor unions, commercial cooperatives, and "sector organizations" among lawyers, women, and other groups. They share with other parties special relationships with big businesses, farmers, clergy, and so forth. Not least among these are the parties' cronies among public employees. On any given day, the headlines in the press will be about interparty and intraparty bargaining over who is to be appointed to what post in what regulatory agency or "parastate" body. Italy, like Sweden, is thus not run by laws interpreted by courts but rather by administrative acts of officials in agencies that owe nothing to Parliament and whose officials are selected by the parties in the ruling coalition.

The state acts as enforcer for private interests—except that they are no longer strictly private. Indeed, the essence of the corporate state is that it abolishes the distinction between public and private—while concomitantly accentuating the distinction between those who have access to state power and those who do not. Thus, an individual who is aggrieved or who merely wants something and petitions the government through formal channels acts unconstitutionally. If he tries to solve his problem by soliciting the cooperation of private citizens to change the laws or to effect officials who will, he acts even more against the spirit of the real constitution. Rather, the correct way, according to the Constitution that really runs things, is to enlist the cooperation of one of the corporate state's constituent organizations— a labor union or a business professional association that is well connected to one of the ruling parties. This is the law, from Crete to North Cape.

In the modern administrative state, then, impartial law is a bother. Social security comes from cozy relations with the gatekeepers of the state's bounty. Whereas law presumes the impartial settlement of contrasting interests by adversarial proceedings and reference to objective truth, social security throughout corporate Europe looks upon law as cold comfort. Instead of law, European regimes offer cooperative striving for consensus and comfortable adjustment. The day-to-day news in Europe consists substantially of which protégé of which politician or, more likely, bureaucrat, has gained temporary control over which fount of favor. To chronicle a fraction of the jobs, contracts, sinecures, licenses, school admissions, exemptions, and exactions retailed through political patronage in Italy alone would fill a library.

The effect on people who live by patronage is clear enough. Because no one presumes that the person behind any given desk earned the position, to get to know a person means to estimate the percentages of usefulness and favor that contributed to that person's getting the position, as well as assessing how useful that person's access to favor might be. Losing a job, contract, or benefit because of shifting powers above carries no onus—but inability to land on one's feet denotes shameful impotence. The only fatherland to which one can repair is one's own faction, and the only right in property or in law becomes the mutual obligation of favors and loyalties.

Italy's way of life is quite tolerable, suffused as it is by the Italians' penchant for pleasant living. But the mildly competitive hedonism of contemporary Europe never generated its own military defense. It is difficult to imagine Europeans nowadays offering their lives for their country. Contemporary Europe's way of life has been possible only because it was protected by the United States.

The Unmaking of Citizenship

Socrates obeyed the laws of Athens unto death, even though he sought virtue higher than the kind that came from civic duty, because that duty, that citizenship, was worthy enough to die for. This chapter has set forth what qualities it takes to be a citizen in several regimes and what civic qualities several kinds of regimes engender. In the end, the possibility of citizenship depends on the presence in the regime of the habits of virtue and freedom, because these are the elements of the rule of law and the rule of law is the bulwark of civil society. However, citizenship also requires the possibility of ruling and being ruled in turn, of sharing decisions big and small. At best, modern regimes engender few of the habits of citizenship.

Law is restraint, and the rule of law is the acceptance of restraint by those who could most easily not accept it. But law requires that this self-restraint be regular and predictable. Most regimes, however, are clusters of discretionary powers and are not suffused with ideas that logically lead people to limit their own discretion. Nothing prevents the Swiss, for example, from using their powers of referendum to sweep away their local prerogatives as mere obstacles to progress. They do not do this, though, because they have grown accustomed to acting as if they did not have the right to take them away even if they wanted to—a virtuous habit. Similarly, the authors of the U.S. Constitution were keenly aware that they had erected mere "parchment barriers" against bad popular government. George Washington dedicated his first inaugural address to the "truth more thoroughly established than [any] that there exists in the economy and course of nature an indissoluble union between virtue and happiness."[35] Jefferson, in his first inaugural address, invoked the principles of natural law that had justified America's struggle for independence to establish "this sacred principle, that though the will of the majority is in all cases to prevail, that will to be rightful must be reasonable, that the minority possess their equal rights which equal law must protect, and to violate must be oppression."[36] Therefore, for the rule of law to exist, not even *vox populi* may be confused with *vox Dei*. Alas, in many modern regimes, the most authoritative voice is that of an official or of a potentate of an organization "close" to a ruling party.

The rule of law is important because it defines who counts equally—that is, who is a citizen—and because it defines the scope of freedom. In some regimes, the label "citizen" properly fits so few people as to be inappropriate. In others, for instance, in the Singaporean regime, those who are equal in their exercise of political power are few but choose to grant unto almost everyone the equal exercise of their economic faculties. In still others, the number of those with political rights is larger, while the number of those with the right to lead nonpolitical lives free from arbitrary force is smaller. Yet more important than differences in scope is the fact that in most places it can be narrowed or broadened, at the whim of the sovereign. That is to say that in most of the world, such citizenship and civil society as exist, do so by sufferance.

Chapter 7
FAMILY

The disciples said to him, "If this is the law of a man with his wife, it is not expedient to marry."

—MATTHEW 19:10

E ACH CULTURE IS LARGELY DEFINED by the ways in which men and women within it come together to raise children, and each regime defines itself substantially by how it affects those ways. That is not to say that every regime has a "family policy"—the very term is a latter-day Western presumption of government power. Seldom do laws place intolerable burdens on families, and never can laws make families. But every regime affects families by making the conditions in which they live. In our time, the passions that surround the relationship between government and families has so obscured it that our discussion must begin by considering what a family is and what it is not.

Family and Nature

Not all arrangements for procreation can properly be called families. Aristotle noted that the barbarians of his time treated women as slaves,[1] using them for the heaviest, meanest tasks as well as for sexual satisfaction. Children were simply another product that the strong got from the weak. But husbands and wives, Aristotle wrote, are natural partners in the household—equally rational beings who adjust their particular contributions to the common good through mutual persuasion.[2] Early Americans also noted that the American Indians used their women like "mules." Why? Thomas Jefferson argued that the Indians did not know the natural law. He wrote: "Were we in equal barbarism . . . our females would be equal drudges."[3] When Western travelers applied the term "wives" to the multiple women taken by African or Asian potentates, they did so for lack of a handier term to describe arrangements that were based on force, were revocable at will, and involved obligation on one side only—or that, at most, were deals between families that exchanged women for goods.

Such arrangements do not involve husbands, wives, and families, properly speaking. They are closer to the practices of four-footed herbivores, among whom the strongest males gather the biggest herds of females. The Muslim harems, however, have an element of family about them because they are entered into, conducted, and broken by law, however imperfect. Some laws, though, such as the old Hindu customary requirement that widows be burned alive on their husband's funeral pyre, cannot naturally coexist with the notion of family. The natural notion of family, of course, is the basis on which the U.S. Supreme Court declared that the practice of polygamy by Mormons in the state of Utah mocked the very basis of family, namely, the full reciprocal commitment on the part of one husband and one wife.[4]

In the particular case of Mormon polygamy, the Court's conclusion went beyond its logic, because the Mormon polygamist husband's allegiance is supposed to be to all wives equally and Mormon law binds all through eternal duties. The Court, however, was responding to the demand by the vast majority of America's husbands and wives to define family strictly by the fullest realization of the natural relationship between men and women, which can only be based on "one to a customer." In the nineteenth century, governments did not imagine the currently fashionable redefinition of family to include any consensual living arrangements, much less were they tempted to entertain any notion that the family might be the root of all social evils.

The very notion of "redefining" families is a thinly disguised argument for the proposition that the natural family is no better than any other human arrangement and is probably the worst of the lot. Thus, practitioners of what were once called "deviant" lifestyles want to pin the family label on relations between homosexuals less because they think there is little difference between homosexual and heterosexual relationships than because they want for homosexual couples whatever deference natural families normally receive. Yet this desire cannot be fulfilled for logical as well as practical reasons. If families are not natural and permanent unions of one man, one woman, and their children, in addition to others related by blood and marriage, they are the products of infinitely variable choices. And if that were the case, how could one deny the label family to sometime unions of one man with many women, of one woman with many men, of many men with many men? Why deny it to any combination of bisexuals, pedophiles, and necrophiliacs or to practitioners of sex with other species or with one's own offspring? Yet to the extent that the label "family" is restricted to some living arrangements and not others, the criterion for the restriction must be natural. The acceptance of nature as the criterion, however, drives us back to one man and one woman united to reproduce and raise children.

The fashion of the most influential Western intellectual circles has long dictated that mankind is composed of discrete individuals whose relations are purely consensual and that when these relationships involve housing and sex, they are called families. Note, however, that where each individual is independent of every other, all individuals must rely on the state alone. To the extent that individuals' relations with their cohabitants—their "families"—are contingent, each individual's relations with the state must be noncontingent. Since within contingent relationships there are always disputes about who is to do what, the state from time to time delegates authority to some over others and calls it family policy. This line of reasoning is based on the twin pillars of modern social thought: autonomous individuals and omnicompetent governments. However, this way of thinking about families hardly resonates beyond contemporary intellectual circles. Ancient barbarians and American Indians gone the way of the buffalo would shake their heads at it for their own reasons, as surely as would Aristotle, Jefferson, or a typical housewife in Omaha.

The modernist line on family matters is expressed in countless tax-subsidized classrooms as well as by advisory groups close to all Western governments. The perspective was never more succinctly stated than in the pages of *Time* magazine by Barbara Ehrenreich, who wrote that the family—and she hastened to specify "*even the ostensibly 'functional,'* non-violent family*"(emphasis mine)—"can be a nest of pathology and a cradle of gruesome violence." For women and children, claims Ehrenreich, "home is statistically speaking, the most dangerous place to be." A husband is a woman's worst enemy, and "for every child . . . who is killed by a deranged criminal on parole, dozens are abused and murdered by their own relatives."

This is highly misleading. All crimes of violence naturally proceed primarily from acquaintance. But the batterers of women are typically not husbands, properly speaking, but "boyfriends" or other kinds of live-in and transient intimates whose relationship was itself a crime until, in recent decades, views like Ehrenreich's became dominant in Western regimes.

Ehrenreich makes clear the reason why she and the Establishment whose views she represents so hate families: "The family, with its deep, impacted tensions and longings can hardly be the foundation of everything else. In fact, many families could use a lot more outside interference in the form of counseling and policing."[5] In other words, the very idea of relationships presumed to be natural is very bad, both because it restricts individual choice and perhaps above all because it presumes itself to be privileged against the state. Any claim of independence from the state is deeply subversive of modern regimes. The state should foster just about any other kind of living arrangement.

This is a succinct statement of modern family policy: The states should improve upon the natural family, or at least free people from it. As early as 1970, Gloria Steinem laid out the basis of a feminism that became a goal for many influential Americans, the overcoming of specifically male and female functions through the power of government. She looked forward to the day when courts would assign to wives (not divorcées) a percentage of their husbands' income, and when government would mandate that housing complexes be designed to force people out of traditional patterns.

However, families are precisely natural, defined neither by governmental nor by private choice but rather by the biological relations between parents and children, who are produced by natural intercourse between men and women who have undergone a process of "naturalization" into one another called marriage. Marriage is indeed a matter of choice. But it is a choice that precludes all such subsequent choices. Indeed, the process by which women leave their parents' homes for new ones has always had the solemn quality of an adoption or a change of allegiance. In ancient Greece and Rome, it involved the renunciation of one set of gods and ancestors to accept another.[6] Being a son or daughter or a father or mother is a fact of nature, not a matter of choice. Marriage is the supposition that husband and wife are related as if by nature. The proper behavior of sons to fathers, of husbands to wives, and so on has been the stuff of the world's philosophy and literature.[7] But until our own time, few who have written on these matters imagined they were doing other than explaining what already exists in nature.

The whole premise of the modern state, of course, is sovereignty—

namely, that nothing is beyond its reach. While some modern regimes have sought to reshape or "redefine" families, others have affected families in the wholehearted pursuit of economic progress without really meaning to. Let us look at how each element of family life can be influenced by regimes and then examine how some exemplar regimes of our time have affected family life.

Law and Marriage

Marriage is the mingling of separate bodies and interests into a common sphere. Although the material goods may be managed by either partner, they are possessed in common. Even to raise the question of each partner's separate material interests is to envisage the dissolution of the marriage. How much more important and less soluble than common property is the sharing of lives, of the only years when we can lay claim to good looks, vigor, hope; the joint bearing of fortune and misfortune, of children who irrevocably belong to both and who concern us from before their birth until our deaths—if not longer. Add to this that being married means living in constant adjustment to another, and it is obvious that to marry is to trade in a life that is one's own for one that is not. No wonder that people who marry want some assurance beyond the other spouse's private promises that they are not spoiling their life. These promises must be public, because both want family, friends, authorities secular and religious, to somehow protect against bigamy, adultery, nonperformance, abandonment. Of course, no third party can guarantee against an unhappy marriage. But the secular difference between marriage and cohabitation is precisely the expectation that to some extent the public will weigh in against whichever partner might be inclined to violate the terms of the deal.

Marriage, therefore, is everywhere a creature of law. But governments just as often affect marriages by not enforcing laws as by enforcing them. The Hindu women who are killed—sometimes by burning—because their families have failed to deliver the proper installment payments on their dowries to their husbands' families are wronged by the government of India, as well as by their assailants, because the government fails to enforce the law banning dowries as legal conditions of marriage that it made, ostensibly to end this practice. In the cities of West Africa, despite widespread protests by women, governments have stopped trying to enforce marriage laws, leading to an informal system of female-headed households in which men are visitors. By contrast, Saudi authorities have enforced the Islamic law by which a man may take a second (or third and fourth) wife only if he can afford to support all as well as one. Hence, any Saudi woman who marries and finds that her husband downgrades her materially and morally by taking another wife has every reason to blame the king. In practice, enforcement of this law has pushed Saudi society increasingly toward monogamy. By the same token, the recent institution of no-fault divorce in Western countries has changed the rules to the disadvantage of those who counted on public support to maintain their marriage so long as they abided by its rules. Thus, Western governments have pushed their societies toward West African lifestyles.

Marriage is as important to society at large as it is to married people. The notion that young men are turned from savages into useful citizens by the women they mate goes back to the earliest Sumerian epics and is a constant theme of literature and sociology. Civilization results from tying sexual satisfaction exclusively to the man producing for others far more than he needs for himself. Marriage—the agreement that a man, no matter how powerful, will take no more than one woman (or up to four in Islam)—also brings peace to society by ensuring that there will be enough mates for everyone, and that no one need worry that one's mate will be taken away. Laws against adultery are the most basic affirmations of social security. But marriage underpins society most of all by turning young men and women into fathers and mothers—people who practice self-sacrifice every day, who have a stake in social order, who are the likeliest to protect it against enemies foreign and domestic, and who alone can ensure that the next generation will not wreck it.[8]

This is why every regime, sooner or later, tries to bolster marriage, each in its own telling way. Even the Soviet regime that openly mocked it in the 1920s and largely destroyed the institution of Russian Orthodox marriage, reversed course in the 1930s and tried to give some substance to its own institution of marriage. It did this not because of any homeyness on Stalin's part, but rather because the country's birth rate was collapsing and communally raised children were proving to be unmanageable. The laws of Middle Eastern and Latin countries treat marriage as a financial deal between two families, making sure that the property that each family puts in through gifts or inheritance flows only to the natural heirs of both. Anglo-Saxon laws deal principally with making sure that common property stays that way.

Marriage laws everywhere deal less with marriage itself than with the disposition of children and property in case of separation or divorce. Islamic law shows two contrary faces. By granting wives divorce in cases of egregious misconduct of their husbands, the law acts as protector of the weak, of the innocent, and arguably of marriage itself. By granting divorce at will to men, however, the law acts as an adjunct to the power of the male, whom nature and society have already endowed with greater power, and provides men with an escape hatch from marriage itself. Similarly, before the Irish people voted narrowly in a 1995 referendum to allow divorce, the advocates of a yes vote argued that divorce was an escape hatch for the oppressed of either sex and that it would increase the chances that surviving marriages would be happy, whereas the opponents' poster read, "Hello divorce, good-bye Daddy"—the contention being that men would use the law to escape their obligations to women and children.[9] In other words, laws on divorce depend on the lawmakers' perception of the problem to be ameliorated, as well as on the interest of those who draw advantage from them. In Western countries, the constituency for no-fault divorce consists disproportionately of people possessing what economists call marketable sexual characteristics—women in their physical prime and successful middle-aged men.[10] By contrast, older women and ordinary men tend to oppose it. Children, of course, hate divorce viscerally.

The rights and duties of husbands and wives differ from regime to regime. Islamic law is unequivocal about the husband's duty to provide material sustenance and is backed by custom, which requires a man to show a certain level of material security before he will be allowed to marry. This requirement, especially given the declining economies of the Middle East and the difficulties of sexual relations outside of marriage in the Islamic world, has made married status the envy of legions of poor young men, many of whom emigrate to the West. In the West, marriage laws compelling husbands to support have been replaced by divorce laws under which ex-husbands are compelled to pay to liquidate their former obligations. This has rendered divorce attractive to wealthy men, as well as to women who expect the settlement to grant them the material bonuses of marriage while shedding the onus of the man. But laws that ease the option to liquidate marriage obviously undercut the imperative to fulfill any of the responsibilities that flow from it. They also neglect the fact that marital and parental obligations go well beyond the writing of checks.

The Old Testament law is that sexual intercourse between an unattached man and woman constitutes indissoluble marriage.[11] And indeed, the very definition of society is that, somehow, a man who lies with a woman assumes for her and for any child who might be conceived a responsibility far beyond money. This proceeds from the natural fact that the offspring of Homo sapiens, unlike that of any other creature, develops his potential only as the result of many years of care by both parents.

The human experience seems to be that where husbands exercise much authority, they bear correspondingly great responsibility, and vice versa. Christianity is as clear as Judaism and Islam: The man is the head of the household. The English common-law principle that "a man's home is his castle" once applied just as much to his authority over wife and children as it did to his property. As a consequence, Anglo-Saxon courts traditionally refused to entertain suits by wives who challenged the husband's authority over domestic matters. For example, the decision about whether the household should move was deemed the husband's prerogative; the wife must follow. The maximum link between lost authority and shed responsibility is found in the case of slave husbands who could hardly be authoritative with their families while their masters showed them no respect, and whose orders regarding their own family they could not gainsay. Likewise, the decrease in the status of husbands in China, which resulted from two decades of life under the Communist agricultural commune system and from the state's one-child policy, also shows the corrosive effects of powerlessness. Early in the twentieth century, Western states began to superintend the family lives of industrial workers on the assumption that minimal standards had to be imposed for the sake of the children. Today, from Helsinki to Perth, women and children have only to wave a hand, and the state, in effect, will take over the husband's role as provider and as source of authority. It is therefore not surprising that throughout the Western world, especially in those sectors of the population that are the biggest consumers of state services, married men are working less and are abandoning their families at unprecedented rates.[12]

While men can slough many of the burdens of husbanding onto women or the state, women are pretty well stuck with the burdens of their sex. Unless they always use contraceptives themselves and live essentially male sexual lives, they can count on pregnancy and then children claiming their strength. The race of men who will help with housework more than occasionally is a figment of modern mythology.[13] Inescapably, then, women must care for children and home. Must they, in addition, work outside the home? And if women can happily provide as well as dispose of material goods, if they can direct as well as nurture—in short, if they can happily perform all the functions of the household—what need have they of husbands? The truth is, few women who have fulfilled all the functions of the household have chosen to do it. Nearly all have been pushed to do so by the death of husbands, by their irresponsibility, or by their inability to make ends meet. And in some cases, they have been pulled by the idea that it would be wrong for them not to try. Could it be that feminism's main result has been to impose more work and loneliness on women?

Marriage is supposed to be a division of labor. And in fact, Gary Becker has shown that in the case of marriage, as in other functions, divided labor is efficient labor.[14] Married men are more productive workers because they bring to work (along with added incentive) the energy they did not have to expend on matters that their wives took care of at home. By the same token, women do a much better job raising children when they are not bothered by the demands of a career. And yet the modern state has promoted the entry into the workforce of women with young children, while teaching by all its means that women should rebel against men who do not do housework. As has often been pointed out, much of the paid work done by women outside the home involves caring for others' children and parents. Thus, women carry out impersonally the same tasks they once performed for their own families. They themselves are clients for the services they provide. The difference is that they pay in taxes for the services they receive and are paid by taxes for the services they provide. The employment of women in public social services is based on the assumption that functions once performed within families can be performed more efficiently by state institutions.

Governments create incentives for this way of life by eliminating laws that give married men advantages in competing for jobs. Furthermore, modern tax systems take no account of the worth of the social services that wives at home provide for their own families. To pay for professional social services taxes must be high. This in itself diminishes family income and pushes women to work outside the home. Tax systems do not take into account the cost of raising children and in some advanced countries actually penalize marriage and children. In Canada, for example, a married couple with three children earning $60,000 per year in 1992 was liable for $17,824 in income taxes if the income came from one worker. But if the husband got a less-demanding job and sent the wife to work, the same income was taxed at only $10,725. If they then got divorced and cohabited, the tax dropped to $7,580.[15]

But surely the greatest incentive for women to work outside the home is the growing expectation by husbands that they do so. The state's official position is that women are quite equal to men and their worth is to be measured on the same scale as men's. This is inherently attractive to men because it allows them to place little value on what women do at home, but above all because it absolves them of the duty to regard women as people to whom they have special duty.

And so, increasingly, men leave marriage, or they shun it, or they use it to exploit women. The outstanding fact of the second half of the twentieth century may be less the collapse of communism than the increasing burdens being placed on women. "The reality," says a study by the New York-based Population Council, "is that trends like unwed motherhood, rising divorce rates, smaller households and the feminization of poverty are not unique to America but are occurring worldwide."[16] All these trends have one thing in common: households that husbands have either left or where they never were. In northern Europe, these account for over one-third of households, and in the United States, for just under one-third. These households are relatively poor, despite the fact that "women tend to work longer hours than men, at home and on the job."[17] Thus, with the exception of Japan and parts of the Islamic world, the rest of mankind, including the Chinese of Singapore, Hong Kong, and Taiwan as well as the Koreans, seems to be following the West, albeit at a slower pace.[18]

Western regimes have further embittered relations between the sexes by encouraging wives to consider husbands as physical threats, thus making them warier of marriage, and by sanctioning their bringing the police into domestic quarrels. States are doing away with ancient customs that prohibited husbands and wives from testifying against one another. But nothing shows the attitude of modern law toward marriage better than the self-contradictory principle established in one way or another in codes and judicial practices that marriage does not entail the presumption of sexual consent. Moreover, Western governments continue to add incentives to the employment of wives outside the home, for instance by subsidizing day care for children. In other words, governments are emphasizing the legal rights of wives vis-à-vis the rest of their families, decreasing their time with their families and shifting their financial dependence from husbands to bureaucrats.

Parents, Children, and the State

During the twentieth century, almost every government on the planet has tried to substitute itself for parents in some way. The practice of uniformed children exercising in unison while mouthing state slogans, and bearing such names as "young pioneers" (Soviet Union), "vanguard" (Syria), "*balilla*" (Italy), and Hitler youth (Germany), has hollowed out the authority of countless parents in the twentieth century. Today, the government of Japan may interfere less with parents' upbringing of children than any other. But before World War II, its effort to make the younger generation into tools of the state was the equal of the Soviet Union's and was even more successful. The schools taught a version of Shinto made to order by the Ministry of the Interior to draw lines of authority directly from the emperor (in practice, the government) to each child, with parents playing supporting roles. The military-style intellectual scheme was bolstered by uniforms and by after-school time filled with military exercises and songs of allegiance to the state.

Western governments' interposition between parents and children has been directed at the same proximate end—the betterment of the next generation by people who think they know better than parents[19] or, in T. S. Eliot's words, toward the creation of "systems so perfect that no one will need to be good."[20] The policy of Western governments has been to proclaim children's rights, then to endow officials with the power to exercise those rights on their behalf against parents. Indeed, one influential author urged that "the legal status of infancy . . . be abolished" and that the state no longer take one person's childhood into account when considering that person's relationship with another.[21]

The first of these children's "rights" is to day care—not only for a few poor abandoned children but for everyone. Every Western government has or has tried to establish such an entitlement and to expand whatever network of state care there already is. The push comes from the class of government employees and social service professionals who run such things and from the imperative inherent in all collectivist ideologies. The second is the right to be free from "child abuse." Most modern states, either by law or regulation, can punish or severely inconvenience parents for inflicting any kind of corporal punishment on their children. Whereas once the policeman would take errant youths home for punishment, now parents are supposed to take errant children to the state for analysis, therapy, and correction. The state, not the parent, has become the ultimate authority. Then there is the right to be free from sexual abuse. In the name of it, modern states have built inquisitorial apparatuses that assume that fathers routinely sexually assault children, and that justify their own existence by finding "telltale signs" of abuse in children, taking these children from their parents, extracting or manufacturing testimony, and prosecuting the parents. Accordingly, throughout the Western world, state schools routinely sow distrust of physical contact with parents. The state also gives children the means to take vengeance for wrongs real or imagined by asking them for confidential reports on their parents' drunkenness and drug use—shades of young Pavel Morozov.

There is no conclusive proof that the state's growing role and parents' diminishing role in the lives of children is the cause of the upsurge in the variety of pathologies affecting children in the modern world. But the correlation between an individual's committing a crime and being raised without a father is high and largely consistent throughout the world. It is even higher for people who have grown up under the direct supervision of the social service authorities.[22] And yet with the exception of the countries in the former Soviet empire, governments are responding to the obvious decline in the condition of children by increasing their involvement in their upbringing.

The modern state has also weakened ties between adults and their aged parents. Social security systems have advanced their stated purpose of making retirees independent of their families. But since the payment of social security pensions depends on collecting taxes from those very children, the dependency on the younger generation is there, in spades. But whereas once the dependency was within individual families, now it is collective dependency through the collection by the state of high taxes on the younger generation. Once the sanction was moral. Now it is political. Moreover, while earlier generations handed down their accumulated wealth to their children and received care in turn, the generation that has dominated modern countries during the last fourth of the twentieth century has paid to the state in "social contributions" large amounts of money that previous generations had laid up for the children's inheritance. Modern states also levy steep taxes on inheritances. Their premise is simply that the community does not mind if an individual dissipates his wealth by gambling, being dissolute, or taking cruises. But if a person attempts to pass that wealth on to the family, the state will take most of it away. In sum, because of the state older people have less to give to their families and can expect less. Thus, while modern retirees look to the state for help, their children bear the state's taxation for social security—without the combination of gratitude and obligation that earlier generations held for their aging parents, realizing instead that the state will not be able to deliver to them what it is delivering to their parents. Both generations seem increasingly united in one sentiment, however: resentment of the state.

No claim of politicians is more fatuous than that the state is a big family or even a "village." Villages, of course, are composed of real families, of churches, schools, and of other associations that take neither orders nor money from the state. Above all, families are bound by blood and serve the natural purpose of raising children. Aristotle described the rule of parents over children as royal—absolute power exercised for the benefit of the ruled.[23] And indeed, during the age of absolutism, kings were wont to describe their peoples as their children. But, unlike fathers, kings granted privileges to some subjects over others, not disinterestedly for their children's benefit but rather to shore up support for themselves. Modern governments, lacking the legitimacy of kings, live by trading privilege for support. To be precise, they purchase the support of whole classes of people by granting privileges, and sometimes jobs, to the entire class. One of the biggest of the constituent classes of modern government is that of the employees of social service agencies—the masses of social workers, psychologists, teachers, consultants, administrators, and hangers-on. If the people at large are the children of the state, then these social service employers are the big brothers and sisters who get the authority and are paid to exercise it—not exactly what happens in natural families and villages. More important, the institutions of pseudofamilies and pseudovillages crowd out those of the real ones.

There are no examples of states that make families. We have seen how the totalitarian Soviet Union well-nigh wrecked Russia's families. Let us now examine how Social Democratic Sweden did it even more thoroughly and how Japanese governments are balancing the contrary pressures of modernity and of their own culture.

Sweden

The fate of the family in Sweden and other modern social democracies since the 1950s shows that government can achieve a relationship between the sexes resembling that of the Soviet Union without Soviet-style brutality—if it is willing to use all the powers of the modern state and if the people are more docile and more trusting of government than Russians. Indeed, although in recent years even Swedes have come to believe that the welfare state must be cut back, there is no sentiment in Sweden or in the rest of Europe for the restoration of the family comparable to the nostalgia for family in Russia.

Swedish family policy began in 1934, ostensibly as an effort (common throughout Europe during the interwar years) to stimulate the birth rate through financial incentives to married couples to have children. The original package of aid to families included assistance for mothers who were looking for work. But this was only a minor part of the Social Democratic Party's agenda, which was fully laid out in Gunnar and Alva Myrdal's book, *Crisis in the Population Question* (1934). The purpose of the Myrdals' book and the party's agenda was the same: to create "the economic independence of married partners." Among other things, that would require a certain kind of sex education as well as the spread of contraception and abortion. Because Swedish society at the time was as familial as any in the West (and more prudish), public opinion caused parliamentary rejection of these proposals. The public would have been even more outraged if the Myrdals' ultimate objectives—the promotion of all kinds of "common living arrangements," the abolition of sex roles, and "living alone"— had been put before Parliament. The Myrdals' agenda lay dormant until the 1960s, when the government set out to pursue it piece by piece, at first under the cover of some traditionalist rhetoric and only gradually avowing its revolutionary implications.

The centerpiece of the government's effort was to push and pull women out of the home into the labor market. The push came from Sweden's steeply progressive income tax. By first permitting married couples to figure their tax bills separately and then mandating them to do it, the government made clear to every Swedish husband that by far the most efficient way to raise his standard of living was not to work harder himself but to send his wife to work. The government also offered women jobs in large numbers in the growing public sector of education, welfare, health, and bureaucracy. Seventy-five percent of public sector employees are now female, making Swedish bureaucracy—the day-to-day control of society—women's work. The government also subsidized jobs for women in the private sector, and in 1992, established quotas for female hirings in private companies. Companies that fail to meet the quotas are fined by special labor courts. So, recruitment of women is heavy. Moreover, the state's schools and public services depict the few women who shun work as "parasites." Thus, 91 percent of Swedish women between 25 and 54 work, although over one-third do so less than thirty-five hours per week.[24]

Second, the state taught Swedes that marriage is just another lifestyle. Swedish sex education, compulsory since 1956, teaches that the sexual urge is to be satisfied like any other and that to limit its satisfaction to marriage is wrong, period. The state teaches sexual technique, encourages sex at will, and provides free contraceptives and abortion. State schools exalt sexual uninhibitedness as the vital proof of personal independence (about the only kind of independence celebrated in the land of social constraint) and of equality between men and women. This is very popular, especially with men. Far from countenancing social disapproval for out-of-wedlock pregnancy, the state offers more support to unmarried mothers than to married ones. Like everyone else, they receive greater allowances for each successive child. But unlike married mothers, they also get preferential housing allowances, welfare allowances, and fully subsidized child care. Not surprisingly, Sweden has the world's lowest marriage rates, one-half of births are now out of wedlock, and one-half of marriages end in divorce. Marriage has become a minority lifestyle. Since the Swedish state also keeps statistics on the behavior of cohabiting couples, it takes note of the fact that they split three times as often as do divorce-prone Swedish married couples. In other words, even cohabitation is losing ground to the dominant lifestyle—casual contact. Perhaps the most significant demographic fact in Sweden is that as of 1980, one-third of all Swedish households were composed of just one person and in progressive Stockholm, 63 percent of inhabitants lived alone.[25] What family?

The government has altered the quality of human contact, too.

State schools teach "gender equality" for the purpose of transcending the differences between men and women. This is not feminism, any kind of exaltation of female peculiarities. It is a tendency, already well known to de Tocqueville,

> to make of man and woman creatures who are, not equal only, but actually similar. They would attribute the same functions to both, impose the same duties, grant the same rights; they would have them share everything—work, pleasure, public affairs.[26]

It is a political project the end of which is to transcend the human condition.

To whittle down the differences between the roles of the sexes, the state has also spent advertising money and has paid fathers to take time off from work so that they might do more child care and housework. But studies have shown that although husbands or live-in men accept the benefits, they do only 7 percent of the housework and 18 percent of the child care.[27] Swedish men then, have it easy. The state, however, has made their status in Swedish homes more precarious by requiring the police to arrest men for domestic violence without evidence or even without complaint, based on mere suspicion. Without formal convictions, men so charged can be compelled to undergo counseling and be deprived of benefits at work. The only way to have relations with a woman without being liable to such treatment is to maintain a separate household—one more reason for the growing popularity of casual contact.

The regime adds physical incentives to the financial and legal ones. Following guidelines of government planners, Swedish architects are designing smaller individual living units, which must share communal facilities such as laundries and play areas. This wealthy imitation of Soviet-style communal poverty discourages mothers, fathers, and children from getting into the habit of behaving as a unit and makes three-generation homes quite impossible.

Swedish family policy is also based on high-quality day-care centers. The cost per child is about $12,000 per year, mostly subsidized by the government. The centers boast ratios of up to one caregiver for four children. If one adds the people who work on buildings and grounds, cooks, cleaners, and administrators, these centers employ up to one person for every two children—roughly the ratio a child might find at home.[28] In the end, then, the industrial method of child rearing does not employ fewer people than the natural family. Swedish arrangements for raising children are not more efficient, even in terms of inputs, not to mention the quality of the product. However, Swedish family policy aims less at socioeconomic efficiency than at a certain kind of social engineering—to train children to focus on people other than their parents as sources of authority. In this it succeeds. The state caps off this policy by offering allowances to adolescents to help them move out of their parents' apartments and begin independent—nay, state-dependent—living as soon as possible. The child's connection with his parents, or indeed with any person he chooses voluntarily, will surely be less substantial than that with the state. About *that* relationship he will have no choice at all.

And just to make sure that no one—either father or mother—wears the pants in a Swedish family, in 1979 the state outlawed spanking of children—only the state may punish. Moreover, the state can decide without formal judicial proceedings to take the children wholly to itself. Even before the child protection wave of the mid 1980s, it did so some 22,000 times every year.[29] At that rate, in the United States almost three quarters of a million children would be removed from their parents every year. If one accepts Swedish claims to have mitigated most social pathologies, the only explanation for such high rates of intervention is that it is an assertion of control. Indeed, the state seems to be stepping up its efforts against what remains of the family by increasing its efforts to get men and women to split household tasks more evenly and to stamp out sexist attitudes altogether. It need hardly bother. As the trend toward single-person households attests, few dissent from its victory.

The consequences of the Swedish state's victory in a generally prosperous and physically healthy setting belie the argument that the way of life in America's black ghettos is due to poverty (much less race). Swedish illegitimate births (the term is not allowed in Sweden) and abortions at close to the rate of American black ghettos are just the beginning.[30] Free-floating men and women who do without each other except for biological purposes are another. Workers whose declining commitment to work results in absentee ratios of 20 percent on Mondays and Fridays are yet another.[31] Teenagers who have the world's highest suicide rate, who drink and take drugs,[32] and who must be disciplined by the police at rates far above those of other native Europeans fill out the picture—except for the fact that the generation to which this applies is the first to have been raised under full-fledged family policy. The full effects of that policy will be felt in subsequent generations.

Japan

The family habits of contemporary Japan result from a combination of the Yamato people's ancient ways and policies adopted by post–World War II governments to imitate to some extent the ways of their American conquerors. In old Japan, women were beasts of burden and objects of pleasure. Visitors to prewar Japan noted that the workforce was heavily female, that the meanest jobs seemed to be reserved for women, and that whether it was a matter of girls rather than boys sweeping school yards, of women giving up train seats to men, or of wives serving husbands in addition to everything else they were doing, the society seemed to run on women's backs.[33] In especially lean years or poor families, girl babies were killed at birth. The only partial exception seemed to be in upper-class families, where women were fully occupied in caring for their families. The Japanese people, however, deviated partially from what one might call standard barbarian practice because regardless of how heavily they used women, they made sure that marriages were universal and honored. In Japan, everyone has a place, no matter how lowly. After World War II, the government reformed Japanese family ways by partially spreading the customs of the upper class to the rest of the country and by elevating marriage still higher in social esteem. As usual, the Japanese reformed themselves in part to become more efficient international competitors, and as usual, they succeeded.

Laws and customs encouraged one-earner households primarily by reserving career-track jobs for men; by giving married men preference in hiring, pay, and promotion; and, secondarily, by taxing married couples at much lower rates than single people. Japanese women went to work in their teens as before and for relatively low pay. But when they got married, which practically all did by their mid-twenties, they retreated to their families, returning to outside employment, if at all, only after their children were grown. The expectation that every young woman was a lady-of-the-house-to-be and that men were to bear the main burdens—which quickly caught on in public opinion—shifted the nature of women's work away from mean labor further toward services. In the Japanese armed forces, for example, women soldiers are taught to arrange flowers, one of the skills required of the traditional upper-class wife. There are career women in Japan. But the norm is that a woman's principal career is the nurture of her family.

Japanese women prepare for marriage systematically with classes in various household skills, including arranging flowers. When they marry (unmarried people in their thirties are looked down on), women become *oku san*, "Mrs. Inside." They run family finances, doling out allowances to their husbands, and do just about everything else necessary in the domestic realm. This domestic support system has made it possible for postwar Japanese men to work incredibly long hours. Women still serve men in ways that make Westerners wince. But one gets the impression that like Japanese workers on the job, they are doing their work to perfection, doing the equivalent of oiling and shining their machines to make them run better.

The new way of marriage is built on the Japanese devotion to duty. Mothers shine their children inside and out to help them compete in the very high-stakes contest to enter higher-ranking schools. They also care for aged parents on either side of the family. It is considered disgraceful for adult children not to care for their parents. The Japanese extend some duty even to the children whom they kill by abortion: They make little clay shrines to them to propitiate their spirits. Everyone has a place in Japan.

The laws—strongly backed by public opinion—discourage single motherhood by not allowing tax deductions for children (except by death of spouse or divorce). Out-of-wedlock children and their mothers also face officially sanctioned discrimination in schools, jobs, and housing. There is enormous social pressure for young unmarried pregnant women to either get married or abort the baby and for adolescents to keep faith with their parents. The government, in short, is very proud of Japan's low rate of single motherhood and believes that the country's success, its very identity, is due to its people coming from two-parent, patriarchal families that take care of both children and grandparents. Because it wants to maintain the status quo, "the Japanese political establishment find the concept of sexual equality about as welcome as smallpox."[34]

Yet the new model Japanese family is eroding. Whether because both mothers and fathers are under too much pressure to perform their roles perfectly or because people are following latter-day Western ways, the fact is that Japan is suffering the same demographic implosion as Western European countries. Couples are marrying later, and the birth rate has fallen to 1.4 per woman, meaning that the county's population will fall by about 60 percent over the next century. As Japanese people grow older, they are less likely to be cared for by their children. The government is offering large financial bonuses to couples that have more than two children.[35] But the bonuses hardly satisfy the financial burden of raising children in Japan, let alone the human cost. The prime minister once even suggested that saving Japan might require discouraging women from seeking higher education. But he quickly retreated.

In fact, the establishment—"out of concern for Japan's cherished international image"—has paid lip service precisely to the need for women to fill traditional male roles. As Robert Christopher has written, "In Japan, where bureaucratic pronouncements are taken considerably more earnestly than in the United States, this sort of thing has impact." Whereas "as recently as the early 1970s polls showed that 80 percent of Japanese women believed that a husband should work and a wife should take care of the house, by 1976 however only 49 percent still held to that belief, and by 1978 the figure had dropped to only 46 percent."[36] Nonetheless, the actual behavior of the Japanese people has been much more oriented toward distinct roles for men and women. But sooner or later, action catches up with words. Moreover, the Japanese government has given substance to its rhetoric by visibly recruiting women for some of its more glamorous bureaucratic posts. The point here is that while a government may earnestly want a particular kind of family behavior, it may get quite another kind, by virtue of its own words and deeds. Mixed signals are always difficult to decipher.

Power and Experience

Anyone who might want to restore family life to Sweden would have to contend less with the laws of that country than with the attitudes that have come to dominate the thinking of Swedish people over the past forty years. They would have to begin by recalling how shocked the Swedish people of the 1930s were when the Myrdals' agenda was partially unveiled and how public opinion was changed gradually over a generation by a determined elite, through a combination of exhortations and concrete incentives. But any non-Swede who thought of imitating such radical surgery on his country's character would have to keep in mind that most peoples are not as docile as the Swedes. In the

Japanese case, any regime that wanted to preserve the Japanese family could count on docility even greater than that of the Swedes and on basic Japanese attitudes that are very approving of families. But the regime would also have to understand which habits made Western society so powerfully imitable in the first place and how these have changed. Then the Japanese would have to do something they have not done since 1868—something original.

Perhaps the most powerful factor in disposing people to accept or reject leadership is massively bitter experience. The Russian people rejected communism's teaching about families—in word if not in deed—because it was part and parcel of an ordeal that the Communist regime imposed on Russia. This does not mean that Russia is about to regrow prerevolutionary families. But it does mean that works and policies aimed at fostering habits of family responsibility are likely to find more favorable responses in Russia than in, say, Sweden, where the attempt to feminize men and androgynize women does not yet have a bad name. In Japan and elsewhere, demographics and other developments are convincing people that, somehow, men should become more manly and women more womanly. But habits seldom reverse course without some impulsive experience, and even then, they do so slowly. In Russia, the argument for male responsibility is convincing mostly women. But it is among women, after all, that civilizations take root or wither.

Chapter 8

THE SOUL

The mores of our fathers produced excellent men, and these excellent men preserved our ancient mores and the institutions of our ancestors.

—CICERO, *De republica*

SINCE PARENTS AND CHILDREN, workers and consumers, rulers and ruled possess the inalienable human tendency to like and dislike, to think about better and worse, to consider where they came from and where they are going, it is not surprising that habits at home, at work, and in public life depend heavily on what is happening in people's souls. Consequently, no issues in public life are more contentious or more defining of regimes than those that deal directly with man's relationship to God, as well as with everything that touches religion.

Religions make people religious—not the other way around. Most of the world's people who marry, raise children, and care for parents do so under some kind of religious injunction. In some places, the secular authorities simply leave such matters to the religious. Any laws in this field are liable to trouble families and to alienate some from the regime. Religion defines the boundaries of economic behavior. No regime in the Islamic or Chinese cultural area has the option of running an economy based on the assumption that people will work, save, and follow rules like the Protestant capitalists described by Max Weber. And since public life is substantially about who or what is to be honored when and how, people are sure to ask whether the choices a regime makes properly reflect the right order of things—an order instilled in most people's minds primarily by religion.

Most regimes affect habits at home, at work, and in public life by acting in the interstices of the predominant religion. Some regimes, however, bet their lives and try to make changes that go beyond the bounds of religion. In a few extreme cases, regimes become partisans in religious struggles or—in what amounts to the same thing—they wage a kind of war on religion. Culture wars, of which religious ones are the most violent, tend to be not good for habits, for religions, or for regimes.

The Wholesale Struggle

In ancient Europe and in much of today's Asia, struggles over the right way of life have not necessarily been religious. Custom and (later) philosophy were guides at least as important as the gods. By contrast, in the Jewish and Islamic traditions all controversy about conduct is fundamentally religious. In Judeo-Christian civilization it is possible to discuss matters of the heart and soul in nonreligious ways. Nevertheless, with all due deference to Aristotle, ethics in Judeo-Christian civilization derive from commandments, and the natural law draws its authority from God. Consequently, all sides in the twentieth century's wars over human conduct have focused on religion.

The very essence of modern Western government has been the attempt to tame and even to eliminate religion. In the sixteenth century, Protestant as well as Catholic princes quickly realized that mere civil life, not to mention the good life, was hardly possible when two or more sects were fighting to the death to impose every item of their confession and ritual on the others. But recall that mere religion was only one among many causes of the wars of religion. Well before the Reformation, Europe's kings had been gathering powers—including, preeminently, power over religious matters—and were bidding for sovereignty. Religious quarrels afforded Catholic and Protestant sovereigns alike the chance to seize the church's lands and the strongest independent organizations in their realms. Whether in France or Scandinavia, the state made itself the *tertius gaudens*, the ultimate winner, of religious strife.

The concept of "established religion" is an early modern *political* concept, not a medieval religious one. Europe's medieval kings did not try to run the church, while the absolute monarchs who followed were not terribly interested in the details of the faiths they managed. They wanted the church's approval of their sexual exploits, of their suppression of rivals, of their taxes, and of their wars. They therefore vested themselves with baroque rituals almost as elaborate as those of the

Caesaropapist Eastern churches. The official churchmen of the absolute monarchs of the sixteenth and seventeenth centuries, both Catholic and Protestant—not the medieval clerics they replaced—elaborated the doctrine of the divine right of kings and began the practice of subsidizing the church with tax monies. The attitude of these regimes toward religion may have been best summarized by Edward Gibbon in his description of attitudes in the early Roman Empire toward various modes of worship: "[They] were all considered by the people as equally true; by the philosopher as equally false, and by the magistrate, as equally useful."[1]

Most observers of society have agreed with Gibbon's emperors about the usefulness of religion. Survey evidence from the United States—roughly replicated in just about every other time and place—shows that religious observance correlates positively with all sorts of desirable human characteristics. According to the 1993 National Longitudinal Survey of Youth, an intact family that attended church weekly averaged an income of $50,000 per year, versus $39,000 for intact families that did not attend church at all.[2] Moreover, it seems that churchgoers make more money because they have the kinds of personal habits that naturally lead to income,[3] since even broken families that attended church weekly made $2,000 more than irreligious intact families.[4] Copious research also shows an unbroken link between religious practice and family stability. And people who go to church commit crimes at a much lower rate than those who do not.[5] In short, there is not now and never has been a better predictor of prosperity, family, and civility than the faithful practice of Christianity or Judaism.[6]

Appreciating religion for its tendency to produce faithful and fruitful subjects is not religion. Even Stalin himself found it useful during World War II to style himself a Defender of the Faith. Thus not just Louis XIV but also Montesquieu, and not just King William but also John Locke sincerely touted the indispensability of faiths they did not necessarily share. Few governments in the world have been overtly hostile to religion and then only until horrid consequences forced them to try something else.[7] Ideas and practices have their own logic, however, and by the end of the eighteenth century, the consensus of European regimes had come to be that useful intellectual and moral habits might best be fostered outside the churches—indeed, that religion itself was a major obstacle to all good things. Hence, modern government's relationship with religion has been one of tension.

In the West, the public struggle for the soul, therefore, is carried on

largely between the state and organized religion. Relationships between church and state fall roughly into the category of embrace, enmity, and neutrality. In the discussion that follows, keep in mind that
religiosity and clericalism are very different things and that regimes
have been friendly to clerics but hostile to religion, and (less fre-
quently) vice versa.

The Red and the Black

Western history, and here the history of Islam must be included,
shows that the state's embrace of religion tends to corrupt both the
state and religion. Few literary passages are more poignant than the
ones near the end of Dante's *Il Purgatorio* that symbolically reenact the
Emperor Constantine's conferral of the status of state religion on
Christianity, upon which event the voice of God himself comments:
"Oh, my poor vessel, how badly you've been loaded!"[8] This is followed by the image of the church as a cart driven by a whore—the
pope—who is engaged in intimacy with a giant (the king of France,
who had just taken the papacy under protection at Avignon); the giant
then beats her whenever she tries to turn her eyes away from him.[9]
Dante's poetic argument is drawn from standard Christian theology:
The functions of church and state are so inherently different that
when either party tries to wield the powers of the other it makes a
mess of both.[10] The church is corrupted both when it exercises secular
power, as the popes did in Italy, and when it accepts a privileged state
in exchange for giving temporal rulers influence in its affairs, as happened in the Greek and Russian Orthodox Churches.

In Europe's absolute monarchies, Protestant and Catholic churches
paid for their official status by compromises that dimmed their spiritual attractiveness. As a result, the former papal states of central Italy
have the lowest rate of church attendance in the country and have bred
Benito Mussolini as well as the Italian Communist movement. In
Protestant Europe, the areas where the church was most closely associated with the state—Sweden and the Netherlands—have the lowest
rates of religious observance.[11] The pattern persists. In Germany, the
Adenauer government's attempt to fuel the country's post-Nazi religious revival by financing churches and synagogues with a church tax
on registered members seems to have discouraged membership.[12]

The limit case of the mingling of religious and secular authority, of course, is that of Islam and, specifically, that of the Islamic Republic of Iran, established by the Ayatollah Khomeini in 1979. Well before he entered politics, Khomeini had earned respect for piety and expertise in Islamic law. Like Islam itself, he embodied leadership in all human affairs. That he brought bloody war and economic decline is incidental; secular leaders in the Middle East have brought their peoples the same. More to the point, Khomeini saddled Iran with a class of rulers who made all kinds of secular decisions (many of them naturally in their own interest) and tried to justify them on the basis of Islam while using secular force to purge the people of impious habits. This simply rang false, and would have even if the decisions had been good and the regime had not been pretending to be holier than its subjects. Moreover, few if any of these governing mullahs had ever made reputations as men holy or wise. Thus, as an astute observer said of Khomeini's successors, "No mullah or religious student . . . nor any Iranian in need of religious counsel would seek a judgment [a *fatwa*] from Khamenei [the ayatollah who succeeded Khomeini]."[13] As a result, the people of Iran have been left poorer spiritually, as well as in every other way.

Direct persecution of religion is seldom as disastrous as outright embrace—as long as the persecution does not amount to the physical extermination of believers, as it did in seventeenth-century Japan's extermination of Christians, as almost happened in Hitler's Holocaust of European Jews, and as happened to the Tibetans under Chinese rule after 1959. Certainly, the Islamic practice of levying a special tax on Christians and Jews—the infidel tax—never stifled the Christian or Jewish faiths in the Ottoman Empire. Nor was it intended to. Often, religious persecution has nothing to do with the soul. Government persecution of non-Muslims in today's Middle East is far more political than it is religious, as evidenced by the fact that Arab governments persecute various Muslim associations even more vigorously. In such cases, persecution has largely neutral effects.

When religious persecution is clearly aimed at destroying a people's identity, however, and the persecution consists of half measures, it often strengthens the faith. This is certainly what happened in Poland under the Communist regime between 1945 and 1989 and in Nicaragua between 1979 and 1990. These regimes taught atheism in the schools, ridiculing and restricting the Catholic Church in innumerable ways. They even established alternative Catholic churches that they controlled. They hoped that the church would wither as society's most ambitious elements moved away from it. But the church fought back by increasing its spiritual demands on believers and offering the people a choice between lives lived in the integrity of the faith and those lived by the standards of a corrupt regime. It gave examples of prelates who put their bodies between the regime and ordinary believers. As a result, the churches, the confessionals, and the seminaries were filled to overflowing.

Neutrality toward religion seldom means that a regime does not care about it, although that seems to have been the case in postwar Japan. The rate at which the Japanese profess affiliation to some religion (19 percent) is comparable to that of modern Europe.[14] But there seems to be no ongoing struggle for the soul of Japan, at least not in the sense of any transcendent truth or the individual's relationship with the creator of the universe. Shinto, the ancient religion of Japan, lacks any concept of an afterlife and any ethical system related thereto. Buddhism is the basis of many Japanese customs and, together with Shinto, encourages a cult of ancestors, prevalent festivals (Japan may have more of these than any other place on earth), and mystical feelings for natural phenomena such as flowers or the moon. In the first part of the twentieth century, the Japanese government effectively fabricated a version of Shinto to reinforce even further the Japanese tendency to obey their superiors. The ploy worked well enough to stifle dissent over a mindless war. In the aftermath of defeat, however, the Japanese people were left spiritually empty. This does not mean that the Japanese lack conscience or character but rather that these come almost exclusively from adherence to the expectations of the group to which an individual belongs. Society is the soul of Japan, and this is where the struggle is.

In sum, then, the prevalence of religion, its substance, and the regime's attitude toward it have affected the character of all nations, enabling them to live certain kinds of lives and disabling them from living others. Let us see how they have done so in ancient Rome, where changing policies over a thousand years went along with radically different ways of life; in twentieth-century Europe, where the ideas and policies of elites have banished religion perhaps more effectively than the Soviet policy of persecution; and in Israel, where the split between observant and nonobservant Jews seems to be creating two peoples out of one. All these experiences shed light on our own.

Many Romes

When the Roman Senate disposed of Romulus, the city's bellicose founding king, at the end of the eighth century B.C., it sought out as his successor Numa Pompilius, who had a well-established reputation for piety and peace. During the next forty years, according to Plutarch, the city gained such "discipline and schooling in religion" that its character was thereafter marked by love of law and reverence for oaths.[15] Numa trained the Romans by establishing countless rites and priestly orders. He even made sure that the private rites of Roman families were consistent with the public rites. In short, he wrapped every facet of life in divine red tape. Numa himself seems to have been the sort who revered nature and who thought, as Greek philosophers were later to write, that decent human behavior is right by nature. He forbade making images of gods, discouraged blood sacrifices, and tried to infuse rituals with ethical content. But his rude countrymen simply got into the habit of religiously following the procedures he prescribed. They associated doing so with what at the time was the greatest good—winning wars—and feared that failure to observe rites and oaths would bring the greatest evil, which was losing wars. Roman religion was an innocent compact between the gods and men: *do ut des*— "I give so that you may give." Abounding tales of ancient Roman justice—of Regulus who delivered himself to death rather than breaking an oath, of Scaevola who burned his hand for having failed to keep one, of countless instances where advantages were forgone or sacrifices endured for the sake of solemn promises—tell the story of a people so mentally tough that they became irresistible.

Livy's account of the later Roman Republic shows us that religion had become more sophisticated and more manageable. Greek influence had brought to Rome a trove of interesting stories about individual gods and goddesses. The Romans superstitiously sought the gods' personal intercession on a wide variety of affairs. But the divine personages of Virgil's *Aeneid* had specific personalities, likes, dislikes, and conflicts. Relationships with them had no ethical content. They were useful, but like Juno who fought Aeneas, they could be defeated. Still, overall, the gods favored Rome; and Rome's advantage was sacred. This was useful to magistrates. Livy wrote approvingly about a Roman consul who pressured the augurs to give favorable omens for battle. When the consul did not get them, he argued publicly that the augurs had botched their job, killed them, and gained a victory. However,

Livy decried another consul in a similar situation who overtly disparaged augury and caused the armies to mutiny. Those were the days, wrote Livy, perhaps without irony, "when disinterest in the gods, common in our century, had not yet become prevalent, nor did everyone interpret laws and oaths to their own advantage."[16] The Romans quickly learned what to do with a religion of success: Use it, but do not believe it.

Livy and Virgil wrote after the Roman republic had died of an overdose of self-seeking on the part of the aristocracy, culminating in civil war. The gods had not brought peace. Augustus had. Thus, the epics and histories of the early empire celebrate the Caesars, not the gods. Imperial Rome's effective religion had become the law itself. The many new religions current among the empire's diverse populations usually did not challenge the law (when they did, they were crushed), but neither did they lend any support to the laws. The old official religion was celebrated with more pomp than ever, but it was believed no more than any other, possibly less. Christian hagiography aside, the policy of the empire, broken only occasionally, was religious tolerance. Nevertheless, the official religion drew more attention from the tastemakers of Rome's high culture. By the time of the empire, however, Rome's cultural leaders had nothing in common with plodding old Numa Pompilius. The theaters were full of plays for every imaginable festival, and the plays were such, as Augustine said, that the actors could not rehearse in front of their mothers. The gods were almost always shown in the throes of debauched sex or engaged in farcical plots. The laws, therefore, were not merely without religious support. Anyone who felt the urge to keep a commitment at his own expense and considered the gods found ambiguous counsel at best. Except under the philosopher-emperor Marcus Aurelius, the laws themselves had only the sanction of force, and force was mitigated only by evasion or corruption. Hence, generous souls increasingly were drawn to unofficial or foreign cults. So it happened that the followers of a crucified Jew taught habits more consonant with the old Roman virtues than did Rome's official religion.

When the barbarians were overrunning the empire, Christians had reason to mock the impotence of both the debauched gods and their debauched followers. Rome's victories had been the old religion's glory. The Romans had even invented a goddess, Victoria, and built altars to her. But, wrote Augustine, Victoria had not made the legions victorious. The legions had made Victoria. And the legions had been made by steady habits forged in the piety of Numa's simple obedience by the great and the humble alike. Those habits had been discredited gradually by people at the top of the regime who had become more sophisticated and less credulous, though also more self-indulgent and better at sloughing their burdens onto others. By A.D. fifth century, Gibbon tells us, the barbarians who came and went through Rome found interesting human qualities only in the Christians and in the whores.

Europe

The French and Italian branches of the liberal tradition that stems from the French Revolution treated religion as an enemy. The German, British, and Scandinavian branch treated it as a competitor. Later, liberals in most places gave up liberal ideas for some amalgam of Marxism and Freudianism, firmly embedded in statism. The pure versions of these doctrines, in addition to the late-nineteenth-century vitalism that merged with other elements to form fascism, have taken European souls from Christianity and Judaism. Indeed, all these doctrines have won converts within the walls of the churches themselves. This unequal struggle for the souls and habits of Europeans has taken place over education, abortion, euthanasia, and the treatment of political enemies, as well as over the very place of religion in public life.

Education used to be the business of clerics, and its ultimate purpose was to enable people to understand God's word. Christian (and Jewish) teachers used to start with Plato's blueprint: The study of practical things would lead to the study of mathematics—the preeminent theoretical discipline—and to astronomy, then to philosophy. On top of this pyramid was theology. This scheme applied from the lowest level of instruction to the great universities of Europe.

The French Revolution's promise of "free and compulsory" secular schools was not redeemed until Jules Ferry's long tenure as minister of education in France's Third Republic after 1875. The schoolmaster, inculcating the curriculum devised by the Ministry of Education, was to free the younger generation from superstition and fill its minds with practical knowledge and zeal for the fatherland. Copied mutatis mutandis throughout Europe, this institution was everywhere acknowledged to be an offensive weapon against religion. In Germany, schools became part of Otto von Bismarck's Kulturkampf against Catholics. In

Italy, the pope urged Catholics to boycott the schools. The public schools divided society sharply between the nonreligious who attended them and the religious who fled them.

Nineteenth-century secular education, however, was not so different from religious education. Not until well into the twentieth century when the schools adopted the gospels of Charles Darwin, Sigmund Freud, and Karl Marx did they teach aggressively different views of man's origin, man's character, and man's relationship to man. Even so, through most of the twentieth century, European secular education taught confinement of sex to marriage, hard work, and fulfillment of civic duty even unto death. During the last one-third of the century, however, secular education has fulfilled its antinomian potential. In Sweden, the high schools teach a compulsory two-year course that presents the world's religions equally as figments of fetishist imagination. They stress the Hegelian-Feurbachian thesis that humans attribute their best qualities to God (that is the meaning of the Marxist concept of alienation), along with the psychoanalytic view of religion as a compulsive neurosis with infantile characteristics. In the second year, they present the practical or ethical side, touting the morality that has been developed in Sweden, which is essentially the platform of the Swedish Social Democratic Party. Everyone is obligated to pay taxes, to show social solidarity by not striving too much or being judgmental, and to avoid being prudish about sex.

This kind of attack has been far more effective than those launched against religion by the century's harsh totalitarians. As we have seen, the Soviet Communists' frontal assault, including explicit indoctrination into atheism, did not succeed fully because it caused people to associate opposition to biblical religion with all sorts of unpleasant things. The Fascists more seductively asked people to worship human vitality in general and in themselves—especially in the nation state.[17] They offered the churches (and in Italy the synagogues, too) a part in this pageantry of ersatz spirituality. Had they held power longer, they might well have succeeded in displacing religion. Still, the French Revolution's altars to *"la patrie,"* fascism's sound-and-light shows, and communism's exorcisms and excommunications (recall East Germany's adulthood ceremonies meant to supplant confirmations and Bar Mitzvahs, which some Germans are now reviving)[18] took their toll and prepared the way for the success of a way of life very close to nihilism.

A recent book by a respected French diplomat notes Europe's moral disorientation and proposes as a remedy nothing less than a "religion without God."[19] But that is a lot like prescribing another drink as a remedy for a hangover, because such a religion is already the official religion of Europe. In every European country, religious practice has waned. Whereas 41 percent of Americans attend church or synagogue weekly and over 80 percent report praying regularly,[20] in Sweden, only 4 percent attend church weekly, while in the EU, weekly attendance averages 18 percent. Without Ireland, where about 60 percent go to church every week, the EU average would be about 12 percent. European tourists gaze at cathedrals as uncomprehendingly as they do at the pyramids, for they are equally products of alien civilization. In the universities, in government service, and in the prestige press, biblical religion is either nonexistent or is treated as a problematic vestige. In its place, European governments promote a thin combination of self-worship (the very word "soul" has been replaced by the word "self") and earth worship.

The new religion's commandments range from the serious to the purely fashionable ("Thou shalt not eat fat, which is bad for you and the environment, nor smoke tobacco"). The serious ones begin with what can be called the First Commandment: "Thou shalt have no truck with the God of the Bible, lest he outshine thee." Its corollary, however, is that the state outshines each of us. "Hence Thou shalt obey the state—the source of all truth, prosperity, and status." Then follow the practical commandments: "Thy children belong in day care, thy parents in nursing homes." "Thou shalt abort," or at least speak of abortions as the ultimate act of liberation and regard denigration of abortion as heinous. Having paid taxes, "Thou shalt struggle with all thy might to get more from and through the government than thou hast paid." Further: "Thou shalt copulate at will, counting this as thy great freedom"; "Thou shalt keep guard over thy neighbor for any sign of evasion of regulations and promptly report the same." Ultimately, "If ever thou dost doubt the authority for these commandments, remember thou that it flows somehow from our Mother Earth, our fragile planet, through Science."

The resulting litany of social ills—the breakdown of families, drug addiction and venereal diseases, increasing willingness to live without working, high crime rates and a demographic crash greater than that caused by the Black Plague of 1385—has spurred Western governments ever further into the logic of secular society. To deal with promiscuity, they have distributed condoms. The government of

France even sponsored a funny TV commercial urging young men to use them "to please Mom." And of course, Western governments provide free abortions. For drug addiction, they provide clean needles. For crime, jails. For those who do not wish to work, subsistence. In short, modern European government is paying to subsidize the way of life that is the consequence of its secular religion and is paying even more heavily to alleviate the discomforts of practicing it. Note, however, that one subsidy comes from abroad. In a nutshell, Europe's official religion has not produced men who even think about defending themselves militarily. For more than half a century, the United States of America has provided Europe with military defense. Had it not done so, European regimes would have been swept away.

The new religion also mandates moral relativism, a progressive disease that the state's prophylactic measures have actually spread. Judaism, Christianity, and Islam taught the world that all men are subject to one God and hence to a single standard. Man-made laws, whether they deal with economics or education, are supposed to discriminate in favor of people who approximate the way of life mandated by the Ten Commandments and against those who do not. Hence, all laws that favor the married over the unmarried, the heterosexual over the homosexual, the faithful over the adulterous, those who save over those who squander, mystics over pornographers, and so forth can be justified only by reference to divine law or its derivative, natural law. Attempts by modern Western governments to construe legal equality while denying religious claims fail because they abolish the reference point of law and hence the very possibility of equitable laws. As authorities drain their societies of the religious preferences that previously defined them, they introduce new ones ad hoc. But they do it on the basis of whim and favor, arbitrated by power.

The great attraction of moral relativism to the powerful is precisely its usefulness in stigmatizing, disadvantaging, or disposing of people who stand in the way of the powerful by denying them reference to a standard to which the powerful also are subject. The most salient fact about the twentieth century's revolts against the Judeo-Christian order of the soul has been the variety of pretexts used to victimize others. The Nazis demonized not only Jews but also Communists and aristocrats, as well as Christians of any denomination who resisted incorporation into the "national religion." The Communists also cast a broad net: the religious, the independent farmer and the independent professional, and even the independent-minded party member. Official

Soviet art and literature, like that of Nazi Germany, the German Democratic Republic, Cuba, and so on, concerned little else than putting the enemy—or the bad attitude du jour—beyond the pale of humanity. Arthur Koestler and George Orwell identified the moral relativists' ultimate enemy: the soul that is stiffly independent because its anchor is beyond the regime's reach.

The moral relativism of the modern welfare states is milder. But as the years pass, its habits of arbitrariness are coarsening it. As these regimes were being established in the 1930s on the basis of economic redistribution, they called their rapacity "economic justice." In France, the ruling Popular Front's explanation for taking over the country's wealth was the same as Willie Sutton's wry reason for robbing banks: "That's where the money is." As the welfare states matured, their ruling coalitions—retirees or the soon-to-be-retired, in addition to various kinds of "disabled" and welfare clients, subsidized industries, government contractors, and government employees—loaded taxes on young workers and called it "social justice." Elsewhere, it has been noted that interest group politics has a logic that drives it toward ever-greater rapacity. But the point of departure for that logic can only be a moral vacuum.

The political ideologies of the past two hundred years—liberalism, nationalism, and the various kinds of socialism that did so much to hollow out Western souls—never managed to fill the void. The new religion is remarkable less for its content than for its ubiquity, uniformity, and political docility. Whatever the treason of the clerics, it happened long ago. Today, the clerics—who represent the European media, the educational establishment, and the ministries of culture—*are* the regime. Biblical religion is as much on the outs in Europe as it ever was in the Soviet Union. Yet because this new religion cannot fill gaps in souls, its chief legacy seems to be to further sharpen the choice between biblical religion and nihilism. Note, however, that because the struggle for Europeans' souls is so one-sided, it is unlikely to lead to civil strife.

Israel

In December 1996, a poll revealed that 42 percent of Israelis thought that a civil war between religious and secular Jews was likely.[21] And in fact, over the past thirty years or so, both religious and secular Israelis

seem to have exacerbated the conflict of visions that has existed since
the conception of the Jewish state at the turn of the twentieth century.
During the generation leading up to the birth of Israel in 1948, both
sides made compromises, on which both sides seem to be reneging
under the pressures of military events and social developments in
Western society. As the years pass, the religious have become more
antisecular, and the secular have become more antireligious. No one
can say now whether the harshness of politics across Israel's religious
divide has passed the point of no return. But no one can deny that
religious politics after the mid-1980s seemed to be producing two
nations.

The Zionist movement that created Israel was largely the creature
of Jews like Theodor Herzl and Chaim Weizmann, fin de siècle Socialists who, like others of their kind, believed in human perfectability
rather than in God. Non-Socialist Zionists, including Zeev Jabotinsky,
a classical liberal, did not share the Socialists' expectation that the Jewish state could come into being without conflict with the Arabs, nor
did they embrace the vision of a society embodying every utopian feature ever dreamed of in the European Enlightenment. All of these
early Zionists were Europeans who happened to be Jews, who had had
enough of attempts at assimilation, and who wanted their own country
for their own nationality. In this they were no different from other
Europeans of their time. They looked on the religion of the Torah as
an embarrassment, quite as much as their post-Christian fellow Socialists looked down upon Christianity.

That is why religious Jews, especially the few already in Palestine,
viewed the Zionists as triple abominations—they were nonobservant
nonbelievers who presumed to hurry the time of the Messiah. They
aimed to set up a society just as foreign to Jewish law as any in Europe,
and they would make a lot of trouble to boot. Nevertheless, the
prospect of resettling the Land of the Promise convinced a few Orthodox rabbis like Samuel Mohlever that the Lord might possibly be
using profane vessels for holy purposes. In the interwar period, as Europe became more menacing, even the anti-Zionists of Agudat Yisrael
joined in the settlement, if only to minimize the damage that the
Zionists might do to Palestine and to Judaism. But although all these
factions worked out compromises, they kept the separate organizations and divergent outlooks that define Israel's four basic political
groups today—two of them secular, labor and Likud; and two religious, those in the National Religious Party and those Hasidim even

further alienated from secularism. Of course, in Israel the religious groups mix promiscuously with the secular ones for political purposes.

It is inherently difficult to sort out the many different relationships that various Israeli Jews have with the laws of the Torah and that each group has with the state of Israel. Perhaps one-fourth of the Jewish population try to live by the whole Halacha, the law of Moses, and send their children either to the state's religious schools or to religious schools of their own supported by the state. Of the remaining three-fourths, broadly termed nonobservant, most follow varying percentages of the law—perhaps four-fifths keep some kind of fast on Yom Kippur, even in secular Tel Aviv—and nearly all accept with some gladness the quiet that descends on the country during the Sabbath, the preholiday preparations, the religious marriages, and other Jewish symbols that pervade society. Aggressive secularists may number no more than one in eight Israelis.

The state of Israel is based on a set of postwar compromises between the secular David Ben-Gurion and Orthodox rabbis, an arrangement since that time called the "status quo." According to this agreement, religious identity, marriage, and divorce would be under religious law administered by Orthodox rabbis. Public transportation would not run in the country as a whole on the Sabbath but would run in non-Orthodox neighborhoods. Most businesses would close. All state eating establishments would follow Jewish dietary laws. Religious schools would be funded by the state, which would also run a more or less secular system. (In the contemporary United States, the Israeli secular system would be insufferably religious.) But Israel as a whole would be a secular state where people could follow their own ways. The state of Israel would emphatically not be a creature of the Covenant but of the United Nations. The state of Israel would never consider razing the Dome of the Rock and rebuilding the Temple. Secularists saw the state of Israel as the affirmation of a Jewish identity whose meaning owed more to lively memories of persecution than to the law and the prophets. Indeed, the only decoration outside the prime minister's office is a painting of the Holocaust, not a menorah. The religious, for their part, were happy enough that the people of the Covenant could worship God in the land of the Covenant. Present dangers helped forge solidarity over the underlying sentiment that others were not true Israelis, nor perhaps even true Jews.

In 1967, when war delivered the Wailing Wall, East Jerusalem, Judea and Samaria, the Sinai, the Golan Heights, and the Gaza Strip to Israel, the status quo began to unravel. Many observant Jews were energized to think that the Lord had given them the whole Promised Land, which they could not now give up. A large number of secular Jews joined them in this belief and formed the Gush Emunim and Tehiya parties, which united the secular and religious Jews in what might be called a new nationalism and pushed politics closer to confrontation with the Arabs. This further discomfited some Socialist Jews who felt that their lives and comforts were being endangered more than necessary in the pursuit of ideals they did not share. The rise of Arab terrorism within Israel pushed both hawkish nationalists and dovish Socialists to see each other as a major obstacle to the different kinds of peace each wanted. During the 1970s and 1980s, secular leftist Israelis underwent the same kind of cultural changes as similar people in Western countries, tending toward growing antimilitarism, diffidence of religion, and sexual liberation. Finally, the immigration of large numbers of Sephardic Jews, who tended to be more observant than Israel's original mix, and the observant Jews' higher birth rates, combined to shift the character of the country in an evermore religious direction. More men were wearing yarmulkes and black hats, more were wearing earrings, and fewer were in between. By the 1990s, Israelis were growling at one another across a religious divide.

Even the army, the institution within which all but a faction of the Orthodox had joined for the common good, began losing the trust of both sides. The Right and the religious opposed the army for carrying out the policy of removing some settlers from the Sinai to implement the peace treaty with Egypt. Some rightists felt that the army might not be counted on to protect settlers in Hebron (some rabbis have called for soldiers to disobey such orders). The secularist Left objected because trust in force was the reason the intransigent part of the population was not eager enough for peace.

Across society, both sides accused the other of encroachment on the status quo. Ugly words were spoken and ugly incidents began to take place. Secular Jews began to drive honking caravans into Orthodox neighborhoods on the Sabbath. Teddy Kollek, Jerusalem's longtime secularist mayor, asked rhetorically what might be done about the Orthodox element's reproductive prowess. And in fact, the city's demographic shift lost him his job. Orthodox rabbis effectively denied Jewish status to the foreign non-Orthodox, implying that their secular brethren could not be classified as Jews, either. And then both factions, supported by friends abroad, began name-calling, blaming each other for the acts of terrorists. In 1995, when Prime Minister Yitzhak Rabin was shot by a deranged settler who claimed that he had done the will of God, the secularists blamed the opposition in general and observant Jews in particular. And after another psychologically unstable Jew committed an act of terrorism against the Arabs and claimed religious authority for it, the Left retaliated by saying that religious Jews are nothing more than interlopers in the Zionist dream.

The constant complaint of the biblical prophets was that the people lived the law with their bodies but not with their souls. Today, many Israeli secularists go so far as to speak ill of the way of life of those who live under the law. Since the Torah is the only possible source of spiritual substance for those who call themselves Jews, the reduction of the Torah to a bone of partisan contention weighs heavily on Israel's spirit. Division into two sets of people habituated to contempt for each other's spiritual substance poses a mortal danger for any country, but most of all for one that rests on a religious foundation. No more than any other, Israel's house cannot stand divided.

Religion and Regimes

What can any regime do with the spiritual habits of the people it governs? Regimes cannot make Christians out of Muslims, nor Jews into Zoroastrians. Few try such nonsense. They can only abet processes by which people become better or worse Christians, Jews, and so on. Nor can regimes create new religions. Those that have tried have ended up with peoples alienated from their old faith and cynical about the new. All religions have civil relevance, but there is no such thing as civil religion. Regimes can work only within the parameters set by the religion. Some, like Shinto, lend themselves to being bent to a regime's purposes more than others. In general, a regime only has the choice of supporting the religion under its domain or trying to weaken it. As we have seen, weakening religion is feasible in several ways. Strengthening religion is probably beyond the reach of any regime, except in the sense that a regime may simply leave some social functions to be carried out by religious authorities. Yet even here, it is important to distinguish between the Saudi practice of leaving matters of morals to the religious police, and the seventeenth-century Swedish practice of deputizing the church to carry out state policy.

Regimes can have the most devastating effects on the spirit of those who live under them, as well as on the body politic, by taking sides in spiritual struggles. Civil wars tend to be the most devastating of wars, and religious civil wars are the worst of civil wars. And yet regimes define themselves precisely by taking sides on the questions most important to those who live under them. Statecraft is also the art of the soul, because it involves choosing which spiritual matters to treat as fundamental. But to choose principles that are right by nature, that intrude minimally on the prevalent religion, and that habituate people to religious peace is most difficult.

Chapter 9

THE ULTIMATE TEST

*It is truer than any other truth that if where there are men there
are not soldiers it is the fault of the prince, and nothing else.*
—NICCOLÒ MACHIAVELLI, *Discourses*

TO THE EXTENT that a people's habits do not produce military
forces that win wars, they amount to a mortal disease. Any
regime's military institutions contribute to habits more or less conducive to healthy civil society, as well as to military survival. The role
that the regime's leading personages play in the preparation and employment of force is perhaps the most important feature of any
regime's institutions. Regardless of the organizational scheme, the task
is always the same: to inspire devotion and to instill quality performance among those responsible for military operations, as well as to
make sure that the forces match the regime's military and civil needs.

Power and Habits

People, not things, generate military power. Regimes that nurture
the proper habits find they have military power when they call on
it, while those that trust in economics or technology to provide it are
disappointed.

No view is more prevalent than that money is the sinew of war. But
history abounds with instances of wealthy peoples defeated by lean
and hungry ones. Alexander's poor Macedonians cut through Darius's
wealthy Persian Empire like a knife through butter. Genghis Khan's
tent-dwelling, dung-burning Mongols did the same to the Chinese
and the Persian plutocrats. George Washington's rag-clothed Conti-
nentals defeated the wealthiest power of the age. Wealthy Americans

were defeated by poor Vietnamese. And of course the wealth of the impotent Romans only excited various barbarians to take it. For this reason, when King Croesus of Lydia threatened Athens' Solon by showing him his gold, Solon told him that war is made with iron. Guns compel butter. Even more to the point, iron is wielded by men, whose ultimate efforts cannot be bought but rather result from certain habits. Nor can money, unlike character, make the difference between the prudent and disastrous conduct of war.

Thucydides' liveliest set of images show Athens, which had all the ingredients of great power, coming to ruin because it lost the key habits of public-spirited moderation. At the outset of the Peloponnesian War, Pericles told the Athenians that they should be confident of victory because of their capacity to draw wealth from their overseas empire. He also told them that their strength lay in their character, which combined lust for magnificence with patriotism and love of right measure. In that regard, he warned them not to try to add to their empire during the war.[1] But because after Pericles' death the intemperate Cleon and the disproportionately ambitious Alcibiades made their respective vices prominent among the Athenian people, Athens' character changed. Quite literally what had been foul became fair, and vice versa. Diodotus found that to get the Athenian Assembly to listen to arguments for decent acts, he had to couch them in indecent terms. When Nicias countered Alcibiades' immoderate suggestion that Athens attack Sicily by showing how inherently senseless, dangerous, and militarily difficult that operation was, as well as how much it would cost, the Athenian people heard only about the cost. They threw stunning amounts of money at the enterprise, but little judgment. The force they sent was magnificent. But its splendor did not make up for its lack of cavalry, the military mission's lack of clarity, or the rifts between its chiefs and the city.[2]

Nor does power come from technology. Probably since before biblical times, when the chariot ruled the battlefields (Egyptians sometimes even attached scythes to the axles), people have been tempted to think that victory belongs to those possessed of the latest wonder weapon. Certain tactics, such as the Greek phalanx and the Roman triple-rank line have led to similar suppositions of invincibility. Today, it is fashionable to think that nuclear weapons or precision-guided munitions have made irrelevant the human ingredients of military power. But believing in the superiority of white-coated, push-button warfare is as much a fancy as previous notions that crossbows, artillery, or machine guns had turned offense or defense into mere technicalities. Machiavelli used the example of fortresses—by also referring to artillery and cavalry he makes clear that he means technical factors per se—to show that one can make few mistakes worse than to regard *any* technical factor as operating independently of human factors.[3] In and of themselves, fortresses can either be useful or not. But the fortress mentality (or the artillery mentality or any other principled reliance on things) is invariably fatal to military habits. We should recall that the Maginot line of fortresses on the northeastern border of the Third Republic of France was inherently quite useful for channeling enemy attacks and economizing French forces. But the Maginot mentality led the French people to think that France's military problems had been solved on the cheap, which fed ruinous habits that spread throughout French society. The same goes for the mentality induced by any other instance of military technolatry.[4]

Even the number and dedication of soldiers is not to be confused with military power. Thus, Mao Tse-tung's assertion that China did not fear nuclear weapons because there were more Chinese than any set of weapons could kill contains only a grain of truth. Even if all Chinese were organized militarily instead of only a minuscule percentage of them (and these, badly), the Chinese have neither the means nor the schemes to prevent any of the world's major powers from doing whatever they might wish to any part of China. By the same token, the Zulu troops that Britain defeated in 1879 were dedicated and trained to a perfection that the Romans might have envied, and they were led well. But run-of-the-mill machine gunners trumped world-class spearmen.

Therefore, where there are proper military habits, able leaders can translate money and high-tech weapons into military power that stands a chance of winning. But where these are lacking, money and matériel are wasted. In 1940, France had more tanks than Germany. But French generals had resisted calls to organize their tanks into armored divisions. The regime could not bring itself to correct the military's smug inertia because it did not want to challenge the country's pacifist habits. Pacifists argued that armored divisions were offensive weapons unworthy of a peace-loving country. Because this sentiment lent support to its narrow self-interest, the military failed to tell the public the truth: that armored divisions—indeed, just about any weapon—may be used for defense as well as offense. Because one set of bad habits at the top of French society abetted another set of bad habits at the bottom, all the money the country spent on tanks could not prevent the Panzer divisions from parading the Nazi eagles on the Champs-Elysées.

The Ultimate Responsibility

Since the regime sets the tone for military institutions as well as for the rest of society, the character of the military depends substantially on that of the regime's leading personages. If they do not lead armies themselves, they must somehow lead both the leaders and the led—the difficulty of which is vastly underrated in modern Western countries and nowhere else. But military institutions also contribute to the tone of society at large.

On a wall in Istanbul's Topkapi Museum are the vestments and swords of the Ottoman sultans. The plain tunic of Mohamed II, conqueror of Constantinople, once fit a fit man. His unadorned sword was obviously dented by steel and bone. As one moves along the exhibit, the vestments get wider and fancier, the swords more ceremonial, until those of nineteenth-century sultans indicate that their owners were fitter for sedan chairs than saddles and that they could no more dent shields than they could lead armies. During these three hundred years, the nature of the Ottoman regime did not change. It was still an Oriental monarchy with an army composed of large numbers of people who were essentially slaves kept in line by dread, and of smaller numbers of special units, especially the Janissaries, who had been raised from childhood to be loyal shock troops and henchmen. When the Janissaries had respected the sultan physically, they focused on winning his battles, whereas when he controlled them by playing some against others, the best they could manage was to oversee the empire's shrinkage. Finally, when the sultans had nothing more in common with military leaders, the "Young Turk" military officers ceased to respect them and their bureaucrats. Thus, these officers first became an interest group within the regime; then they set up their own.

Even though the soldiers in the Prussian army were hirelings (and then under the unified German Reich, conscripts) and its officers were aristocrats, Prussia underwent an evolution analogous to Turkey's. Quite simply, whereas until the mid-nineteenth century the senior officer corps had been broadly representative of the aristocracy, its social base thereafter narrowed to a sector of East Prussian landholders who came to think of the army's interests as more important than those of the regime. Conversely, the rest of the regime, from the Kaiser down, progressively lost confidence in its own military judgments and received less and less respect from generals, gradually losing control over them even as they gained greater weight within the regime. That is why during World War I, General Ludendorff was able to take over the Reich effectively without either the army or the regime realizing that anything radical had happened. But that army, although efficient enough in operations, wrecked the country by pursuing a two-front war that the most elementary tenets of statecraft—of which it was ignorant—would have counseled against.

The experience of Nazi Germany shows the obverse of the same predicament. In this case, a group of chaotically undisciplined civilians whose führer was the epitome of personal indiscipline imposed their ways on the armed forces. Special units proliferated, not only to perform the standard tyrannical functions of slaughter and counterchecking, but also because any number of military leaders were corrupted into seeking special channels of influence and privilege. After July 1940, Hitler's management of World War II became militarily indefensible and was harming the professional military as much as the country in general. Yet the regime had so impressed its own chaos, mistrust, and lack of honor on the military that it never seriously resisted.

Sometimes armies influence the character of regimes more than regimes influence that of armies, and sometimes armies pass their peculiar disease—or health—on to society at large. Ever since Juan Perón reshaped Argentina in 1943, every part of the regime—government agencies, parties, and allied organizations—has exercised some exclusive economic privileges. The armed forces, too, have run dozens of companies and profited from it. By contrast, the armed forces of neighboring Chile accepted the earmarked taxes on the copper industry but managed nothing, holding themselves aloof from the country's politics, preserving old-fashioned, modest probity. In 1973, when the congress asked the armed forces to overthrow Salvador Allende's rapacious regime, Chilean tanks literally stopped at traffic lights, and the subsequent military regime remade the country in its image. In 1982, when Chile's military ruler Augusto Pinochet built a luxurious presidential palace, the frugal habits of the public and of the military as well made it impossible for him to move in. Nor have his successors.

In the ancient republics, military service was synonymous with citizenship, and rightly so, because the ultimate practical question in public life anywhere is "Who will uphold the laws, arms in hand?" Even in the ancient world, especially in Carthage, the argument was made that other kinds of contribution—especially money—could be just as valuable to the community; therefore, such contributions entitle those who make them to as full a voice in civic life as those with military service. But this argument is most convincing to those who have not given or are not about to give up the best years of their lives to the discomfort and danger of military service.

A set of difficulties arises when regimes purchase the military service of citizens or foreigners. As we shall see, various schemes have been tried with varying degrees of success to alleviate some of the consequences of straightforward purchases. The best-known instances of straightforward purchases—by city-states in Renaissance Italy—were the object of Machiavelli's historic critique: By not fighting for themselves, citizens do not form patriotic habits of the heart and never learn military skills, while governments do not form links of habitual command and obedience with citizens. Worse, bought armies seldom fight as well as armies composed of citizens, and when they win (rarely), they often replace the government.[5]

Common sense has always prescribed a cure for such ills, namely, citizen officers as well as citizen soldiers. But these words are difficult to translate into reality, regardless of whether the regime is an oligarchy or a democracy, because citizens who have gained the power to rule others seldom allot to themselves any of society's unpleasant functions, let alone the dangerous ones. And no function is less pleasant or more dangerous than soldiering. Where low-ranking soldiers are concerned, it is possible for regimes to have the advantages of citizen soldiers without inconveniencing the powerful of the land by taking the young and the poor. More rarely, leading citizens have been able to convince the population at large to pressure its children to give their lives as soldiers. But, as World War I and its aftermath in Europe showed, even the perception that the blood tax is being assessed unfairly or for insufficiently worthy reasons is the stuff of revolution or outright social dissolution. In sum, officers are either the same kind of people who run the country or they are not. And that makes for big differences in society.

The Israeli experience is a reminder that what the classics taught about the role of military forces within civil societies is still valid. Although Israel today extends to Arabs all civil privileges of citizenship, it denies them military service. Because the rest of the Israelis cannot rely on them when the chips are down, the Arabs are not really citizens. Because it is difficult for a man to rise in Israeli society without fulfilling thirty-three days of military service every year, military experience is a closely examined part of resumes, and marks of military distinction are marks of social distinction. Thus, at the top of Israeli society are men habituated to physical courage and responsibility for life and death. At a minimum, foreign affairs is not a spectator sport for any Israeli. Also, perhaps the concept of the common good is not as abstract for them as it otherwise might be. Since the most prestigious military units—the special forces who scale rocks and rescue hostages—require special physical performance, teenagers from the best Israeli families pay for and sweat through courses to prepare to compete for the privilege of serving in them. Hence, there flows toward the top a stream of young men habituated to expose themselves to risk. Finally, societies where almost every man is a soldier are always pervaded by a radical sense of equality because nothing so entitles a man to look upon his fellows as no more than equals than does the hardship suffered and the danger incurred in military service. The resulting informality is often mistaken for a lack of respect. But it really signifies that respect is spread rather evenly. One of the peculiarities of Israel is that this spirit of equality exists in a people whose economy runs on patronage and who therefore have to make their way by wheedling favors. Anybody can "get to" just about anybody else through some mutual acquaintance made in the army. Also, while Israel's Socialist economics tend to push women out of the home, Israeli families receive a patriarchal push from the fact that men are the society's obviously indispensable protectors.

Soldiers and veterans are not always pillars of the rule of law. In the Roman Empire, especially after military service had ceased to be an act of citizenship and became a profession, the military and ex-military simply composed the dominant interest group. But when citizens are soldiers, they are in the best moral position to assert the basic demands of citizenship: to be treated as fairly as anybody and to be left to run their own lives. They are also in a good practical position to press their claims because through their years of service, they have acquired the capacity to lead and to follow according to rules. They have also learned how to accomplish the most unpleasant civic duty of all: rebellion. Even Stalin had to be a little careful of veterans. The defense of the Russian Parliament that sealed the Soviet Union's fate in 1991 was possible only because a large number of Red Army veterans, and some active units as well, defected to the Russian rebels. The defense of the Lithuanian Parliament in 1990 against KGB forces was organized by a Lithuanian American who had served in the U.S. Special Forces.

Machiavelli explained definitively that a society that takes to hiring soldiers learns to devalue and diminish patriotism and soon loses realistic perspective about peace and war, ultimately forfeiting respect at home and abroad. Some disagree. But few have recognized the importance of military service to the formation of citizens while dispensing with it. In recent decades, the countries of Western Europe have maintained conscription while allowing about one-half the eligible young men (almost all from the upper classes) to simply not show up when called. Political leaders just do not believe in the necessity of service enough to enforce conscription of their own kind. By the 1990s, such blatant discrimination against the poor was dividing European societies rather than bringing them together, much as it had done in the United States during the Vietnam War. Moreover, European governments were redistributing so much of society's money to political constituents and thought so little about military matters that they could fill their thin military ranks without imposing service on anyone who did not want to perform it. Thus, in May 1996, the government of France gave up two centuries of conscription, which it had valued for habituating different classes to equal and joint endeavor. For this, it substituted a one-week class on civic obligation, compulsory for all young men and women. One wonders how the audiences will be affected by the contrast between official words and deeds.

Arms and the Regime

Just as any regime's reach must not exceed its grasp, its military forces must fit its character and its objectives. Before the Punic Wars, republican Rome seldom sent armies of more than fifty thousand men beyond the Apennines. Because these armies were relatively small, hordes of barbarians would occasionally defeat them. But as the barbarians drew closer to Rome, the city and its peninsular hinterland turned populations into masses of soldiers. In 347 B.C., near today's city of Pisa, one band of Gauls was annihilated by 1.5 million Romans. And one century later, whenever Hannibal wiped out a Roman army, the extended city would bring forth another as if nothing had happened. Early republican Rome could not send big armies far because the legions were made up of ordinary citizens whose family fields and shops could not spare them for long. But since every man was a soldier, emergencies could bring out masses for short periods. Rome did not have to send big armies far away because the only faraway wars it undertook were those its generals planned on winning with relatively small forces. The armies did not have to stay long after the victory because the Romans quickly inserted colonists into newly conquered lands, who could defend them to some extent. The colonists did not have to fight often because Rome let potential attackers know that the penalty for attacking Roman colonies would be sure, swift, and terrible. In short, ancient Rome drew a very sharp line between peace and war, and none at all between citizen and soldier.

By contrast, as soldiering was becoming common only among the dispossessed who were willing to exchange ten years in the legions for the promise of land in the provinces, late republican Rome began the practice of stationing large armies far away. Large standing armies abroad allowed Roman generals the luxury of long campaigns. This made it possible for Roman consuls to deal with peoples such as the northeastern Germans, the Scythians, and the Goths by making a little peace and a little war. The provincial legions remained strong well into the imperial era. But their vigor, the growing practice of hiring barbarians into the ranks, combined with the loss of military habits in Italy, caused the Roman Empire to implode many times before the center rotted completely and the barbarians put it out of its misery.

The point here is to recognize the necessary proportion between any regime's military organization and the regime's objectives. Consider that nineteenth-century Britain was able to control a vast empire, including such warlike people as the Afghans, with fewer than twenty thousand men abroad at any given time. For this, the organization described below sufficed. By contrast, note that the Soviet Union occupied its East European empire with almost 1 million soldiers and that a superbly equipped Soviet force of two hundred and fifty thousand was unable to hold Afghanistan. Maintaining the Soviet empire required near-universal conscription and the economic militarization of society. The reason these two empires required such different levels of effort and such different kinds of relationships between society and the military lies in the very different purposes of the two empires. Whereas the British worked through the local power structure wherever possible, did not dream of threatening what the locals held dearest, and offered them a way of life that many found attractive, the

Soviets backed locals who sought to force their countrymen into uncomfortable molds. The Afghan mujahideens' war made sense only as a defense of threatened Islam. And the Russian people's rejection of their regime's war shows a disconnection between the mentality of the conscript army that had to be used in a conflict of that size and the purposes for which the regime fought the war.

Europe's Ancien Régime

Prior to the French Revolution, Europe's regimes fostered a set of habits at both the top and the bottom of society that fit the regimes' domestic order and served the pursuit of their moderate international objectives.

In Britain, where the military habits of the seventeenth and eighteenth centuries lasted through the nineteenth, Rudyard Kipling wrote that "Sergeant Whatshisname" could "make soldiers out of mud."[6] The duke of Wellington had described that mud as "the scum of the earth" and had been happy to say that the British system had turned into useful fellows men who otherwise would have been useless or worse. A generation earlier, Frederick the Great had described his recruits as "the dregs of society." But he, too, was confident that training would turn them into useful soldiers. And so were his French counterparts. The soldiers of Europe's ancien régimes—up to one-third of whom were foreign adventurers—were enticed or forcibly impressed into regiments, where sergeants drilled them in loading and firing muzzle loaders regardless of the carnage around them. They were also taught to march and to make bayonet charges. Discipline was everywhere enforced by horrible physical punishment. Yet by the turn of the eighteenth century, Britain's duke of Marlborough and Louis XIV's minister François Michel Le Tellier, Marquis de Louvois had discovered that soldiers who believed that their officers cared about them fought better than those who did not. Thus, both Britain and France sought to make enlisted military service something that would enmesh the soldier or sailor in habits of obedience. The regiment or the ship would become the enlistee's only real family and country. Punishment would then become less important as a motivator. The liberal British preferred enlistments for twenty-one years but often abandoned old soldiers to pitiful conditions. The paternalistic

French went further and established the chain of old soldiers' homes, of which the magnificent Invalides in Paris is the centerpiece.

The middle classes and ordinary farmers would not have stood for attempts to recruit them into such lives—which is why the free English of America were so horrified when the British navy kidnapped some of *them* for service. Nor would ordinary British or French subjects have stood for impressment. Ordinary people served in the very part-time militias that were relics of the old feudal retainers. But the ancien régimes relied ever less on armed representatives of a free society, whom they feared as breeding possible resistance and as militarily unreliable. Adam Smith, applying the Hobbesian ideology typical of the period, believed that men motivated by dread would face danger more surely than men accustomed to freedom. Hence, the old regimes relied ever more on men who could be counted on to behave as if they had been bred to obedience. Ironically, the exploits of royal armies, composed of society's dregs and led by its cream, inspired middle-class spectators to think nationalistic thoughts, thus paving the way for the nationalist regimes and mass armies of the nineteenth and early twentieth century.

The most significant aspect of the old regimes' military arrangements, however, is how they trained officers, almost all of whom were noblemen, to be loyal to the king. Military leadership had been the old nobility's raison d'être. Many, if not most, nobles were all too eager to lead troops. Their families cultivated habits of courage and honor aplenty. And recall that the sixteenth and seventeenth centuries had been full of wars between nobles and kings. By the eighteenth century, however, European kings were selling to their nobles the right to pay to equip the regiments they would lead, under the superintendence of royal bureaucrats. Still, the great nobles were not easy to train. The Prince de Condé and the Vicomte de Turenne were loyal enough to Louis XIV. But the first was a prince and the other a count. Although Louvois was Louis's minister, he could no more order such blue bloods around than William III could push Marlborough after the victory of Blenheim. Leadership had to be subtle. The domestication of the military nobility was accomplished not just through repeated acquiescence to royal wish but also through the introduction into the officer ranks of commoners who had shown merit. The Prussians led the way here, followed by the French. But when the British took up the practice, they went the others one better and granted knighthoods to able commoners. The old regimes thereby trained a class of military leaders that was identical with themselves.

The military tools at the disposal of the old regimes fit their objectives of survival and limited aggrandizement. They wanted to avoid radical changes abroad quite as much as at home. Soldiers were relatively difficult to rake up and were expensive to maintain for life. In campaigns, the ranks of armies were cut between one-third and one-half by disease, desertion, and casualties. There was thus every reason to use armies sparingly. Still, they would go anywhere and do anything asked of them. The officers, too, were even more willing to go for glory. But the idea was not to let them get too much of it, nor too much rapport with their troops. Such armies and navies were just right for genteel, limited warfare. The grand prizes were the succession to the thrones of Spain or Austria, the allegiance of the Netherlands or some princeling in Germany or Italy, or the possession of some colony. Thus, though there was bloodshed and bravery and honor aplenty, commanders also recognized when someone else's timely march or placement of artillery had so prejudiced the survival of a fortress or the outcome of a battle that surrender was an honorable option. And a safe one. In the Franco-British war over the Netherlands, for example, captured officers would go home after promising in writing to abstain from further action during the current conflict. Instances of cruel imprisonment such as the British inflicted on Americans aboard ships in Charleston harbor in 1778 were most rare. In this way, the old regimes' military practices fostered habits consistent with themselves.

Napoleonic France

Appetite comes from eating. So goes an old French proverb. Just so, Napoleon's appetite for conquest grew with each victory—and so did his military needs. In the end, those needs outstripped the capacity of the regime to supply them, even though the regime had been organized primarily for that.

The Napoleonic regime really was organized like an army. The old regime had slowly substituted feudal functions and powers that had been vested in countless guilds, towns, and nobles by royal officials. These assumed responsibility for roads, bridges, public health, basic industries, and even the breeding of quality draft horses. Not least of the kings' motives for this had been to increase their capacity to draw military power from society. The revolution swept away the remainder of society's spontaneous hierarchies—what de Tocqueville called "intermediary bodies" and Burke, the "little platoons." It pasted the label *"commissaires"* onto royal officials, while multiplying their functions and powers. Since their regime was fighting for its life from beginning to end, the revolutionaries were even more militarily motivated. For this reason as well as to imitate the ancient republics, the revolution introduced universal conscription. Napoleon, First Consul and then Emperor who claimed to be in the line of the Caesars, took these trends to their logical conclusion and created the first modern regime conceived for people-to-people war. No Caesar had ever established a network of schools to qualify the best of society's young for administration, health, and all the useful trades. The Napoleonic regime marshaled society's many occupations and functions into "corps." Every part of society was encouraged to think of itself as an organ in a body marching forward. Napoleon had organized a Ministry of the Interior to make sure that the various social functions were coordinated and delivered matériel. Conscription delivered the personnel. The country was cut into departments, within which towns were marked out, roads named, and houses numbered, so that orders from the very top could move the very bottom. The Parliament itself was the "legislative corps," with its assigned function, just like every other part of society, in a scheme intended to produce military power.

War is supposed to be one of the means of statecraft. But the Napoleonic regime—thereafter widely copied throughout the Western world—had no end other than war. A regime's purpose is supposed to transcend that of the army, but in this case, the purposes were identical. Therefore, while the army triumphed and society was well trained to supply its needs, triumph fed habits of spiraling ambitions that could never be satisfied.

Napoleon asked a lot of the regime. In 1804, he drafted 60,000 men. The following year, he took not only 80,000 from the newly eligible but 100,000 from among young men who had become eligible in earlier years but not been taken. Six months later, he asked for another 80,000. In 1811, as he prepared for the Russian campaign, he took 120,000 from the current crop of eligibles and 100,000 from all the preceding ones. In 1812, he took 120,000 and incorporated another 100,000 from the old territorial militias. As he began to suffer more defeats than victories, the demands grew even larger. But even the victories were costly: The campaigns of 1806 and 1807 killed 200,000, and the Russian campaign alone wiped out 300,000.

Making such sacrifices required a particular set of habits. Napoleon instilled them in officers and men alike quite simply by running the army, according to de Gaulle, as "a perpetual contest, of which the emperor was the organizer and judge, the reward of which was glory."[7] And, he might have added, profit as well. Just as men advanced in the various civilian corps by demonstrating competence in competitive exams, they advanced in the armed corps by demonstrating superior performance in combat. Napoleon's descent upon the most heavily bloodied regiment after the battle of Abensberg was typical: He asked for the bravest officer and made him a baron with a lifetime pension. Then he asked for the bravest soldier and made him a knight of the Legion of Honor, also with a lifetime pension. The emperor, in short, built a brand-new, endowed nobility. He made some of his marshals into kings (Sweden and Naples); others into dukes. He made counts out of colonels and barons out of captains. And formerly humble farmers who had earned their way into the guard or who had been decorated with the Croix de Guerre could count on prestige that would compel the respect of officials throughout the regime. Napoleonic France was truly the land of opportunity, where nobodies could become princes by their own valor. To entice the many to keep trying for rewards that could only go to the few, the emperor freely handed out symbols of recognition, such as special hats or rations of wine or decorations for the musket. He taught his senior officers to spread downward the impression that the leader sees all, appreciates all, and gives a just reward. And so, because restless daring flowed downward, Napoleon's armies moved faster and fought harder than others.

The regime's denial of just measure, however, destroyed the habits on which its success rested. The source of the trouble was that Napoleon only pretended to aim at a peace with which his country could live. His army and his country gradually found out that he was lying to them. His first campaigns had been continuations of the wars of the revolution, caused as much by France's neighbors as by the French. Between 1800 and 1806, Napoleon aggrandized France beyond the hopes of its kings, though not wholly without reason. Before every battle, he would tell his troops that after this one, they could go home. But after every battle, there was a bigger war. As Napoleon threw more men and more guns into battle, he ceased to care about the quality of his instruments or about what would happen to them.

His expressions of concern for his men had begun to ring hollow. In the end, the regime and the army crashed at the same time because recruits did not know how to fire muskets that in any case were defective, because cannons fell off carriages built out of green wood, because society began tolerating draft evasion, and because some officers quite naturally began to enjoy some of the rewards of their efforts. Still, at Waterloo, the outcome was a near thing.

Switzerland

Life in Switzerland is much less exciting than it was in Napoleonic France, and the Swiss army is no more fit to hurl masses of conscripts against great powers than it is to send small numbers to hold down foreign posts. It is fit for only one mission: to defeat invaders. For this, a country of 6.7 million can generate an army of twelve divisions (the U.S. army has ten) and twenty-six brigades, armed with some of the world's best equipment. Of course, Swiss forces completely lack, among many other things, the mobility and capacity to sustain the long supply lines that the armies of great powers possess. But the Swiss army's civil function and military mission require steadiness rather than mobility, teeth rather than tail.

The Swiss regime consists of provincial burghers who have no desire to be anything else. Even bankers in Zurich and Basel, as well as people in the universities and the media, share that mentality. Long ago, they realized that they would have to pay for their peace and quiet by getting rich and poor to cooperate in a mighty army capable of defense, but nothing else. Until the seventeenth century, poor Swiss boys had hired out all over Europe as state-of-the-art pikemen. During Europe's wars of religion, the fact that different bands of Swiss served with Catholic and Protestant princes fostered strife among the cantons. The Swiss therefore came to realize that given their own religious and ethnic diversity (they speak German, French, Italian, and Romansch and practice both branches of Protestantism as well as Catholicism), to have peace among themselves they would have to take no part in foreign quarrels. Hence, the Swiss regime became characterized by its pursuit of internal social peace and international peace, traits that have become habits. The superabundance of guns in Swiss hands contributes to both.

The Swiss army is a militia that requires every fit man to perform twenty-eight years of service—forty years in cases of emergency. No one is allowed to refuse promotion to higher rank (and responsibility). Men who are exempted for good reason pay extra taxes, and refusal to serve may be punished by expulsion from the country. This means that for twenty-eight days for twenty-eight years of their lives, men of every socioeconomic category have to practice entrusting their lives to one another. Since military units are small and each draws mainly from its own locality, the men get to know one another very well, and there naturally arises among them the same kind of bond that old regime armies tried to manufacture among their low-class recruits. But Swiss soldiers come from all classes, meaning that the bonds are formed on a higher human level and that the society as a whole, and not just the regiment, benefits from widespread mutual confidence. Beyond the army the regime also produces habits of mutual trust because people in each locality administer their own affairs and national as well as cantonal issues are often settled by referendum. Switzerland certainly does not have the kind of divergence in tastes and manners among men in the upper reaches of society, especially the media and the universities, that one finds in other advanced societies.

By design, these common tastes and manners include violence. In Zurich, for example, a holiday is set aside to introduce young boys to shooting at human silhouettes. And can one even imagine a college professor or a TV news anchor in America who is also an artilleryman? In Switzerland, such people are common. Thus, while no one would describe the Swiss as particularly jolly or loose, relations among them are remarkably smooth; and though the Swiss are anything but egalitarians, their habit of treating one another with respect and by the rules is well established. In sum, then, the habits generated by the recruitment and training of the armed forces concur with those generated by the rest of the regime.

The Swiss military has not been fully tested in war since the time of Napoleon, when it gave a good account of itself. But its skills and dedication have been sufficient to deter attack ever since. During both World Wars, the German military simply figured that taking Switzerland would cost more than the country—never mind mere passage through it—was worth. In 1940, the German plan for conquering Switzerland, dubbed "Tannenbaum," called for using twenty-one divisions against the Swiss. Given the advantage inherent in defensive positions and short supply lines, even twenty-one divisions might not have been enough—especially since in the only trial between Swiss and German forces, the Swiss came out ahead: On their way to France, German aircraft violated Swiss air space. In the ensuing fight, the Luftwaffe lost seven planes to one for the Swiss. The amateurs beat the pros.

Note also that the Swiss enjoy in unusual measure the usual advantage that accrues to military forces that are operating on known terrain. Not only are passes, roads, and bridges mined, but any enemy would be operating in effect on the Swiss army's training ground, where every artilleryman knows by heart the settings for hitting precisely every point in his field of fire, where the field of fire emanating from every bunker has been studied for generations, every line of communication covered optimally by generations of reservists, and every tactic rehearsed on the very battlefield where it must be employed. Some of the Swiss preparations—such as airplanes stored in mountain tunnels—are so expensive that they can be paid for only over many years. But because the Swiss regime's commitment to military matters does not depend on shifting perceptions of external threats and opportunities but rather because it depends on constant attention to one mission, that commitment can be steady.

Because Switzerland is the land of steady habits, where nothing exciting ever happens, many regard it as dull—even as many thought Sparta dull. But in Switzerland as in Sparta, dullness and longevity go hand in hand by design—and the army serves to keep it that way.

Part III

OUR CHARACTER

Chapter 10
DE TOCQUEVILLE'S AMERICA

The foundations of our national policy will be laid in the pure and immutable principles of private morality.
— GEORGE WASHINGTON,
FIRST INAUGURAL

A MERICA'S IMAGE, albeit hazily perceived, has drawn much of the world to transform itself. But it is less an image of America as it actually is today than a portrait drawn from a reality best described by Alexis de Tocqueville over a century and a half ago, much of which is forever past.

De Tocqueville described a way of life that combined characteristics that Europeans had thought incompatible: unprecedented freedom and popular participation in government, along with unprecedented respect for law and morality. The American phenomenon, he explained, is due to the prevalence of habits of equality, of devotion to religion, and of practical responsibility in the exercise of local government. He showed that the founders' thoughts reflected the country's ways, and vice versa. The original American regime's prosperity is to be understood in terms of its civility and its religion, while its religious habits are to be understood on their own terms as well as those of civil equality. The whole combination of these elements can only be understood as the peculiar result of religious and economic practices. Finally, Americans became "most free" because, like the Swiss, they were "most armed."

American Prosperity

Every Thanksgiving, the *Wall Street Journal* runs as its editorial two descriptions of Massachusetts by its earliest settlers. The first, written

213

upon the Pilgrims' arrival in 1620 and entitled "The Desolate Wilderness," describes a place that promised hunger and cold, as well as danger from "wilde beasts and wilde men." The second, written a few years later and entitled "The Fair Land," describes solid prosperity and boundless confidence. What turned one into the other? Certainly not any economic "plan" or any economic policy whatever. The very words would have been incomprehensible. Nor did prosperity come through any transfers of wealth to the poor colonists. If anything, the mother country's stewardship was exploitative. Nor did prosperity come from extraordinarily available natural resources. Massachusetts' soil is poor, its weather worse, and making farm land out of virgin forest with hand tools is enormously laborious. The colonists surely worked hard, but probably no harder than the Russian peasants who carved out of the Siberian forests nothing that attracted the world. So, neither superior connections, resources, circumstances, nor even mere effort—much less wiser economic policy—turned America's subpoverty into superprosperity. Rather, the yoked disciplines of self-interest and freedom, driven by Christian morality, built habits of disciplined and thoughtful labor. Material plenty came from a wealth of human qualities unleashed.

The American founders wrote often of what had to be done to foster prosperity. But few of their utterances on the subject strike modern readers as economics. Rather, they look like political moralizing. And indeed they are. From countless pulpits, Americans heard the king of England's claims on them denied in words similar to those of John Allen:

> As a fly or a worm, by the law of nature has as great a right to liberty and freedom (according to their little sphere in life) as the most potent monarch upon the earth: And as there can be no other difference between your lordship and myself, but what is political, I . . . take leave to ask . . . whether anyone who fears God will oppress his fellow creatures?[1]

Such expressions restated John Locke's premise that whosoever mixes his labor with anything thereby acquires a natural right to it. Thus countless orators rhetorically asked whether the king had plowed their fields and if not, what right he had to any of their produce. Thus also Francisco de Miranda told the story of an ordinary Virginia farmer who demanded of General Rochambeau payment for fields trampled by his troops and, when rebuffed, returned with a humble sheriff to vindicate his property rights against the great man. A people so imbued with the combination of equality, righteousness, and industriousness, remarked Miranda—like de Tocqueville after him—could not but prosper.

The effect of the so-called Protestant ethic on America is often remarked upon, usually with some reference to grim determination. But there was nothing grim about early American economics. First, it is impossible to read early Americans' accounts of their economic exploits without being struck by the joy they took in their accomplishments. From the days of John Winthrop until the 1920s, America grew on the exuberant sense that human accomplishment serves the will of God. Second, early Americans acted on the belief that economic activity—so long as it was conducted on the basis of equality and without the admixture of compulsion—is the path to domestic and international peace. "Our plan is commerce" wrote Thomas Paine, in his capacity as America's first secretary of state, eschewing power politics.[2] Economic freedom at home and free trade abroad were more than paths to wealth and peace: They were the paths of righteousness, into which the Good Shepherd of the Twenty-third Psalm leads mankind for his name's sake.

Just like property rights and free trade, sound money and frugal budgeting were not matters of economic policy but of morality. Thus the Reverend Samuel Cooper, preaching on the day on which the Massachusetts Constitution took effect, used the expression about America having "a national character to establish," a phrase George Washington had made famous in his campaign for payment of debts owed to the Continental army, in a sermon largely about sound money and the maintenance of national credit through minimal expenditure. Cooper also reminded his economically eager parishioners that there is a big moral difference between making money through honest labor and doing so through the acquisition of privilege. The latter, he said, breeds habits of servility: "Servility is not only dishonorable to human nature, but commonly accompanied with the meanest vices, such as adulation, deceit, falsehood, treachery, cruelty, and the basest methods of supporting and procuring the favor of the power upon which it depends."[3] Cooper would not have been surprised at the economic results of communism and Third Worldism. His fellow Americans would have diagnosed the poverty of these systems as a moral rather than as an economic dysfunction.

The founders were not unanimous on economics. Alexander Hamilton was a mercantilist who thought that trade was about getting special deals. He also wanted to make the U.S. government into the country's most potent investment banker. But he was overruled on these matters by most of the rest of his fellows, with whom he generally agreed on the moral bases of economic action. Jefferson was deeply suspicious of the habits that nonfarming occupations would bring to America. Nonetheless, at the end of his life, fifty years after having written the Declaration of Independence, he rejoiced that his country was becoming a hive of industry and commerce because it was happening on moral bases of which he approved.

America's Civility

America had been made town by town. Physical isolation made it likely that local government would be the only real government, that factions too out of tune would simply set up their own town, and hence that higher levels of government would be built on cooperation among localities. American public life, in short, was not made by conquerors or delegates but by free citizens. By the mid-seventeenth century, no one had to try to build citizenship in the colonies—only not to erode it.

The authors of the U.S. Constitution expressed the strongest fears about the effects of popular government on the national level. That is why they enumerated the specific tasks of the federal government and why the Constitution does not even contain the most important word in the language of modern politics, *sovereignty*, nor does it refer to sovereignty's substance, the capacity to define one's own power. They were happy enough to leave sovereignty where it already existed—with the inhabitants of localities and states.

De Tocqueville was thus moved to explain why the colonists thought popular sovereignty on the national level was inconsistent with good citizenship:

> The general business of a country keeps only the leading citizens occupied. . . . It is difficult to force a man out of himself and get him to take an interest in the affairs of the whole state, for he has little understanding of the way in which the fate of the state can influence his own lot.[4]

The American founders knew that since most people had neither the knowledge nor the personal affection needed to deal responsibly with national affairs, they would do so as party and prey to some faction. But they also knew that in regard to matters close to them, people have

> an infinite number of occasions . . . to act together; and [to] feel that they depend on one another. That is, the same people are always meeting and . . . they are forced in a manner to adapt themselves to one another. . . . Some brilliant achievement may win a people's favor at one stroke. But to gain the affection and respect of your immediate neighbors, a long succession of little services rendered and of obscure good deeds, a constant habit of kindness and an established reputation for disinterestedness are required.[5]

De Tocqueville aimed his explanation at European statesmen, some of whom were already bemoaning ordinary citizens' sullen indifference and exhorting them to revive local civic life. But de Tocqueville noted that such statesmen

> [i]n making municipalities strong and independent . . . fear sharing their social power and exposing the state to anarchy. However, if you take power and independence from a municipality, you may have docile subjects but you will not have citizens.[6]

European politicians, in short, would tell people to be vigorous and to participate. But since they reserved all important matters to their bureaucrats, they were effectively telling people to get excited about trivia or about the things that the leaders wanted them to be excited about. Meanwhile, they were imposing school curricula, urban planning, and the agendas of interest groups as well as social reformers on localities. Just as during the French Revolution, European states had hired prefects to oversee mayors in their administration of central directives.

De Tocqueville, however, reported that New England towns (whose population of working-age men was typically in the low hundreds) had nineteen elected officials and yearly elections. Most men would have several turns in some office. In de Tocqueville's America, as in Aristotle's *Politeia*, the distinction between "the people" and "the officials" was primarily chronological. Thus, New Englanders fulfilled Aristotle's definition of citizens—equals who rule and are ruled in turn and who are fully responsible for the city. When the public safety was threatened by crime, they did not merely call the police. As de Tocqueville noted:

> In America the means available to the authorities for the discovery of crimes and arrest of criminals are few—Nevertheless, I doubt whether in any other country crime so seldom escapes punishment. The reason is that everyone thinks he has an interest in furnishing proofs of an offense and in arresting the guilty man. . . . In Europe the criminal is a luckless man fighting to save his head from the authorities; in a sense the population are mere spectators of the struggle. In America he is an enemy of the human race and every human being is against him.[7]

It made sense: The same people who made the laws enforced them. The legislative, executive, and judicial powers were separate in theory. But the same people who voted for ordinances acted as officials and served on juries. For the same reason, when it was time to fight the Indians or the British, they formed their militias much as Roman citizens had, elected their officers, and went out to fight. They were no more paid to fight than they were paid to vote or to serve as jurors.[8]

The various localities not only erected peculiar rules about the Sabbath. They established religion, regulated speech, and, yes, tolerated slavery or not. De Tocqueville was by no means enthusiastic about the "wisdom and quality" of American local legislation. But he recognized that "there is prodigious force in the wills of a whole people"[9] and that officials backed by popular laws "dare to do things which astonish a European, astonished though he be to the spectacle of arbitrary power." He therefore warned, "Habits formed in freedom may one day become fatal to that freedom."[10]

All of this is to say that citizenship is a good, relative to the objectives of the city at any given time. De Tocqueville, like many Americans, saw different kinds of polity arising in the South and the North. The Civil War that eventually engulfed both regions was all the fiercer because it was fought by young men brought up to treat the res publica as their own. But de Tocqueville used the American example to teach that local independence, however dangerous, is the key irreplaceable ingredient of citizenship. At the turn of the twentieth century, when urbanization and the ideology of efficiency through scale had diminished many Americans' participation in meaningful local affairs, the direct democracy movement (initiative, referendum, recall) tried with modest success to resuscitate civic involvement in an America where the distinctions between ruler and ruled had become clearer and more solid. But neither these reforms nor subsequent ones ever restored Tocquevillean vigor and civic life in America.

De Tocqueville had also noted that vigorous political life at the local level is a useful guardian against the excesses of representative government at the national level. He had observed various interested parties trying to influence government in America. But because they could not capture—no one could—a government so diffuse, they were reduced to trying to gain the attention of a variety of legislators, officials, and their successors. This, too, was very difficult. In short, because they had to deal with public opinions, American interest groups had to talk a lot and moderate their demands. By contrast, as de Tocqueville said, interest groups and political parties in Europe were organized

> to act and not to talk, to fight and not to convince. . . . There is nothing civilian about their organization and indeed military ways and maxims are introduced therein; one also finds them centralizing control of their forces as much as they can and placing the whole authority in very few hands.[11]

In America, however, or in any country where local politics is meaningful and where representatives are elected one by one, each representative must pay more attention to the needs of constituents than to the demands of any party.[12] To get a grip on many representatives, the party would first have to gain control over many constituencies—and this is what James Madison bet would be hard to do. But Madison's confidence in the people's disinterest in nationwide factions is based on his assumption that they would severally be absorbed by the politics of their districts. By contrast, when people become accustomed to focusing on political matters that do not involve local cooperation and to obeying rules made by people they do not know and cannot control, said de Tocqueville, "their habits too are trained; they are isolated [from one another] and then dropped one by one into the common mass."[13]

Among such peoples the capacity for citizenship will gradually atrophy. It does not matter that the agenda imposed on them is more enlightened than the one they would have imposed on themselves or that the professional officials to whom they turn are more competent than the amateurs or part-timers they replaced. De Tocqueville did not report that America in the early nineteenth century was administered neatly, nor did he enumerate the social services that local governments delivered. But he did tell his European readers that the American system produced free men, citizens such as Europe could barely imagine.

The French Revolution had just swept Europe with the claim that its version of equality and liberty would produce a brotherhood of citizens such as the world had not seen since the Roman republic. Hence, throughout Europe, officials took on Roman names: prefects, consuls, procurators, tribunes, censors, and so on. Yet the Europe of de Tocqueville's time had nothing in common with the Rome of Cincinnatus and Cato. With the exception of Switzerland and parts of Germany, Europeans had long since forgotten how to look to one another. So when they overthrew one set of masters, they simply accepted another.[14] Throughout Europe, administrative organization quickly came to resemble that of the early Roman Empire—orderly, capable of marshaling human energies, and passionate about foreign wars, but devoid of citizenship and always liable to disruptive popular movements. Napoleon, in short, had been the revolution's legitimate heir.

The Americans were not Romans because Christianity did not allow Roman-style single-mindedness about aggrandizing the city. Nonetheless, the Americans cultivated the Romans' civic virtues—the self-sufficiency of families made for real equality and liberty, while constant cooperation in local affairs built habits of fraternity.

The American Family

In America as elsewhere, habits of fraternity begin at home. America's economy and its civic life were strong because America's families taught piety, the sanctity of commitment, the performance of duty, the pursuit of righteousness, and the value of work. American families were strong in part because the founders treated marriage as a preeminent part of the divine order of nature and as the foundation of private morality. Since the founders had no doubt that popular government is possible only among virtuous people, they revered marriage as few people before or since.

Members of the founders' generation got married in church, where they heard the familiar injunctions from the King James Bible: "[W]ives, submit yourselves unto your own husbands . . . Husbands, love your wives even as Christ also loved the Church."[15] They also heard: "The wife hath not power of her own body, but the husband; and likewise also the husband hath not power of his own body but the wife"[16] and "What therefore God hath joined together, let not man put asunder."[17] They kept Aristotle in mind, who wrote that marriage is a friendship both useful and pleasant and also "a friendship of virtue if [husband and wife] are good."[18] Thomas Jefferson wrote of marriage in these very terms: "While one considers them [women] as useful and rational companions, one cannot forget that they are also the objects of our pleasures."[19] In short, the founders' generation believed that men's and women's interests were complementary, and they saw marriage as the divinely ordained, naturally good way to organize life. George Washington had started his presidency by pointing out that public life must be grounded on private morality. His successor, John Adams, devoted husband of Abigail, was even more specific: the "foundation of national morality must be laid in private families."[20] He went on to say that children learn the meaning of morality, religion, and respect for law from the habitual fidelity of their parents to one another.

The founders had no doubt that marriage meant a monopoly of lawful sex. Every colony and town had laws against sex outside of marriage and, of course, against sodomy in all its forms. Fornication was often punished by exhibition in stocks. Adultery was punished by heavy corporal punishment and heavier fines. Marriage laws obliged husbands to support their wives and pay the debts they incurred. When Jefferson supported a local ordinance for punishing deficient husbands by confinement at hard labor, he did nothing remarkable.[21] Since divorce could be granted only in outrageous cases—mainly adultery, in which case the adulterer was not allowed to remarry—ordinary women could be sure that their men would not go when wrinkles came. The law built a community of interest on the expectation of mutual performance and permanence.

That interest, according to de Tocqueville, was pursued according to

the great principle of political economy. . . . They have separated the functions of man and woman so that the great work of society may be better performed. . . . You will never find American women in charge of the external relations of the family, managing a business or interfering in politics; but they are also never obliged to undertake rough laborers' work or any task requiring hard physical exertion. No family is so poor that it makes an exception to this rule.[22]

This is why Jefferson, James Wilson, and their contemporaries were so shocked at the sight of Indian women bearing the brunt of labor, and would have been even more shocked at Soviet labor practices than latter-day Americans—not because using women for labor is inefficient but because it violates the order of nature. De Tocqueville made clear that Americans of both sexes concurred wholeheartedly in this assessment of the natural role of each. Americans thought that human associations large and small must have a head, that the natural head of the household is the husband, and that the purpose of democratic equality is to regulate necessary powers, not to destroy them. American men, he noted, "constantly display complete confidence in their spouses' judgment and deep respect for their freedom because they relied on their wives for management of the household. Wives in turn took pride in their husbands' authority and hold him accountable for it."[23] Just as each level of government—federal, state, and local—was supreme in its own jurisdiction, American women ruled the "domestic sphere" autonomously as nowhere else.

De Tocqueville also noted that Americans applied to relations between the sexes the same kind of spirit that they applied to legal matters in general, namely, equal treatment. Adultery was punished equally, and American husbands no more than wives boasted of amorous exploits. But the Americans tempered equal treatment with recognition of the sexes' physical inequality. Whereas in Europe rapists were treated leniently and juries often refused to convict, Americans hanged them routinely. De Tocqueville found this remarkable because in general America's criminal laws were milder than Europe's. Americans were so adamant about rape not because of any unusual possessiveness about women—Europeans were more so—but rather because "as the Americans think nothing more precious than a woman's honor and nothing deserving more respect than her freedom, they think no punishment could be too severe for those who take both from her against her will."[24]

De Tocqueville did not imagine that the laws did anything more than defend the American family. Rather, he argued that the American family was bound by natural ties and that the greatest contribution the laws had made to these ties was to let nature take its course. Had Americans tried by law to make the family what it was, they probably would have failed, because "trying to add something, [the law] almost always takes something away."[25]

Far from suggesting that American-style families would spring up among any and all peoples if they were left in some kind of lawless state of nature, de Tocqueville was careful to point out not only the powerful penalties against nonmarital sex but also that as both Puritans and traders, Americans were accustomed to "a continual sacrifice of pleasure for the sake of business."[26] Americans valued high standards of human performance and were accustomed to holding themselves and others responsible for meeting them with "great strictness." Freedom left no excuse for bad performance. The American way of consensual marriage left no room for extramarital love. As de Tocqueville noted, "there is hardly a way of persuading a girl that you love her when you are perfectly free to marry her but will not do so."[27]

Early America, then, was a network of families. American cities, like all cities, had prostitutes and some amorphous people on the margins. But to grow up into a normal adult, a boy had to become a husband, and to become a woman, a girl had to become a wife. Few men or women stayed out of marriage—because to do so was to stay out of society. The occasional out-of-wedlock birth produced "bastards," most of whom were quickly adopted. Not until the late nineteenth century did the need arise for social institutions to deal with "foundlings." No doubt some parents were abusive toward their children as well as toward one another. But the Americans of de Tocqueville's day did not understand, much less believe, his warning that government might someday try to superintend their domestic lives. Nor would they have taken seriously anyone who told them that their way of life itself was abusive. The American men and women of that age would not have understood (as many Europeans already did understand) the notion that people should make up their own definition of a good man or a good woman, nor that these definitions might change with government policy or that anyone might command them to become gender neutral. They knew they were free, and believed the Declaration of Independence that their freedom derived from "the laws of nature and nature's God."

The American Religion

"The religious atmosphere of the country was the first thing that struck me on arrival in the United States,"[28] wrote de Tocqueville, and throughout his account, he reiterated that to make sense of America, his readers had to realize that religion really did pervade every aspect of life, that religion was "the first [of America's] political institutions." That was true precisely because clerics had no official power. Even more strangely, the pastors and priests liked it that way.

De Tocqueville knew the difference between religion and religiosity. He looked for hypocrisy and found little. He wrote:

> [I]n the United States the sovereign authority is religious, and consequently hypocrisy should be common. Nonetheless, America is still the place where the Christian religion has kept the greatest real power over men's souls; and nothing better demonstrates how useful and natural to man it is, since the country where it now has widest sway is both the most enlightened and the freest.[29]

He found religious fervor in the depth of the forest, where pioneers would travel for days to encamp around the tent of a circuit-riding preacher, and in the homes of rich New Englanders, who would give up comfort to preach the gospel in the wilderness. He found it in the schools—almost universally run by clerics. He found it in private as well as in public; in short, everywhere, and everywhere without compulsion.

To be sure, the very earliest settlers in Massachusetts had come from Christian sects on the edge of heresy, which had made little distinction between secular and divine law. But neither Plymouth's William Bradford nor Boston's John Winthrop had been theocrats in the mold of Mohammed or even Calvin. None ignored, much less repudiated, Christ's distinction between duties to God and to Caesar. The confusion of ecclesiastical and secular authority in the earliest settlements—people were in fact whipped and fined for sin—was naturally due to the fact that each settler band was simultaneously a practically sovereign civil polity and a self-governing religious congregation. It would have been a lot to expect of any given bunch of dog-tired people living on the edge of survival and meeting to transact their common business that they would draw fine lines between the civil and religious items on their agenda.

The settlers were motivated both to freedom and to a greater degree of civil and ecclesiastical perfection. John Donne's sermon to the Virginia Company in 1622 was a typical mixture of exhortation to add to "this kingdom," meaning England, and "to the kingdom of heaven." The Mayflower Compact of 1620 also dedicates the signers to "the glory of God and advancement of our Christian faith, and honor of our king and country." As the colonies grew, the two sets of ends were reconciled rather quickly in terms of practical tolerance, because dissidents could always move out—as Roger Williams moved from Massachusetts to found Rhode Island. Just as important, the practical necessity for each congregation—Protestant, Catholic, or Jewish—to be self-supporting and self-governing led Americans of different religious persuasions to spread out and live profitably side by side. Thus, George Washington could write to the Jewish congregation in Newport, wishing it success in its own house and supposing that it wished Christians success in theirs. Consequently, as Paul Johnson has argued, "America was born Protestant"[30]—Protestants, Catholics, and Jews developed Protestant habits—and each congregation vied with the others for civic success and godly lives. This pluralism was not, as some claim, a "collapse of the idea of total Christian society."[31] The very notion that society, much less the polity, should be Christian had been relegated to heresy ever since St. Augustine published *The City of God* in A.D. fifth century. In America, each congregation was as free to be as Christian as it wished, in the way that it wished, and so was every other. Nor should anyone read as religious indifference Washington's assurance to the Jews of Newport that in America they observed their religion not by tolerance but by right. On the contrary, American Christians welcomed Jews because they were the senior branch of America's religious family. Washington would not have written a similar letter to Muslims, much less to an organization of Thuggees, peyote smokers, or militant atheists.

So, while the laws of the several colonies did not force anyone to belong to any congregation or to perform any religious rite, it was impossible to take part in public life except as a member of some congregation—just as it was difficult to do so unless one was married. Since the country was built by, of, and for the faithful, anyone who was faithless was very much a stranger. Moreover, every town and every colony had some ordinances that put certain forms of ungodly behavior beyond the pale. Maryland's 1649 act concerning religion, later known as the Toleration Act, for example, set fines for denying the existence of God and for various acts of blasphemy.[32] Such laws, however, were nonsectarian and were indeed less religious than civic, since they defined the common denominator on which the polity stood. They did not force anyone to revere Jesus. But they kept irreverence private and out of public squares dominated by reverence. Hence, de Tocqueville wrote that "Christianity itself is an established and irresistible fact which no one seeks to attack or to defend."[33] Merely to stand away from God, however, was to cease being part of the body politic because all ranks of society identified with Christianity and liberty and judged them essential to their institution. He added an example:

> While I was in America, a witness called at assizes of the county of Chester (state of New York) declared that he did not believe in the existence of God and the immortality of the soul. The judge refused to allow him to be sworn in, on the grounds that the witness had destroyed beforehand all possible confidence in his testimony.[34]

De Tocqueville wrote that he had "met no one, lay or cleric," who did not agree that "the main reason for the quiet sway of religion over their country was the complete separation of church and state." Clerics and laymen alike quickly came to realize that involvement with politics burdens the faith with "the ill feelings that must necessarily attach to political enterprises from time to time."[35] Moreover, when a church is in any way subject to political authority, it loses the one claim by which it can trump politics—namely, that it speaks for the transcendent authority of God. State churches, he wrote, tend to serve the interests of the state and are always sooner or later fatal for the faith. Hence, the state constitutions of New York, Virginia, North and South Carolina, Tennessee, and Louisiana explicitly excluded clergymen from public office. All the others did so by custom. This was so even in the states (nine of them in 1775) that extended special favors of "establishment" to one or more sects. Thus, while the political sermon was a major fixture of American life, the cleric who delivered it could not himself touch public business.

Even before the first Great Awakening of the 1730s, clergymen were the best known—indeed, the only widely known—people in the colonies, and the advancement of piety was a prime goal of public policy. James Madison's 1789 speech on behalf of the First Amendment to the Constitution made clear that the amendment was being introduced at the behest of several states to protect the several states' peculiar religious arrangements—all meant to foster the practice of religion. Paul Johnson summed it up as follows:

> Hence, though the Constitution and the Bill of Rights made no provision for a state church—quite the contrary—there was an implied and unchallenged understanding that the republic was religious, not necessarily in its form, but in its bones, that it was inconceivable that it could have come into being or continue to flourish, without an overriding religious sentiment pervading every nook and cranny of its society.[36]

Religion influenced America from within. From the beginning, religion in America had been less ritualistic and more literal, and hence more intellectual, than elsewhere. Protestant services were substantially lessons. Catholics and Jews imitated them. De Tocqueville noted that on the Sabbath, America came to a halt and that after church the typical American read the Bible. Nowhere else in Christendom was the Old Testament read so much and the notion of God as lawgiver so widespread. The tendency of Americans to equate themselves with the children of Israel was so great (note the predominance of Old Testament names) that it spread to Negro slaves as well. By the time of the Great Awakening, preachers, notably Jonathan Edwards, were already linking this re-Judaized Christianity to natural law. This kind of preaching substantially stiffened morals—something immediately obvious to visitors.

In the public realm, this religion of law fostered the notion that all power under God must be accountable to Him. Hence, anyone who could understand the laws that God had written in nature and in the hearts of men could and should judge the actions of the powerful. The American Revolution and the tradition of limited government that flows from it can only be understood in this light. Anyone suggesting that the American Revolution was about claiming the "rights of Englishmen" either is unacquainted with the fact that ever since Henry VII, English law had been neither more nor less than the will of the

Crown and that after 1688, this absolute sovereign power had passed to Parliament, or else is referring to the medieval conception of right, which proceeded from natural law. De Tocqueville did not think the U.S. Constitution was as powerful a guarantee of limited government as religion, which "prevents [Americans] from imagining" and forbids them to dare "all sorts of usurpations." "And if anyone," he wrote, "managed to conquer his own scruples, he could not likely conquer those of their partisans."[37]

The litany of American statesmen's invocations to God, of their reminders to their fellow citizens to stick close to the divine laws because they are the only bases for good republican laws is long, repetitive, and beside the point here—that point being, what did early American statesmen do to foster the religion on which their regime depended? The answer seems to be "everything and nothing." De Tocqueville, too, after lengthy treatment of the importance of religion to the American regime, has only the following to say about its preservation:

> What I am going to say will certainly do me harm in the eyes of politicians. I think the only effective means which governments can use to make the doctrine of the immortality of the soul respected is daily to act as if they believed it themselves.
>
> I think that it is only by conforming scrupulously to religious morality in great affairs that they can flatter themselves that they are teaching the citizens to understand it and love it in little matters.[38]

Not by accident did American politicians, especially presidents, come to speak of their offices as "pulpits." Nor is it an accident that long after the founding generation had passed away, American political discourse was suffused not just with Christian symbols—America (with Canada tagging along) is the only country that observes a national day of Thanksgiving—but also with the framing of issues in terms of natural law. Perhaps the best illustration of this is the coincidence that the House of Representatives passed the resolution asking President Washington to proclaim a National Day of Prayer and Thanksgiving[39] on the very day, September 24, 1789, after it had passed the First Amendment to the Constitution, by which it had shielded America's massive, public, and fervent practice of religion against the interference of the federal government. It is worthwhile noting the lack of ambiguity in Washington's response:

The providence of Almighty God, to obey His will, to be grateful for his benefits, and humbly to implore His protection and favor . . . that great and glorious being who is the beneficent author of all the good that was, that is, or that ever will be, that we may then unite in rendering unto Him our sincere and humble thanks for his kind care and protection of the people.[40]

Shakespeare and the newspaper—the two pieces of writing that de Tocqueville found everywhere in the forests, towns, and cities—filled the space in the souls of early Americans that was not filled by religion. In sum, the early American soul was not terribly complex. Its pleasures were "simple and natural," seeming to consist of success, both material and spiritual.

The Human Product

The founders made the laws and the laws made the founders. And they were the wonder of Europe. George Washington was probably the first international celebrity, receiving awed letters and visitors from throughout the Old World. Europeans marveled at the Americans' bearing. Their walk and their manners bespoke freedom, dignity, and confidence. Europeans knew that although the Americans did not live in splendor, they were somehow richer than they. They also knew that the Americans were righteous, happy, and free. Alexis de Tocqueville was only one of an endless series of foreigners who traveled to America to find out its "secret" recipe. The most perceptive of them, however, focused on human qualities, as de Tocqueville did. From the very first, Americans themselves have considered how to spread their way of life to the rest of mankind. But the sober judgment of America's founding generation was that the American way of life was made possible by a set of qualities that other peoples did not possess. Might they ever?

The deepest reflection on this subject was John Adams's in his *A Defense of the Constitutions of Government of the United States of America*, a veritable survey of mores and laws around the world.[41] Adams saw mankind's prosperity everywhere eroded by greed, laziness, and rapacity. He saw freedom rendered impossible by lack of self-restraint on the part of great and humble men alike. He saw debauchery and luxury ruining domestic life, and ignorance, superstition, and hardheartedness barring man's way to God. In short, all mankind was drowning in sin, and the American people were blessed to have their heads just a bit above the muck. If the Americans were diligent, if their laws continued to encourage hard work, self-control, fidelity, and piety, they might retain their present happiness and be the city set on a hill, the city that might enlighten the world.

As for the rest of the world, Adams's analysis added only Christian morality to the advice of Greek and Roman manuals for liberal education, that is, for training man in the habits necessary to get and maintain freedom.[42] These maxims, along with the Christian faith, were known in Europe long before the founding of the American republic. The Europeans never put them into practice, but perhaps the sight of America's happiness might inspire them to do it.

Chapter 11

WHAT ARE WE DOING
TO OURSELVES?

We have now a national character to establish.
—GEORGE WASHINGTON,
LETTER, APRIL 4, 1783

WHILE NO ONE WOULD ARGUE that the U.S. government set
out to engineer the vast differences in civic and economic life,
family customs, and souls that separate contemporary America from
the nation of the founders, the government's leading role is well-nigh
self-evident. It is difficult to think of any ideas and practices that have
become part of American life despite the government's strenuous fight
against them. Rather, whether deliberately or through unintended
consequences, government has been an important engine of innovation. As we have seen, it is natural that this should be so, because
government is the forceful expression of what sets the tone anywhere—the Establishment, the regime.

Outside of the struggle over slavery, few Americans before our time
have argued that one part of society had enlisted government in an effort to shove an alien way of life down its throat—much less that it had
succeeded in doing so. (William Jennings Bryan's "cross of gold"
speech is a notable exception.) Even the heated controversies over the
New Deal economic policy were about implications for the future.
The impact of New Deal social policy was even more theoretical. In
the 1930s no one of either party could have conceived of Supreme
Court decisions that would take schools out of the hands of local citizens, drive religion out of public life, safeguard obscenity, create "protected classes," establish abortion, and ordain a host of other changes
in American life. All of these changes have long intellectual or social

pedigrees. But the massive innovations in American life beginning circa 1965 were wrought upon America from the top, preeminently by a liberal regime that used government—and preeminently the least representative branches of government—to carve the larger society in its own image. But social engineering begets counterengineering. Since the 1980s, the liveliest products of American political thought have come from conservative think tanks concerned with using the power of government to push their recipes down liberal throats.

The American Regime

Like any country anytime, anywhere, modern America has a regime. The modern American regime—the Establishment—contains most of the officials of the U.S. government, as well as the majority of state and local officials of both parties. Also included is the leadership of countless business and nonprofit groups who profit from their connection with any level of government and who generally share the proclivities of government officials. As the regime changes, it pushes some groups out and pulls others in. Excluded are those of whatever rank or station who oppose "mainstream" trends or who otherwise will not acknowledge the Establishment's right to its privileges. Even the president of the United States may find himself beyond the Establishment's pale. In 1981 and 1982, when President Ronald Reagan spoke of the Soviet Union as an "evil empire" on its way to the scrap heap, his nominal subordinates disregarded him because Reagan was entirely contradicting the conventional wisdom of America's tastemakers as well as of the U.S. government itself. By the same token, senators, congressmen, and other officials do not receive the deference normally accorded to persons of their rank if they hold antiestablishment views, do not honor establishment symbols, or perhaps worse, do not cooperate in funding the "private sector" of the Establishment. Thus, in September 1983, when Congressman Larry MacDonald of Georgia was killed along with sixty other Americans aboard a Korean airliner shot down by the Soviet Union, the regime did not react as it would have to the killing of a *real* member of the legislative branch, say, Senator Ted Kennedy.

The private sector of the regime includes all those organizations and individuals who have their position in society because officials favor them. Companies like Archer Daniel Midlands, the nation's biggest grain broker, and Tyson Foods, the biggest processor of poultry, prosper as they do because of the U.S. government's special provisions—among many others—for using grain alcohol as a fuel and for pushing American poultry into foreign markets. The major automakers, which have "helped" to set tariffs and environmental regulations and have joined with the Department of Transportation to produce the "car of the future" and innumerable other similarly connected businesses, also contribute money to politicians as well as support to officials by testifying before Congress and helping to form public opinion. In the nonprofit sector, hundreds of "public interest groups" are wholly or largely financed by government. Without exception, such groups happen to be politically liberal. These groups objected to a law requiring them to disclose their financial relationship with the U.S. government whenever they testify before Congress on the grounds that they are in the same business as the government, are seeking the same ends, and are effectively extensions of it.

They have a point. We can see that point most clearly when the character of the regime changes: some groups that had been in are pushed out, while others that had been outside become pillars of the regime. Until the 1960s, the National Rifle Association (NRA) was part of the regime. It received surplus U.S. government guns and ammunition, its members were allowed to use government ranges, and were encouraged to run shooting clubs in schools. The association was close to officials at all levels of government. During the same period, the Boy Scouts of America were similarly intertwined with government, especially with schools. During the 1970s, however, the rest of the regime decided that the way of life associated with hunting, with individual and collective defense, was bad. The Boy Scouts' promotion of morality and religion became suspect. The NRA became a pariah, then an enemy, and courts began to take seriously arguments that the Boy Scouts are a nursery of inappropriate attitudes toward women and homosexuals. By the same token, during the years when the NRA and the Boy Scouts were in, groups such as Planned Parenthood and the Sex Information and Education Council of the United States (SIECUS) were not. Since the 1970s, these groups have been part of America's schools more than the NRA ever was.

Just like advocacy groups, some media organizations are in and others out of the Establishment. The *Washington Post*, the *New York Times*, and the major broadcast networks are in. Officials fall over themselves to talk to them. The Central Intelligence Agency itself gives regular inside briefings to its favorites from what it designates as the major media. For U.S. government officials, talking to a reporter from the *Washington Post* is a sign of distinction. Talking to one from the *Washington Times* is a sign of disloyalty. Nothing frightens the media establishment more than the prospect that it might not get special treatment. Thus, in 1980, the media greats gave a collective sigh of relief when Ronald Reagan, having lambasted the establishment media during his campaign for president, sought an invitation to dine with the owner of the *Washington Post* as soon as he got to Washington. The order of the regime would not be upset after all.

After the election of Ronald Reagan, the *Washington Post*'s Style section, true mirror of the regime's tastes, published a front-page article, only slightly tongue-in-cheek, about how the new administration's appointment of thousands of role models very different from their predecessors would make a long list of people, institutions, customs, magazines, foods, culinary habits, and so forth passé, while making others the new standard. Cohabitation, for example, was to be replaced by marriage and children. The *Post*'s fears did not become reality. Neither it, its favorite people, nor its favorite habits went out of style because in fact the new president appointed mostly establishmentarians. Nevertheless, the *Post*'s publication of the contrasting lists of customs and tastes was close to the mark.[1]

Being in or out of the regime makes a big difference. Take universities and other intellectual institutions. "The best and the brightest" are not defined by competitive exams but rather by residence in places where officials go between stints in office, where the grant money goes, and where ambitious young people know they can find ladders to climb. The very notion that admission to and employment in them should be determined by impersonal exams is socially intolerable. These places are the academic analogues of well-connected businesses: When government officials need members of advisory panels to justify saying yes or no to whatever projects they want or don't want, they go to the very same people in the very same places—Massachusetts Institute of Technology, the Council on Foreign Relations, and so forth.

Not being part of the regime means being liable to all sorts of hostility—ranging from press attacks to prosecution—whenever one tries to exercise any of the functions the regime reserves for itself. Three years of criminal prosecution (ending in complete exoneration) made it impossible for Ronald Reagan's secretary of labor Ray Donovan to function, thereby negating his appointment. Appointees of similar persuasion or inclination got similar treatment. Unsurprisingly, most of the appointees of the most antiestablishment president in recent times quickly made friends with the Establishment. By contrast, being in means that unless you are caught with both hands in the cookie jar, you have a right to exercise power. Thus, while Robert Bork and Clarence Thomas, antiestablishment nominees to the U.S. Supreme Court, endured public pillorying, the proper way to treat members of the Establishment is to disregard their errors. Their membership alone validates any behavior. For example, on April 28, 1997, U.S. Attorney Eric Holder filed an argument before Judge Royce Lambeth asking the judge not to consider a suit arising from a government wiretap in which Secretary of Commerce Ron Brown had selected private participants in a U.S. trade mission according to their record of contributions to the Democratic party. Ten days before, Mr. Holder had said of Secretary Brown: "He played a substantial role in my becoming U.S. Attorney. He's the guy who made the calls . . . when the names were being sent up."[2] Whereas once upon a time the U.S. government used to prosecute improprieties at least as vigorously in its upper as in its lower ranks, in the 1990s a host of cases ranging from adultery to untruthfulness illustrate that being a part of the establishment means seldom having to be sorry.

The regime's sheer weight is more important than its orientation. Like America's previous regimes, the current one sets society's dominant tone. Unlike previous ones, however, the current one is backed by the power of modern government. Until the mid nineteenth century, those who wished to set America's tone had to appeal to countless almost autonomous individuals, families, and localities. One century ago, the J. P. Morgans and Jay Goulds were economically more important than Archer Daniel Midlands's Duane Andreas or Microsoft's Bill Gates. But today's tycoons have more power over ordinary people than the trusts of a century ago, because unlike them, they get to help make government rules and pay for the privilege. The turn-of-the-century regime allowed more economic choice than the regime does now. One century ago, Horace Mann and John Dewey set the tone for American education. But these men exercised their sway by persuasion alone. Government did not funnel one-tenth of America's GDP to them as it does to today's teachers' unions.[3] Because government accreditation was in its infancy, as was government financing of universities, starting a new school or college was much easier then.

It is not necessary to multiply examples to understand that until fairly recently, the line between those who are part of the regime and those who are not was not so significant or so distinct as it is today. Never has it been so necessary as today for an American to be part of the Establishment to exercise his full human powers. As the late Christopher Lasch pointed out, whereas once upon a time the "American dream" consisted of making one's way without being burdened by people with more privileges than oneself, now it consists of the prospect of climbing out of the ranks of the ruled into those of the rulers, from the ranks of those who count only theoretically to the ranks of people who count because they've got connections.

What ways of life, then, does the new, power-heavy American regime foster? What kinds of people are likeliest to tread the paths to wealth and power that it offers? What standards of behavior does it foster? The U.S. Constitution, said Washington, Madison, and their fellows, was written for people of a certain character. As our leading characters change, the words of the Constitution—which the founders knew were always mere "parchment barriers" to evil ways—must become ever thinner barriers.

It is important to reemphasize that the following account of how our regime is affecting the habits that affect our prosperity and so on is no more than that. It is emphatically *not* a complete picture of America in our time. It is not, except tangentially, an account of the many forces working in the opposite direction. Those forces have affected not only society but also the regime itself—at least as it presents itself. In fact, ever since 1976, every major presidential candidate and nearly all candidates for major office have pledged to decrease the size of government, or at least not to increase it. President Clinton even declared in 1996 that "the era of big government is over." Those postures certainly reflect an aspect of the American people's resentment of government that no one who seeks votes can afford to ignore. But that has not stopped the expansion of government nor changed the regime's identity in the least. What follows is an account of the regime's effects.

Power and Prosperity

The U.S. economy today is being shaped not so much by economic policies as by a degradation of economically useful habits caused by the ever-increasing injection of government power in the world of work. Both liberal and conservative economists have largely missed this.

Liberal economists have argued that America's prosperity is being undermined by policies that encourage excessive private consumption, shortchange public and other investments, and contribute to deficits in the international balance of payments, thus turning America into the world's biggest debtor. They argue that private profligacy is deindustrializing America. They urge higher taxes to rein in consumption and to provide the funds for "industrial policy" to get us out of debt and set a firm foundation for our children's future. But America is very much a creditor when the worth of investments is figured at market value rather than "book value." Also, total income from overseas investments is greater than total payments to foreign investors.[4] Large corporations have indeed shed middle managers and moved manufacturing to lower-wage countries. But this has coincided with the creation of new jobs here at a very respectable rate. The claim that these are lousy jobs at falling wages is based on one very misleading statistic—the average nonfarm, nonsupervisory wage—and on the now widely acknowledged overestimation of inflation.

Liberals write of the need to repair America's crumbling infrastructure. Yet the proposition that the American economy is hampered by crumbling roads and bridges and that it is more difficult to move people, goods, and data around the United States than elsewhere is ludicrous to anyone who has traveled the world. And indeed, liberal proposals for "investments" have much less to do with bricks and mortar (read: indirect patronage to favored contractors and unions) than with "human investment" (read: direct patronage to social service providers and their clients). President Clinton claimed that each dollar spent on education, early childhood vaccination, and job training would pay $3 or even $10 in increased production and reduced government costs.[5] This is part of the argument that President Lyndon Johnson made a generation earlier for expanding welfare and job training as part of the "war on poverty." When President Clinton makes this argument now, few take him seriously, for it is generally accepted that the populations targeted by these huge investments became more economically dependent and produced greater burdens for the criminal justice system. Realistically, such investments pay off only in the coin of political support.

Nevertheless, the liberals' talk of social investments at least addresses the key relationship between prosperity and human capital. The bulk of conservative economists nowadays—the neoclassical public choice theorists—ignore the warnings of their intellectual ancestor

Wilhelm Ropke about the indispensability of good character for the proper functioning of markets. Instead, they assume the constancy of character, and that all people rationally seek to maximize their material well-being. This has led them to the correct but ultimately unfulfilling observation that when the government pays people for not working, it will wind up with more nonworkers and that if the government raises price supports for any given crop, more of that crop will be produced. But unlike their forebears, the neoclassicists cannot account for the farsighted self-restraint and discipline that lead some utility-maximizers to make economic contributions to themselves and others and the short-sightedness that turns other utility-maximizers into consumers of social services. Public choice economists usually do not understand that the meaning of free enterprise differs radically for people of different moral disposition. Therefore, although the conservatives' policy recipes—they prefer private to public investment, free trade to managed trade, and low taxes to high ones—tend to be better than those of the liberals, conservative economists are apt to ignore what is gnawing at the habits of the heart of a people that once turned a "desolate wilderness" into a "fair land." Thus, Gary Becker has recalled to his fraternity something of the moral emphasis of an earlier generation of economists. "The effects of a free market system on self-reliance, initiative, and other virtues," wrote Becker, may be more important to prosperity than technical market arrangements. Becker has pointed to welfare as a destroyer of economically essential virtues but also to

> affirmative action initiatives that help people get ahead not through their own accomplishments but because they belong to favored groups, aid to small and large businesses that subsidizes their profits and insures them against losses, and regulations that protect companies against competition. Social security is another example, because it encourages many families to count on government to provide their retirement income.[6]

The best economists, then, look to noneconomic causes and effects.

The Real Issue

In fact, whole classes are losing the personal discipline traditionally imparted by families, are succumbing to self-indulgent New Age beliefs, and are being enervated by welfare for the poor, by welfare for the middle class, and especially by welfare for the rich. At stake in the struggle between different sets of economically relevant habits is not just the amount of material possessions that the American people will enjoy but also the extent to which the American people will have at their disposal the material means of personal independence and habits of self-control. At stake is also whether modern America, like the America of the founders, will value the habits that make for productive lives or whether, like so many other regimes, it will teach people that having is better than producing, thereby fostering mutual depredation.

The temptation to redistribution is inherent in all government. But in a democracy, that temptation affects more people, and those on society's lower rungs are freer to imitate those above them. That is why corporate favoritism is more dangerous than welfare for the poor. The rich and the upper middle class, not the poor, have driven the process first sketched by Mancur Olson and described by Jonathan Rauch,[7] by which interest groups have hardened the arteries of the American economy and are turning it notch by notch from a machine for production into one for redistribution. Here, as elsewhere, "as a society becomes more and more dense with networks of interest groups, as the benefits secured by groups accumulate, the economy rigidifies."[8] Entrenched interests use the government to collect more while working less; individuals learn that productive activity is less rewarding than government-related activity. Of course, a government that lives by redistribution is itself first paralyzed and then destroyed by it. The recipients of benefits cannot possibly be satisfied. As their demands grow, the government is compelled to become more "taxy" and to alienate society's producers into sullen passivity or worse.[9]

It is a mistake to calculate the economic cost of government merely by adding to government expenditures the direct cost of complying with the regulations. As Rauch points out, the Washington University Center for the Study of American Business once calculated that cost at $137 billion per year, while the Rochester Institute of Technology estimated it at between $400 and $500 billion. In addition, the U.S. Office of Management and Budget estimated that compliance with government paperwork costs Americans 5 billion hours per year. But such estimates, large as they are, do not touch the heart of the problem, namely, the growing portion of every individual's attention and effort that is devoted to profiting from friendly regulations and defending against unfriendly ones. Rauch has written about businesses that have found they could make more money by cutting down on the number of production workers and hiring more government affairs consultants, as well as substantive experts who have found more remunerative careers as experts in government relations. He estimates that rent seeking—what he calls "the parasite economy"—costs the country some 5–12 percent of GDP.[10] In comparison with most of the world, that is not bad. By previous American standards, it is awful. Even worse is that the U.S. economy is moving farther into the orbit of government.

While enriching some at the expense of others, government corrupts habits and wastes effort. After all is said and done, every socio-economic category ends up getting a percentage share of direct government benefits (as distinguished from advantages, which go almost exclusively to people at the top of society) that is roughly equal to its percentage share of the population. But to get the benefits—that is, to stay relatively even—Americans increasingly have to deal with lawyers, consultants, go-betweens: In other words, they have to pay in time, money, and habits. And through this striving, Americans are making sure that the economy will involve ever more rules, exceptions, and appropriations each successive year. As we issue more regulations, more of us will have to go to law school than to schools of science and engineering. That is because, as James L. Payne has shown, the legislative process is close to monopolized by witnesses who are petitioning for more rules and expenditures. Only one witness out of 145 wants less of them.[11] Congress calls such witnesses precisely because they are claimants.

The costs are both material and moral. The aerospace-defense industry is an extreme example. During the 1980s, the press was indignant that contractors had charged $500 for a hammer, $600 for a toilet seat, and $7,000 for a coffee pot. But it wrongly assumed that someone had pocketed the difference between these sums and the $15 or so that these items should have cost. Nor were the toilet seats made of gold or "unobtanium" by herds of Ph.D.'s. Rather, they were produced under government contracts that required literally mountains of paperwork. But above all, they involved several sets of reviews by different government committees at different stages of the job. This means that entire factories march in place as engineers who could be building products are instead shuttling on airplanes between the factory and Washington. By the same token, the high cost of drugs reflects the years and somersaults required to gain approval by the Food and Drug Administration. One can only sympathize with the aerospace vice president who told me: "If the government wants paper instead of metal, we'll take the money to the bank just the same."

Knowing what the government wants is the surest path to riches. Thus, employment in the Department of Justice or the federal court system doubles the market value of a lawyer. A biotechnologist who has worked for the Food and Drug Administration (FDA) can name his price with a drug company. And what utility would not pay top dollar to someone who had worked for the Environmental Protection Agency (EPA) on approving smokestack scrubbers? Lest anyone think that such high salaries (passed on to the public through higher prices) are fair recompense for substantive expertise, consider why the Lockheed Corporation management hired one John MacMahon, deputy director of central intelligence, to be president of its Missiles and Space Company. The company builds high-tech products, and MacMahon, whose career had been in personnel security, did not know a pixel from a pixie. But his knowledge of the people who give out contracts justified every penny of his astronomic salary.

Corruption at the Top

The broadening reach of government is changing the way big money is made in America. Since the New Deal, America has come to know what other countries know even better: the political entrepreneur. The first of this kind in America, Henry J. Kaiser got close to the Roosevelt administration's lobbyist Tommy Corcoran and garnered through him almost one-third of America's war production—all on government credit—"cheap at twice the loan," he would say. Since he worked on cost-plus contracts and was allowed to buy his facilities at a few cents on the dollar at war's end, he resembled a modern Russian privatizing nomenklaturist more than a character from a Horatio Alger story who made money by adding value.

The flood of accusations and denials that surround President Clinton's financial dealings have shed much light on the relationship between power and wealth in the state of Arkansas, where power over business has long been as strong as it is now becoming in the rest of America. The essence of the story is that Tyson Foods, the state's largest poultry processor and several banks and savings and loans had special relationships with the state's first family, from which the first family gained financially. There is no record of Tyson, whose chief counsel was instrumental in multiplying the first lady's investments, having had any problems with the state's environmental regulators. Nor did Madison Savings and Loan, whose president paid the governor's personal campaign debts, have any problems with the state's banking examiner, appointed by the governor. The fact that the savings and loan was represented by the governor's wife (at a high consulting fee) to the governor's appointee may have helped.[12]

What the great do in a grand way, lesser folks do as they may. Thus President Clinton's secretary of labor, Alexis Herman, made between $500,000 and $1 million, according to her federal disclosure form, on a silent partnership with a man whose interests she recommended to her mentor, Secretary of Commerce Ron Brown, who then—after the man had made a $50,000 campaign contribution—used the power of the United States to obtain special treatment for him in Japan.[13] The point here is not that those in power seek opportunities for self-enrichment. On the contrary, such opportunities knock at their doors and well-nigh knock them in. The legal definition of bribery requires explicit, specific governmental quids for explicit, specific quos. But the trade of favorable treatment in exchange for marvelous opportunity—sometimes called "access capitalism" in Washington and not so different from Chinese *Guanxi*—is the essential reality of the new American economic regime at the top.

Corrupting the Bottom

Lower-class corruption is straightforward. In the 1960s, the U.S. government began the transformation of public assistance, or "welfare," from a locally administered safety net for the lame, the blind, and the temporarily distressed into a set of federal programs to whose benefits people in certain categories would be entitled. Today, approximately 5 million "families," amounting to roughly 15 million people, receive Aid to Families with Dependent Children (AFDC)—up more than threefold since 1970. Some 15 percent of American children are on welfare, and fully 10.4 percent of all Americans now receive food stamps.[14] Other welfare programs—housing assistance that pays the rent, energy assistance that pays the utility bills, and Medicaid that pays the doctor bills—have grown even faster. In twelve states, the combined worth of just these five programs (there are seventy others to choose from) to a welfare mother of two amounts to over 90 percent of the mean wage in the area. In Hawaii, Alaska, Massachusetts, Rhode Island, and the District of Columbia, these combined benefits actually exceed the after-tax income of the average worker. And in each of the fifty states, the combined benefits exceed (in some by a factor of three) the take-home pay from a minimum wage job. To this must be added the fastest-growing welfare program of all, Social Security Disability Insurance (SSDI) and Supplemental Security Income (SSI). In 1994, the number of people supported by these programs, which affect the middle class as well as the poor, actually exceeded those supported by AFDC.[15]

The effects of these programs on the economic habits of recipients and potential recipients are more appalling than the figures. If the welfare relationship were merely a quantitative economic transaction, the habits it fosters would not be so debilitating. (Note, for example, that in southern Europe welfare is often just a way fraudulently to add to income from honest work.) The quality of the welfare transaction in America, however, may be glimpsed in the fact that roughly 40 percent of those eligible for benefits have not taken them because they are too proud to take up a very particular lifestyle. The government tells them they are entitled to be relieved of worries and toil. But, like the bedraggled wolf in Aesop's fable who chose not to share the well-fed dog's dish—and collar—they prefer to eat whatever meager portion they can earn. Once upon a time, private and local charities separated worthy recipients (the lame, the blind, the injured) from the able-bodied of questionable character. To the latter, they offered minimal sustenance in exchange for hard labor, thereby fostering personal honor and the habits that flow therefrom. By making welfare an entitlement, the U.S. government has effectively labeled such scruples as stupid and has validated the habits of the takers.

Now consider the economic consequences of the moral content of the welfare culture. Quite contrary to the intent of the statute that created it, AFDC has become the main support for the sexually irresponsible. But it is worse than that. Social workers and police know very well that welfare mothers are not really "single," that is, bereft of men, and that the money that the government pays for the children's support actually goes in substantial part to men. Typically, these itinerant "boyfriends" make sure that they are with their women on the day the check arrives, popularly called "mothers' day." The U.S. government in fact makes it possible for such males to hang out, fight, and deal drugs. While the church on the corner may tell them to be productive, the U.S. government gives them the material and moral means to disdain the jobs for which they qualify as unworthy sources of "chump change."

This is not a racial problem. Most of the Americans who live this way are white, and the *percentage* of lower-class whites who live this life is climbing rapidly toward black levels. Indeed, as Charles Murray points out, the biggest difference between the black underclass and the growing white underclass is the geographic concentration of the former and the geographic dispersion of the latter.[16] Most important, the welfare culture is multiplying among all races because bit by bit, social workers are breaking down the moral stigmas that all races used to attach to the culture. It is also growing biologically through growing rates of illegitimate births. The main economic consequence is that if the trends identified by Murray continue, one in seven Americans, soon more—will be noncontributors, mere consumers, or worse.

Social Security's welfare programs (especially SSI) may be the most harmful of all. Whereas in other countries disability programs mainly support the otherwise decent grassroots clients of politicians, in America they have grown into support mechanisms for social pathologies. That is because the government has classified alcoholism, drug addiction, and various kinds of personality disorders (aggressiveness, boorishness, tendency to steal) as federally subsidizable disabilities. Children, too, are eligible to be classified as "disabled" if they exhibit "mental impairment." In 1990, the Supreme Court redefined this category to include children who do not act in an "age-appropriate" manner. Thus, whereas once parents had only incentives to make their children act their age or better, the U.S. government now gives them $458 per month or more for every child who can demonstrate immaturity or below-grade performance.[17]

Subsidies to bad habits and the official erasure of stigmas on behavior that civil society once discouraged are raising up more and more people who are more likely to turn the fair land into a desolate wilderness than the other way around.

Corrupting the Middle

The U.S. government's corruption of the great American middle class's economic habits—the geese that have laid history's greatest trove of golden eggs—has been more subtle. As elsewhere, the promise of security has been the effective bait. Middle-class entitlement programs, especially Social Security and Medicare, have led people to believe that in exchange for substantial contributions, they will receive, absolutely guaranteed, services that are worth more than what they pay. This might be called the "insurance plus" mentality. Reality, however, amounts to "insurance minus." And the minus consists of lost habits as well as lost money.

For its first three decades, the Social Security's Old Age and Survivor's Insurance, established in 1937, was a pay-as-you-go, chain-letter scheme. Workers and employees paid in tiny amounts (one-half of 1 percent of wages) and a relative handful of people received benefits that though modest, were much greater than what they had put in. More than satisfied, recipients were convinced easily enough that they had a right to what they got because they had "earned it." They learned to treat as sacrilege questions about how the increase had come about. The increase, however, came from the fact that most payers had not yet become beneficiaries and from an increase in population that was increasing the ratio of young workers to retirees. Twentieth-century American politicians, precisely like Otto von Bismarck, who invented social security at the end of the previous century, used the young workers' contributions to buy the votes of retirees, while promising young workers that their time would come. However, since the government spends the money taken in by social security the moment it comes in, these promises are backed by nothing. The contributor has no property right whatever in any of the money he pays in. The government's implicit promise that everyone would get much more than they put in trained people not to ask to whom the money belonged or precisely what happened to it.

After the baby bust of the 1960s, however, when the system was kept alive only by increases in the social security tax, which soon exceeded the average worker's income tax, it became possible to ask what happens to a worker's money between the time it is taken by the government and the time it is returned as social security benefit payments.

The government's answer, embodied in the bipartisan Social Security Commission of 1983 and in the Reform Act of that year, was mumbo jumbo about putting the "trust fund" on a sound basis nearly forever and included a whopping increase in the payroll tax. As a consequence, the Social Security system began to take in lots more money than it paid out—according to the Social Security Administration, some $30 billion in 1993.[18] Yet politicians do not go on television to discuss what happens to this money. They avoid this because talk of "trust funds" thinly veils the fact that the Internal Revenue Service (IRS) turns the money over to the treasury, which spends it as it does all other moneys. In return, the treasury gives the Social Security Administration a set of IOUs. But those IOUs can only be redeemed by the willingness of future politicians to tax future workers to pay future retirees. And since it is known with near certainty how many retirees and workers there will be between now and roughly the year 2020 (they have been born already), the inexorable truth is either that taxes in America will rise to Swedish levels or that the U.S. government will repudiate the promises of social security.

Like any Ponzi scheme, social security yielded enormous increases to those who were the first to collect. A typical worker retiring in the early 1970s before the big jumps in social security taxes and surviving into the 1990s may have received a hundred times more than what he or she contributed. Between the early 1970s and the early 1990s, the odds reversed rapidly. A nominal worker retiring in the mid-1990s and surviving for twenty years will be lucky to get an increase of 2 percent on the money contributed. A typical baby boomer retiring in 2010 may get 40 cents on the dollar compared to money invested. From there, the curve will drop steeply. In short, the U.S. government has led millions of Americans to lose trillions of dollars. Consider what a middle class social security contribution of $3,000 invested and compounded each year for forty years at the stock market's historic 9 percent return would yield had that money been invested Chilean style.[19] The resulting $1,880,000 would provide some $126,000 per year for a fifteen-year life expectancy after age sixty-five, whereas social security will have a difficult time keeping its promise of a maximum of some $14,000 per year.

Social security has been a smashing success, however, in changing the economic habits of America. Prior to social security, Americans secured their old age through savings and through their children. Families planned to pass on their nest eggs to their children insofar as they could. Social security, however, promised people independence from their children. True, until the late 1960s, the benefits it paid were insufficient for any but the most penurious independent living. Nor, until the 1970s, did social security taxes take enough from personal income to hamper the building of private nest eggs. Nevertheless, social security pointed the way to a new model of family economics. The government encouraged adults to dream of retirement not among the children and grandchildren who would be their heirs but in Winnebagos heading into the sunset bearing the standard bumper sticker: "We are spending our children's inheritance." Ironically, of course, although the folks in the Winnebagos may be independent of the younger generation on the individual level, they are very much dependent on the collective level. Moreover, social payments are a growing negative inheritance pressed upon their children and grandchildren by the U.S. government. But that negative inheritance is passed on in the name of an anonymous generation rather than in that of beloved parents. Hence, rather than encouraging generosity, the government is encouraging people's natural tendency to be even less generous collectively than individually.

The other major middle-class entitlement, Medicare, is to be understood as the prototype of social services. Its operative feature—individuals pay some third party that then guarantees the delivery of services—has long since conquered the habits of middle-class Americans. Before the Medicare law was passed in 1965, there was only one major health maintenance organization (HMO) in America, and health insurance was the exception. By the 1990s, health insurance was the rule and HMOs the model. The habits associated with the new way of medicine are very different from those fostered by the old. Under the new system, even people who have a wide choice of doctors, as under Medicare, are claimants.

In the old days, people went to the doctor and contracted fees for each service. They might or might not consider price, but in any case, they hired the doctor. Under the new systems of "managed care," middle-class Americans and their employees pay month after month to insurance companies or HMOs that then hire and pay the doctors. The contributor (who, ironically, is no longer considered a payer) then goes to see "gatekeeper" physicians who decide what, if any, treatment the patient should receive.

Middle-class Americans have been attracted to managed care for some of the reasons they were attracted to social security, among them the promise of unlimited benefits in exchange for limited payments. Earlier forms of health insurance paid only a percentage of costs and then only after the patient had paid substantial amounts out of pocket. The HMOs promised to pay for everything. Pay a small premium and get unlimited use of the miracles of modern medicine! But: The premiums turned out to be not so small, and the gatekeeper physicians, whose future now depends on satisfying their employers rather than their patients, were encouraged to make cutting costs their first priority. Thus, when middle-class Americans now walk into a doctor's office looking for medical care, they do so as petitioners. For those upper-middle-class people who either have personal relationships with the doctors or with the "payers," or who can expect to have their arguments taken seriously because of their status, the new system does not require behavior much different from the old. But lesser beings now have to cajole and often to plead, first with doctors and then with insurance companies.[20] To make their case, they have to research their health problem themselves and may be forced to hire a lawyer. To get their money's worth, and in the illusory pursuit of a bit more, middle-class Americans now need bureaucratic skills that their parents did reasonably well without.

In sum, then, the U.S. government is habituating Americans to pursue national well-being in ways that would have seemed strange to the country's founders and, indeed, to most Americans before the 1960s. The economic habits being fostered in the upper, lower, and middle classes, though different, share two features: the search for security and advantage; and the rejection of personal responsibility. These features are destructive not only of prosperity but of civic, family, and spiritual life as well.

Citizenship

If de Tocqueville were to return to America at the turn of the twentieth century, he would find the Constitution he had described dead in all but formal and vestigial aspects. Instead of few laws to which citizens adhered with pride of authorship, he would find an incomprehensible infinity of regulations and hordes of haughty officials propitiated by a nation of increasingly resentful subjects. He would find that a government with so many favors to give and to withhold was producing a nation of favor seekers, that the government that had taken upon itself to right social wrongs had so stimulated the articulation of grievances that it was producing a nation of whiners and enemies. De Tocqueville would find that inhabitants of American towns were taking their concerns to the state or national capitals just like the Europeans of his day. He would find legislators elected from districts designed to be "safe" for blacks, whites, or Hispanics, and he would conclude that the American people were being divided to be ruled. De Tocqueville would notice the scarcity of prominent citizens in public places. He would find they had retreated into buildings, suburbs, and gated communities governed for practical purposes as if the public laws did not exist. He would be struck by how much citizens concerned about crime talked about the police and the courts and how little they considered their own responsibility for public safety; and he would conclude that Americans were becoming Europeans.

From the Rule of Law to the Whim of Man

The rule of law in America is eroding in theory and in practice. It long ago ceased to be a secret confined to the law schools or to readers of Texas law professor Lino Graglia that the rulings of the Supreme Court have nothing to do with the text of the Constitution or the intentions of those who wrote it, but rather reflect the political preferences of the judges and their political associates off the bench. There is little support in the legal establishment for the proposition that judges should be restrained by the text of law. Also, the attack on the 1991 nomination of Clarence Thomas to the Supreme Court showed that liberals are universally hostile to natural-law restraints on government power—though they often use natural law-type arguments to expand it.[21] As for conservatives, though they tend to oppose the expansion of government power, they also seem to do so as a mere assertion of will. Chief Justice William Rehnquist, for example, tried to argue that federal courts should not substitute their will for that of the framers of the Constitution. But by writing that the "Constitution's safeguards for individual liberty . . . assume a general social acceptance neither because of any intrinsic worth nor because of any unique origins in someone's ideas of natural justice, but instead simply because they have been incorporated in a constitution by a people,"[22] he granted that all such judgments are of inherently equal worth. This left his colleagues in government asking: If you agree that the will of the founders is no better than ours, why should we not push ours à outrance? Indeed they push, and in so doing set a willful tone for the rest of the country.

Congress, too, has abandoned constitutional restraint. It no longer bothers to cite authorization from Article 1, Section 8 of the Constitution when it legislates national speed limits or a national drinking age, makes nationwide rules for the health-care industry, mandates hospital stays for specific conditions, sets rules regarding the environment or disabled people, or whatever. But Congress's propensity to legislate is a small part of the problem.

In practice, since 1935 most "laws" in America have not been of the sort taught in civics class—passed by the Congress and state legislatures elected by the people and enforced in detail by courts that hand down the judgment of juries composed of one's peers. Instead, for the most part, citizens are not governed by laws but by regulations. Bureaucracies make the actual rules, then administer and enforce them. Most often, ordinary people get the treatment they do not even because of published rules, never mind laws, but rather because of "agency policy." That is because when the Supreme Court let pass into oblivion its ruling in the Schechter case (1935) that Congress could not delegate legislative and judicial powers to its creature, the National Recovery Agency, it effectively amended the Constitution to allow Congress to delegate its powers to bureaucracies both unelected and unlimited by the Constitution.

This was the beginning of "alphabet soup" agencies that exercise quasi-legislative and quasi-judicial powers—as well as executive power, of course. From the citizen's standpoint, there is nothing "quasi" about these powers. They are more absolute than ordinary criminal and civil law, and far less accountable. Often, officials choose to impose via regulatory agencies rules that they have failed to impose through legislation. Thus Massachusetts Attorney General Scott Harshbarger, having failed to convince the legislature to ban the manufacture and sale of handguns with certain characteristics, simply prevailed on the state's consumer protection agency to do it. People in the know in today's America no longer bother with legislatures. They go where results are easy—the bureaucracies or the courts.

The rules for dealing with bureaucrats are not written in any civics book. These rules fall under two headings: first, "rules are for outsiders," and second, "[expletive deleted] flows downhill." In practice, this means that if one succeeds in rising to the level of those who sit on agencies' advisory boards, there is no need to fear rules, or bureaucrats, for that matter—because they know you can always have a chat with their boss and make rule no. 2 work against them, very personally. Most people, however, are not able to influence the bureaucrats' bosses. So they are stuck.

The rule of law means that the government is bound by rules

known to all and administered equally "by the book." But modern American bureaucracy has so many rules that not even the officials who administer them can know them all or apply them consistently, while those who live under them cannot possibly take refuge behind compliance. The Federal Register issues 200 pages of densely written regulations every day. The Internal Revenue Service manual consists of 260 incomprehensible volumes. The Occupational Safety and Health Administration rule book has some 4,000 chapters. Any willful official or simply one under pressure to get ahead can find a taxpayer, a homeowner, or a business in violation of some regulation because of how he filed his tax return, how he modified his house, or how he runs his business. This is easy enough, especially since some agencies hand out a majority of their citations not for substantive violations of regulations but for faulty record keeping or inadequate filing of forms. In today's America, any business can be shut down, every individual can be mightily inconvenienced, if not ruined, at the mere discretion of a couple of officials. And if one inspector or auditor thinks something is OK, that is no guarantee that another inspector will not wreck you. That is because different officials know and care about different rules, or they understand them differently on any given day. Nor can a taxpayer, even if armed with the Internal Revenue Code, or a landowner, likewise prepared with EPA regulations, confidently cite a regulation in defense because the courts have consistently held that agency regulations and, a fortiori, policies are merely guides to administrative action. And since administrative judges are hired, fired, transferred, and promoted by the agencies whose conflicts with the individual they are supposed to review, modern American bureaucrats increasingly look at citizens as if to say: "I can do anything I want to you, and there's not a damn thing you can do to me, so when I say, 'Jump,' you had better ask, 'How high?'" Prudent individuals quickly realize that the best chance for safety before a force they cannot control is to humor it.

The irony is that Judge J. Skelly Wright and others who originally advocated the explosion of rule making in the 1960s thought that they would thereby be protecting the citizen against bureaucratic discretion.[23] But the contrary has happened. Between 1978 and 1992, the number of penalties assessed by the IRS jumped tenfold, and the number of liens it placed against property jumped by a factor of three, as has its preemptive (that is, prior to any court judgment) seizure of assets.[24]

Seizure has also become the standard mode of procedure of other regulatory agencies, thanks to the recent and very radical revival of the old but long-dormant legal principle, known as civil forfeiture, that a criminal forfeits the property used in the commission of a crime. In today's America, a bureaucrat armed with that principle can seize property, even without ever bringing formal charges, simply on the allegation that it might be used in the commission of a crime; and the citizen must obey the will of the bureaucrat in order to get part of the property back.

Civil forfeiture was revived as a measure against drug dealers. But according to James Bovard, 80 percent of the people whose property is seized under the drug laws are never formally charged with any crime. The percentage of those whose property is seized by the Environmental Protection Agency and the U.S. Fish and Wildlife Service and who are never even charged, much less convicted, is even higher. The Supreme Court has ruled that even a person's total innocence does not protect that person's property.[25] What a weapon against a citizen! For whatever motive, an official accuses a citizen of a vague or unsubstantiated offense, then inflicts punishment on the spot by seizing the person's land, machinery, or transportation. A livelihood is ruined. The citizen can go to an ordinary court to try to prove his innocence. But that costs money he does not always have, to fight bureaucrats who stand to lose nothing. The citizen who is unlucky enough to draw the attention of a willful bureaucrat is typically reduced to doing at least part of what the bureaucrat wanted, plus signing a waiver of his right to sue.

Since 1965, American legal procedure has increasingly turned citizens into resentful subjects and wheedlers. Nowhere is this clearer than in regard to economic regulation. Take agriculture. Since the 1930s, American agriculture has been effectively run by government-mandated marketing boards, composed of leading growers in each crop who advise the Department of Agriculture about such vital matters as arbitrary standards of quality below which products may not be sold at any price. This system has turned into a machine for driving small farmers out of business. The system is supposedly legitimized by periodic referenda of the growers, run by the department. But the department itself collects and counts the ballots and permits no opponent to verify the honesty of the process. So, as in the rest of modern American administration, there is a lot less money in fighting the system than in going along with it, and if possible, joining it.

Receiving the Food and Drug Administration's seal of approval is fraught with even more arbitrary rewards and punishments. Evaluations of both "safety" and "effectiveness" depend on subjective criteria. What percentage of laboratory animals must be free of what symptoms after what dose was taken for how long in order for the drug to be considered safe? How much improvement must human testers show with what dose before it can be considered effective? Depending on the subjective answers, people in business can become wealthy or poor. Arguing for test criteria can only be done by people who are familiar with the process and on good terms with those who run it. Any drug company would be foolish if it did not hire—for a lot of money—the most prestigious, well-connected consultants it could. Former employees of the FDA are best, in no small measure because their prosperous presence tells current employees that if they act right, then they, too, can get high-paying jobs with drug companies.

When a company tries to stand on its rights, however, terrible things happen. Thus in 1990, Sporidicin, a well-established producer of disinfectants approved by the EPA, was notified that its product now had to be certified by the FDA as well. The company was not pliant enough, arguing that its product had been sufficiently tested. Thus, on December 13, 1991, the FDA and the EPA together raided its headquarters and seized all its products. The pretext? The product had passed 239 tests, but the FDA said it had failed number 240. The government had no case, but it had the power to keep the company shut down. In the final settlement, the company only had to agree not to violate federal advertising rules in the future—and of course not to sue. But the damage had been done.[26] How does one avoid trouble with the regime when one is not a member? In America as elsewhere, one hires members—legislative lobbyists, bureaucratic lobbyists, lawyers, and, at the bottom of the food chain, the prudent builder will hire from a list of expediters or contractors who have good personal (read: financial) relationships with the inspectors.[27] In the Soviet Union, they called such people *tolkachi*.

The U.S. bureaucracy's new discretionary powers are all the more galling because the government is so loath to punish its employees for harming citizens. Even when, in a highly publicized incident, an FBI sniper murdered the wife of a fugitive who was standing in a doorway holding her baby, the government issued mild reprimands to its own. It did not even apologize to Richard Jewell, the security guard whom the FBI ruined by publicly accusing him on the basis of precisely no evidence (unfortunately for him he fit a profile) of setting off a bomb in Atlanta during the 1996 Olympics. Federal prosecutors now obtain indictments in 99 percent of the cases they bring to grand juries, the case of *Moore v. Valder* being a rare instance in which judges have punished the unethical methods prosecutors routinely use to get such indictments.[28] That is why when the IRS agent who is auditing you laughs in your face, it makes little sense for you to think of the *Federalist Papers*. In such instances, it is easier to understand why so many Russians still have such affection for Stalin, who regularly threw to his subjects the bones of those who oppressed them directly.[29] Alas, it is easiest of all to think the servile thought: "To get along, go along, minimize the damage, and look for a way to get yours." That is how subjects nurse their grudges.

The Rule of Spite

As the rule of law recedes, it becomes easier to get satisfaction at the expense of one's fellow citizens. Thus, Lance Morrow summed up the new pseudo-legal litigiousness in *Time* magazine:

> The busybody and the crybaby are getting to be the most conspicuous children on the American playground. The busybody is the bully with the Ayatollah shine in his eyes, gauleiter of correctness, who barges around telling the other kids that they cannot smoke, be fat, drink booze, wear furs, eat meat or otherwise non-conform to the new tribal rules taking shape. The crybaby, on the other hand, is the abject, manipulative little devil with the lawyer and so to speak the actionable diaper rash. . . . Both these types are fashioning some odd new malformations of American character. It all adds up to what the *Economist* perceptively calls a "decadent Puritanism within America: an odd combination of ducking responsibility and telling everyone else what to do."[30]

These latter-day American epigones would just be sad fun if they were not part of the regime. In fact, their actions are significant primarily because certain classes of Americans now enjoy legally "protected status" over others. It all began with the civil rights movement of the 1960s, when some Americans found moral satisfaction, personal power, and careers in branding some of their fellow citizens as racist. Racially motivated injustices have always been part of American society—though less than of any other multiethnic society in history. Reducing them is a noble objective. Surely for a substantial part of the civil rights movement, that objective was uncontaminated by ignoble motives. However, no movement could be an exception to the rule that power corrupts. As Congress was passing the Civil Rights Bill of 1964, its sincere, ingenuous sponsor, Hubert Humphrey, already felt compelled to deny in the strongest possible terms that the bill might be used to advantage some at the expense of others in jobs and education. But Howard Smith, the bitter segregationist Virginia congressman, knew that Humphrey's followers had every intention of flaunting their power, that they would quickly turn power gained in the name of discrimination into power to discriminate, and that this would cause massive troubles in American society. Therefore, to cause trouble among those who had caused him trouble, to foster litigiousness among the liberals themselves, he added the word "sex" to the list of bases on which discrimination would be prohibited. He need not have bothered, because the movement was heading on its own toward expanding the bases on which the judiciary and the bureaucracy—meaning themselves—could interfere in interpersonal affairs. In 1967, Congress added the stipulation that workers over forty years old had the right to sue for discrimination in employment—and in practice, for everything else. Since then, the list of protected classes has lengthened, and more Americans have learned the joy of gnawing on one another.

What this meant became unmistakable in 1976 when the Supreme Court, in *Meritor Bank v. Vinson*, established a woman employee's right to sue for sexual discrimination not on the basis of a tort (as specific intentional damage recognized in common law) but rather on the basis of subjective feelings of discomfort. Protected status means that some people have the right to get mad at others and hurt them, while the others don't have the same right against them. In 1990, Congress followed that logic to its *pons asinorum*, its point of absurdity, by adding people with various handicaps to the list of the protected.

It is hardly surprising that many people, offered the advantages of protected status, quickly learned to flaunt it. Thus, in the womb of the federal bureaucracy, the judiciary, and its allied groups in society, the germ of the Civil Rights Bill begat affirmative action, and affirmative action begat race norming, sexual quotas, suits for racial and sexual harassment, and sensitivity programs, the legions of officials who make their living in them (Alexis Herman began her rise to fortune as one of them), as well as the making and breaking of careers through everything but honest labor. One nice grievance and one can be rid of an enemy, lock in a career, or just make enough money to retire. And to think that once upon a time you had to make a better mousetrap!

As Mary Ann Glendon has pointed out, defining any contest in terms of rights "impedes compromise, mutual understanding, and the discovery of common ground."[31] It makes not for fairness but for haughty winners and sore losers. Perhaps above all, it makes government power the arbiter of the contest. Robert Reich and many other liberals knew that the expansion of special rights would increase the level of contention in society and make lawyers as a class the managers of the new conflicts. They got more or less the results they wanted.

Unequal Equality

"Affirmative action" became a part of American life immediately in universities, and was quickly taken up by government itself as well as large corporations. The pretense was soon dropped that it involved only aggressive searches for qualified, now-protected-but-heretofore-victimized students or employees, and a system of outright preferences was instituted. Even in the rare cases where the brokering of preferences actually attempts to balance the presumed right to advantage of two reasonably qualified, relatively disadvantaged individuals,[32] the presumption of adversarial proceedings that weigh the worth of human categories is a recipe for strife. Most who advocate preferences for protected classes try hard to obfuscate the fact that a governmental preference extended to one individual is a government-inflicted injury on another individual. Almost anyone can recite an accurate schedule of racial-sexual handicaps for jobs, promotions, and schools in his or her field. Yet rare in the literature is a straightforward defense of preferences.[33] Among politicians, it simply does not happen. And so, to the corrosive effects of the policy must be added the corrosive effects of dissimulation.

Almost simultaneously with the practice of preference, there arose the practice of penalizing dissent with it. Labeled "racism," "sexism," "ageism," and so forth, the New Age crime of discomforting a protected person through speech can now be prosecuted formally by lawsuits (which have increased manyfold since 1969) for compensatory (and, since 1992, for punitive) damages. But the number of suits is dwarfed by informal actions brought before kangaroo courts within the workplace. No impartial juries, no rules of evidence apply to these proceedings. The offenses are defined only by the feelings and the status of the parties involved. Opposition to preferences for protected classes is prima facie proof of guilt (a position supported by the Supreme Court's decision in the *Romer* case [1996]), as is humor about the whole matter.[34] At stake are promotions and demotions, who is up and who is down, who gets what—but above all, who "gets" whom. A reporter for the *New York Times*, obviously not realizing the self-indicting nature of the claim that there is a class of human controversy in which one side is right 95 percent of the time, breathlessly reported the following as typical: "A. T. and T., which has won considerable respect for its policies, says that 19 out of every 20 complaints received [for sexual harassment, discrimination] are valid." Almost by definition, the only accusations for New Age crimes that get to first base are those levied against people who lack the proper support within the workplace to turn them against the accuser. They are another unaccountable, pseudo-legal weapon of the preferred against the unpreferred, of the politically powerful against the politically weak.

Academic, governmental, and corporate America quickly came to love affirmative action precisely because it gives officials (still overwhelmingly white men) the capacity to dispense with objective criteria in hiring and promoting in general not simply with regard to particular classes of employees but with regard to every employee. Affirmative action makes it possible to reward friends, to punish enemies, and to safeguard one's own position. Some years ago, following Judge Stephen Reinhardt's (Ninth Circuit Court) impassioned plea to a Stanford Law School audience for acceptance of affirmative action because there are too many white men in high positions in the legal profession, I asked Judge Reinhardt whether he would agree to resign his post if the president would assure him that it would be filled by a qualified nonwhite female. As the audience laughed at his embarrassment, he evaded by answering that the interaction between the concepts of professional qualifications and affirmative action is more complex than it seems. It is also very simple.

In practice, the distinction is not between formally protected classes and formally unprotected ones. In practice, not just any black gets preference over just any white, nor just any woman over any man. Under the system, lots of whites of both sexes get preference over other whites of the same or the opposite sex as well as over people of other races. In practice, affirmative action is neither about race nor about sex. It is about politics—not the grand kind, but the seamy variety. People like Judge Reinhardt would prefer to work with another white man who belonged to his personal or political *khvost* than to have a black woman who was not pliant enough personally or politically. Still others use the freedom from standards that affirmative action provides to hire people who will not threaten to outshine anyone. In sum, then, affirmative action is about adding to the power of those who already have power and obliging those under them to build the personal political relationships that override objective criteria and immunize against New Age accusations. If liberal education is the formation of minds and hearts fit for freedom, affirmative action teaches some very illiberal habits.

The fading of the American tradition of the rule of law has produced new "rights"; the beneficiaries of such rights are resentful,[35] and the new victims are bitter at having been deprived of theirs. It is producing a people increasingly habituated to using power to get theirs at others' expense. Thus, the civil rights industry has produced "unprotected classes" that publicly nod and privately simmer at charges against them that they know are not true. Moreover, as court decision after court decision emboldens homosexuals and feminists to condemn the lifestyle of the average American, these feel increasingly as if they live in hostile territory.

Local Prerogatives

A local tradition as strong as America's is not erased easily. But the U.S. government has gone a long way toward accomplishing it.

Demography helped. As cities grew, each to the size of an empire, classic American civic life became impossible in them. Thus, by the middle of the nineteenth century, New York City's school board was dominated by aristocrats, and by the turn of the twentieth, the class of bureaucrats whom the aristocrats had hired had become the new rulers. But in most of America, local government remained largely Tocquevillean through the 1950s. In fact, as city dwellers moved to the suburbs after World War II, they reestablished—at least for a few years—something resembling the kind of civic life they had lost in cities. A commuter to a job with a large corporation could still be a volunteer fireman and a power on the school board or city council. By the late 1950s, however, as the suburbs expanded into one another, the idea gained ground that services such as zoning, police, fire, sanitation, and schools had to be handled professionally and on a larger scale. Elected mayors gave way to city managers, all but the most important of whom became liaisons with county departments that were really extensions of state bureaucracies responding to federal priorities. By 1990, in one of the most extreme of these steps, the state of Washington, through its Growth Management Act, mandated county governments to adopt countywide policies binding on the cities within them. In effect, the state abolished local government.[36]

The biggest abolition of citizenship came in the administration of schools. Whereas at the turn of the century in an America of 80 million people there had been some 105,000 school districts, by 1990 an America of 260 million had only 16,000 school districts. When the roughly 9,000 districts that serve tiny populations are subtracted from this number, it becomes clear that most Americans live in school districts with populations as large as those of states in James Madison's era and that leaders regard local governments as incompetent to rule themselves. Thus, New York schools chancellor Joseph Fernandez declared in 1995 that individual parents could not be allowed to stand in the way of the distribution of condoms, even to their own children. If parents could thwart the professionals on that, said the chancellor, they might do anything. He had a point.

Federal courts accelerated the breakdown of American federalism and literally turned the Constitution on its head by pushing local government out of the regulation of behavior. By declaring unconstitutional those laws that prohibited loitering, disorderly conduct, and the sale of pornographic material, and by restricting authority over zoning, the courts made it impossible for those local voters who wanted to maintain control of their community to do so. The federal courts laid down detailed rules on everything from the extent to which a citizen may defend himself to what indignities he must suffer from those who flaunt loud music or obscenities "in his face." As these rulings took effect, American towns and cities began to segregate themselves by price of housing as never before. The reason is straightforward: The capacity to move to a more expensive neighborhood, among similarly expensive neighbors, had become the last way in which an American could affect the quality of his surroundings.

For many people, however, the courts curtailed even that freedom.

The main device was court-ordered busing of schoolchildren from one part of a district—or in some cases of a county or even a metropolitan area—to another for the purpose of achieving racial balance or simply to overcome economic geography. City public school districts thus lost all but the poorest of their white students. In Boston, the National Guard had to be called out to restrain parents who realized that because of Federal Judge Arthur Garrity, they would henceforth have to choose between moving away, paying private school tuition, or letting their children be used as guinea pigs. "White flight," the government called it, indicting as racists those who would not submit to its policies. Hartford, Connecticut, is typical. Ninety percent of the city's public school students are black or Hispanic. In 1993, the Federal courts began crafting a plan to forcibly bus suburban children into the central city. By 1996, the bargaining and the appeals had ended, the luckless districts were identified, the usual rituals about stable neighborhoods were intoned, and another sad round in the game of musical neighborhoods began.

Those who cannot afford to move are condemned to be antisocial. This is what happened to people in the lower-middle-class community of Yonkers, New York, during the 1980s, when the federal government and the courts brought their full pressure to bear on them to force them to accept a federal low-income housing project in the community. The courts declared the Yonkers city council vacant, deposing its elected members. But new elections brought in even fiercer opponents. Finally, the federal government simply dispensed with the fiction that the people of Yonkers had anything to say about the quality of their lives or the value of their homes. Of course, the judges did not choose to put the project in nearby wealthy Scarsdale, where their own kind live. In the same vein, courts and bureaucracies do not release convicted felons to the neighborhoods where judges and court officials live.

The ultimate form of flight is the gated community—groups of houses surrounded by walls with guarded entrances. There are some 150,000 of them in America today, along with countless apartment buildings with equivalent security arrangements, and the number is rising. Inside, the pathways, even the landscaping, are the private property of the corporation to which the residents belong, and are ruled by the corporation's bylaws, enforced by private guards. The guards know the difference between citizens—those who pay them—and everybody else. In places like this, and indeed within the private shopping malls that have replaced public shopping districts, some of the judicial revolution that occurred between the 1960s and 1990s might as well not have happened. Parks do not have to be designed to eliminate the nooks where people can find privacy but where criminals can hide. Packs of youths cannot loiter and intimidate, and parents can let children play without guard. Some of these "communities" have their own private schools. Such places, however, should not be confused with the American local governments of de Tocqueville's time. They are not places where mutual obligations are exercised, where people rule and are ruled in turn, where they can enforce their views of the good life. Rather, their residents are purchasers and consumers of minimal order. And the courts may not long permit the arrangement.

Nothing shows the growing lawlessness of the American regime more than its reaction to Proposition 209, passed by the voters of California in 1996 to prohibit racial preferences. The words of 209 are precisely those of the Civil Rights Act of 1964, whose authors also indisputably intended to banish racial preferences thereby. Yet the very courts and executive branch that enforce the 1964 act regard that act as if it had said precisely the opposite of what it says. Not surprisingly, within days of 209's passage a federal judge ruled that 209 is unconstitutional for attempting to apply the very words of the 1964 act in their plain meaning. The Clinton administration joined the American Civil Liberties Union, the National Education Association—indeed, practically the entire regime—in asking that the appellate courts overturn Proposition 209. The fundamental, practical reason why it did so is that, as we have mentioned, group preferences are a legal shield behind which one can run a patronage system. The underlying theoretical reason is that 209 seeks to reinstate the older American legal principle that rights and duties pertain to individuals alone, whereas the federal courts have increasingly placed group rights over individual rights.[37] Clearly, the modern American regime lives by a constitution of group rights administered by the government, a constitution that increasingly substitutes will for law.

Crime and Criminals

Nothing wipes away civics textbook illusions about the relationship between citizens and public servants so thoroughly as a typical encounter with the police. Here is an account of one by a writer for the *New York Times Magazine* who was strolling down a street in Los Angeles:

An immaculately groomed patrolman came up and, as his glance took me in, planted a meaty paw on my chest. "Get off the street," he said, and shoved me back. . . . The casual nature of both words and gesture, the arrogance of it, I suppose as well as the hostility . . . took the breath away.[38]

Except in small towns, this herding attitude is typical of modern American bureaucracy, extending from federal agencies down to lowly airport security, and unless such bureaucrats get unlucky and bully someone from the regime, they just throw their weight around. Most Americans over forty can remember when police were blue-clad, lightly armed, nonthreatening figures who seemed to know the difference between their masters and the bad guys. They were eager to solve crimes and seemed upset if a single burglar in their area went uncaught. The paradigm shifted one generation ago. In part because of the war on drugs, police became heavily armed. Perhaps in part, the civil rights movement and the Supreme Court's expansion of the rights of criminals made it more difficult for them to do their job, but in any case they began to apply harsh procedures to all. Perhaps their unionization insulated them from complaints, but their bureaucratization and the expansion of jurisdictions insulated them from their fellow citizens. Perhaps the practice of riding around in patrol cars or watching movies about paramilitary operations did, too. But whatever the reason, they now run around wearing windbreakers and baseball caps with their agency's name on them, or sport paramilitary gear, and they do not give out names or badge numbers. If they were as effective at maintaining the public safety as the police in Singapore, the average American might not mind so much.

But Los Angeles is also the paradigm for perhaps the most typical police behavior of our time: During the riots that blackened a square mile of that city in 1992, the police absented themselves for about twenty-four hours and left store owners to defend lives and property as best they could with their own weapons. When the police returned as the rioters retreated, they did not try to arrest every rioter. But they did handcuff and take away such store owners as they found standing armed guard over their life's work, earning again the label that the area's Spanish-speaking residents pin on them: "los cobardes," the cowards. The paradigm is this: American police in general seem to have designated their main enemy—the criminal they cannot tolerate—as citizens who arm to protect themselves.

De Tocqueville had found America the safest and most law-abiding of places because citizens defended their own lives, property, and honor with their own arms. Now, American cities may be among the world's most unsafe places because in these cities, the police have effectively lobbied for the disarmament of law-abiding citizens and for punishment of those who "take the law into their own hands." Courts have consistently held individuals acting in undeniable self-defense liable for injuries to the assailant. Courts will protect a loudmouthed youth who shouts obscenities at a woman and punish the woman's husband or the youth's father who punches that mouth. Carlos Bea, the San Francisco judge who vacated a judgment against a cab driver who had pinned an armed robber to a wall with his cab, became a popular hero in 1992. But his career stopped right there.

The law enforcement establishment's constant refrain is that the country is violent because ordinary citizens are too violent and that controlling citizen violence through gun control is the key to safety. Thus, a perceptive observer has written:

Crime is rampant because the law-abiding, each of us, condone it, excuse it, permit it, submit to it. We permit and encourage it because we do not fight back, immediately, then and there, where it happens. Crime is not rampant because we do not have enough prisons, because judges and prosecutors are too soft, because the police are hamstrung with absurd technicalities. The defect is there in our character. We are a nation of cowards and shirkers.[39]

The point is only slightly overdrawn. While the so-called underlying causes of crime have continued to rise, homicide rates in Florida and Oregon dropped by one-third within a year of the passage of laws permitting ordinary citizens to carry concealed firearms.[40] This effect occurred even though only a tiny percentage of the population has availed itself of the privilege. It occurred because the mere prospect that victims might be "hard targets" has given potential criminals an immediate incentive to restrain their appetites.

Controversies over crime are part of a cultural struggle. When Mario Cuomo was governor of New York, he felt strongly enough to denounce his state's numerous gun owners—who, after all, had committed no crime—as "hunters who drink beer, don't vote, and lie to their wives about where they were all weekend."[41] By Governor Cuomo's and others' measure of civilization, such people are worse than criminals because they exhibit insufficient faith in the regime and adhere to ways now alien. For many gun owners, by contrast, the likes of Governor Cuomo are the aliens.

In sum, the replacement of the rule of law by the rule of rights as defined by the regime has given new meaning to citizenship in America. Liberals and conservatives now battle essentially within a society framed by, in the words of a wise contemporary, a

> confiscatory nanny state run by people who "know what is best" for everyone; a state that promotes class envy, which in turn causes social unrest, and which in turn "requires" government "solutions" concocted by the same social engineers that created the problem; a state that bestows "rights" on favored groups and individuals and confiscates those of others less favored, with all the pomp, ceremony, and arbitrariness of a feudal lord blessing or punishing a serf.[42]

Chapter 12
THE CULTURE WARS

[One man's] vulgarity is another's lyric.
— U.S. SUPREME COURT, *Cohen v. California*

IN MOST PLACES AND TIMES, the differences in manners and morals—what we call lifestyle—between the members of the regime and the rest of the people have been quantitative. The richer and more influential have done the same things that those on the lower rungs have, only with greater abundance and ease. When such differences are extreme, however, they call forth mutual contempt. In rare historical cases—the Jacqueries of the late Middle Ages or the French Revolution—they break up societies. But even small differences in manners and morals can cause big troubles when they are rooted in religious differences. In the rare cases when regimes differ substantially from their population and try to press the manners and morals of their religion on society, that population is likely to see the process as a corruption of its ways and view the regime as an enemy. Thus, the shah of Iran made his regime liable to revolution when he flaunted the elite's non-Islamic ways and tried to press them onto the general population. In short, cultural splits between the regime and large numbers of the people are always troublesome, and culture wars are doubly so.

Cultural conflict in today's America is not a figment of the imagination. Whereas in 1948 three-fourths of the American people said they trusted the U.S. government to do the right thing by them, by 1994 three-fourths answered that they did not trust the government.[1] Much of the shift would surely have occurred regardless of the cultural context and policies of the regime, simply because the government takes and gives much more than it did fifty years ago and because the distance between ruler and ruled has grown. But the gap would not have grown so large had there not been a growing recognition on both sides of differences in manners and morals—and a growing mutual dislike. In the world's most diverse society, parts of which retain some of the ways of its founders, the distinction between ordinary people and the regime is anything but neat. Still, there is no mistaking the messages that have permeated American society from the top about family and religious matters: Marriage, for example, is a temporary contract of convenience, in no way preferable to "alternative" lifestyles. All human relationships are contingent on consent except those with the state. The public schools and social service agencies know better than parents what is good for children. Religion may be all right for commoners so long as they do not take it seriously and keep it out of public places, where they must practice the regime's secular religion. The purpose here is not to gauge how far cultural conflict has advanced but rather to note how cultural differences have engendered public policies that are dividing Americans.

The Village v. the Family

Although families and the idea of family still set the tone for most Americans, the modern American family wields less authority over its members and is less important in their lives than ever before. It is smaller because fewer children are born into it, adolescents move out of it sooner, and aged parents seldom move in. And because of divorce, it has a shorter life expectancy than just one generation ago. Most important, fewer Americans over 18 (61 percent) are married than ever before—a drop of 11 percent in just twenty years. And for a substantial sector of the population—the blacks—marriage (at 43 percent) has become a minority lifestyle.[2]

Although American families are still unusually strong in some respects—fewer than 2 percent of married people report having had extramarital affairs during the previous year—they are generally weaker than ever. Divorce is so prevalent that by some estimates, a white child has only a 30 percent chance of reaching the age of eighteen with both natural parents, and a black child a 6 percent chance. Because mothers now work, children get some 40 percent less time with their parents than they did a generation ago.

Far from decrying the weakening of the American family, the modern American regime seeks to hasten it by word and deed. Elite spokesmen have treated the traditional American family as a bad myth, an anomaly that is not passing quickly enough into the dustbin of history. Congresswoman Patricia Schroeder (D-CO) made notorious the proposition that only 7 percent of American families now fit the "Ozzie and Harriet" model, which in her circles is a model of hell. But that proposition is mistaken. Representative Schroeder meant that in only 7 percent of households are *two* children present—not one or three—and the mother has never earned a penny. In fact, however, most households with children have a working father and a predominantly homemaker mother. Another figure often cited to show the demise of the traditional family is that only 27 percent of American households with children under eighteen are headed by a married couple. According to the 1990 U.S. census, however, twenty-seven percent is the figure for U.S. households that have two parents and children. Another 9 percent of households have children with only one parent or guardians. The remaining households—a large and growing percentage—are classified as singles, empty nesters, and so on. The point, however, is that according to the census 72.5 percent of households where children are present are headed by a married couple. Nevertheless, the census revealed that a fast-growing proportion—22 percent of white and 68 percent of black children—are not born into two-parent families at all. That is because the kinds of relationships between men and women that used to produce families are less and less evident, from the ghettos to the campuses of elite universities. And that, in turn, is because the modern American regime gives examples, makes laws, and runs programs hostile to all that marriage implies.

Marriage

The tone that the American regime has set regarding how men, women, and children ought to relate to one another comes through clearly in the academic literature. Marriage is one "lifestyle choice" among others—and far from the most satisfying. Open marriages, same-sex marriages, and cohabitation are often portrayed as involving more sharing and opportunities for individual development—especially for women—than male-headed heterosexual households. To become less oppressive, traditional male-female arrangements must take on some of the characteristics of these others. That is why U.S. government agencies and courts, for whom the expert community is the lodestone, usually speak of fostering the plural "families." As for children, the regime view stated in innumerable places is that the state should treat children on the same legal basis as their parents, with neither having special rights or claims on the other. In this same vein, Barbara Bennett Woodhouse, professor of law at the University of Pennsylvania, has written that the law should regard children as "having a direct relationship with government," that the relationship between children, parents, and the state should be regulated by the state, and that "children's welfare bureaus, juvenile courts, and of course the expansion of public schools [should push] at the borders of the domestic realm."[3] Children belong first and foremost to a community defined by something other than marriage—that is the point that Hillary Rodham made in 1974 in the *Harvard Law Review* and that she made again in her book *It Takes a Village*, albeit with an anesthetic coating. That is the received wisdom that the modern American regime is pressing on the American people with notable success, and it is the source of the ongoing culture war over the American family.

There is no dispute over findings that marriage is the healthiest form of life. A recent survey of obituary pages showed that the median age of death for married women is 79 but only 71 for unmarried ones. For men, marriage made an even bigger difference: The married died at age 75, whereas the single died at 57. This greater discrepancy may be due in part to the very high mortality of homosexual men. A check of the *Washington Blade* (a paper for male homosexuals) obituaries showed that the median age of death was 43 for those without AIDS and 39 for those with it. Nor is there any doubt about the very positive effect of marriage on the prosperity of men, but even more on the prosperity of women and children. The "feminization of poverty" and the dramatic rise in the proportion of children living in poverty, about which so much has been written, result quite simply from the growing separation of women and children from men. Indeed, the great divide in the economy, politics, and society in this country is between those who are part of families (including, interestingly, widows) and those who are divorced or have never married. Even the socioeconomic gap between blacks and whites nearly disappears when marriage is taken into account: Black married couples earned 87 percent as much as white married couples in 1995.[4] The presence or absence of marriage literally creates two different nations.[5]

In the minds of those who set the tone and make the laws, however, the undisputed benefits of marriage weigh less than its congenital sins: Marriage is based on unequal gender roles, limits the professional development of women and the sexual freedom of all, and shuts people off from the wider community. That is why the modern American regime sometimes "supports" families as a rope supports a hanged man.

In *Griswold v. Connecticut* (1961), the Supreme Court began to use the notion of the sacred privacy of the marriage-based family to read into the Constitution a right of personal sexual privacy that it later applied to all people, whether married or not, and that subsequently led it to diminish the status of natural families in American law.[6] In *Roe v. Wade* (1973), the Court used an "emanation" from the "penumbra" of this right to deny not just the humanity of the unborn child but to reject the notion that marriage might give a man any role in deciding the life or death of a child he fathered within the marriage. In *Romer v. Evans* (1996), the Court applied this doctrine to erase the distinction between married sex and homosexual sex. The Court does not have to follow the logic any further to reduce marriage to one idiosyncrasy among others—a point recently made by Hillary Rodham Clinton and backed by the Beliefs column of the *New York Times*.[7] In 1997 the regime—from Senate majority leader Trent Lott to the secretary of defense to the *New York Times*—poured scorn on the military's practice of severely punishing members who have adulterous affairs. Disregarding the individuals against whose marriages the adulterers transgressed, as well as the discord that marital poaching produces on military bases, the *Times* condemned the prosecution of adultery as an offense against "current societal mores."[8] It did not think to specify that it was speaking for the rulers, not the retrograde ruled.

Marriage is not the regime's favorite idiosyncrasy. Betty Friedan described it as "a comfortable concentration camp," and Hillary Rodham called it "a dependence relationship" and likened it to "slavery and the Indian reservation system." Quite as much as in Sweden, elite opinion in America despises the young woman, especially if she proves her talent with something like a Phi Beta Kappa, who chooses to stay at home and, in Hillary Rodham Clinton's derisive expression, "bake cookies." And so elite opinion has demanded of young women that they be so gender-liberated as to act precisely as sexually demanding men want them to, while paying half the rent.

In sum, the regime has demanded more effort and responsibility from women and less from men. To be a woman now means doing the job of a man—and raising children, too—while being a man no longer means supporting a family. True, three-fourths of married people agree with the proposition "If there is no financial necessity for her to work, a mother of small children should stay home full time to raise the children."[9] That means the old American ethos is far from dead, especially among those who are married and raising children. Nevertheless, nowadays fewer and fewer American men include in their proposal of marriage the promise to support the woman and any children she may bear. Less often does financial necessity mean two jobs for him than it does another one for her. David Gelertner aptly summed it up this way:

> The typical husband would always have been happy to pack his wife off to work; he did not need Betty Friedan to convince him that better income in exchange for worse child care was a deal he could live with. Society used to restrain husbands from pressuring their wives (overtly or subtly) to leave the children and get a job. No more.[10]

The regime, then, has devalued marriage for both sides. Men no longer need it to satisfy and legitimate their sexual urges. To women, it is increasingly a set of burdens uncompensated for by economic or social security.

The biggest change in the American way of marriage is, of course, no-fault divorce. Like so many other parts of the revolution in America's habits, it originated at the top. In 1966, only 13 percent of respondents thought that divorce should be made easier to obtain.[11] There was no popular pressure for granting divorce merely on the demand of both parties. Pollsters did not even ask about divorce requested by one party only. Yet this was the ideal for which judges, lawyers, psychologists—that is, the regime—strove. They got it, and divorce rates doubled overall. In some categories (divorce after long marriages) they quintupled. Perhaps changes in the law were not responsible. But the coincidence of changes in habits subsequent to changes in law is probably more significant than that of planetary alignments.

No-fault divorce produced a kind of serial polygamy among successful men—one trophy wife after another. It also imposed injustices on people who thought they had entered into a lifetime commitment that could only be broken for exceptional cause, who had given no cause, and who found themselves dumped. And of course it brought tragedy on millions of still-more-innocent children. But the biggest impact of no-fault divorce may have been the changed expectations of all married people. Marriage had differed from cohabitation in that one couldn't just walk away. But if one can walk away from it, why call it marriage? Naturally, the spreading realization that the ceremony had been emptied of legal standing and that it had become legally (and soon, socially) acceptable to abandon a spouse led people to act and think defensively to supplement the now unenforceable contract of marriage with enforceable prenuptial agreements, which the courts treat as ordinary contracts. Limited protection is better than none.

The fading of the expectation of lifetime marriages has had a profound impact on the attitudes of young men and women. After nearly forty years spent around college campuses, I (and just about everyone else) have noticed a decline in romance. Nowadays, especially at elite colleges, it is bad form for couples to walk hand in hand. By all accounts, there is far more sexual activity than ever. But romance—a complex trial of emotions and judgment both wonderful and terrifying because its logical end is the irrevocable commitment of one's one and only life—is a lot more than sex. But with lifetime commitment legally impossible, politically incorrect, and even "corny," young people increasingly look on each other as short-term resources.

There is in America a reaction against no-fault divorce. The legislatures of several states are considering bills to reinstate a limited concept of fault, especially when there are children involved, or at least to impose waiting periods.[12] Much as such proposals aim at correcting somewhat the balance between the modern passion for autonomy and the interests of innocent parties, they do not begin to question the regime's basic preference for consensual rather than natural relationships. To really strengthen the institution of marriage, one would have to go beyond recognizing its utility, to appreciating its goodness.

There is also a reaction against girls who bear babies to whom they give perfunctory care, if any. In 1995, Congress passed a bill that would have required unmarried pregnant girls, on condition of receiving government benefits, to live in some kind of supervised environment—either in a privately run group home or with a relative's family, but pointedly not in their own apartments. President Clinton vetoed it, to the acclaim of most of the regime.

There has always been a consensus for forcing men to pay to support the children they have fathered. In the 1992 presidential campaign, both Bill Clinton and George Bush excoriated "deadbeat dads" as the bane of society. Some 38,000 officials and $1.8 billion are devoted to enforcing child support payments. But the very notion that "the major problem the children have in a single parent family is not the lack of a male image, but rather the lack of a male income" con-fuses child support with family support. Many middle-class divorces nowadays are initiated by women enticed by the prospect of getting most of the financial benefits of marriage without the troublesome guy. In such circumstances, men feel justified in evading payments. Hence, a tenfold increase in collection effort has yielded little.[13] For the majority of cases (and the number is growing) in which men sire children out of wedlock, the very notion of payment is fanciful. Noth-ing short of imprisonment on a chain gang would have the slightest chance of making them pay, any more than of forcing them to perform the role of husband and father. Law might, however, prevent the siring of children out of wedlock by defining it as statutory rape.[14] That is what certain localities are trying. But such laws are swimming against the tide of the regime's moral foundations: First, the Good Family Man—that typically masculine combination of sacrifice and author-ity—is a dangerous, repressive, reactionary figure. Second, sex is sport.

Thomas Hobbes described with characteristic bluntness the neces-sary consequences of these attitudes:

> If there be no Contract, the Dominion [over the child] is in the Mother. For in the condition of mere Nature, where there are no Matrimonial laws, it cannot be known who is the Father, unless it be declared by the Mother: and therefore the right of Dominion over the child dependeth on her will, and is consequently, hers. Again, seeing the infant is first in the power of the Mother, she may either nourish it or expose it; if she nourish it, it oweth its life to the Mother; and is therefore obliged to obey her rather than any other; and by consequence the Dominion over it is hers.[15]

The Supreme Court would have done well to consider the social con-sequences portended by Hobbes before writing its opinion on *Roe v. Wade*.

Sex and Responsibility

The Supreme Court's imposition of abortion on demand of the mother only, at all times and for any reason or no reason, wholly pre-cludes any and all notions of family. Predatory young men grasp this with a directness that surpasses even Hobbes's: "Her choice, her kid," they say about the results of their sport. In so saying, they are truly the modern American regime's law-abiding citizens. Just as truly, any man who asserts his responsibility for the child he fathered and objects to a woman's decision to have the child killed is a hostile, disruptive stranger to the regime. So are the grandparents who might object to the killing of their grandchildren and the brothers and sisters who might object to siblings being killed. The regime, you see, says that family does not matter. And, of course, any children who make it to the age of reason and wonder how close their mother came to having them killed are similarly out of tune with a regime that puts one person's choice above natural responsibility. Families are about mutual responsibilities. Abortion trains everyone to disregard the most fundamental responsibility of all.

The U.S. and state governments attack the natural attachment of family members not just by making abortion into literally the most unqualified right in the land but indeed by paying for most abortions. Despite a legal ban on direct federal funding, the U.S. government funds them by directly paying some 30 percent of the budget of the nation's largest abortion provider, Planned Parenthood. Planned Parenthood also runs some 33,000 of the public schools' sex education programs, paid for by federal, state, or local governments. This private organization, then, is paid for almost exclusively by public funds. Here is what the standard instruction book of this extension of government in the Rocky Mountain region has to say:

> Sex is fun, and joyful and courting is fun and joyful, and it comes in all types and styles, all of which are OK. Relax about loving. Do what gives pleasure and ask for what gives pleasure. Don't rob yourself of joy by focusing on old fashioned ideas about what's "normal" or "nice." Just communicate and enjoy.

Not all public school sex education programs are run by Planned Parenthood. Most of the rest are run by the Sex Information and Education Council of the United States. Originally funded by the Playboy Foundation, it is now funded by the U.S. government as a contractor for the Centers for Disease Control, whose officials wear pseudo-military uniforms. Compared with the official SIECUS program, which includes condom distribution, the Planned Parenthood's semi-official version seems family-friendly.

What the regime actually does with programs that push in opposite directions makes its thrust even more unmistakable. In 1985 Congress passed the Adolescent Family Act, specifically to encourage the teaching of sexual abstinence outside marriage. The federal district and circuit courts stayed the act's application for four years on the ground that it unconstitutionally established religion. After the Supreme Court vacated constitutional objections to the program, the bureaucracy of the Department of Health and Human Services and of the relevant congressional committees nevertheless kept its 1994 funding at a token $6 million per year, while at the same time funding "hard" sex education (Title X) at $199 million.

Therefore, if you are a local school official and you want to make money teaching that sex belongs in families, forget it. But if you want to make money teaching the joys of sex at will and then shuttling girls to abortion clinics without their parents' knowledge, you can count on being able to keep up your payments on your BMW. And if you are on the local council and you want to regulate the sale of cigarettes and beer to minors, so be it. But don't even think of trying to regulate the sale of condoms to minors. That is strictly against national family policy, as is failure to make unmarried pregnant teenagers—or their impregnators—feel welcome in the new America. A 1972 federal law made sure they must be included in cheerleading, football, and all that.[16] Despite superficial presidential rhetoric to the contrary, adoption, too, is against family policy. Despite a surplus of couples so eager to adopt that thousands go overseas to do it, adoptions in America have fallen since 1970 because the courts and the various social service bureaucracies have thrown up barrier after barrier to adoption—chief among them the new doctrine that natural parents may assert the legal rights to the child regardless of any prior renunciation on their part. In sum, if you live the kind of reproductive life they lived in de Tocqueville's time, you will be doing so against family policy.

Children

Raising children as in de Tocqueville's time is also against family policy. First of all, the regime does not want children raised by their mothers. Look closely at the instructions to IRS Form 1040. Since 1989, if you pay someone else to raise your two children, the IRS will let you take $1,800 off your tax bill. Thus, one-earner families subsidize two-earner couples, who typically earn 60 percent more than they do. If one adds to this equation the marriage penalty built into the earned-income credit, a couple with two children and earning $27,000 per year loses $4,142 by being married rather than cohabiting. In other words, the difference between living in accord with or against modern American family policy can add up to one-fourth of some couples' income.

If you raise your children yourself, you should know that although the law allows no interference in a mother's decision to abort a child, administrative practice forbids a mother from slapping a foul mouth, spanking a recalcitrant bottom, or punishing a character fault with a beating. "The first thing a child learns here," complained a recent immigrant, "if you spank me, I'll call 911." Another immigrant was more specific: "The state comes between you and your children. Americans don't discipline their children well, and when you do it the right way, there's the danger your kids can call social services on you."[17] The difference, however, is not geographic. Americans used to take children "to the woodshed" regularly. Many still do. The difference now is that the administrative bureaucracy, often outside the framework of law, penalizes it.

This is not out of excessive tenderness: Police and juvenile officers today handcuff, strip-search (including body cavities), and otherwise "process" preadolescent children as a routine part of taking charge of them—something they did not do a generation ago. Nor are the authorities simply enforcing ways of handling children that are known to produce good or even quiescent behavior. On the contrary, while serious criminal behavior by adults has decreased somewhat in recent years from the fearful peaks of 1970–1995, there is no argument that juvenile behavior in America has worsened to the point that the country is threatened by young people whom James Q. Wilson calls feral presocial beings. His point is that they were never socialized. The data are clear: Where families are in charge of their children, the authorities are not needed, and where families are not in charge, the authorities are powerless to ensure elementary safety.[18] The fact is, the authorities are trying to inculcate a certain way of raising children, not for its results but because they value it for its own sake. They despise the alternative more than they fear the results.

America's social service bureaucracies do not lack power. They are big enough and well connected enough with police and prosecutors to exercise enormous discretion. During the late 1980s, social service agencies in New Jersey, Massachusetts, California, and Florida mounted a series of high-profile prosecutions for sexual abuse of children based on testimony coached from toddlers. In 1994–1995, the epidemic hit tiny Wenatchee, Washington. Dozens of innocent lives were wrecked. But in the end, almost all convictions in these high-profile cases were reversed.[19] Hundreds of defendants around the country who did not rate attention from the national press, however, were deeply victimized by charges of sexual molestation or for fitting the wrong "profile" in the social service agencies' operating manuals (being overweight, it seems, is prima facie evidence of being an abuser). The most remarkable feature of these incidents is the utter unity that the social service bureaucracies show in the face of their enemies in the culture wars. In 1995 in Florida, after a jury acquitted one such falsely accused victim, Grant Snowden, a district attorney named Janet Reno ordered a chain of new charges against him and kept the jury from knowing about the previous acquittal. He got five life terms.[20] Sexual molestation and "recovered memory" are yesterday's bureaucratic fads. But the social service bureaucracies are sure to invent new reasons for meddling. Unless one has friends in social services, anyone who deals with children, including their own, is only one accusation away from very big trouble.

What is the safe, politically correct method of disciplining children? What positive child-rearing habits are the social service agencies pushing? How can one restrain an unruly child in America today without getting in trouble? Use the prescription drug Ritalin, sales of which have increased 500 percent since 1991. It is routinely prescribed for something called Attention Deficit Disorder (ADD), diagnosis of which has boomed to the point that 5 percent of American boys and 2 percent of American girls are now said to be afflicted with it. In the nation's trendy prestige suburbs, the ratio is several times that. Moreover, adults are being diagnosed with ADD at a rate that Dr. Alan Zametkin of the National Institute of Mental Health and a major figure in the field describes as "just chaos," and "a cottage industry."[21] ADD is not an objective fact like a viral infection or a severed nerve. Rather, it is a label that some physicians have recently begun to use for behavioral traits known in children since time immemorial: short attention span, restlessness, distractibility, and impulsiveness. As Zametkin has noted, "Even procrastination is now said to be a sign of ADD."[22] Although Ritalin is a stimulant related to amphetamines, it undoubtedly has a calming effect and often improves performance. The schools are typically the first to point out that a child does not sit still, underperforms, or whatever. Doctors diagnose ADD. Parents increasingly agree with the diagnosis and buy the Ritalin. ADD has become socially acceptable because it relieves schools, parents, and children themselves of responsibility. Inattention was once thought to be caused by the boring nature of the material or by the child's ordinary disinterest in it. Lack of discipline was once thought to be due to bad parenting, bad character, or both. Bad performance spoke for itself. But judgments about performance, whether the school's or the child's or the parents', call for effort at self-improvement. But now, the relief from responsibility and effort for everyone comes in little bottles of value-free pills.

The issue of parental responsibility also divides those Americans who are in tune with the regime from those who are not. The legal struggle, however, is full of contradictions. About one-half the states and many localities have passed laws that hold parents liable to varying extents for the criminal acts of their minor children. The premise of such laws is that the parents must exercise control. But parental control, of course, is precisely what the public schools and the social service agencies have been working so hard to undermine. In a recent case of parental conviction, the prosecutor argued that the parents had failed to send a larcenous, violent, armed youth to counseling.[23] What good would that have done? What could have restrained such a youth? Ritalin? Nothing could have stood a chance short of memorable physical thrashings combined with strong incentives to religious conversion. But if the parents had inflicted such things on him, the social service agencies could well have prosecuted them for violating what they regard as the child's right to be free from religious compulsion and parental physical abuse. However, the secular priesthood of the state's counselors and the "procedures" of prison guards are acceptable.

To be consistent, parental responsibility laws would have to be coupled with laws that establish parental rights over children. Had such laws been proposed in de Tocqueville's America, they would have been regarded as superfluous because the notion that anyone other than parents should be responsible for the upbringing of children would have been incomprehensible. Yet in 1996, Senator Charles Grassley of Iowa proposed a law (modeled after a dozen similar ones working their way through state legislatures) that would prohibit federal, state, or local governments from interfering with or usurping "the right of a parent to direct the upbringing of the child." Grassley's proposal was rightly described by its opponents as disruptive of the established order.[24] Under the proposed law, parents could sue governmental agencies to stop their interference with the family's social, religious, and disciplinary practices. Opponents' charges that such laws would allow parents to chase Shakespeare out of school curricula and make it impossible to protect children from murderous parents are smoke-screens. In fact, home schoolers are likelier to read Shakespeare than public school attendees. But charges that parental rights laws would chase sex education and abortion counseling—indeed, all mandatory counseling—out of the public schools while reinstituting the rule of the rod in many homes are right on the mark. That is what struggles for habits are all about: One man's civilization is another's barbarism.

This is not to deny objective differences between habits on either side of the struggle. The readiest evidence of such differences consists of scores in standardized tests. Although such scores are not compre-hensive measures of human worth, they are the only widespread, ob-jective measures of performance at the same task. The test scores' first lesson is that school funding and student-teacher ratios correlate neg-atively with performance. In 1959, when the pupil-teacher ratio in the public schools was 26:1 and per pupil expenditure was in real terms one-third what it is today, SAT scores were 80 points higher.[25] The next lesson is that if socioeconomic background is controlled for, pri-vate and parochial schools perform better than public schools, but home schools do best of all.[26] This suggests that the greater the degree of parental control, the better the educational performance. This be-comes even clearer when you consider that the highest average scores come from states like Iowa, Utah, and the Dakotas, where private schools are rare, pupil-teacher ratios are high, and per capita expendi-tures are among the lowest in the country.[27] In these states, public schools are tiny, the bureaucracies weak, and parents exercise the greatest control over school policy. The clincher is the performance of recent Asian immigrants. Their socioeconomic status is very low. They attend schools where the average performance is extremely low and the modern American regime is giving its numbing, dumbing, coarsening cultural messages in their most undiluted form. Yet these children's scores typically lead the country. The one and only explana-tion is that the grip of their families is so tight it overcomes all else.

The upshot is that the modern American regime's antifamily cul-ture has an unbroken correlation with the dissipation of social capital in all its forms: the alienation of man from woman, of parent from child, of young people from the community (vice and crime) and, in the end, of young people from their own minds. It is possible to make the case that divorce, women raising children alone, and even high rates of crime are the price we should be glad to pay for wider sexual and personal choices. It is somewhat more difficult to argue that the new postfamilial American way of life is a step up in civilization, given that the package includes fostering mental debility.

Aged Parents

No account of changing American family habits would be complete without reference to the new American way of aging and dying: in the tender bosom of government-regulated institutions.

Inspired and supported by social security and Medicare's ideal of independence and pushed by their children's increasing desire for hassle-free living, aging Americans began to move into nursing homes en masse around 1970. By the 1990s, however, the *Wall Street Journal* reported:

> The current crop of older Americans appears to be more averse to nursing homes than their parents were. They are the first generation to have seen their own parents in large numbers survive into their 70s. They anguished over sending parents to nursing homes 20 or 30 years ago and now facing a similar fate, are determined not to go.[28]

And in fact, stories of subhuman ends to human lives in factorylike nursing homes staffed by "slave drivers and lion tamers" have become *images d'épinal*, goading symbols powerful enough to drive the elderly to search for just about any alternative. However, government regulations—driven as always by the private groups closest to the operating agencies, in this case operators of nursing homes and hospitals—are making it more difficult to avoid this fate. And so are many adult children. In a nutshell, new regulations are forcing the closing of many small establishments for the elderly, places like the Swiss Home in Mount Kisco, New York, that cared for people unto death through all stages of debility. New regulations require such things as "team planning of patient care"[29] and other features characteristic of the large institutions people try to avoid. This is not surprising because the rules were designed by large institutions. Similarly, when the Florida legislature passed an "aging in place" law that specifically permitted "assisted living" homes to keep frail residents there rather than turning them over to big nursing homes, the state health department—on the advice of such big homes—issued regulations to gut the intent of the law.[30]

Thus, on the one side, the elderly are finding that the government is not the family substitute it was cracked up to be, but on the other side, they are finding that their families have become less familial. The American Association of Retired Persons recently reported on the spreading phenomenon it calls "granny dumping"—the abandonment of frail elderly people by their adult children. By some estimates, in 1993, 70,000 elderly suffered a fate similar to that of John Kingery, an eighty-two-year-old suffering from Alzheimer's disease, who was abandoned at an Idaho dog track in a wheelchair with a note pinned to his chest.[31] No doubt, dumping such unwanted elderly people relieves the dumpers of an imposition on their constitutionally guaranteed right to privacy, of a restriction of their choices. One might say that such dumping amounts to aborting a family relationship—and constitutes an exercise of choice. Within the intellectual framework and habits fostered by the modern American regime, such treatment of the elderly is impeccable and even logically necessary.

Struggling for the Soul of America

De Tocqueville's America had the kind of family, economic, and civil life it did because the souls of Americans were arranged mostly by biblical religion. American life today is the way it is because a significant part of the American people order their souls according to a remarkably seamless combination of the teachings of the Supreme Court and Hugh Hefner's *Playboy* philosophy. The U.S. government is the prime combatant in a bitter war to establish—in the strict, old-fashioned European sense of the term—a new religion, complete with government-paid priests and acolytes. This, however, may strengthen contrary tendencies so much that the course of the war may resemble less the metamorphosis of Sweden in the twentieth century than America's internecine struggle in the middle of the nineteenth.

It is a commonplace that America's culture is up for grabs, that there is a "crisis of values" or a "culture war."[32] Some argue that this multiculturalism is the result of a wave of immigration almost as big as that of the turn of the twentieth century, a wave that has brought to America peoples much less in tune with the souls of the founders. The turbaned Sikhs and Hindus who are now running so many motels and

Seven-Elevens, the varied Southeast Asians of Confucian background so prevalent in the computer business, the Mexican laborers who seem less the product of Spanish than of Aztec or Mayan traditions, and the generic Middle Easterners who seem to have taken over the country's taxicabs, so goes the argument, are not interested in biblical religion. Therefore, it is impossible to impose traditional American moral standards upon them, "and because Americans cannot enforce them upon immigrants, they will tend to enforce them less on themselves."[33] The argument concludes that while monoethnic societies can survive multiculturalism, ethnically pluralistic ones must be ruined by it quickly. Hence, the proponents of this view call for a long pause in immigration to absorb such disparate cultures into the American *forma mentis*. Yet the conclusion has more merit than some of the premises because most of the new immigrants were drawn by a dim but accurate understanding of America's original culture, are more or less eager to join it, and are by no means waging war on it.

The Protagonists

In fact, neither Hinduism, nor Islam, nor Confucius, much less Quetzalcoatl, are protagonists in the struggle for the soul of America. What is preached in America's universities as multiculturalism has nothing to do with learning or affirming any foreign culture or language, let alone religion, and has everything to do with some Americans' denigration of the Judeo-Christian civilization of other Americans. America's cultural war is very strictly a domestic war. The judges and bureaucrats who are the principal aggressors in this war are hardly moved by love of foreign gods. Rather, they are moved by visceral antagonism to biblical religion, as well as by the vision of a good society ruled by themselves.

Elected officials seem to be on both sides at once. Thus, even politicians who appoint the most antireligious judges extol the importance to America of religious practice.[34] Speaking well of religion is not only smart politics in a country where the majority are churchgoers and where, according to a major survey, the overwhelming majority pray regularly.[35] It is downright unavoidable in a country where all but a few believe that whatever decline there has been in the overall quality of life—increase in crime, worsening relations between the sexes, between parents and children, and so on—is due to a decline in what just about everyone now calls "values."

Social science amply backs this popular perception that love of neighbor as well as of self depends in practice on love of God. Survey after survey correlates churchgoing with every possible index of social and personal well-being and estrangement from churches with the opposite.[36] There is little doubt that even politicians who lead personally dissolute lives and have the greatest contempt for the average God-fearing family find it convenient to preside over people who exhibit more rather than fewer of the behavioral characteristics associated with religion. If charges for social services—police, welfare, and the rest—were assessed on the basis of statistical propensity to use the services, it would be child's play to make the case that non-churchgoers should be taxed at a higher rate than their churchgoing neighbors—a kind of infidel tax.

And yet surely the most remarkable feature of contemporary American public life is the total, unrelenting consistency of the regime's attack on religion, even when the target of the attacks are the very secular consequences that even antireligious politicians themselves desire. Thus in 1980 the Supreme Court forbade the state of Kentucky from posting the Ten Commandments in schools and other public buildings, and in 1996 a federal district court in Alabama ordered a facsimile of the Ten Commandments removed from the courtroom of an Alabama judge.[37] Kentucky had argued that it has a secular interest in promoting the acts and forbearances on the list, and that by posting the list it was not thereby establishing any confession over any other. The Court agreed that the state had an interest in a population more likely to honor parents than to lie, kill, cheat, and steal. But it said, in no uncertain terms, that pursuit of such personal characteristics through a code said to have been promulgated by God is impermissible. Kentucky would have to find a way of teaching the same things that was wholly untainted by belief in God—assuming the same tenets could come from another authority with the same force. By the same token, the Court has branded as a violation of the First Amendment the use of Alcoholics Anonymous (AA) as a treatment for alcoholic prison inmates.[38] True, AA has proved to be the only successful cure for alcoholism. But since AA cures through daily, confessional prayer, the Court held that exposure to it violated the rights of convicted felons. Better that they keep their destructive habit than that they be exposed to the unconstitutional wiles of prayer.

Prayer and public observance have been the Court's most immediate target. As recently as the 1960s, every day in almost every public school in America began with a reading, usually from the Old Testament, and with some nondenominational invocation to God. The Court outlawed this.[39] Society never voted on it. In addition, almost everywhere else in the world parents who send their children to religious schools (thereby relieving the state of the burden of educating them) somehow have their tuition paid or their taxes remitted, but American parents who send their children to religious schools (mostly Catholics, Baptists, and Orthodox Jews) must pay taxes as well as tuition. Again, no vote has determined this, just court decisions. The Court has outlawed student references to God in graduation speeches, "moments of silence" during which students might pray, and even a teacher's habit of keeping a bible—along with the Koran and the Bhagavad Gita—on the desk (the Court saw through that ruse, too). In a recent case, the Court struck down a Mississippi school's practice of turning over the public address system to students who would pray aloud through it, as well as the school's providing classrooms where local clerics could conduct bible studies.[40] As one might expect, officials have acted mostly within the antireligious spirit of these judicial laws, going so far as prohibiting students from reading the Bible on school buses. Why, they should have been reading their Planned Parenthood guides to condom use instead. In what may be the most extreme manifestation of all, police in southern Illinois handcuffed and threatened with mace a fifteen-year-old girl who had gathered with others around the school's flagpole to pray before the beginning of school.[41] The regime treats as subversives those who try to practice religion more or less as it was practiced during the first three hundred years of America's history. Given the new character of the American regime, they are indeed subversives.

The U.S. government considers any public act contaminated, to the extent it is derived from Judeo-Christian religion—meaning that it must allow nothing to happen in the public realm that lends the slightest support to such acts. This results in actions by lower officials that range from the awful to the ridiculous. In the latter category, consider a typical regulation promulgated by the county counsel of Monterey County, California, for public employees for the "holiday season" (née Christmas) of 1992. It says:

Secular, or non-religious decorations and activities are appropriate decorative items in public buildings. Secular and permitted decorations include Christmas trees, and religious-neutral ornaments, tinsel, poinsettias, greenery and wreaths, reindeer, Santa Clauses, and snow-persons. Religious displays or symbols, including nativity scenes, however, are not appropriate for display in public buildings.

The memo concludes with wishes for "a joyful Holiday season, a Merry Christmas, and a Happy New Year," as well as with a warning that "no employee or visiting member of the public be offended by the use of patently religious symbols, activities, music, language, or decorations in our workplace."[42] Never mind the offense inherent in prohibiting the expression of individual employees' religious sentiments and in delegitimizing the public's desire to see its own heart and soul expressed in its own buildings. Ironically, his own memo could have been used to take action against him for saying "Merry Christmas."

The Regime's Religion

But why does the regime spread what Stephen Carter has called "a culture of disbelief?" The reason is that by and large, American elites long ago set themselves apart from the biblical religion of the common herd. When surveys of Americans' religious practices account for occupation, it becomes clear that the small percentage of nonbelievers is concentrated among nonscientific academics, lawyers, senior civil servants, the media, the arts, and the entertainment industry. Within these sectors of the population, ignorance of and contempt for religion are de rigueur. When American elites refer to people who actually believe the Christian Nicene Creed or Jewish law, they tend to use the adjectives "ultra" or "fundamentalist," implying that there are "moderate" modes of religion that they might not despise. But they themselves adhere passionately to a this-worldly religion wholly contrary to that of the Bible. This religion, not Hinduism or Zoroastrianism, is the true contender for American souls.

Whereas biblical religion requires believers to restrain their appetites and attune themselves to God's commandments, the religion of American elites commands the fulfillment of rights through demands by individuals upon government to manipulate society. In short, the establishment's secular humanism celebrates the indulgence of one's own desires and the control of others'. It subsidizes its priesthood with tax monies, requires reverence of its own icons (feminism, abortion, homosexuality, and so on), and punishes questions about the character of its saints (try mentioning the fact that Martin Luther King plagiarized his doctoral dissertation and cheated on his wife).

Above all, this religion requires vanquishing the social manifestations of the faith of the uncouth masses. The typical American elite's vision of hell is an "Ozzie and Harriet" life of distinct sex roles, no therapists, and marital fidelity, of raising children without nannies and going to church. The very pit of hell would be if this family ate red meat, smoked, and told ethnic jokes. And yet old habits die hard. Many of the elite live very conventional, industrious lives. Much of their radicalism is a matter of chic symbolism. Descended from ancestors who were "holier than thou," the adepts of today's secular religion now claim the right to look down on lesser beings because they themselves are "trendier than thou."

Liberation and sex are the main ingredients of the elite religion. One of the pillars of modern psychology, celebrated in high literature and sitcoms alike, is the desire to be free from metaphysical responsibility, from a sense of shortcoming (née, sin), to think well of one's self regardless of what one does. The serpent in this garden of self-esteem is the legacy of dysfunctional relationships with parents, spouses, and others. Thus, millions of people engage in "therapy" to overcome their legacies as "adult children," "codependents," and so forth. In the new religion, "therapy groups" and even television talk shows have replaced confessionals. The first big step to self-esteem is to project onto others responsibility for one's own imperfections confession of others' sins is a neat reversal of biblical religion.

Today's elites hardly invented extramarital sex. But they did wellnigh invent the notion that everyone has a right to it. The courts have used the civil rights laws to prohibit renters from discriminating against the unmarried. Sexual freedom requires freedom from the main consequence of sex—children. Renunciation of responsibility has always been easier for men than for women. But even for men such renunciation used to carry guilt. Guiltless freedom for men and almost the same for women could come about only if the child could be disposed of, sight unseen. This is why abortion, in addition to being a matter of convenience, is a spiritual icon.

Freedom also means not being burdened by aging parents. The welfare state has taken material responsibility for them. But so long as they live, they are a claim on consciences. That is why euthanasia, too, is a cultural icon.

The effects of the successful affirmation of these icons are straight-forward. Public opinion has accommodated itself to some extent to the reality of abortion. In 1973, after centuries during which abortion had been a heinous crime or "grave misprision," polls showed that some three-fourths thought it wrong; by 1996, after two decades during which abortion had been a basic constitutional right, only two-thirds thought it wrong, and these respondents were split many ways on what, if anything, to do about it. The American Medical Association, which once strenuously opposed abortion, now officially endorses it and has abolished the 2,400-year-old Hippocratic Oath (which for-swears abortion and euthanasia and pledges the physician to work ex-clusively for the interest of the patient) as a requirement for entry into the profession. Still, nearly all physicians and nurses will have nothing to do with it, which is why abortion is unavailable in 83 percent of America's counties—abortionists work long days and fly a lot. But the logic of the law continues to push. The American College of Obstetri-cians and Gynecologists, which is reluctant to train new abortionists, has been shy about stating its position and incurs the wrath of the Establishment's voice—the *New York Times*'s editorial page—for "avoid[ing] responsibility to train doctors in a legal procedure."[43]

The greatest consequences of the legalization of abortion—other than the destruction of some 30 million innocents—stem from the ar-guments the Court has used to justify its actions. As it had done in Dred Scott (1857) when it declared slaves to be property rather than humans, the Court in *Roe v. Wade* declared the unborn to be mere parts of their mothers, wholly at their disposal. Just as Dred Scott's de-humanization of slaves tended to take away such little human regard as society had for them, so the Court's reasoning in Roe has reduced the high human regard and legal status that society once granted the un-born. The unborn are still legal persons in that they can inherit prop-erty. But whereas assailants of pregnant women who killed a child in utero were once routinely prosecuted for murder, the criminal courts nowadays understandably have become reluctant to protect against a stranger a being whom the mother has an untrammeled right to kill at any time for any reason and in any manner she chooses. Certainly, therefore, the mother has the right to kill her child to alter the succes-sion of inheritance rights to an estate. That practically negates the un-born's right to inherit. So it appears that abortion is creating a legal category of outlaw and a category of individuals who have the right to act toward that outlaw outside the restraints of law.

Above all, of course, abortion abolishes the whole concept of innocence or guilt from discussions of what may be legitimately done to whom. Anyone in the outlaw category need not have done anything to be condemned to the ultimate penalty. He need merely be in the charge of someone who desires to inflict it.

The change in American public opinion has been even more drastic as regards euthanasia, the putting to death of the terminally ill. Whereas in 1973 the topic was unmentionable, ten years later Colorado's governor, Richard Lamm,[44] made it a constant theme that old people were burdening the younger generations and had a duty to get out of the way. By 1996, this concept had sunk so far into Americans' souls that no jury could be found to convict Dr. Jack Kevorkian of manslaughter for admitting to having helped to dispatch dozens of willing patients. America's acceptance of euthanasia, combined with the high cost of health care, the high value of most elderly people's real estate, and America's commercial culture, combine to form a logic that frightens even Dutch practitioners of it. One told an interviewer that "in view of the financial cost that the care of patients imposes on relatives and society under the U.S. health care system, the legalization of euthanasia in America would be 'an open door to get rid of these patients.'" Another said that when American doctors asked him how to introduce euthanasia into the United States, he always replied: "Don't . . . I wouldn't trust myself as a patient if your medical profession, with their commercial outlook, should have that power."[45]

THE TEMPLES AND THE PRIESTS
The temples and priesthoods of these cults, at universities and in the arts and humanities, are largely funded by the U.S. government, which enforces their great powers over American culture. Even many private universities receive one-half of their funds from the U.S. government through various grants and federally guaranteed student loans. The U.S. government does not lack power over the temples of culture and routinely uses it to force universities to do a variety of things, for instance, de-funding men's wrestling and track teams so that a variety of women's teams might be established, as well as making sure that "protected classes" get special treatment. Therefore, it would be hard to argue that government is not responsible for the universities' uniform hostility to religion, to Western culture, and to America in general.

That hostility is a consequence of the fact that since the late 1960s, outside the hard sciences and with few exceptions, university faculties have hired only political leftists and adepts of the elite religion. A 1984 comparison by Hoover Institution fellow George Marotta of voter registration records in the vicinity of Stanford University with the membership of the university's departments of humanities and social sciences found that only 11 percent of faculty in these departments were registered as Republicans, most of whom had been hired prior to the mid-1960s. Some departments had no Republicans at all. In the 1990s, with the exception of economics, it was inconceivable that any Stanford humanities department would hire a white male Republican—never mind an overtly religious one. With very few exceptions, these figures would be the same for Princeton or for Podunk U. The U.S. government does not worry about this because it approves.

The universities teach the nation's schoolteachers, who are the backbone of the Democratic Party. At the party's 1992 convention, 13 percent of the delegates were members of teachers' unions, and many other delegates were spouses, parents, or children of members of the teachers' unions.[46] At the 1996 Republican convention, presidential candidate Bob Dole briefly touched on the relationship between the educational establishment, the U.S. government, and the Democratic party. But he was quickly persuaded that to speak this way is to put oneself outside the establishment. And so it is.

The lack of diversity of the universities and the views of teachers' unions on matters of the soul may be seen most easily in the standards for the teaching of world and American history in the nation's public schools, amounting to a veritable antihistory, developed by university professors appointed by a government panel.[47]

The U.S. government abets this near monopoly of the new secular religion with the nearly $400 million it grants each year through the National Endowment for the Arts (NEA). In their practical aspects, these endowments are straightforward patronage mills operated with taxpayer funds by cliques. The chances of an artist who is a realist and works on religious themes being supported through this agency make those of a white conservative professor at Harvard look great by comparison. President John F. Kennedy dedicated the NEA to "grace and beauty" and told Americans that their tax dollars would buy "contributions to the human spirit." Instead, the endowment has subsidized a class at war with the culture of the average American. Pictures of Christ and of the pope submerged in urine, artists whose performance consists of urinating on a picture of Christ, or of interactive genital contact with the audience, of naked people covered with paint rolling on paper, of black masses, or of homoeroticism, pedophilia, and so on, are the rule rather than the exception.[48] The endowment enables people to do things they would not otherwise have the leisure to do and puts the government-approved stamp of high culture on things that were, and in many cases still are, crimes. They also shut nonconforming artists out of, say, the theater and art shows by enabling subsidized artists to tie up the schedules of theaters and galleries. In short, through the NEA, the U.S. government puts Gresham's law to work in American culture.

The Consequences

It is impossible to objectify the spiritual effects of a culture. Aristotle wrote that the only path to true happiness is doing the right things for the right reasons. But while one cannot measure from within the happiness of the adherents of the new American religion, it is easy enough to measure their behavior. Gross statistics on crime, child abuse, drug use, suicide, and even SAT scores do not identify the different mentalities behind the figures. But they make clear that, over the past generation, as the new religion has claimed a greater share of America's souls, life has become nastier. Moreover, the indices of nastiness have climbed (or dived) most steeply precisely in those sectors of the population most receptive of government guidance. As Myron Magnet has shown, the underclass—defined not by income but by a debilitating set of attitudes—resulted from the acceptance by the poor in general and the black community in particular of the new secular religion's main tenets, which are very different from those that ministers had been preaching in the black churches.[49]

The changing mix of the American soul is reflected by behavior in the rest of society as well. The sextupling of cases of child abuse that has accompanied the quintupling of abortions since 1973 and that affects all classes cannot but be related to the idea that children are a bothersome occasional byproduct of the exercise of the inalienably private right of self-fulfillment. Since there is no essential difference between a prebirth and a postbirth baby, it was inevitable that as the law habituated people to sacrifice preborn babies to their convenience, they would learn quickly enough to do the same thing with ones who are older and more bothersome. More and more, one reads of girls, sometimes aided by boyfriends, giving birth in college dorms or movie theaters and then either killing the baby outright or putting the remains in a garbage bag. More disturbing are the predictable reactions of the elite media and public officials. In November 1996, the governor of New Jersey said of a couple of high-born college students who had crushed their newborn's skull that they should have considered their options more carefully. Indeed. Had they managed to crush the skull while it was still inside the mother, they would have performed a partial birth abortion, something endorsed by the president of the United States, the Supreme Court, and any number of governors. The *New York Times* suggested that a charge of murder was unwarranted because other times and places have been more tolerant of such things.[50] That is the point: The regime is fostering quite another civilization among us.

America's great epidemic of drug use—roughly one-half of high-school seniors have at least tried marijuana—is the matrix of almost every kind of dysfunction. But it is necessary to keep in mind that these all-too-familiar dysfunctions affect least of all people whose souls are filled by biblical religion and most of all those who follow the regime's religion. For our purposes, it is not necessary to show that a causal relationship exists between the government-sponsored secular religion and the many and varied manifestations of spiritual emptiness, but only to note their correlation.

Because America's culture wars are about two sets of separate and unequal beliefs and ways of life, they are leading to a progressive sorting out of the population according to religion—not any separation among Protestants, Catholics, and Jews but rather the drawing together of people who strive to live under the Ten Commandments in the face of those who live by the new religion. The legalization of abortion, for example, has led to a natural sorting of marrying couples according to their radically incompatible views on how to treat the products of their union. The trivialization of the marriage contract is also naturally separating those whose religion mandates permanent unions from those under no such inner constraint. Marriage, and indeed friendship, are possible only when people share the things that are dearest to them, from art to personal habits. Even music is becoming partisan.[51] Since the differences between the two cannot possibly be bridged, we are likely to see two populations living out the increasingly different consequences of their cultures.

Every crime, every outrage, every instance of unfulfilled responsibility naturally raises the cry, "There oughta be a law," or a tougher law, or at least elicits the response that more government money and attention should be devoted to the problem. Natural as this is, however, one must remember that it is easier for government to spread than to cure pathologies. James Q. Wilson has reminded us that

> there are only two restraints on behavior—morality enforced by individual conscience or social rebuke, and law, enforced by the police and the courts. If society is to maintain a behavioral equilibrium, any decline in the former must be matched by a rise in the latter (or vice versa). If familial and traditional restraints on wrongful behavior are eroded, it becomes necessary to increase the legal restraints.[52]

True, at any given time any people must choose between more morality and more government. But what lessons does government teach when it punishes, exalts, and spends? If its lessons lessen the soul's own capacity to discipline itself, society can easily spiral into greater repression, yielding ever less order.

Note that since 1965, the United States has increased spending on social uplift programs by 800 percent and has increased the rate of incarceration fourfold, while reaping a fivefold increase in felonies and leaving people less happy than before. The failure of this impeccable quantity of carrots and sticks indicts their soulless quality. The U.S. government has been trying, in Senator Joseph Biden's words, to provide something to which people can say yes. The problem is precisely that in so doing it has been tearing down the things to which America had been saying Amen.

Machiavelli's teaching on these matters—"fear of the prince . . . may temporarily supply the want of religion"[53]—further cautions that any attempt to drive out religion or supplant it works against the grain of reality. Yet Machiavelli missed a bigger point—that the social consequences of bad soulcraft pale in comparison with the spiritual consequences.

Chapter 13
AMERICA'S DEFENDERS

[War is] the gravedigger of decadences.
—CHARLES DE GAULLE, *The Edge of the Sword*

THE ULTIMATE TEST of any regime is its capacity to "summon up the blood"—to draw out of itself and its people the willingness to kill and be killed, the coherent preparations and the wise operations that win wars. Especially in democracies, war and preparations for war test a people's character—its capacity to produce high-quality goods, its capacity for order and self-sacrifice, the authority by which families send their sons to fight, the spiritual strength of fighters and leaders alike.

On the eve of World War II, Adolf Hitler fatally underestimated America's character. On the basis of static economic analysis, he thought the American people could spare little of their $100 billion GDP to affect the war in Europe. But the American people miraculously doubled their GDP and devoted one-half of it to the war, producing more armaments than the rest of the world combined. Hitler thought that the Americans were mongrels. Instead, as Lincoln had hoped, the American people had become "blood of the blood and flesh of the flesh" with the founders, through the acceptance of the Declaration of Independence's "self-evident" truths. Their unity amazed the world. Hitler thought that American families would not give their sons and could not muster a fighting spirit because they were in the grip of a pacifist religion. But the American people mounted a crusade to kill him. When the war was over, the Americans fed their defeated enemies. This break with the custom of conquerors, which awed the world even further, also proceeded from a uniquely religious character. In sum, the American people of the mid-twentieth century were no less the world's wonders than their de Tocquevillean forefathers had been.

In the half century after World War II, much has happened that has altered the American people's habits about work and government, about family and religion. At the top of society, the American regime has changed even more. No one can be sure how the Americans of the year 2000 would react to a challenge of World War II's magnitude. But they could not deal with the crisis as did their grandparents because the regime has instilled in many of today's Americans habits different from those of their grandparents, and even more so than those of their forebears of Washington's or de Tocqueville's time.

Contemporary Americans are not as likely as their grandparents were to see a need and take charge of a project to fill that need. How could they be, after decades of training in making sure that "all the players are on board," especially the government regulators? Contemporary Americans know that to start a project without, say, an environmental impact statement, could lead to jail. Much like Europeans or Japanese, they have reason to believe that certain contracts, jobs, roles, and activities are set aside for people specially designated from above. Although the storehouse of interpersonal trust is fuller in America than just about anywhere, the very fact that the American legal profession has been mushrooming shows that decisions, agreements, and transactions are taking more time and have become more complex than ever before. Add to this the fact that the proportion of Americans doing useful work has declined, and it is difficult to imagine countless new factories, new processes, and redoubled results springing up overnight as they did during World War II.

Contemporary Americans also lack their grandparents' experience in civic responsibility. As the number of school boards, companies of volunteer firemen, and all manner of local officials has shrunk, the percentage of the population habituated to exercising leadership and responsibility for others has also plummeted. In irreducible personal ways, government has become something that "they" do rather than something "we" do. One of the essential elements of military power, whether on the home front or the fighting fronts, is that as many individuals as possible must behave as if everything depended on them. Of all the advantages over other combatants that America enjoyed in World War II, perhaps the greatest was the tendency of Americans to take matters into their own hands. One corollary of civic responsibility, of course, is the sentiment that everyone is doing his fair share. Contemporary Americans have become accustomed to the proposition that war is the business of those whom we hire to wage it.

As the years pass, American families are becoming less and less like the families for whom American fighting men fought in World War II. Nearly all who fought then had grown up with their mothers and fathers and did not want to shame them. Even more ominous than the fact that, as already noted, white children born nowadays stand only a 30 percent chance of growing up with both natural parents (and black children a 6 percent chance) is the near-total replacement of the concept of shame in the raising of children with that of a self-esteem not tied to behavior. Military recruits raised without habituation in honor and shame could not be trained quickly and could not be expected to perform with as little supervision as the Americans of World War II. Like the low-life recruits of Europe's ancien régimes, they would have to be given artificial families and artificial courage. Even harsher discipline would be needed to make deracinated modern youths risk their lives because, of course, so many lack faith in life after death.

But surely the greatest reason that the America of the year 2000 could not duplicate America's feat in World War II is that its regime, in addition to inculcating habits that are not conducive to military efficiency, itself has a character less than fit for the ultimate test. In a nutshell, the modern American regime is constitutionally not oriented to generating military power and has substantially alienated itself from those in American society—people attuned to the America of yesteryear—who do produce military power.

The New Elites

The character and mentality of officials in charge of foreign and defense policy have diverged from the original American pattern no less radically than those of the federal judiciary. By the 1990s, the senior levels of the Departments of State and Defense, the Central Intelligence Agency, not to mention the major foundations concerned with these matters, were staffed by people who for the most part did not serve in the military and share deep aversion to military matters as well as social aversion to military people. They either worked for or admired Senator J. William Fulbright, author of *The Arrogance of Power*. They made their careers helping to defeat the United States in Vietnam, worked to diminish and restrain American military power in the Cold War, and jeered Ronald Reagan's call to cast communism on the scrap heap of history. By all means at their disposal they delay and denature programs to defend America against missiles. They came to power gradually through the government's front door, through the best schools and through the patronage of elders who advanced them precisely to promote their ways. Hence, their accession to power amounted to a transmutation of the Establishment.[1]

People like Anthony Lake and Strobe Talbott—like their friend President Bill Clinton—learned about America's role in the world from William Appleman Williams's *The Tragedy of American Diplomacy*. Like their mentors and patrons, the extreme Left of the 1950s and 1960s, the future monopolizers of the foreign policy establishment thought the American people ignorant, violence-prone jingoists and believed that America stood in the path of the world's progress toward peace and socialism. They believed that modernity, and especially nuclear weapons, dictated a new approach to international relations based on the widest possible collective security arrangements rather than on American military power.[2] They therefore believed that the biggest threats to peace lay, first, in the tendency of Americans to believe that carrying "the free man's burden"[3] gave them the right to pursue their interests and, second, in the American military leaders who clung to outdated notions about winning wars. They saw themselves as the indispensable sophisticates who would make the American people safe for the world. Their mission also was to restrain a nuclear trigger-happy military as well as to "crack" its noxious culture. They thought themselves entitled to lead because they had weaned themselves from their fellow Americans' retrograde morality, militarism, and interestedness, because they were open to the Socialist world and the Third World—and yes—because their differences from their fellow Americans made them morally superior.

In sum, they were eager to manage America's wide involvement in the world, but they neither knew nor appreciated military things, and they had at heart the opposite of their country's grandeur. Hence, as their influence on American policy increased, a gap opened between the ends of American policy and the means by which those ends were pursued.

Insolvency

In the Korean War, American elites began the practice of sending their fellow citizens to kill and be killed, not to win wars for America's interest, righteousness, or glory but rather to pressure other governments to negotiate terms that would be in the best interest of the world community. That is, they began to use their fellow Americans' lives to try realizing such figments of the imagination as "collective security" and "stability." While both the troops and the professional military of the age thought that the Korean War was worth winning if it was worth dying for, and that if it was not worth winning no one should die for it, the Establishment deemed these thoughts laughably unsophisticated. Ordinary Americans damned the regime's management of the Korean War with the label "no-win war." In the end, the Korean War taught few lessons because both the Establishment and the American people thought the other would not act that way again, and neither understood how deeply the other was committed to its ways.

While ordinary Americans saw nuclear weapons as more effective means for limiting damage to America and winning wars—the Eisenhower administration described them as "more bang for the buck"—the growing consensus of elite opinion saw them as thaumaturgic instruments for transcending the human condition. By building a U.S.-Soviet nuclear balance that would be stable to eternity, the Establishment judged that we could make the Soviet regime a partner and, indeed, that we could act as if, for all practical purposes, nuclear weapons had never been invented. We could thus banish major war forever. The regime cast its policies about nuclear matters in pseudotechnical arms control lingo impenetrable by the American people. After 1963, the Establishment built and planned to use nuclear weapons to maximize civilian casualties in the Soviet Union, while making sure that Soviet nuclear weapons would have unimpeded access to America. This is why the regime has always regarded attempts to build American antimissile defenses as threats to peace. Ever since pollsters have probed these matters, the American people have shown that they do not know—and when told, they do not believe—that their government has no means and no intention to defend their lives in case of nuclear or missile attack. Consequently, were even one missile to land on a deliberately undefended America, it would destroy the social contract just as surely as lives.

Americans did not want the Cold War to turn hot. And if it did, they wanted the fighting to be done as much as possible by nuclear weapons, as far away as possible. The American people never really grasped that beginning in 1961, the Kennedy administration's policy of "flexible response" meant that thenceforth it would counter Soviet aggression with European and American bodies rather than with nuclear weapons and that the result of the Establishment's nuclear phobia had been to make the world safe for conventional war—and for even more personal kinds of war as well. Then came Vietnam.

In Vietnam, the American people came to learn that "limited war" meant that the Establishment would balance its foreign policy with the people's bodies. The Establishment learned that while it was OK for people like themselves to direct such wars as Vietnam, they would not send their own children to fight in them. They sent the sons of the middle and lower classes. But the elite would not even consider letting them win. Ever since the Vietnam War, the regime has promulgated the proposition that public opinion hampered America's conduct of military operations and made victory impossible. Not so. In 1968, 70 percent of Americans opposed any cessation of bombing of North Vietnam, while only 23 percent identified themselves as "doves."[4] Alas, the regime's heart and mind was with the 23 percent. As then Secretary of Defense Robert McNamara explained (much later) in his book *In Retrospect*, he and his colleagues were trying above all to forestall the majority of Americans who wanted victory because they themselves wanted no such thing.

The Kennedy and Johnson administrations refused to identify the government of North Vietnam as the enemy or as evil—President Johnson taught Americans to see poverty and disease as the real culprit—and while American administrations wanted to pressure North Vietnam, they rejected any military plans that would have threatened its regime. They (and only they) believed that military victory was impossible for either side and that the struggle would end in amicable negotiations. Thus, America's self-described "best and brightest" would fight the Vietnam War on the new model: value-free and under peacetime conditions. They expected America's unwashed to lend themselves to the regime's delicate maneuvers. Therefore, they strongly decried those who urged them to choose between victory and withdrawal, refused to declare a state of war, and vigorously upheld the legitimacy of those in their own political and social circles who were working to defeat the armed forces they were sending into battle.[5] Indeed, the regime convinced itself that it was fighting on the wrong side of the war, that the real enemy was America's arrogant anticommunism, and that the greatest service it could render to humanity would be to scuttle the American effort. In 1977, in a speech at the University of Notre Dame written by that paragon of the regime, Henry Kissinger's former assistant Anthony Lake, later to be President Clinton's national security adviser, President Jimmy Carter explained that only by losing the Vietnam War did Americans "find our way back to our own values." Thus convinced, the regime sent 50,000 men to die and six times that many to be wounded, until the American people forced the regime into political bankruptcy.

But the bankruptcy led to a complete takeover of the regime by precisely those elements of the Establishment—personified by Anthony Lake himself and replicated in high office throughout the foreign policy establishment—that embodied the greatest discrepancy between the ends they sought, the means they could muster, and the willingness of the American people to lend themselves to either. What Americans and their leaders learned about themselves and one another in Vietnam caused wounds that have only widened.

The Secession of the Elite

By withdrawing its bodies from a war it was conscious of waging in its own peculiar way, the regime taught the American people the most corrosive of lessons. By the early 1960s, the American people had become comfortable with the military draft. Knowing that the fittest stood a good chance of serving, college boys filled the Reserve Officers Training Corps (ROTC), and recent graduates who felt the draft's hot breath often signed up for Officer Candidate School. But beginning in 1965, the sentiment flowed down from the highest toward the lower parts of American society that evading the draft was socially preferable to going to Vietnam. As trendy entertainers urged college girls to "say yes to the boys who say no," college deans released girls from the parietal arrangements that were then universal to attend all-night antiwar events. Deferments for education (originally meant as postponements of service) became upper-middle-class exemptions. American elites tended to see the end of the draft as a release from the responsibility of conducting foreign policies that the American people would have to approve of enough to commit their own lives. But those who most wanted volunteer armed forces were surest not to volunteer. They remained almost as eager as ever to have a muscular foreign policy. But foreign policy became a spectator sport. The regime would play global chess with hired hands.

The end of the draft was only the beginning of the elite's secession from the military. In subsequent years, as the elite demilitarized itself, the military became ever more distinct from the rest of society. Since 1973, the Pentagon and Congress have marshaled figures to argue that America's armed forces are not unrepresentative of society. Perhaps the most subtle of these efforts shows that (based on average family income within particular zip codes) the proportion of youth from any given income bracket in the general population differs from the proportion of the youth from those brackets in the armed forces by only a few percentage points—except for the top sixth of the income scale, which gives only about one-half its expected share of members.[6] Even leaving aside that the volunteers from high-income zip codes are likeliest to come from low-income enclaves therein, the argument's basic proposition is refuted easily enough by ordinary observation of American society. At Stanford, Harvard, and similar training grounds for the Establishment, perhaps one in one thousand graduates enters the military. The professoriate, the legal profession, the media, finance, and even corporate bureaucracy (except for military contractors) are now almost exclusively without veterans younger than age sixty. Nor do their families serve. Seldom do they have friends who do. So, the policymaking class deliberates about what risks and burdens are acceptable for the U.S. military as if its members were what they are—strangers.

Whereas prior to the Vietnam War streams of new veterans were flowing into country clubs and Congress as well as into blue-collar American Legion posts, today fewer than one-third of members of Congress have ever served, and the proportion is dropping. Four percent of the Clinton administration's political appointees were veterans.

Nor is this a matter of revocable policies. The young elites who do not enter the military are part of a regime culture that inculcates value-free nonviolence starting in preschool, that frowns on toy guns for tots, treats hunting as semicriminally as smoking, and labels the very notion of citizen militias subversive. The members of today's American regime lack the capacity to serve, as well as the moral authority to lead in things military. So war, which is too important to be left to the military—especially in democracies—is becoming the military's exclusive business.

The military has contributed to this separation by discouraging all but long-term enlistments and by nearly shutting down the sources of noncareer officers. Officer Candidate schools function primarily to process physicians and lawyers. Scholarships have transformed ROTC into a source of mostly regular commissions. Pilots must now commit for at least nine years. Even as the military downsizes, classes at the military academies are near all-time highs and seem to have more children of military officers than ever. The military has become accustomed to blaming the decadence of civilian society for problems in its own ranks. Thus when the U.S. Naval Academy discovered massive academic dishonesty among cadets in 1995, its spokesmen blamed civilian society rather than any shortcoming of the academy's. The military, in short, does not want to be mixed up with civilian society any more than the regime wants it to be.

The regime has also fostered changes in the military's internal ways. Beginning in 1961, Secretary of Defense Robert McNamara changed the criteria for promoting officers. Whereas the post–World War II military had sought to elevate men with the potential to become like Admirals Arleigh Burke and Hyman Rickover or General George Patton—hard-charging types who would gain the love of their men, get the job done, and ask about regulations later—McNamara sought to weed such people out in favor of those who get advanced degrees, serve in Washington, and compete for the favor of civilian officials.

The Vietnam War massively sorted out the officer corps by drawing a line between those who thought it unethical to hazard lives without seeking victory—who left—and those who were persuaded easily enough to regard the war as a chance to "punch tickets" for advancement in rank. The Vietnam War produced a big crop of morally emasculated officers. Soldiers and sailors, but especially officers, have learned to live with superiors who are out for themselves. Since McNamara, Republican and Democratic administrations alike have appointed to the top ranks that shape the culture below them such quintessential briefcase carriers as Alexander Haig and Colin Powell—men more at ease leaking to reporters than leaking in the woods. The new tone of the officer corps sharpened the contrast that had long existed between it and the senior enlisted ranks by reason of the fact that advancement therein is by competitive examination rather than by competitive favor seeking. Finally, the tone of the lower ranks has been set by the promise tendered for recruitment—a well-paid opportunity for interesting but not dangerous self-development. War would disabuse such a military structure of many illusions, and devastate its leadership.

In sum, because of divergent political personalities and interests, the regime and the military have been developing clashing ways.

The Great Divorce

The regime has reduced the size of the armed forces while sending its members to the ends of the earth on nonwar missions that have required them to be away from home for unprecedented periods of time. It has also imposed on them the kind of sexual integration typical of contemporary coed college dorms. But unlike colleges, the military has punished its members (much less often women) for the kind of sexual behavior that occurs naturally in such circumstances. From the top of the armed forces have come calls for restraint in deployments, while top and bottom are ever less reticent about their political disrespect for the regime.

In the 1990s, the U.S. government has sent naval, ground, and air forces to the Middle East, to Africa, to Bosnia, and to Haiti. True, such troops have suffered violent deaths at rates inferior to those of their cohorts in civilian life. But by spending ten-month-long unaccompanied deployments in rapid succession, they have been inconvenienced far more than the recruiting pitches led them to expect. By 1997 the Pentagon had concluded that one-third of the personnel serving in Bosnia had become "psychological casualties" as a result of privations suffered for no evident sufficient reason.[7] As such "long and lite" missions proliferate and as the troops lose their combat skills, senior officers worry that they are going to be put into situations they will not be able to cope with and that since the troops no longer train with tactical nuclear weapons, they would certainly not be able to cope, outnumbered, with a determined enemy like North Korea. Troops and officers also resent being put into liaison situations that amount to subordination to United Nations officials. For all these reasons, the military has become the biggest lobby for limiting military commitments. As a popular recruiting ad on television shows, the regime regards the military as tools by which it can play global chess. Hence it resents the military's reticence to lend itself as a mixture of cowardice and insubordination.

Insubordinate sentiment and habits are certainly a result of the regime's sexual rules for the armed forces. One out of eight persons in uniform is now female. Women enter the services through the same avenues as men and undergo the same training, though it is neither as much nor as hard. They fill nearly all military occupational specialties, process battlefield intelligence, drive trucks (with power steering), and fly transports (and some fly fighter planes), although they are officially not allowed in combat. Men who serve alongside them complain that women do not perform as well and that they have to pick up the slack without even the privilege of complaining. Pregnancy rates vary according to the type of unit and deployment. During Desert Storm it was about 10 percent. The army officially states that 12 percent of its women are pregnant at any given time, while on some extended navy cruises the rate has reached one-third.[8] Sexual relations between men and women of all ranks are so pervasive in the field that the U.S. Army Medical Research and Materiel Command issued a Guidance for Small Unit Leaders (July 1996) urging them to pass on such military lore as "ensure partners use a new condom," "urinary directors minimize disrobing during urination," and "avoid anal intercourse." Yet there is widespread recognition that the military has become a sexual jungle. Men complain that the presence of women creates sexual bonanzas for some and tantalizing situations full of danger for others. Mere accusations of sexual harassment or of failing to be appropriately attentive to accusations thereof has ended hard-won careers.[9] Like all purges, this one provides opportunities to settle personal scores and lays up rancor for the future. To all this, President Clinton added the prospect that the services might have to tolerate open homosexuality in the ranks. At any rate, it seems that the services may be more occupied with sexual recriminations than with preparing to fight enemies.

There is no doubt that members of the U.S. armed forces vote Republican as overwhelmingly as public schoolteachers vote Democratic. Nor can one miss the growing contempt with which, from private to general, the armed forces refer to President Clinton and to civilian leaders in general, sometimes to their faces. They surely do not regard them as fountains of wisdom or as having their best interests at heart. The shallowness of the reservoirs of habitual respect is evident in the reaction of American troops in Saudi Arabia to Secretary of State James A. Baker III on a pre-Thanksgiving visit during Operation Desert Shield. Troops who had been in hot tents for two months without prospect of an end or of a reasonable purpose greeted him with expletives and invited him to drink hot water with them.[10] They are nowhere near mutiny, but then again neither have they suffered the kinds of misfortunes that usually trigger such things.

There has been much discussion of late on how civilian control over the armed forces may be strengthened. Suggestions include "rebuild[ing] the diversity of the officer corps, particularly with respect to prevailing attitudes and perspectives."[11] In practice, this means an increase in indoctrination sessions (all personnel are already required to attend "training" sessions on sexual etiquette) and perhaps the establishment of officers specifically charged with the task of ensuring the reliability of other officers. This would be quite foreign to America, and to republics in general. But there seems to be no consideration given to returning to the republican tradition that citizen control of the military means participation in the military by prominent citizens. Indeed, it is inconceivable that the children of Clinton officials or of the Harvard faculty might ever decide to join the military en masse for any reason whatever. They just do not have that in them. In any event, history teaches that regimes that bemoan the diffidence of their armed forces while refusing to take part in them might as well bemoan the law of gravity.

The modern American regime's fostering of habits not particularly conducive to military power will matter only when a serious military challenge arises. The very belief that such a challenge will not arise in our lifetime, as many have come to think since the end of the Cold War, is most likely to bring one about. Still, America's size and geography make Lincoln's statement that "all the armies of Europe, Asia, and Africa combined, with a Bonaparte at their head, disposing of all the treasure of the earth (our own excepted) in their military chest . . . could not by force take a drink from the Ohio or make a track upon the Blue Ridge in a trial of a thousand years" as valid at the turn of the twenty-first century as in 1838.[12] Appropriately, Lincoln went on to warn that if destruction was to be America's lot, we ourselves would have to be its author and finisher. In short, even if we are fortunate enough that foreigners do not take advantage of our debilities, the habits that the regime has been pressing upon the American people diminish us and foster strife among us.

Commerce, Montesquieu taught, is the profession of equals. As our regime lowers barriers between business and politics, it fosters unearned inequality and thus renders us less fit for the kind of economics our forefathers preached. It trains us to get ahead by getting close to power and to seek security over self-reliance. We thus acquire some of the thirst for privilege that sank the Soviet economy, some of the reliance on bureaucracy that has robbed the Japanese of the fruits of their labors, some of the passion for security that has hardened Europe's economic arteries, and some of the craving for unearned money that makes the Third World what it is.

Ruling and being ruled in turn, taught Aristotle, is the essence of citizenship, and citizens are people who share equally the privileges of the regime. As our regime increases the number of rules and bureaucrats and as it transfers power to the judiciary, it trains us to be subjects. The metal detectors that shield the entrances to federal buildings set aside for nonfederal employees, like the security barriers that now close the streets around the White House against a domestic threat presumed to be greater than that of our enemies in World War II, teach civilians and government workers alike that they are each other's natural enemies.

As we let go of the old American view that law is somehow the expression of right and get into the habit of thinking of it as a means of gaining advantage, we learn, like republican Romans, to argue about who ought to live off whom and who should be treated as a human being and who should be proscribed. By getting out of the habit of running our own locality and ensuring our own safety and becoming consumers of government, some of us are gaining a taste for Singapore-style efficiency. Having learned that equality and modern government are incompatible, we focus on social mobility.

Nature and religion make family ties that bind and chafe. Our regime, like so many others in the modern world, teaches that those bonds are dysfunctional and offers help to those who want to loosen them or live without them. Hence, with our regime's help, men and women are learning that they do not have to marry and that they do not have to bear responsibility for the children they conceive. We are acquiring some aspects of the Swedish lifestyle, though laced with the bitterness that characterizes relations between the sexes in Russia.

George Washington and his colleagues taught that the American regime is built on the foundation of biblical religion. Our regime, by contrast, has sought to remove that religious foundation from public life and to train us in the exercise of a new, secular religion. But like the citizens of the Roman republic, we are losing the old while not acquiring the new. Indeed, like the modern Israelis, we are dividing along religious lines.

The purpose of this long essay has been to explore the effects of regimes on the habits that most affect the quality of human lives. Nowhere is the regime anything like the sole influence on these habits. In America, resistance to the influences of the regime is particularly strong. Throughout American society, there is plentiful evidence of secession from the regime and of countercurrents against it. The computer software industry has raised up a set of products that change too fast to be regulated. The government's postal system has been overwhelmed by undisciplined private initiatives. A passion for deregulation does battle with environmental pretexts for regulation. To regain control over their lives, people move to gated communities or to exurbs. Tax avoidance is growing. More and more families are opting out of public education, and networks of families are springing up to keep the official culture at bay. For some, Branson, Missouri, has replaced Hollywood as the standard for entertainment. And, of course, people are sorting themselves out according to religious practice. But secessions, however numerous, and the countercurrents, however powerful and ominous, are no more than that. Even in America, there is only one regime at a time.

Notes

Introduction

1. U.S. Department of Commerce, Bureau of the Census, 1991.

2. Sophocles. *The Plays and Fragments*, vol. 3, trans. R. C. Jebb (Cambridge: Cambridge University Press, 1891), 126–127 (ll. 662–663 in Greek text).

3. Norman J. Ornstein, Thomas E. Mann, Michael J. Malbin. *Vital Statistics of Congress 1995–1996* (Washington, D.C.: Congressional Quarterly, 1996), 22, 28.

4. John Leo. "Bust Those Candy Cane Felons," *Newsweek*, December 30, 1996, 26.

5. 1 Sam. 8. The corruption begins with King David's appropriation of Bathsheba, extends to the civil wars between David and Saul and David and Absalom, and is detailed in the book of Kings. This divine warning was the centerpiece of Thomas Paine's argument against monarchy in *Common Sense*, the most influential and least original piece of writing ever published in America. Less well known and more pervasive were countless similar references from America's pulpits. See Ellis Sandoz, ed., *Political Sermons of the American Revolution* (Indianapolis: Liberty Press, 1991).

6. In the modern world several of the categories of regimes mentioned by the classics—real monarchies and timocratic warrior regimes—hardly exist. In addition, while some might want to characterize the Islamic Republic of Iran as a theocracy, comparison with the real thing—ancient Egypt or pre-1950 Tibet—shows that modern Iran has a government well within the normal range of Muslim statecraft. As for the Aristotelian category of the mixed regime, I treat most actual regimes as belonging to that category broadly conceived.

7. This commonsense principle, known as the *via negativa*, is the basis of the structure of, among other works, Dante's *Divine Comedy*. The *Purgatorio*'s discrimination of the mixture of evil and good, never mind the *Paradiso*'s grasp at the sublime were made possible by the *Inferno*'s confrontation with unmasked evil. For a contemporary application, see George Will, *Statecraft as Soulcraft* (New York: Simon and Schuster, 1983), 68: "Begin at the outer edges of the awful. Begin from circumstances that are so intolerable that they drive many persons to desperation. Then work in, by small inferences, toward an understanding of political excellence."

8. Gannett News Service. "Census Bureau Reports Rate of Out of Wedlock Births Holding Steady," November 7, 1995.

Chapter 1

1. Cf. Leo Strauss, *Natural Right and History* (Chicago: University of Chicago Press, 1950), 36–42. Contrast perhaps the urtext of modern social

science methodology: Quincy Wright, *A Study of War* (Chicago: University of Chicago Press, 1964).

2. Thomas Sowell. *Race and Culture* (New York: Basic Books, 1994).

3. Robert D. Kaplan. "The Coming Anarchy," *Atlantic Monthly*, February 1994, 44–75.

4. Richard Herrnstein and Charles Murray. *The Bell Curve* (New York: Free Press, 1994).

5. Ralph Reed. Op-ed, *Wall Street Journal*, December 15, 1994.

6. In February 1992, Prime Minister Kiichi Miyazawa of Japan remarked that Americans' lack of a work ethic contributed to the nation's current economic slump. *Boston Globe*, February 4, 1992.

7. Xenophon. *Oeconomicus*, vol. 4, Loeb Classical Library (Boston: Harvard University Press, 1923), 168. Language and style aside, Xenophon's argument is very close to that of Gary Becker in *A Treatise on the Family* (Cambridge: Harvard University Press, 1981).

8. Jonathan Rauch. *Demosclerosis* (New York: Times Books, 1994).

9. Scott Shane. *Dismantling Utopia: How Information Ended the Soviet Union* (Chicago: Ivan R. Dye, 1994).

10. T. S. Eliot. *Christianity and Culture: The Idea of a Christian Society and Notes Towards the Definition of Culture* (New York: Harcourt Brace, 1968).

11. Myron Magnet. *The Dream and the Nightmare: The Sixties' Legacy to the Underclass* (New York: W. Morrow, 1993).

12. St. Augustine. *City of God*, vol. 19, Loeb Classical Library (Boston: Harvard University Press, 1957), 24, 411–417.

13. William Shakespeare. *Henry V*, 5.2. (Oxford: Clarendon Press, 1971).

14. Norman Cohn. *Pursuit of the Millennium* (Cambridge: Harvard University Press, 1970).

15. See Edward Goerner, *Peter and Caesar* (New York: Herder and Herder, 1965).

16. Plato. *Republic*, trans. Allan Bloom (New York: Basic Books, 1968), 368c–369b, 544e.

17. Thucydides. *The Peloponnesian War* (Ann Arbor: University of Michigan Press, 1959), bk. 3, chaps. 81–85.

18. Aristotle. *Politics*, trans. Carnes Lord (Chicago: University of Chicago Press, 1984), 1290a.7–11.

19. Ibid., 1279a.26–31.

20. George Will. *Statecraft As Soulcraft* (New York: Simon and Schuster, 1983).

21. Plato, *Republic*, 553e–555a.

22. Ibid., 547d–548d.

23. Ibid., 539c–541b.

24. See Harvey Mansfield, *America's Constitutional Soul* (Baltimore: John Hopkins University Press, 1991).

25. Charles de Gaulle. *Le fil de l'épee* (Paris: Union Générale d'Editions, 1902), 96.

26. Angelo Codevilla. "A Second Italian Republic," *Foreign Affairs* 71 (summer 1992).

27. Harry V. Jaffa. *Crisis of the House Divided* (Chicago: University of Chicago Press, 1958).

Chapter 2

1. Edward Banfield. *The Moral Basis of a Backward Society* (Glencoe, Ill.: Free Press, 1958).

2. Needless to say, these battles take place in every culture, hence rulers know that a society's literary appetites make a difference. For a discussion of this phenomenon in the American context, see Allan Bloom's *The Closing of the American Mind* (New York: Simon and Schuster, 1987), 55–60.

3. See Chris Black, "GOP Senator Denounces Fan Pier as 'Taj Mahal' and 'Obscene Waste,'" *Boston Globe*, November 9, 1995. According to this article, Senator John McCain denounced the planned $220 million federal courthouse in Boston as a "Taj Mahal" and a "shrine." In response, General Services Administration officials (the construction arm of the federal government) argued that they "were attempting to strike a balance between budgetary constraints and construction of long-lasting buildings that convey the dignity and majesty of the law."

4. Comic strip heroes such as Batman and Superman recall the ingrained American preference for people who fight crime at their own peril, following standards of common decency rather than statutes or (possibly corrupt) officials.

5. Alan Erenhalt. *The Lost City: Discovering the Forgotten Virtues of Community in the Chicago of the 1950s* (New York: Basic Books, 1995).

6. James Q. Wilson and George L. Kelling. "Broken Windows," *Atlantic Monthly* (March 1982): 29–36.

7. Samuel Huntington. "Clash of Civilizations?" *Foreign Affairs* 72 (summer 1993).

8. See Leo Strauss's *Natural Right and History* (Chicago: University of Chicago Press, 1950), 1.

9. John Rawls. *Theory of Justice* (Cambridge: Harvard University Press, 1971).

10. Aristotle. *Politics*, trans. Carnes Lord (Chicago: University of Chicago Press, 1984), 1294b.14–16.

11. See Xenophon's *Hiero* (London: Macmillan, 1935), 5.3–4.

12. Niccolò Machiavelli. *The Prince*, trans. Angelo Codevilla (New Haven: Yale University Press, 1997), chap. 7. Stalin took note of Borgia's use of Messer Remirro de Orco. See Paul Johnson, *Modern Times* (New York: Harper Perennial, 1991), 300–304.

13. Machiavelli, *Prince*, chap. 17. "Men forget the death of a father more quickly than the loss of patrimony." In most regimes, there must be at least a seeming respect for the property of one's subjects.

14. See Stephen Handelman, *Comrade Criminal* (New Haven: Yale University Press, 1995).

15. See N. S. Timasheff, *Religion in Soviet Russia, 1917–1942* (New York: Sheed and Ward, 1942); see also Daniela Deane, "Chinese Army, Police Overshadow Tibetan Monks: Decaying Monasteries, Once Revered Religious Centers, House Fear and Divisiveness," *Washington Post*, July 3, 1991.

16. James L. Payne. *Why Nations Arm* (New York: Basil Blackwell, 1989).

Chapter 3

1. Francis Fukuyama. *The End of History and the Last Man* (New York: Free Press, 1992).

2. Cf. Aristotle, *Politics*, trans. Carnes Lord (Chicago: University of Chicago Press, 1984), 1305a.28–36. Also, for the best-known prescriptive document against the danger of this tendency, see *The Federalist Papers*, no. 10 (Boston: University of New England Press, 1982), 51.

3. "A Nationwide Study of Home Education," The National Home Education Research Institute, Salem, Oregon, 1990. The average scores of home-schooled students showed that the national percentile mean for home-schooled students was 84 for reading, 80 for language, 81 for math, and 84 for science. See also press release by Home School Legal Defense Association, December 7, 1994, citing a study by Dr. Brian Ray of student performance in the Iowa Test of Basic Skills. The national average for home-schooled students is at the seventy-seventh percentile. The "grand mean percentile in language and math" is 73 percent.

4. In the *Politics* (1337a.11–22), Aristotle assumes this is the case.

5. Cf. *The Federalist Papers*. Hamilton attributes (Papers 1–9) the idea of federalism to Montesquieu, whom he cites as the author of "the new science of politics." Burke is justly famous for his reference to "the little platoons" of society that hold the whole together.

6. Alexis de Tocqueville. *Democracy in America*, vol. 1 (New York: Alfred A. Knopf, 1945), 91–92.

7. Cf. David Hume, "Of the Parties of Great Britain," in *Essays: Moral, Political, and Literary*, ed. Eugene Miller (Indianapolis, Ind.: Liberty Press, 1985). Hume's discussion of the Tory and Whig parties is pertinent here. Also see Harvey Mansfield, *Statesmanship and Party Government* (Chicago: University of Chicago Press, 1974).

8. Cf. Plato, *Republic*, trans. Allan Bloom (New York: Basic Books, 1968), 488a–489c.

9. However, if they had looked at the Roman republic, they would have seen how quickly shifting economic policies change a people's way of life. Cf. David Hume, "Of Taxes," in *Essays: Moral, Political, Literary*, ed. Eugene Miller. See also Edward Gibbon, *The Decline and Fall of the Roman Empire* (New York: Heritage Press, 1946), chap. 17.

10. Cf. Aristotle, *Politics*, 1259b.18–21. Also see John Locke, "Of Paternal Power," in the *Second Treatise of Government* (Buffalo: Prometheus Books, 1986), as well as Xenophon's *Oeconomicus*.

11. One can see the roots of this conceptual transformation in the writings of Karl Marx and Friedrich Engels. But even they, to a certain extent, accepted the natural basis of gender differences. Their followers, on the contrary, take a different approach. While Eleanor Marx (Marx's daughter) could write that Shakespeare was the Bible in their home, Jonathan Dollimore, a modern Marxist Shakespearean scholar, calls for a rewriting of *Antony and Cleopatra*—in which gender roles are switched and Cleopatra has a "same-sex" and "cross-class" relationship with one of her attendants (Dollimore, "Shakespeare, Cultural Materialism, Feminism, and Marxist Humanism," *New Literary History* 21 [spring 1990]: 471–493).

Chapter 4

1. This is most obvious in Karl Marx's *The Economic and Philosophical Manuscripts of 1844*, *The Communist Manifesto*, and *Critique of the Gotha Programme*, as well as in Karl Marx and Friedrich Engels, *The Origins of Family, Private Property, and the State*.

2. B. P. Pockney. *Soviet Statistics Since 1950* (New York: St. Martin's Press, 1991), 101.

3. Mikhail Bernstam. "Economic Systems, Demographic Change and Global Conflict," in *Population Change and European Security*, ed. Lawrence Freedman and John Saunders (London: Brassey's, 1991), 169. I am deeply indebted to Mr. Bernstam, a former colleague at the Hoover Institution, for many insights into the Soviet economy drawn from this seminal article and from countless conversations over many years.

4. Ibid., 165–167.

5. Mikhail Voslensky. *The Nomenklatura* (New York: Doubleday, 1984).

6. Stephen Handelman. *Comrade Criminal: Russia's New Mafiya* (New Haven: Yale University Press, 1995), 110.

7. Ibid., 104.

8. Georgii Arbatov. *The System* (New York: Random House, 1992).

9. In an instance that shows the peculiar viciousness of Russian criminals, Sherry Jones, in an op-ed piece (*New York Times*, November 25, 1995), tells about a businessman friend who was being extorted by two officially connected gangs, tried to give up his business when the payments got too high, but was forced to continue paying lest his family be killed. Having exhausted loans from friends, he committed suicide (which was reported as an apparent heart attack).

10. "Smuggling Raw Materials to West Creates Huge Fortunes," *Washington Post*, February 2, 1993.

11. Steven Erlanger. "Corrupt Tide in Russia from State–Business Ties," *New York Times*, January 3, 1995.

12. Andrei Amalrik. *Will the Soviet Union Survive Until 1984?* (New York: Harper and Row, 1970).

13. See Erik Von Kuhnhelt-Ledihn's *Liberty or Equality* (Front Royal, Wash.: Christendom Press, 1993) for a full exposition of this argument.

14. Robert Putnam. *Making Democracy Work: Civic Traditions in Modern Italy* (Princeton, N.J.: Princeton University Press, 1993).

15. Abdurakman Avtorkanov's *The Communist Party Apparatus* (Chicago: Regnery, 1964), 49, 60–61, 73, 84.

16. From Josef Stalin's *Works*, as cited in ibid.

17. This is the point of vol. 3 of Aleksandr Solzhenitsyn's *The Gulag Archipelago* (New York: Harper and Row, 1976), pt. 7, chaps. 1 and 2.

18. Solzhenitsyn. *The Gulag Archipelago*, vol. 3, p. 524.

19. Hedrick Smith. *The Russians* (New York: Ballantine Books, 1976), p. 352.

20. Ibid.

21. Robert Conquest. "The Importance of Historical Truth," *Freedom Review* (November-December 1992): 36.

22. Alessandra Stanley. "Russian Mothers, from All Walks, Walk Alone," *New York Times*, October 21, 1995.

23. Francine Duplessix Gray. *Soviet Women* (New York: Doubleday, 1989), 45–48.

24. See "Loyal Wives, Virtuous Mothers: Women's Day and Russian Women of the '90s," *Russian Life* 39 (March 1996): 4.

25. Mikhail Gorbachev. *Perestroika: New Thinking for Our Country and the World* (New York: Harper and Row, 1987), 117.

26. See Katherine P. Henry, "Registration of Churches in Soviet Union,"

Religious and Communist Dominated Areas 1 (winter 1987): 14; see also Radio Liberty Research Bulletin RL 171/88 (April 22, 1988); and Dmitry V. Pospielovsky, *A History of Marxist-Leninist Atheism and Soviet Anti-Religious Policies*, vol. 1 (London: Macmillan, 1987).

27. Smith, *The Russians*, 434.

28. Ibid., 580–581.

29. Niccolò Machiavelli. *Discorso a dialago interno alla nostra lingua*, ed. Bortolo Tommaso Sozzi (Torino: G. Einaudi, 1976).

30. *Le Monde*, March 28, 1995.

31. This is also the opinion of Condoleeza Rice, provost of Stanford University, who followed Soviet military affairs for the National Security Council between 1989 and 1992, as expressed in an address to the Hoover Institution, Stanford University, June 21, 1993.

32. J. Michael Waller. *Secret Empire: The KGB in Russia Today* (Oxford: Westview Press, 1994), 113.

33. Bill Keller. "Cry of 'Won't Give My Son!' and Soviets End Call-Up," *New York Times*, January 20, 1990.

Chapter 5

1. Kenneth A. Schultz and Barry Weingast. *The Democratic Advantage* (Stanford: Hoover Institution Press, 1996).

2. Lester Theroux, Chalmers Johnson, James Fallows. "Head to Head Containing Japan," *Atlantic Monthly* (May 1989); Clyde Prestowitz, Ronald Morse, and Alan Tonelson. *Powernomics: Economics and Strategy After the Cold War* (Washington, D.C.: Economic Strategy Institute, 1981).

3. See John Locke, "Of Property," chap. 5 in the *Second Treatise of Government* (Buffalo: Prometheus Books, 1986). In this chapter, Locke bases lawful government and property rights on the fact that all people mix their labor with nature. Because all people have an equal interest in their property, all property must be treated equally.

4. See Plato, *Republic*, trans. Allan Bloom (Basic Books, 1968), 367b–372c.

5. Paul Kennedy. *The Rise and Fall of the Great Powers* (New York: Random House, 1986). This oversight reminds one of André Malraux's lines in *Man's Fate*: "Europeans never understand anything of China that does not resemble themselves" (New York: Vintage, 1934), 111.

6. This is the theme of John Kenneth Galbraith's *The Affluent Society* (Boston: Houghton Mifflin, 1960).

7. See *1997 Index of Economic Freedom* (Washington, D.C.: Heritage Foundation, 1997).

8. In *The Immoralist*, André Gide wrote: "The honest Swiss! All their prosperity is worthless. Without crimes, without history, without literature, without art, what are they but an overgrown rosebush that bears neither thorns nor bloom!" (Paris: Mercure de France, 1921), 146–147. Gide understood, like many before and after him, that the prosperity of a people and the relative success of government depends more on the quality of the souls composing a state than on quantifiable economic factors.

9. Indeed, the authors of the "Third World" concept and the managers of the programs meant to uplift it included countries that had never been Western colonies (for example, Taiwan, South Korea, and Latin American countries). Indeed, they even included Argentina, a country that had once been among the world's richest but had fallen on hard times. For a moving account

of the character of Third World leaders and what they have wrought, see Paul Johnson, *Modern Times* (New York: Harper and Row, 1983), especially the chapters entitled "The Bandung Generation" and "Caliban's Kingdoms."

10. David Landes. "Rich Country, Poor Country," *New Republic*, November 20, 1989.

11. John H. Coatsworth. "Obstacles to Economic Growth in Nineteenth-Century Mexico," *American Historical Review* 83 (1978): 94.

12. See Hilton Root, "Institutional Foundations for a Market Economy in Tropical Africa," Stanford University, Hoover Institution, March 1994, chap. 1. I am indebted to Hilton Root for countless insights on the relationship between power and money.

13. In this regard, note the intriguing suggestion by R. Emmet Tyrell in *Boy Clinton, the Political Biography* (Washington, D.C.: Regnery, 1996) that under Governor Bill Clinton, the state of Arkansas effectively franchised Donald Lasater to import drugs and a variety of other well-connected people to loot its banks.

14. Edward A. Gargan. "Family Ties That Bind Growth," *New York Times*, April 9, 1996.

15. Dan A. Cothran. *Political Stability and Democracy in Mexico: The "Perfect Dictatorship"?* (Westport, Conn.: Praeger, 1994), 193–198. Arrested ostensibly for murder, La Quina has never been tried.

16. Steven Greenhouse. "Comparing Wealth as Money Fluctuates," *New York Times*, August 23, 1987.

17. E. H. Norman. *Origins of the Modern Japanese State* (New York: Pantheon Books, 1975), 233; and Walter McDougall, *Let the Sea Make a Noise* (New York: Basic Books, 1994), 353–362, 531–539, 663–673.

18. In a 1991 Mainichi Press poll, 62 percent of Japanese respondents believed that "it was strange" that products manufactured in Japan are less expensive in other countries than in their own. See *Index to International Public Opinion 1990–1991* (New York: Greenwood Press, 1992), 69.

19. Nicolas Kristoff and Sheryl WuDunn. *China Wakes* (New York: Times Books, 1990)

20. See, e.g., the lead article in the March 1997 *National Geographic*, "China's Gold Coast."

21. Ramon H. Myers. "The Socialist Market Economy in the People's Republic of China," *Fifty-fifth Morrison Lecture*, Australian National University, November 8, 1994, 11. "Shared Cooperative Systems" is from Gao Lu, "Call for Reform of Ownership, Property Rights—Brief Account of Seventh, Eighth Symposiums at 'Forum on China's Market Economy,'" *Jingji Ribao*, November 2, 1993, in *JPRS Report: China*, January 21, 1993.

22. Hilton L. Root. "Has China Lost Its Way? Political Risk and Financial Intermediation in the PRC," Hoover Institution, Stanford University, 1995, 33. I am indebted to Hilton Root in general and to this paper in particular for insight into the systemic importance of China's *guanxi* (4, 13–15).

23. Ibid.

24. Sheryl WuDunn. "China's Rush to Riches," *New York Times Magazine*, September 4, 1994, 39.

25. Ibid., 41.

26. "China, the Art of the (Raw) Deal," *New York Times*, February 12, 1995.

27. Root, "Has China Lost Its Way?" 19.

28. Here is how the *Economic Daily* described it: "'Leaping into the sea' is to

march into the central battlefield of economic construction. . . . If it had not been for the Party Central Committee Third Plenum and Eleventh Meeting and Deng Xiaoping's southern tour, leaping into the sea would never have been possible." See also Ruhying Chen, ed., *The Mania for Leaping into the Sea* (Beijing: University of Beijing Press, 1993), 47.

29. Alternatively, some hypothesize that a new contest is taking place in China to see which regime can be friendliest to business. Barry Weingast has called this "market-preserving federalism." See Yingyi Quian and Barry Weingast, *China's Transition to Markets* (Stanford: Hoover Institution Press, 1995).

30. *1996 Information Please Almanac* (Boston: Houghton Mifflin, 1996), 167, 287.

31. See *New York Times*, December 22, 1993. They average under $1,000 per (good) worker per year. See also "Art of the (Raw) Deal," *New York Times*, February 12, 1995.

32. World Bank. *World Development Report, 1992* (New York: Oxford University Press, 1992).

33. In one of the more clamorous cases of discovery, an armed robber, caught in the Rome suburbs after a high-speed chase by car and on foot, was found to have been on the disability rolls for total blindness. See *Il Tempo* (Rome), September 4, 1994.

34. Wilfried Prewo. "Germany Is Not a Model," *Wall Street Journal*, February 1, 1994.

35. De Tocqueville wrote, "In fact, the nobility was regarded in the age of feudalism much as the government is regarded by everyone today; its exactions were tolerated in view of the protection and security it provided." *The Ancien Regime and the French Revolution*, trans. Stuart Gilbert (Garden City, N.Y.: Doubleday, 1955), pt. 2, chap. 1, 30.

36. *Sweden's Prosperity in Comparison with Other Countries* (Stockholm: Ekonomipakta, 1989), 9.

37. George Melloan. "Looted Banks, One-Eared Cows, and Moral Fog," *Wall Street Journal*, August 15, 1994.

38. See chap. 6 in this work for a discussion of the relationship between the welfare state and demographic trends.

39. Francisco Orrgeo Vicuna. *Chile: The Balanced View* (Santiago: University of Chile, 1975), 185, table 18.

40. Between 1965 and 1970, food imports averaged $100 million per year. By 1972, the figure had risen to $450 million, and in 1973, it hit $600 million (Sergio de Castro, ed., *El Ladrillo* [Santiago: Centro de Estudios Publicos, 1992], 36–37).

41. Figures from Banco Central de Chile, quoted in Jorge Rodriguez Grossi, ed., *Perspectivas economicas para la democracia* (Santiago: Instituto Chileno de Estudios Humanisticos, 1984), 32.

42. Official Chilean government figures cited in James R. Whelan, *Out of the Ashes* (Washington, D.C.: Regnery Gateway, 1989), 308.

43. *El Ladrillo*, 32.

44. Declaration of the Supreme Court of Chile, May 26, 1973, quoted in Whelan, *Out of the Ashes*, 413.

45. Angelo M. Codevilla. "Is Pinochet the Model?" *Foreign Affairs* (November-December 1993), 129.

46. Ibid., 30.

47. In 1988, the government and opposition established a commission under Raul Rettig Guissen, a respected jurist, to compile a definitive report on the actions of all sides in the civil war. According to the Rettig Report published in March 1991 and accepted by all sides as definitive, 2,115 people had been killed. See *The Report of the Chilean National Commission on Truth and Reconciliation* (London: Notre Dame Press, 1993).

Chapter 6

1. John Fortescue. *De laudibus legum Angliae* (Cambridge: Cambridge University Press, 1942).

2. Robert William Fogel and Stanley L. Engerman. *Time on the Cross: The Economics of American Negro Slavery* (Boston: Little, Brown, 1974).

3. Aristotle. *Politics*, trans. Carnes Lord (Chicago: University of Chicago Press, 1984), 1277b.7–15.

4. De Tocqueville remarks in *Democracy in America* (New York: Alfred A. Knopf, 1945), vol. 2, bk. 4, chap. 6, 435: "It is vain to summon a people who have been rendered so dependent on the central power to choose from time to time the representatives of that power; this rare and brief exercise of their free choice, however important it may be, will not prevent them from gradually losing the faculties of thinking, feeling, and acting for themselves, and thus gradually falling below the level of humanity."

5. Plato. *Republic*, trans. Allan Bloom (New York: Basic Books, 1968), 388c.

6. "The Notion of a Living Constitution," *Texas Law Review*, 54 (1976): 693. This is the revised text of the ninth annual Will E. Orgain Lecture, delivered at the University of Texas Law School, March 12, 1976.

7. José Pedroni, quoted in William Ratliff and Roger Fontaine, *Changing Course: The Capitalist Revolution in Argentina* (Stanford: Hoover Institution Press, 1990), 19. See also Carlos Weisman, "Argentina, Autarkic Industrialization and Illegitimacy," in *Democracy in Developing Countries*, ed. Larry Diamond, Juan Lunz, and Martin Lipset (Boulder, Colo.: Lynne Rienner, 1988).

8. Homer. *The Odyssey*, bk. 23, ll. 208–230. Upon returning home, Odysseus objects to Penelope's test of his identity—the suggested moving of their bed away from the trunk of an olive tree—by stating: "Woman, by heaven you have stung me now! Who dared to move my bed? No builder had the skill for that—unless a god came down to turn the trick. No mortal in his best days could budge it with a crowbar. There is our pact and pledge, our secret sign, built into that bed—my handiwork and no one else's!" Homer shows us the suitors as worthy of death because they had been eating Odysseus's property.

9. Plato, *Republic*, 553d–556a.

10. Cf. Jean-Jacques Rousseau, *The Social Contract*, trans. Charles Frankel (New York: Hafner, 1947), bk. 4. See also Montesquieu, *Considerations on the Causes of the Greatness of the Romans and Their Decline*, trans. David Lowenthal (New York: Free Press, 1965).

11. Titus Livius. *Ab Urbe Condita Libri*, trans. B. O. Foster (Cambridge, Mass.: Harvard University Press, 1970).

12. Fragment (August 1, 1858). From Roy P. Basler, *The Collected Works of Abraham Lincoln*, vol. 2 (New Brunswick, N.J.: Rutgers University Press, 1953), 532.

13. The finest summary account of this is in Norman Cohn, *Pursuit of the Millennium* (New York: Harper & Row, 1960).

14. John Stuart Mill. *Considerations on Representative Government* (Buffalo: Prometheus Books, 1991), especially the chapter titled "Of True and False Democracy; Representation of All and Representation of the Majority Only."

15. The classic discussion of how proportional representation destroys democracy at all levels in the organization of parties is in Ferdinand A. Hermens, *Democracy or Anarchy* (South Bend, Ind.: Notre Dame University Press, 1941), 51–58. Hermens's discussion of the role of proportional representation in the rise of fascism and nazism is on 178–246.

16. Simon Schama. *Citizens: A Chronicle of the French Revolution* (New York: Knopf, 1989).

17. Charles de Gaulle. *La France et Son Armée* (Paris: Plon, 1938), 271.

18. Ralf Dahrendorf. *Society and Democracy in Germany* (Garden City, N.Y.: Doubleday, 1969), 397–411. As the late Lewis Gann used to say, every German truck driver, every cleaning lady, knew that the German Democratic Republic was a fraud. But few of the elites did, and after 1970 none said so publicly.

19. Nicholas D. Kristof. "A Lesson in Heroics Is Lost on Many," *New York Times*, November 2, 1990. Such campaigns are indistinguishable from countless similar Soviet efforts (e.g., the glorification of Pavel Morozov) to teach unnatural morality. The Chinese seem to "buy" such teachings even less than the Russians. Kristof reported a Chinese teacher's comment: "Nobody believes that rubbish."

20. Zhisui Li. *The Private Life of Chairman Mao*, trans. Tai Hung-Chao (New York: Random House, 1994).

21. John Byron and Robert Pack. *The Claws of the Dragon: Kang Sheng, the Evil Genius Behind Mao and His Legacy of Terror in People's China* (New York: Simon and Schuster, 1992).

22. Kenneth Lieberthal. *Governing China* (New York: W. W. Norton, 1996).

23. Hu Chang. "Impressions of Mainland China Carried Back by Mainland Visitors," in *Two Societies in Opposition*, ed. Ramon H. Myers (Stanford: Hoover Institution Press, 1991), 144–153.

24. Thomas A. Metzger et al. "Understanding the Taiwan Experience, an Historical Perspective," *Pacific Review* 2, no. 4 (1989): 300. Estimates of the number of Taiwanese killed in the repression of the anti-Kuomintang riots of 1947 range between eight and ten thousand. This great bloodshed is to be compared with that of the Communists on the mainland, who killed by uncountable millions.

25. Sidney H. Chang and Leonard H. D. Gordon, eds. *All Under Heaven: Sun Yat-sen and His Revolutionary Thought* (Stanford: Hoover Institution Press, 1991).

26. Ed Campos and Hilton Root. "Rethinking the Asian Miracle," Stanford University, Hoover Institution, June 1994, 71.

27. "Taiwan's Prosperity Is Exacting a Heavy Toll," *Los Angeles Times*, May 14, 1995. Note that mainland Chinese officials do not worry about divorce rates—it would hardly make sense for officials who three decades ago forced the physical separation of hundreds of millions of Chinese couples. However, as with the Taiwanese, between 1982 and 1990, the Chinese divorce rate in-

creased 42 percent (*Los Angeles Times,* July 18, 1995). For a comprehensive discussion of this recent development in Asia, see Ken Davies and Graham Richards, "Asian Values Myth Debunked," *Plain Dealer,* December 24, 1995.

28. Seth Mydans. "Good Life Guide: To Five Cs, Add Clout," *New York Times,* June 5, 1996.

29. Philip Shenon. "Models for China: Either Filthy and Free or Clean and Mean," *New York Times,* February 6, 1995.

30. The positivist movement, founded by the French founder of sociology, Auguste Comte (1798–1857) preached the scientific management of society. Its motto, "Order and Progress," and its philosophical premise, that reality consists only of measurable data, and its militant secularism became the foundations of modern social science. Only Brazil has "Order and Progress" written on its flag. But most modern regimes have the premises of positivism in their bones.

31. See Javier Livas, *Confesion de un ingenier electoral* (Monterrey, Mexico, 1992). This is an account of how Francisco Loredo Valdes fixed elections for the PRI in Monterrey between 1976 and 1991. Note that the electorate's "pride in Mexico" is about triple its "pride in the Mexican political system." Cf. Jorge I. Dominguez and James McCann, *Democratizing Mexico: Public Opinion and Electoral Choices* (Baltimore: Johns Hopkins University Press, 1996), 38–39.

32. *La mordida es institución nacional,* or "graft is a national institution," is a popular saying in Mexico. But note that while in Mexico more money can buy some elbow room within the system, in honest social democracies like Sweden, nothing can substitute for connections.

33. See Brian Latell, *Mexico at the Crossroads* (Stanford: Hoover Institution Press, 1986). Latell, a senior analyst at the Central Intelligence Agency, was the author of a highly regarded national intelligence estimate on Mexico in 1985. This unclassified version retains all the author's insights into the revolutionary significance of changing attitudes in Mexico. In northern Mexico there is probably a majority in favor of joining the United States.

34. The government's typical response to the exposure of a bureaucrat caught red-handed in corruption or violence is simply to transfer him laterally and geographically. See Alicia Ely-Yamin, *Justice Corrupted, Justice Denied* (New York: Mexico Project, World Policy Institute, 1992).

35. George Washington, "First Inaugural Address," in *Writings,* ed. John Rhodehames (New York: Library of America, 1997), 732–33. Note the parallel with the theme of Aristotle's *Nicomachean Ethics.*

36. Thomas Jefferson. *Thomas Jefferson, Writings,* ed. Merrill D. Peterson (New York: Library of America, 1984), 492–93.

Chapter 7

1. Aristotle. *Politics,* trans. Carnes Lord (Chicago: University of Chicago Press, 1984), 1252a37–38.

2. Ibid., 1259a37–1259b10, 1260b8–1260b19.

3. Thomas Jefferson. *Notes on Virginia* (New York: Library of America, 1984), 186. See also Francis Parkman, *France, England, and North America,* vol. 1, ed. David Levin (New York: Viking Press, 1983). Writing a half century after the founding, Parkman described the life of Huron women as beginning with "a youth of license" followed by "an age of drudgery." "Female life

among the Hurons," he wrote, "has no bright side" (358). I am indebted to Thomas G. West for pointing me to Parkman's judgment on the Indians' treatment of women.

4. *Cleveland v. United States* 329 US 14 (1946). The court ruled that the Mann Act—which made illegal the transportation of women "for the purpose of prostitution or for any other immoral purpose"—also included polygamous practices. In essence, it affirmed the decision of *Reynolds v. United States* 98 US 145 (1878), in which the court ruled that "from the earliest history of England polygamy has been treated as an offense against society."

5. *Time*, July 18, 1994.

6. Fustel de Coulanges. *The Ancient City* (New York: Doubleday, 1965), bk. 2, chap. 2. In this chapter, de Coulanges stresses the aspect of rebirth. The custom of carrying the bride across the threshold dates to these times and symbolizes that the wife did not walk into the husband's house but rather was born there.

7. Take, for example, Sophocles's *Antigone*, whose tragedy consists precisely in refusing the process of alienation and rebirth implicit in marriage. She tells the Chorus: "O, but I would not have done the forbidden thing for any husband or for any son. For why? I could have had another husband and by him other sons, if one were lost; But father and mother lost, where would I get another brother? For thus preferring you, My brother, Creon condemns me and hales me away, never a bride, never a mother, unfriended, condemned alive a solitary death." In *The Theban Plays* (New York: Penguin, 1947), 150.

8. A recent survey—albeit a summary one—by *Reader's Digest* (July 1992, 48–54) shows that Americans who are married with children have substantially different and much more conservative opinions on social and political matters than do other Americans. This is non-news. Even among the animals, those with young behave very differently than those who do not have them.

9. Cf. "Ireland Should Vote No," *Daily Telegraph*, November 23, 1995.

10. "Family Values to Shift; Divorce Rate to Climb," *Trends Research Institute* 5 (summer 1996): 4. Anyone frequenting an expensive restaurant will be likely to note the prevalence of couples consisting of middle-aged men and women half their age.

11. Deut. 22:28–29.

12. "More Men in Prime Not Working," *New York Times*, December 1, 1994. In the United States since the end of the 1960s, the share of prime-age men who are not in school, on the job, or looking for work has tripled, moving from 3 percent to 9 percent, according to Robert H. Haverman, an economist at the University of Wisconsin: "The decline in men's work is concentrated at the bottom of socioeconomic scales." Note Myron Magnet's thesis that upper-class ideas have had devastating effects on the lower classes. See Myron Magnet, *The Dream and the Nightmare: The Sixties' Legacy to the Underclass* (New York: W. Morrow, 1993).

13. Even those who favor these recent developments, for example, Jane Wheelock, *Husbands at Home: The Domestic Economy in Post-Industrial Society* (New York: Routledge, 1990), admit these tendencies—although their slogan is "give it time."

14. Gary Becker. *A Treatise on the Family* (Cambridge, Mass.: Harvard University Press, 1981). See *The Family Wage: Work, Gender and Children in the Modern Economy* (Rockford, Ill.: Rockford Institute, 1988). The domestic divi-

sion of labor is efficient in part because mothers will agonize over the best ways to care for their own, while a day care worker will not, and that husbands will care for their homes as hired maintenance workers will not.

15. From *Taxpayer* (winter 1992), as quoted by William Gairdner, *The War Against the Family* (Toronto: Stoddart, 1992), 178.

16. Tamar Lewin. "The Decay of Families Is Global, Study Says," *New York Times*, May 30, 1995.

17. Ibid.

18. "Fings Ain't Wot They Used to Be," *Economist*, May 28, 1994, 31.

19. The idea that "the best trained practitioners of both sexes," namely, scientifically trained government employees, know better about children than parents has been popularized by such authors as Kate Millet, *Sexual Politics* (Garden City, N.Y.: Doubleday, 1970).

20. T. S. Eliot. *The Rock* (London: Faber & Faber, 1934), 42.

21. Hillary Rodham. "Children Under the Law," *Harvard Educational Review* 43 (November 1973): 508. The full statement reads: "If the law were to abolish the status of minority and to reverse its underlying presumption of children's incompetency, the result would be an implicit presumption that children, like other persons, are capable of exercising rights and assuming responsibilities until proven otherwise. Empirical differences among children would then serve as the grounds for making exemptions to the presumption and for justifying rational state restrictions."

22. The litany is just about the same, regardless of where one gets the statistics. In the United States, some 70 percent of men in state and federal prisons come from homes where there had never been a husband. One can argue that children of criminals or children who live in criminal-infested neighborhoods have a higher tendency to commit crime than those who do not. But that only pushes the correlation back one logical step. Most impressive is the consistency of the phenomenon around the world.

23. Aristotle, *Politics*, 1259b12–17.

24. Sheila B. Kamerman and Alfred J. Kahn, eds. *Child Care, Parental Leave, and the Under 3's: Policy Innovation in Europe* (New York: Auburn House, 1991), 173–176.

25. David Popenoe. *Disturbing the Nest: Family Change and Decline in Modern Societies* (New York: Aldine de Gruyter, 1988), 175.

26. Alexis de Tocqueville. *Democracy in America*, vol. 2 (New York: Alfred A. Knopf, 1945), chap. 12, n. 3. De Tocqueville thought that this can only "degrade both" and "produce nothing but feeble men and unseemly women."

27. Linda Haas. "Family Policy in Sweden," *Journal of Family and Economic Issues* 113 (spring 1966): 75.

28. Ibid., 78. The quality is so high that according to one of Sweden's admirers, the Swedes have achieved something that intuitively appears to be physically impossible: "the amount of time parents spend directly interacting with their children is not lessened by Swedish children's time spent in day care."

29. Roland Huntford. *The New Totalitarians* (New York: Stein and Day, 1992), p. 84.

30. See *Basic Statistics of the Community: Comparison with Some European Countries, Canada, the USA, Japan, and Russia* (Luxembourg: Office for Official Publication of the European Community, 1993).

31. "A Change of Course: The Model Starts to Show Her Age," *The Economist*, March 3, 1990, 5.

32. The newest craze is a drug named "Special K" or Ketamin—a veterinary anesthetic given to dogs and cats. ("Party Craze for Cats' Drug," *Guardian*, July 7, 1996).

33. Mary Nourse. "Women's Work in Japan," *National Geographic* (January 1938): 99.

34. Robert C. Christopher. *The Japanese Mind* (New York: Random House, 1983), 114.

35. Nicholas D. Kristof. "Baby May Make 3, but in Japan That's Not Enough," *New York Times*, October 6, 1996.

36. Christopher, *The Japanese Mind*, 115.

Chapter 8

1. Edward Gibbon. *Decline and Fall of the Roman Empire*, vol. 1 (Chicago: Encyclopedia Brittanica, 1955), chap. 2, 12.

2. *National Longitudinal Survey of Youth* (Washington, D.C.: U.S. Department of Labor, 1993).

3. This old story in social science applies even to "black male inner-city youths." See National Bureau of Economic Research, Working Paper Series no. 1656 (Cambridge, Mass.: NBER, 1985).

4. "Incentive Pay, Information and Earnings Evidence from the *National Longitudinal Survey of Youth*" (Washington, D.C.: U.S. Department of Labor, 1995).

5. Howard M. Bahr and Bruce A. Chadwick. "Religion and Family in Middletown, U.S.A.," *Journal of Marriage and the Family* 47 (May 1985): 407–414.

6. It is not appropriate to say the faithful practice of religion of any sort predicts this because, after all, the Thuggees (from which the word "thug" derives) worshiped Siva, the Hindu god of violent death, at least according to the Thuggees' testimony-in-deed. The murderous followers of the medieval heresiarchs described by Norman Cohn and the suicidal followers of the Reverend James Jones in the 1970s are among many examples of the sad consequences of bad theology.

7. The Turkish government of Mustafa Kemal (1923–1938) waged a war against Islam almost as violent as that which the Soviet regime waged against Russia's religions. Turkey appeared to have won that war with relatively few ill effects. Then in 1995, Turkey's Islamic Welfare party won a plurality in parliamentary elections, and the Turkish regime began to ask how ready the army was to wage another civil war on behalf of secularism.

8. Dante. *Il Purgatorio*, Canto 32: 129. The translation is mine.

9. Ibid.

10. The Mughal emperor Akhbar's attempt to confuse himself with Allah is interestingly described in Douglas E. Streusand, *The Formation of the Mughal Empire* (Delhi: Oxford University Press, 1989).

11. In Sweden, a 1990 poll showed that only 38 percent of the people had trust in the church (lower than in any other Western European country). Correspondingly, trust in the police force was twice as high. See Hans-Dieter Klingemann and Dieter Fuchs, eds., *Citizens and the State* (New York: Oxford University Press, 1991).

12. On the effects of the German church tax, see Dennis L. Bark and David

Gress-Wright, *A History of the Federal Republic* (London: Basil Blackwell, 1990).

13. Edward G. Shirely. "Is Iran's Present Algeria's Future?" *Foreign Affairs* 74, no. 3 (May-June 1995): 38.

14. Bill Broadway. "Poll Finds America 'As Churched as Ever'," *Washington Post*, May 31, 1997; see also Larry Witham, "Europeans Forge New Religious Paths; Boomers Tilt Traditions to Fit Their Needs," *Washington Times*, March 11, 1996.

15. Plutarch. *Lives*, vol. 1, trans. John Dryden et al. (Philadelphia: Henry T. Coates, 1896), 113.

16. Titus Livius. *Ab Urbe Condita Libri*, trans. B. O. Foster (Cambridge, Mass.: Harvard University Press, 1970), 3.20.5.

17. Benito Mussolini. *Fascism* (Rome: Arditi, 1932).

18. Stephen Kinzer. "Coming of Age, Unideologically," *New York Times* (international edition), June 11, 1994. Kinzer describes the Jugendweihe's being revived "to promote good citizenship."

19. Jean-Marie Guehenno. *The End of the Nation-State* (St. Paul: University of Minnesota Press, 1996).

20. "The Counterattack of God," *The Economist*, July 8, 1995, 19.

21. Poll conducted by *Yediot Ahronot*, December 2, 1996. Significantly, 51 percent of the secularists thought so, but only 38 percent of the religious. Eighty-three percent of the respondents thought the best way to avoid such a war is for secularists and the religious to study the Torah together.

Chapter 9

1. Thucydides. *The Peloponnesian War* (Ann Arbor: University of Michigan Press, 1959), bk. 1, 140–144.

2. Ibid., bk. 6, 8–31.

3. Niccolò Machiavelli. *The Prince*, trans. Angelo Codevilla (New Haven: Yale University Press, 1997), chaps. 20, 24.

4. See also William McNeill, *The Pursuit of Power* (Chicago: University of Chicago Press, 1982), for a discussion of how the changing technology of weapons affects those who use them.

5. Machiavelli, *Prince*, chaps. 6, 8, 13, 24.

6. Rudyard Kipling. "Pharaoh and the Sergeant," in *Rudyard Kipling's Verse Inclusive Edition, 1885–1926* (Garden City, N.Y.: Doubleday, 1929), 227.

7. Charles de Gaulle. *La France et Son Armée* (Paris: Plon, 1938), 138. My account of the Napoleonic regime owes much to de Gaulle's admirable chapter.

Chapter 10

1. John Allen. "An Oration upon the Beauties of Liberty," preached in Boston, December 3, 1772, and widely circulated, in *Political Sermons of the American Revolution*, ed. Ellis Sandoz (Indianapolis, Ind.: Liberty Press, 1991), 305.

2. Thomas Paine. *Common Sense* (New York: Knopf, 1994).

3. Samuel Cooper, October 25, 1788, in Sandoz, ed., *Political Sermons*, 639.

4. Alexis de Tocqueville. *Democracy in America*, vol. 2 (New York: Alfred A. Knopf, 1945), pt. 2, chap. 4, 482–483.

5. Ibid.

6. Ibid., vol. 1, pt. 1, chap. 5, 61.

7. Ibid., 86.

8. See James Thomas Flexner, *Washington, the Indispensable Man* (Boston: Little, Brown, 1974), parts of chaps. 11–13, 16, and 17.

9. De Tocqueville, *Democracy in America*, vol. 1, pt. 2, chap. 6, 221–222.

10. Ibid., chap. 7, 234.

11. Ibid., chap. 4, 179. Note de Tocqueville's foreshadowing of the Leninist practice of "democratic centralism."

12. Ibid., vol. 2, pt. 2, chap. 21, 487.

13. Ibid., vol. 1, pt. 1, chap. 5, 79.

14. See Alexis de Tocqueville, *The Ancien Régime and the French Revolution*, trans. Stuart Gilbert (Garden City, N.Y.: Doubleday, 1955), for a broader analysis of this phenomenon.

15. Eph. 6:22–24.

16. 1 Cor. 7:4.

17. Matt. 19:6.

18. Aristotle, *Nicomachean Ethics*, 1162.

19. Memorandum on a tour from Paris to Amsterdam (1778). See chapter on "Women and the Family" in Thomas G. West, *Vindicating the Founders: Race, Sex, Class, and Poverty in the Origins of America* (Lanham, Md.: Roman and Littlefield, 1997). I am indebted to Professor West for numerous insights on the American founding generation's family ways.

20. John Adams, *The Works of John Adams, Second President of the United States: with a life of the author, notes and illustrations by his grandson Charles Francis Adams*, vol. 3 (Boston: Little, Brown, 1850–56), 171.

21. West, *Liberalism*, 74.

22. De Tocqueville, *Democracy in America*, vol. 2, pt. 3, chap. 12, 576–577.

23. Ibid.

24. Ibid., 578.

25. Ibid., 564.

26. Ibid., 568.

27. Ibid., 571.

28. De Tocqueville, *Democracy in America*, vol. 1, pt. 2, chap. 9, 271.

29. Ibid., 268.

30. Paul Johnson. "God and the Americans," *Commentary* (January 1995): 25–45.

31. Ibid., 28.

32. Ibid., 29.

33. De Tocqueville, *Democracy in America*, vol. 2, pt. 1, chap. 1, 396.

34. De Tocqueville, *Democracy in America*, vol. 1, pt. 2, chap. 9, 266–270.

35. Ibid., 272.

36. Johnson, "God and the Americans," 31.

37. De Tocqueville, *Democracy in America*, vol. 1, pt. 2, chap. 9, 269.

38. De Tocqueville, *Democracy in America*, vol. 2, pt. 2, chap. 15, 517.

39. Saxe Comins, ed. *Basic Writings of George Washington* (New York: Random House, 1948).

40. Thanksgiving proclamation, October 3, 1789, in W. B. Allen, ed., *George Washington: A Collection* (Indianapolis: Liberty Classics, 1988), 534.

41. John Adams. *A Defense of the Constitutions of Government of the United States of America: Against the Attack of M. Turgot in His Letter to Dr. Price, Dated 22nd March, 1778* (Philadelphia: Budd & Bartram, 1797).

42. See Werner Jaeger, *Paideia: The Ideals of Greek Culture* (New York: Oxford University Press, 1939).

Chapter 11

1. Elizabeth Bumiller. "The Elephant's Ecstasy and Washington in Wait; Now Get Ready for the Country Club Presidency," *Washington Post*, November 6, 1980. See also Henry Allen, "The Fifties Are Coming; Say Hello to Reagan Retro, So Long to Liberal Chick," *Washington Post*, November 12, 1980.

2. Quoted in editorial, "Review and Outlook: Vacuum of Justice," *Wall Street Journal*, April 30, 1997, 14.

3. Gary S. Becker. "Why the Dole Plan Will Work," *Business Week* (August 26, 1996), 16.

4. The United States supposedly became the world's largest debtor in 1986. That year, however, Americans netted $20.8 billion from overseas investments. See Charles Wolf and Sarah Hooker, "Who Owes Whom, and How Much," *Wall Street Journal*, January 6, 1988.

5. Jason DeParle. "Social Investment Programs: Comparing the Past with the Promised Payoff," *New York Times*, March 1, 1993.

6. Gary Becker. "The Best Reason to Get People Off the Dole," *Business Week*, May 1, 1995.

7. See Mancur Olson, *The Logic of Collective Action: Public Goods and the Theory of Groups* (Cambridge, Mass.: Harvard University Press, 1971), and Jonathan Rauch, *Demosclerosis* (New York: New York Times Books, 1994).

8. Ibid., 30.

9. Niccolò Machiavelli. *The Prince*, trans. Angelo Codevilla (New Haven: Yale University Press, 1997), chap. 16. The recipients of benefits cannot possibly be satisfied. As their demands grow, the government is compelled to become more tax prone and to alienate society's producers, who retreat into sullen passivity or worse.

10. Rauch, *Demosclerosis*, 67.

11. James L. Payne. *The Culture of Spending* (San Francisco: Institute for Contemporary Studies, 1991), 13. See also "Where Experience Doesn't Count: Arguments for Limiting Congressional Terms," *Across the Board* 28, no. 9 (September 1991): 21.

12. The most complete account of the complex of dealings known as "Whitewater" is a three-volume series, *Whitewater (A Journal Briefing)*, from the editorial pages of the *Wall Street Journal* (New York: Login Pub. Consortium, 1984). See also Alexander Cockburn and Jeffrey St. Clair. "Is Hillary a Crook?" *New Statesman and Society*, April 12, 1996, 20.

13. Paul Gigot. "The Fine Art of Helping Political Friends," *Wall Street Journal*, March 28, 1997.

14. Jason DeParle. "Social Investment Programs: Comparing the Past with the Promised Payoff," *New York Times*, March 2, 1993.

15. See Heather MacDonald's report titled "Welfare's Next Vietnam" from Manhattan Institute's *City Journal*, cited in *Wall Street Journal*, January 20, 1995.

16. Charles Murray. "The Coming White Underclass," *Wall Street Journal*, October 29, 1993.

17. In "Welfare's Next Vietnam," MacDonald reported: "Stories abound of parents coaching their kids to misbehave in school or fail their tests. A child in

Wynne, Arkansas asked his teacher if doing well on an exam would affect his 'crazy check.' According to Morton Gold of the Social Security Administration's Savannah, Georgia, office, parents sometimes hold their children out of school to ensure that they will fall back several grades and thus fail the age appropriate test."

18. Carolyn L. Weaver. "Social Security's Infirmity," *The American Enterprise* 4, no. 2 (March-April 1993): 30.

19. See Sylvester J. Schieber, "Your Retirement, Your Social Security," *Wall Street Journal*, January 8, 1997, for one proposal for transitioning from the current social security system to something closer to the Chilean model.

20. Lisa Belkin. "Under New Health Plans Patients Change Habits," *New York Times*, January 6, 1993.

21. During the Thomas confirmation, Senator Joe Biden and other liberal senators on the Judiciary Committee, following counsel by Harvard law professor Laurence H. Tribe—who had argued for "natural" rights to privacy during the Bork proceedings—attacked Thomas's position that the Constitution is an expansion of natural law. See Jacob Weisberg, "Supreme Courtier: Larry Tribe's Hopeless Quest," in *The New Republic*, September 30, 1991, 16. Biden could not understand how it would be possible for Thomas to serve on the Supreme Court if he held the position that natural law arguments against the institution of slavery—embodied in the Declaration of Independence— were true. Confused, Biden argued, "I find it hard to understand how you can say what you're now saying, that natural law was only, you were only talking about the philosophy in a general philosophic sense, and not how it informed or impacted upon Constitutional interpretation" (as stated in a recording of the confirmation hearings by the *MacNeil/Lehrer News Hour* on September 10, 1991). As with many others like him, Biden fails to recognize in his understanding of natural law that "self-evident truths" have a natural law foundation; in essence, humans comprehend truth through reason. Also see "'Lord Biden'—Font of Natural Law," *Washington Times*, September 22, 1991.

22. See the debate between Lino A. Graglia and Harry V. Jaffa in *National Review*, August 14, 1995, 27, 31.

23. Philip K. Howard. *The Death of Common Sense* (New York: Basic Books, 1995), 10.

24. Internal Revenue Service. *Annual Report, 1992*, 42.

25. James Bovard. *Lost Rights* (New York: St. Martin's Press, 1994), 268, 270.

26. Ibid., 65.

27. Cf. Gene Wirges's *Conflict of Interest: The Gene Wirges Story* (North Little Rock, Ark.: Riverboat, 1992). To a lesser extent, the lessons apply elsewhere. Also see Kevin Sachs, "The Great Incumbency Machine," *New York Times Magazine*, September 27, 1992.

28. *Moore v. Valder* 314 US App. D.C. 209 (1995).

29. Note that Cokie Roberts of ABC News reported that members of a test audience responded most passionately when speakers at the 1996 Republican National Convention called for the abolition of the IRS. See transcript, *This Week with David Brinkley*, August 18, 1996.

30. Lance Morrow. "A Nation of Finger Pointers," *Time*, August 12, 1991, 18–22.

31. Mary Ann Glendon. *Rights Talk: The Impoverishment of Political Discourse* (New York: Free Press, 1991).

32. See the case of Diane Joyce versus Paul Johnson, the subject of *Johnson v. Santa Clara County* (1987), in Melvin Urovsky, *A Conflict of Rights* (New York: Charles Scribner's Sons, 1994). At stake was a road dispatcher's job.

33. Charles A. Reich. "Individual Rights and Social Welfare," *Yale Law Journal* 74 (April 1965).

34. See, e.g., Dan Levy, "San Jose Coaches Upset by Spoof of Sexual Harassment," *San Francisco Chronicle*, November 22, 1990.

35. Ellis Cose. *The Rage of the Privileged Class* (New York: HarperCollins, 1993).

36. Tom Brune. "Washington State: Want Your Check? Draft a Growth Plan," *Christian Science Monitor*, August 5, 1996.

37. Two of the landmark cases were *Plessy v. Ferguson* (1896), in which the Supreme Court allowed government-mandated racial separation in public transportation, and *Brown v. Board of Education* (1954), in which it ruled for government-mandated integration of schools. In both cases the Court rejected Justice Harlan's argument that "our Constitution is color blind" and that rights inhere in individuals rather than groups.

38. Richard Raymer. "Wanted, a Kinder, Gentler Cop," *New York Times Magazine*, January 22, 1995, 26.

39. Jeffrey Snyder. "A Nation of Cowards," *Public Interest* (fall 1993): 42.

40. David Kopel. "The Untold Triumph of Concealed Carry Permits," *Policy Review* (July-August 1996): 9.

41. Samuel Francis. "Elites Are Prosperous Amid the Slaughter," *Washington Times*, December 17, 1993.

42. Mark Melcher. *Potomac Perspectives* (Washington, D.C.: Prudential Securities, 1995).

Chapter 12

1. Inter-University Consortium for Political and Social Research. *American National Election Studies, 1948–1994* (Ann Arbor: University of Michigan Press, 1994).

2. U.S. Bureau of the Census. *Marital Status and Living Arrangements: March 1990*. Current Population Report Series, 15–25.

3. Barbara Bennett Woodhouse. "Who Owns the Child? Meyer and Pierce and the Child as Property," *William and Mary Law Review* 33, no. 4 (summer 1992): 1051.

4. Steven A. Holmes. "Quality of Life Is Up," *New York Times*, November 18, 1996.

5. "The Marriage Gap." *Wall Street Journal*, November 15, 1996; "The Family—A Reader's Digest Poll," *Reader's Digest* (July 1992): 48–54.

6. I am much indebted for this insight to David Wagner, "The Family and the Constitution," *First Things* (August-September, 1994).

7. Peter Steinfels. "Unmarried Couples, Single-Sex Couples, Triads and Quintets, Why Marriage Norms?" *New York Times*, May 14, 1994, Beliefs.

8. Editorial. *New York Times*, June 6, 1997.

9. Reader's Digest poll on "The Family Gap," *Reader's Digest* (July 1992): 52.

10. David Gelertner. "Why Mothers Should Stay at Home," *Commentary*, February 1996, 28.

11. Herbert Jacob. *Silent Revolution: The Transformation of Divorce Law in the United States* (Chicago: University of Chicago Press, 1988), 28.

12. William A. Galston. "Needed, a Not So Fast Divorce Law," *New York Times*, December 27, 1995.

13. See testimony by Andrew J. Cherlin before the House Select Committee on Children, Youth, and Families, cited in David Blankenhorn, *Fatherless America* (New York: Basic Books, 1995).

14. See Bill Callahan, "DA gives Priority to Statutory Rape Law; Case Against Man, 19, Launches Offensive," *San Diego Union-Tribune*, February 5, 1996.

15. See Thomas Hobbes, "Of Dominion Paternall, Despoticall," in *Leviathan* (New York: Penguin, 1968), chap. 20, 254.

16. Lena Williams. "Pregnant Teens Are Outcasts No Longer," *New York Times*, December 2, 1993.

17. Celia W. Dugger. "A Cultural Reluctance to Spare the Rod," *New York Times*, March 1, 1996.

18. Patrick Fagan. "The Real Root Causes of Violent Crime: The Breakdown of Marriage, Family, and Community," *Heritage Foundation*, March 17, 1995.

19. Timothy Egan. "Child Sex Abuse Charges Tear at Scandal-Shaken Community," *Houston Chronicle*, April 19, 1995.

20. Dorothy Rabinowitz. "Justice in Dade County," *Wall Street Journal*, October 26, 1996.

21. Gina Kolata. "Boom in Ritalin Sales Raises Ethical Issues," *New York Times*, May 16, 1996.

22. Ibid.

23. See, e.g., Robyn Meredith, "Parents Convicted for a Youth's Misconduct," *New York Times*, May 10, 1995.

24. Editorial. *New York Times*, May 5, 1996.

25. "After surveying 65 studies on the influence of expenditures per pupil, Professor Eric A. Hanushek of the University of Rochester reported in the *Journal of Economic Literature* that 49 showed no statistical significance and that of the 16 that showed significance, 3 indicated a negative relationship. Of 112 studies on the influence of changing teacher-pupil ratios, only 23 were statistically significant, 9 in the positive direction, and 14 in the negative direction" (Edwin G. West, "Restoring Family Autonomy in Education," *Chronicles* [October 1990]: 17).

26. On the performance of private and Catholic schools, see the classic work by James S. Coleman and Thomas Hoffer, *Public and Private High Schools: The Impact of Community* (New York: Basic Books, 1987).

27. Dirk Johnson. "Study Says Small Schools Are Key to Learning," *New York Times*, September 21, 1994.

28. Michael J. McCarthy. "Grim Prospect: Aged Try Mightily to Avoid the Nursing Home," *Wall Street Journal*, December 3, 1992.

29. Melinda Herneberger. "Losing the 'Home' in 'Nursing Home,'" *New York Times*, December 17, 1992.

30. Michael J. McCarthy. "Many States Await Result of Florida Attempt to Support 'Aging in Place'," *Wall Street Journal*, March 4, 1992.

31. Timothy Egan. "When Children Can't Afford Parent," *New York Times*, March 29, 1992.

32. Richard Grenier. "The America You Don't Know," *Washington Times*, October 31, 1995. See also Edward Rothstein, "As Culture Wars Go On, Battle Lines Blur a Bit," *New York Times*, May 27, 1997; and Clifford D. May,

"America's Culture Wars, Society Engaged in an Intellectual Battle over the Country's Moral Direction," *Rocky Mountain News*, May 7, 1995. But above all, see the debate between the magazine *First Things* (October-November 1996) and *Commentary* (February 1997) on whether and to what extent the American establishment's hostility to the mores and religion of most Americans is depriving the regime of its legitimacy.

33. Peter Brimelow. "America's Identity Crisis: On the Importance of Immigration; Why Kemp and Bennett are Wrong," *National Review*, November 21, 1994.

34. Thus, Bill Clinton has delivered several moving speeches on the subject. See, e.g., his speech in the *New York Times*, July 12, 1995.

35. Kenneth Woodward. "Talking to God," *Newsweek* January 6, 1992. Apparently, some 78 percent of Americans pray at least weekly, and 57 percent do so at least once per day. Ninety-one percent of women and 85 percent of men report that they "pray regularly."

36. See Allen E. Bergin, "Values and Religious Issues in Psychotherapy and Mental Health," *American Psychologist* 46 (1991): 394–403; David B. Larsen et al., "Dimensions and Valences of Religious Commitment," *American Journal of Psychiatry* 149 (1978).

37. *Stone v. Graham* 449 US 39 (1980). For the confrontation in Alabama, see Katherine Q. Seelye, "House Republicans Back Judge on Display of 10 Commandments," *New York Times*, March 5, 1997.

38. *Jones v. North Carolina Prisoners' Labor Union* 433 US 119 (1977).

39. *Wallance v. Jaffree* 472 US 38 (1985) is the latest significant case.

40. "Herndahl v. Pontontoc Co.," *New York Times*, June 4, 1996.

41. As retold in a speech by Ralph Reed, Laguna Beach, Calif., January 21, 1995. See the prepared testimony of Jay Alan Sekulow, chief counsel, American Center for Law and Justice, before the House Committee on the Judiciary Subcommittee on the Constitution, July 23, 1996.

42. Douglas C. Holland, county counsel, Monterey County, Calif. Memo dated December 8, 1992.

43. Editorial. *New York Times*, October 13, 1994.

44. "Lamm Dispenses Bitter Pills Not Likely Swallowed," *Palm Beach Post*, August 10, 1996.

45. John Keown. "Dutch Slide Down Euthanasia's Slippery Slope," *Wall Street Journal*, November 5, 1991.

46. Editorial. "Educators or Lobbyists," *Washington Times*, September 1, 1996. Moreover, the *Times* reports "Half of all unionized delegates were teachers. The NEA delegation, about the size of California's, again represented the largest special-interest block, a distinction it has prized for each of the last six Democratic conventions."

47. *National Standards for United States History: Exploring the American Experience* (Los Angeles: National Center for History in the Schools/UCLA, 1994).

48. James F. Cooper. "Art Censors: A Closer Look at the NEA," *New Dimensions*, June 1991, 26–29. See also Robert Knight, "The NEA," *Heritage Foundation*, January 18, 1991; and Mark Lasswell, "Not All AIDS Dramas Are on Broadway," *Wall Street Journal*, April 29, 1996.

49. Myron Magnet. *The Dream and the Nightmare: The Sixties' Legacy to the Underclass* (New York: W. Morrow, 1993).

50. *New York Times*, December 22, 1996, News of the Week in Review.

51. Terry Teachout. "Abortion, Set to Music," *First Things* 65 (August-September 1996): 42.

52. James Q. Wilson. "Tales of Virtue: Moral and Development of Children," *Current* 365 (September 1994): 4.

53. Niccolò Machiavelli. *Discorso a dialago interno alla nostra lingua*, ed. Bortolo Tommaso Sozzi (Torino: Einaudi, 1976), bk. 1, 11–15.

Chapter 13

1. See Angelo M. Codevilla, "Birds of a Feather," *National Interest* 35 (spring 1994).

2. See John Lewis Gaddis, "The Tragedy of Cold War History," *Diplomatic History* 17, no. 1 (January/February 1993): 1–16, for a friendly acknowledgment of the establishment's orthodoxy.

3. See Anthony Lake, ed., *The Vietnam Legacy: The War, American Society, and the Future of American Foreign Policy* (New York: New York University Press, 1976), xxi.

4. Polls cited in Arthur M. Schlesinger, Jr., *Robert Kennedy and His Times* (Boston: Houghton Mifflin, 1978), 843.

5. Perhaps the most poignant document is Robert McNamara's memoir, *In Retrospect: The Tragedy and Lessons of Vietnam* (New York: Times Books, 1995), in which the former secretary of defense explains how family and friends persuaded him that he was on the wrong side of the war but that he nevertheless continued to order men to fight and die in it.

6. *Social Representation in the U.S. Military* (Washington, D.C.: Congressional Budget Office, 1989), 41.

7. Chris Hedges. "Studying Bosnia's Prisoners of Peace." *New York Times*, March 30, 1997.

8. K. L. Billingsley, "Booty Camp. On Maneuvers with the Co-Ed Military," *Heterodoxy* (April-May 1997): 6–8.

9. Editorial. "Overly Friendly Fire," *Washington Times*, June 6, 1997; see also Philip Gold, "Feminist Agenda Setters Take Aim at Truth Teller," *Washington Times*, March 10, 1997.

10. *New York Times*, November 4, 1990; see also Owen Ullman, "Baker's Vagueness Does Little to Relieve Frustration of Troops," *Orange County Register*, November 5, 1990.

11. See Richard H. Kohn, "The Crisis in Civil-Military Relations," *National Interest* 36 (spring 1994); and Colin Powell, John Lehman, William Odom, Samuel Huntington, "Civil-Military Relations Debated," *National Interest* 36 (summer 1994).

12. Young Men's Lyceum address, January 27, 1838. In *Abraham Lincoln, Collected Works*, vol. 1, ed. Roy P. Basler (New Brunswick, N.J.: Rutgers University Press, 1953), 109.

Index

Abortion, 74; America (modern) and, 9, 18, 39, 231, 272–73, 274, 285, 286–87, 289–90; Japan and, 172; Soviet Union and, 91, 92; Sweden and, 170

Adams, Abigail, 221

Adams, John, 221, 229–30

Adenauer, Konrad, 6, 23, 178

Adoption, America (modern) and, 274

Adultery, 159; America (early) and, 221, 222, 223

Aeroflot, 82

Affirmative action, America (modern) and, 255–58, 261

Afghanistan, 99, 201, 202

Africa, 25, 26, 27; civilizations in, 50; tyranny and, 54; women and, 155

Aged parents, 35; America (modern) and, 279–80, 285; Japan and, 172, 173

Agency for International Development, 101–2, 107

Agnelli, 120

Agudat Yisrael, 188

Aid to Families with Dependent Children (AFDC), 242, 243–44

Alcibiades, 60, 194

Alcoholics Anonymous (AA), 282

Alexander, 29, 193

Alexis II, Patriarch, 95

Algeria, 33

Allen, John, 214

Allende, Salvador, 122, 123, 197

Amalrik, Andrei, 85

America, early, 16–17, 213–30, 229–30; civility and, 5, 6, 16–17, 47, 66, 67–68, 130, 132, 135, 136–37, 140, 153, 216–20, 222–23, 309n4, 315n4; Civil War and, 19, 218; decency and, 74–75; democracy and, 60; family and, 17,

220–23; government and, 5, 6, 63–64, 72, 307n5; leadership and, 37, 38; military and, 193, 218; moralism and, 19; pluralism and, 19; prosperity and, 16, 213–16; religion and, 16, 47, 67, 224–29; Revolution, 193, 227; slavery and, 39, 68, 129–30; tone and, 45

America, modern, 1–4, 9, 17, 27, 61–63, 231–305; arts and, 288–89, 290, 305; civility and, 2, 3–4, 18, 37, 38–39, 40–41, 46–47, 67, 132, 136, 231, 239, 248–64, 304, 309n4; civil rights and, 38–39, 254–58, 260, 261, 325n37; corruption and, 240, 241–48, 323n17; culture and, 27, 34–35; decency and, 75; education and, 231, 234, 258, 259, 260, 278, 282–83, 287–88, 305, 310n3, 326n25; family and, 2–3, 18, 19, 37, 163, 231, 238, 265–80, 285–87, 289–90, 304; government and, 9, 18, 72, 236; interest groups and, 233, 239; media and, 233–34; military and, 3, 18–19, 194, 200, 292–303; pluralism and, 19; prosperity and, 17, 52, 103, 105, 236–48, 303–4; regimes of, 232–36; regulation and, 238–41, 250–54, 305; religion and, 3, 35, 47, 185, 231, 280–91, 304, 305; tone and, 45, 46–48; violence and, 47–48; welfare and, 237, 238–39, 242–44, 323n17

American Association of Retired Persons, 280

American Civil Liberties Union, 261

American College of Obstetricians and Gynecologists, 286

American Indians, women and, 154, 222, 317n3

329